THE NEW GLOBAL TRADING ORDER

The international institutions that have governed global trade since the end of World War II have lost their effectiveness, and global trade governance is fractured. The need for new institutions is obvious, and yet, few proposals seem to be on offer. The key to understanding the global trading order lies in uncovering the relationship between trade and the State, and how the inner constitution of Statecraft drives the architecture of the global order and requires structural changes as the State traverses successive cycles. The current trade order, focused on the liberalization of trade in goods and services and the management of related issues, is predicated on policies and practices that were the product of a global trading order of the twentieth-century modern nation-states. Today, a new form of the State – the post-modern State – is evolving. In this book, the authors propose a new trade norm – the enablement of global economic opportunity – and a new institution – the Trade Council – to overhaul the global trading order.

Dennis Patterson holds the Chair in Legal Theory and Legal Philosophy at the European University Institute in Florence. He is Board of Governors Professor of Law and Philosophy at Rutgers University School of Law (Camden) and Professor of Jurisprudence and International Trade at Swansea University, UK. His previous work includes *Law and Truth* (1996), the *Blackwell Companion to Philosophy of Law and Legal Theory* (1996), and numerous articles in a wide variety of academic journals, including the *Oxford Journal of Legal Studies, Columbia Law Review, Texas Law Review*, and *The Modern Law Review.*

Ari Afilalo is Associate Professor of Law at Rutgers University School of Law (Camden). His work has appeared in the *New York University Journal of International Law and Politics, The Chicago Journal of International Law, Northwestern International Law and Business Journal, Georgetown International Environmental Law Review*, and the *European Journal of International Law.*

The New Global Trading Order

The Evolving State and the Future of Trade

Dennis Patterson

Rutgers University
Swansea University, Wales, UK

Ari Afilalo

Rutgers University

CAMBRIDGE
UNIVERSITY PRESS

CAMBRIDGE UNIVERSITY PRESS
Cambridge, New York, Melbourne, Madrid, Cape Town, Singapore,
São Paulo, Delhi, Dubai, Tokyo

Cambridge University Press
32 Avenue of the Americas, New York, NY 10013-2473, USA

www.cambridge.org
Information on this title: www.cambridge.org/9780521124683

First published 2008
First paperback edition 2010

Printed in the United States of America

A catalog record for this publication is available from the British Library.

Library of Congress Cataloging in Publication Data

Patterson, Dennis M. (Dennis Michael), 1955–
The new global trading order : the evolving state and the future of trade /
Dennis Patterson, Ari Afilalo.
   p. cm.
Includes bibliographical references and index.
ISBN 978-0-521-87518-9 (hardback)
1. International trade. 2. International economic relations. 3. International
finance. 4. United Nations Monetary and Financial Conference (1944 : Bretton
Woods, N.H.) I. Afilalo, Ari. II. Title.
HF1379.P378   2008
382–dc22   2007040544

ISBN   978-0-521-87518-9 Hardback
ISBN   978-0-521-12468-3 Paperback

Dennis dedicates this book to Barbara, Sarah, and Graham.

Ari dedicates it to his mother, Suzanne Afilalo, and to the memory of his father, Moshe Afilalo.

Contents

Preface to the Paperback Edition   *page* ix

1   Introduction 1

2   The Evolving State 11

3   The Changing Nature of Welfare 41

4   Disaster and Redemption: 1930s and Bretton Woods 67

5   The Transformation of the Bretton Woods World and
    the Rise of a New Economic Order 81

6   The End of Bretton Woods and the Beginning of a
    New Global Trading Order 110

7   The Enablement of Global Economic Opportunity 147

8   Trade and Security 186

    Conclusion 203

Notes   209
Bibliography   239
Index   265

Preface to the Paperback Edition

We wrote this book in a time of great portent. Global trade was a contentious topic in general and in American electoral politics in particular. We aimed at changing the parameters of the conversation about the role of government in economic and social life, and to warn that the global trading order needed a constitutional overhaul if it was to continue to thrive in the transformed geopolitical order of the twenty-first century. We advanced a theoretical construct that defines the concrete shape and content of trade law and the global institutions that give it life. We argued that the architecture of global law-making, crafted after World War II at Bretton Woods, was eminently suitable to structure the commercial relations of the nation-states of the modern twentieth century but needed reconstruction for the post-modern states of the twenty-first century. Comparative advantage, which presupposes "national" assets and discrete economic components associated with nation-states' boundaries, ceased to provide a viable animating theory of trade in a kaleidoscopic world in which cross-border actors ignored national boundaries to form a "flat economic world" of interloped ownership and activity. Instead of comparative advantage, we argued, states should join to enact ad hoc regulatory schemes, joining national and international legal rules in regulatory packages that would ignore the classic international legal insistence on national sovereignty and international law's increasingly artificial divide between the "municipal" and the "international," aimed at achieving "global enablement of economic opportunity."

In addition to agreeing with the conventional wisdom that global trade was fractured, we sounded a Cassandra warning. We posited that the constitutional moment of change had arrived. The trading world had to either adapt its norms and its institutions to a fundamentally different landscape, or face a fate as dire as that of the modern liberal democracies last century, when they failed to reject protectionism and refused to choose comparative advantage in the days of the Great Depression. Our project, we argued, was a component of a greater effort to reject the notion that, with the advent of democracy, we had reached the "end of history." The great Western conceit had long been to view history as a series of advances leading to the ultimate good life and form of government: ours. That form of government, democratic orthodoxy told us, included a number of doctrinal mainstays, including comparative advantage and the notion of free trade tempered only by countervailing concerns for fairness and human rights. Our project was driven by a belief that history never ends but instead traverses epochal cycles during which the foundational hallmarks of government or "Statecraft" must be overhauled and infused anew with principles necessary for the viability of trade architecture.

Statecraft is a concept that we develop, nuance, and analyze in this book. It lies at the root of our theory. We believe that, in each era, Statecraft defines the two "faces" – outer and inner – of the state participants in the global order. The inner face of a state is its law and constitutional order. For example, in the twentieth century, "modern" liberal democracies followed a welfare democratic form of Statecraft, in which regulation, government intervention, and other regulatory tools were intended to protect the welfare of the nation and give it rights and entitlements. In the nineteenth century "pre-modern" era, a State-centric form of government, designed to amass wealth and consolidate the power of the State, had prevailed. Conscription, lack of social regulation, and the absence of State intervention in cycles of boom and bust exemplify this form of pre-modern government.

The global order of states and its trade structure (strategy and trade, respectively) form what we call the outer face of Statecraft. In the pre-modern era, colonization of foreign resources and "beggar thy neighbor" protectionist policies furthered the State-centric impulse of the time. In the twentieth century, comparative advantage and the explosion of freer trading among nation-states furthered their drive to protect their national welfare. States could work together to increase the global economic pie while sheltering internal redistributive policy choices from international interference. Whether following a cradle-to-grave (as was the case in France and England), tax-and-spend (the preferred method in the United States), or indicative planning (used by Japan's famed MIT) route to welfare, the modern liberal democracies had relatively unfettered regulatory space to further their welfare aspirations. In turn, the interaction between the outer and inner faces of the State generates a transformation of each realm that, in turn, requires an affirmative overhaul of the foundational elements of Statecraft. Thus, the State-centric activities of the pre-modern era created a nation, which bred a new Statecraft ethos whereby the State would unleash its power and resources for the nation's welfare, engendering a need to reject mercantilist policies and the establishment of a comparative advantage–based system of trading.

These are the themes that we develop in this book, informed by the lessons of history, law, economics, and political science. Our theory has particular relevance today because, as was the case in the first half of the twentieth century, we have reached an epochal constitutional crossroads, one that the global trading actors must affirmatively traverse. We call these epochal landmarks "constitutional moments." With each constitutional moment, the world must articulate and adopt a new set of animating principles of Statecraft. Bretton Woods was such a constitutional moment. At the dawn of the modern era – the outbreak of World War I, the first battle of the Long War – it became necessary for the maturing nation-states to cement their relationship through a rejection of mercantilist policies. Instead of selling as much as possible to one's neighbor and buying as little as possible, it made sense for nation-states to open their borders to trade and develop their comparative advantage. The ethos of the modern liberal democratic states, the protection of the "nation" and of its rights and entitlements, was thus embedded and in large part replicated in an international system that treated each nation-state as a "sovereign" member of a compact that respected its national redistributive rights but prohibited any form of discrimination.

When we first published this book, we argued that the early twenty-first century presents us with one of the constitutional crossroads that requires a constitutional moment of transformation, and we advocated that transformation be put in motion while time was still on our side. We explained that by opening up global trade, the modern era created a "flat world" that rendered comparative advantage obsolete and made it unlikely that the welfare state, in the form that we know it, would continue to provide the organizational basis for domestic Statecraft. Nations, boundaries, national assets, and domestic tools of State intervention have become largely ineffective, irrelevant, or nonexistent in the post-modern globalized world of trade. In turn, because the interaction between discrete modern nation-states lay at the root of the comparative advantage system, that principle had to give way to a new animating norm, which we called the "enablement of global economic opportunity."

We are rewriting the preface to this book in a time of tremendous upheaval, one that hit globalized markets faster and harder than we had anticipated. Sadly, our predictions have come true, and we find ourselves revising this preface in a time of economic and financial disaster. Instead of suggestions for the betterment of our collective future, the prescriptions we advance are now indispensable components to economic recovery. We write in the midst of a global economic crisis that has been misunderstood, misdiagnosed, and mishandled. The American administrations, voices of the right and the left, have applied remedies of a prior era and used the opportunity to settle accounts with one another. European and Asian policy makers have followed suit. The left can now take comfort in the belief that neo-liberal theories of limited government have been repudiated. For their part, the right is preparing to blame future problems on the left's application of interventionist and redistributionist policies that choke economic growth. Both are wrong.

The root of the problem is not addressed by the question whether government should act "compassionately" and support the people, or whether it should leave it to private market mechanisms to get the work done. The root of the problem is not how much or how little regulation we need or should retain. Rather, the fundamental questions relate to how a post-modern State intervenes in interloped markets and relates to the post-modern society of states, and to the pockets of modern and pre-modern countries that, owing to accidents of their history (such as colonization), did not traverse the same pre-modern, modern, and maturing post-modern tracks that the liberal democracies have traveled.

Yet, even as they rigorously and thoroughly address existing problems, the State actors of the day continue to act as modern nation-states. Alas, like their pre-modern predecessors of the twentieth century, they are impeding effective solutions to the very problems they need to address by adhering to an outdated model of Statecraft.

The "bailouts" of various mainstays of American and European industry and finance provide good examples to illustrate our claim. The governments of the United States and major European states have every incentive to intervene in an effort to avoid market crashes and the correlative long-term injury that would surely be visited on crucial industrial and financial sectors. If banks disappear, and unemployment increases sharply because of massive layoffs and shutdowns, economic opportunity will wither away. However, State intervention has used the language and tools of the modern nation-state era to intervene: as a result, states are not putting economic activity on the right path (or are doing it only as a coincidental byproduct of policies designed for other purposes) and are merely staunching the bleeding.

The very word "bailout" is eminently modern. Consider General Motors. That company has been a mainstay of "American" national industry in the modern epoch. Its disappearance would of course send shock waves through the U.S. economy, owing in part to psychological reactions associated with the loss of such an American cultural symbol, and in part to the economic impact on several American states and industrial sectors of the drowning of an undertaking that spans several industries and employs a substantial number of American workers. The ripple effect would be disastrous, just like the American and global economies would have a very difficult time coping with and recovering from the death of more financial institutions and banks.

The government response to this very real problem, however, is driven by notions of national entitlement rather than enablement of global economic opportunity. The General Motors bailout was predictable in its adherence to a nationalization model with which twentieth-century observers are all too familiar. An important company loses money, market positioning, and viability. Public funds are injected into the company to subsidize its losses. The public takes an equity stake and essentially ensures the survival of a company that does not have the competitive edge necessary to keep its market stake without substantial assistance. The rationale is that the company's workers and those who depend on them are entitled to the economic benefits that it confers, and if it cannot make it on its own, then the public should shore it up. We have seen this process in action in Europe in the twentieth century, and it is being replicated for the crisis of the American twenty-first century.

A better approach would be to fashion a "bailout" based not on welfare and entitlements but on the enablement of economic opportunity with a global reach. Such a bailout plan would ignore the traditional divide between national and international realms and involve global as well as local actors. Instead of infusing cash to make up for operational losses, and to employ bankruptcy laws solely to discharge and restructure debts, the bailout could have been structured along the following lines:

- A bankruptcy process designed to enable economic opportunity of interested actors.
- Breakup and sale of General Motors divisions, such as component parts or the financial services division, financed in part by public funds.
- Preferential treatment to bidders agreeing to employ current workers and to give equity stakes to workers.
- "Higher and better offers" evaluated not solely in terms of benefits to creditors, employees, and equity holders, but in relation to the ongoing profitability of the surviving entities.
- Conversion of debt into equity of surviving entities for creditors willing to finance ongoing operations.

- Incentive for strategic partnership with foreign groups, who could open up new markets for the restructured entities. (The Obama administration directed Chrysler to seek to form a partnership with Fiat; the GM process would use domestic U.S. incentives to attract bids from foreign undertakings with access to markets that are useful to that company. As we argue in the book, these incentives could be extended in regulatory realms such as intellectual property, taxes, antitrust, or securities laws.)

Likewise, a bailout of the financial industry should not have focused solely on infusing cash to bolster the capital needs of institutions plagued with "toxic assets." Again, the regulatory reflex is grounded in a nation-state, welfare legislative paradigm of deploying the power of the State to protect and provide entitlements to the nation. If an institution of sufficiently significant market standing is allowed to fail, the thinking goes, the ripple effects on the welfare of the affected nationals will be too harmful to tolerate. Hence, government needs to intervene by drawing on the collective resources to shore up the failing institution. This State intervention is justified by a utilitarian, welfare-driven rationale, informed by Keynesian economics: the role of government in tough economic times is to inject enough capital into the economy to stimulate activity and to avert a spiraling-down effect. Thus, the "national assets" have to be strengthened by the national government in times of stress; this is the essence of modern Statecraft.

A better, post-modern way of achieving a financial bailout would identify the needs of the actors relying on failing financial institutions and deploy the power of government to meet those needs, providing economic opportunity rather than a liquidity injection. It goes without saying that insuring private deposits lies at the core of financial stability and economic opportunity. In all instances, the Federal Deposit Insurance Corporation should step in and provide depositors with access to their funds. However, the massive spending of public funds that the current and past administrations undertook could certainly have gone to better post-modern uses than straight welfare checks to banks.

Consider the following scenarios:

- Community-based banks with a commitment to micro-lending are given access to public capital (loans) to buy out failed institutions at a relatively low cost, with a condition subsequent that a certain portion of their capital be used to finance micro-lending projects.
- A number of national commercial banks, publicly held and gradually sold off to private interests, are established to provide businesses with

ordinary course financial facilities, including letters of credit, factoring, and revolving lines. These facilities are provided to them at low cost and would go a much longer way toward stimulating economic activity than saving banks who clean up their balance sheets but do not reactivate commercial activity.

- Bankruptcy court–supervised purchases of assets of failed companies are financed. For example, concerns selected to acquire assets of GM in the conditions described previously would be infused with public funds and be required to grant equity interests either to groups designated by the government (such as workers) or to a public corporation charged with infusing the necessary cash.

A shift in our approach to regulation is necessary for us to resolve our current crisis, and to retool our commercial architecture to match the times. By adhering to a modern, twentieth-century regulatory mode, we will fail to solve these problems in a sound and lasting fashion – just as protectionism and mercantilism failed in the 1930s. Indeed, modern regulation is today's functional equivalent of twentieth-century protectionism. Instead of spreading economic opportunity and enabling it globally, we are insisting on salvaging institutions that were symbols of the twentieth-century "national strength." Far better to give way today to a diffuse set of interactive and dynamic global economic interests, for only these can guarantee long-term growth in a post-modern context.

By resisting this transformation, we not only hurt our economy but fail to solidify our relationship with the powers of the day (such as China). Instead, we are alienating them. Here again we find ourselves in a situation similar to the early 1930s. When we wrote this book, although we did not accept the superficial comparisons between fascism and religious fundamentalism and global networked terror, we warned that the trade architecture of the early twenty-first century was as deficient as that of the early 1930s. Our contention was that, much as the states that came to be known as the Allies faced their worst economic crisis at a time when strategic considerations demanded economic strength, so would we face famine if we failed to revamp our international commercial architecture. Today, we have already bound the modern liberal democracies to free trade. In the process, we have created a flat and kaleidoscopic world that, as we explain, includes emerging new powers. Our mission, consistent with the evolution of Statecraft, is to bind these powers to the modern liberal democracies by enabling global economic opportunity to spread to them.

This book is non-partisan, inclining neither left nor right. Rather, we are offering a method of thinking about governance in the twenty-first century that transcends and leaves behind the obsolete debates of the twentieth century. Our approach, we maintain, would allow us to act decisively to shore up the global markets and bind them in an alliance that would make war among them "not only unthinkable, but also materially impossible."

1   *Introduction*

The international institutions that have governed global trade since the end of World War II have lost their effectiveness. Global trade governance is fractured. The need for new institutions is obvious and, yet, few proposals seem to be on offer.[1] The stubborn problem of the inequality gap between the developing nations and the nations of the first world remains a centerpiece of the international agenda. Current battles over trade policy are both intense and serious, for a great deal is at stake.[2] The way to break out of the endless debates between the advocates of free trade and their critics is to move beyond the terms of the current discourse. To do so requires an understanding of why the current trade order was successful in fulfilling its role in international relations for as long as it did and why it is in need of a transformation to retain currency and effectiveness. This book will answer these two questions and more.

In this book, we present fresh proposals for tackling the issues presented by global trade. We argue that neither politics nor economics alone hold the key to unlocking solutions to the problems presented by global trade. Global trade is not principally a matter of economics. Though we certainly do not prescind from matters of politics and economics, we believe that *ideas* are the fundamental tools both for understanding trade and for crafting solutions to the problems of inequality and fairness that lie at the heart of the great questions of the day.

But this is not a study in political theory alone. No account of the global trading order can be adequate if concrete reform proposals do not accompany the theoretical analysis. To that end, we start with an account of the ideas that have shaped the global trading order since the eighteenth century. We use these ideas to trace the development of trade discourse through its various iterations, reaching all the way down to the level of institutions. At each turn in our analysis, we unearth connections between the politics and institutions of trade and the deeper theoretical ideas to which the global institutions of trade give expression. In short, our argument is complete, as it starts from the abstract plane of political theory and ends with concrete institutional and normative proposals for effecting these ideas.

The first, and most important, claim we defend is that the key to understanding the global trading order lies in uncovering the relationship between trade and the State.[3] A central aspect of this understanding is that the victors of war or states that otherwise dominate the strategic playing field have the opportunity to establish a trade system that accords with their Statecraft. The trade order between states is connected to a larger order of states, an order we identify as "constitutional." The current trade order is predicated on policies and practices that were the product of a global trading order of nation-states. When the current trade order was conceived and implemented in the middle of the twentieth century, the world was comprised of nation-states. Each nation-state contained an infrastructure and a wealth of industries that were located in a place and connected to markets regulated by the states where those industries were found. For the nation-state, the nature of its Statecraft accorded with the trade system put in place at Bretton Woods, and it was in the interests of the victors of World War II to adopt such a system. This world, which comprised the material background for the institutions conceived at Bretton Woods, is not the one we live in. Yet, the policies, practices, and institutions of the global trading order are all predicated on this world. Given that the rules and institutions of trade are the product of a world that no longer exists, new norms and institutions are urgently needed. As we will show, not only does trade hang in the balance but global security as well.

In this book, we explain how the global trading order developed from the eighteenth- and nineteenth-century trade policies of mercantilism, through the twentieth-century era of comparative advantage to the present and how the structure of the trade order between states is a function of the *type* of states that comprise the trade order. We believe that the trade order of states follows the constitutional order of states, and that the states that dominate the global strategic order, whether through victory in war or otherwise, will be the powers that structure the global trading order. As the internal constitutional order of the global society of states changes, so too does the global trading order. It is the connection between the State and the trade order that is the key to understanding the global trading order.[4] As we will show, once we understand how trade reflects the inner logic of the State, we will understand both why the trade order developed as it did and why the rules and institutions of the current global trade order are faltering and in need of replacement.

We begin our story with Francis Fukuyama's 1989 claim for "the end of history." Although criticized and often dismissed, we think Fukuyama was on to something in his claim for "the end of history." When the Berlin Wall fell in 1989, communism was vanquished. This was a "transitional end of history" moment, for after the defeat of fascism in World War II, communism was the last challenge to the supremacy of democracy as the preferred mode of State governance. What Fukuyama got right was that the century-long struggle between democracy, fascism, and communism was over. What he failed to see was that history had simply taken a turn down a new road. It is that road we intend to traverse.[5]

Fukuyama is not alone in recognizing the significance of 1989. The British diplomat Robert Cooper argues that 1989 set the stage for the emergence of a new form of the State, the "post-modern state."[6] In *The Shield of Achilles*, Philip Bobbitt not only disputes that 1989 is the end of history, he further argues that it ushers in a new form of the State, the "market-state," which will succeed the nation-state. These two theorists of the State agree on a number of defining characteristics of the new form of State that, in their view, confirm the continuing evolution of the State.[7] Further, their theories point to a nexus and an interplay between a particular form of the State (currently the nation-state) and its strategic foreign policy and military objectives. We think Bobbitt and Cooper are right about the State. Although each has made an enormous contribution to our basic understanding of the role and importance of strategy in the current era, they do not address the role of the global trading order. That is the story we tell in this book.

The State has two faces, an inner and an outer. The outer face of the State has two dimensions: strategy and trade. The inner face of the State also has two dimensions: law and welfare. "Statecraft" names the outer and the inner faces of the State. We shall now detail how these dimensions of the State interact with one another over time.

The outer dimension of the State is comprised of two principal features: strategy and trade. At all times, states have a strategic relationship to other states. The most basic of these are peace and war. In the twentieth century, sovereignty and balance of power were the two central attributes of the strategic relationship between states. Each of these aspects of the outer face of the State is in irreversible transition.

Trade is the second dimension of the outer face of the State. Trade ideology (e.g., mercantilism or comparative advantage) follows the constitutional order of states in that each form of the State is complemented by a particular trade regime. For instance, mercantilism is complementary to the state-nation form[8] of the State. In the twentieth century, comparative advantage was a natural trade ideology for the era of the nation-state.

Thus, when we say that the trade order "follows" the constitutional order of states, we mean that each constitutional order of states (i.e., each iteration of the State) embraces a complementary trade ideology.

The inner dimensions of the State, law and welfare, are directly linked to the outer face of the State. Law is the means by which the State maintains domestic peace and provides an orderly structure for life and commerce. Welfare represents the State's promise of providing for the health and well-being of the nation. "Welfare" names a wide range of policies and entitlements. In addition to support in the form of unemployment insurance, health care, and pension funding, the State also protects minority rights and provides regulation for everything from the environment to interstate commerce.

The State legitimates itself by delivering on its promises of security and welfare.[9] In matters of security, modern nation-states delivered on the promise of security with two principal devices: sovereignty and balance of power.[10] The notion of balance of power was linked to the concepts of sovereignty and of the nation as the interlocutor of the State in its quest for legitimacy. In the modern system, global order between strong sovereign powers was achieved by maintaining the balance of power between nations rather than the hegemonic domination of an empire or superpower.

With respect to welfare, there is great variation between the cradle-to-grave systems of the European nations and the leaner American approach to the social safety net. But there is more to welfare[11] than subsistence and aid from the State. In addition to delivering social support, the State must produce and manage a legal regime that preserves and protects the infrastructure of the nation. Thus, everything from the environment to regulation of markets and intellectual property falls within the purview of law. Most importantly, through law the State provides rights for everyone, but above all civil rights protections, especially for minorities. These protections constitute an all-important component of the "welfare" of the nation.

In matters of both strategy and welfare, the State is undergoing a process of irreversible change. Let us start with strategy. The year 1989 marks the end of the great struggle of the twentieth century between fascism, communism, and democracy. With the demise of fascism at the end of World War II, it remained for democracy to defeat communism in the struggle for the preferred model of Statecraft. The year 1989 – specifically the fall of the Berlin Wall – saw communism finally falter as a contender for global dominance. Henceforth, democracy would be the governance model for the State.

But the evolution of the State did not end with the triumph of democracy. As Cooper details, the states of the European Union have now relinquished sovereignty and embraced transparency in matters of strategy. States, Cooper argues, have now become "post-modern" in that the attributes of the State during the nation-state era are fading and being replaced with a cooperative, interloping strategy regime.[12]

Philip Bobbitt has an even stronger argument than Cooper. Bobbitt maintains that the growth of global networked terrorism and the commodification of weapons of mass destruction pose an unprecedented strategic challenge to the State. As the State can no longer deliver on its promise to protect the homeland from external attack, the strategic ground of its legitimacy is changing.[13] This development, Bobbitt argues, portends a move from the nation-state to what he calls the "market state." Like Cooper, Bobbitt sees the State evolving, not ending.

Now, to trade. The system of trade that was put in place after World War II reflected the inner constitutional order of the states that were its main actors. At the time, the world was subdivided into national economies coextensive with the nation-states that formed the General Agreement on Tariffs and Trade, and its successor World Trade Organization (GATT/WTO) system. The theoretical foundations of the system respected sovereignty, and left it to internal domestic policy to control the redistribution of wealth, with the essential caveat that trade restrictions should not be used for any protectionist purpose.[14] However, fiscal policy, monetary policy, and welfare policies were means of domestic control over redistributive justice that, at least in theory, trade left untouched.[15]

At present, the world can no longer be viewed as a subdivision of national economies coextensive with nation-states and dominated by the World War II victors. Whether driven by the WTO or by other factors, the twenty-first century has inherited a multipolar economic (as well as strategic) world. Countries like Brazil, India, China, and South Korea, just to name a few, have increasingly become world economic centers. The output of the non-OECD countries has reached 45% today, and is expected to reach 60% by 2015. The old Second World, made up of communist countries, is being replaced by a new Second World made up of economies formerly classified under the global heading of "developing countries." Lying within and alongside the first (post-modern) and second (modern) economies are pre-modern societies that lack the education, infrastructure, and other conditions to benefit from the liberalization of trade that the WTO has effected.

The ontological centerpiece of the global trading order – an aggregation of nation-states governed by the sovereignty, welfare, and balance of power principles of the twentieth century – is eroding. To be sure, the overlapping of ownership and spread of production has for quite some time made it difficult to identify a particular product as belonging to one nation versus another. But there is more to the story than these developments.

At the same time, the State has lost control over fundamental tools of wealth transfer and protection of the domestic economy unrelated to trade. Monetary policy, for example, is increasingly escaping control by states. The sheer magnitude of markets for currencies is gradually resulting in the transformation of money from a tool of exchange, which can be manipulated domestically, to a mere commodity. Public debt is increasingly held by foreign actors, and is being regulated more by the interplay of commercial interests than by domestic choices.

To the citizens of a nation, the State's promise of the delivery of welfare constitutes the most visible aspect of the evolving dynamic of states in the global order of the society of states. Part of our thesis that the nature of the State is changing is tied to changes in the way the State delivers on its promise of welfare. As we explain, we have a capacious view of the meaning of "welfare."[16] Briefly, the welfare of a nation is a function of the degree to which the State maintains legal regimes for the enhancement of commerce (for example, a legal system wedded to the Rule of Law) and the protection of the nation in matters of health (e.g., public health regulations) and entitlements.[17] With respect to the latter, entitlements, the State is evolving in its delivery on the promise of benefits to the nation. Succinctly, the State is moving from a regime of (legal) entitlements to one of incentives. This change is most evident in the states of the European Union and the United States but it can be seen as well in indicative planning states such as Japan. As we explain, we believe the move to a new global economic norm of enablement of global economic opportunity will manifest itself both in the domestic sphere (that is, within states) as well as globally (between states). That is to say, both domestic and international policy will reflect an increasing embrace of this new norm.

The consequences for trade of the erosion of the nation-state, the gradual decline of the model of a world subdivided into national economies, and the transformation of the means of production are manifold. We believe that the nexus between the inner face of the State and its outer trade face is gradually pushing the trade world to embrace both an institutional framework and a norm that will supplement and to a large extent work hand-in-hand with comparative advantage: that norm is the enablement of global economic opportunity. This move, together with the multi-polarity and diffuseness of the new world, are bound to create new protectionist pressures on domestic governments, which the institutional tools of the WTO are not adequately equipped to handle. The flow of industry to the multi-polar world is bound to affect industries that are sensitive to the economies of the United States, Europe, and the other main GATT trading partners. Technology, software, services, and other functions may be serviced by the developing countries. At the same time, the huge comparative advantage enjoyed in the labor field by actors such as China (especially in light of China's increasing attention to infrastructure) will increase the pressure to protect domestic competitors in the United States and Europe through anti-dumping or safeguard measures.

Our claim is that Statecraft transforms itself through successive epochal iterations, and the victors of war (or states that otherwise dominate the international strategic order) have the opportunity in each era to devise a trade system that reflects their epochal Statecraft. The Bretton Woods Order[18] accorded with the hallmarks of what we call "modern Statecraft": a State grounded in the nation, legitimating itself through the delivery of welfare, resting on an industrial base that was associated with the nation, cemented in the era of the state-nation, and trading with other, similarly situated nation-states. Like the preceding pre-modern order, however, Bretton Woods set in motion the seeds of its own demise. Bretton Woods inherited and shaped a world subdivided into national economies coextensive with the nation-states that established the trade order of GATT. The GATT/WTO opened up borders to trade in goods and services, an openness that lies at the heart of comparative advantage. This resulted in interloping ownership of production units across nation-states' borders, the correlative spread of production throughout the world, and the replacement of essentially "national" products and industries with global, diffuse goods and cross-border associations of economic interests that created a global market divided along industrial or sectoral, rather than national, lines. This transformation of patterns of economic activity was compounded by the revolution in global communications and, further, it was an important causal factor in to the gradual shift of fundamental policy tools of economic regulation and wealth transfer from the domestic to the international realm.

The transformation of the international economic order of states wrought by Bretton Woods contributed to the erosion of the essential domestic attributes of Statecraft in the modern world and to the passage from the age of the welfare nation-state to the age of the "enablement of

economic opportunity." In turn, just as the Bretton Woods system ushered in an international system that accorded with the nation-state, a
new constitutional moment is needed to usher in the international commercial order of post-modern states. We do not believe that the age of
comparative advantage signals the end of trade history. Rather, comparative advantage is an historically efficacious trade norm, one that made
sense in the era of the nation-state but, today, is in need of supplemen-
tation or more. As the State fulfills its welfare commitment through the
enablement of economic opportunity more than through the supply of
entitlements, so too will the global trading order of states dedicate and
legitimize itself by enabling economic opportunity across borders more
than through the mere liberalization of international trade in goods and
services.

We believe the modern liberal democracies that won World War II
must establish a new global trading order that "embeds" the post-modern
states into the evolving trade order. John Ruggie famously observed
that the Bretton Woods Order embedded the modern liberal democratic
ethos by facilitating trade and enlarging the global economic pie, all the
while leaving it to the nation-state to redistribute resources through its
sovereign welfare system. Consistent with this structure, the institutions
of trade of the twentieth century were dedicated to structuring rounds of
negotiation for lowering barriers to trade, adjudicating tensions between
free trade principles and countervailing domestic regulation, and implementing a minimal level of harmonization in fields (such as intellectual
property) affecting the free movement of goods and services. Today's international marketplace is diffuse, globalized, and interloped. We believe a
new trade organization needs to be embedded in this new marketplace,
one that should be comprised of a shifting representation of states and
their governments, dictated by the industries at issue (we will call this new
organization the "Trade Council"), delegating responsible persons based
on expertise in a given subject matter area to work jointly with industry
representatives and other international organizations.

In each instance, the Trade Council will establish programs designed
to engender the conditions necessary for the enablement of global economic opportunity. Consistent with diffuseness and post-modern Statecraft, the Trade Council will coordinate with a wide variety of international institutions. In addition, the Council could determine which
topical areas (beyond the traditional areas that are dealt with by the
WTO) are good candidates for trade linkage or other action. The norm
of enablement of global economic opportunity carries in its penumbra
other norms, such as anti-corruption rules, that could be more effectively enforced by cooperation between the Trade Council and, say, the

International Criminal Court or *ad hoc* tribunals. Likewise, together with central banks and other financial institutions, the Trade Council could coordinate financial and other monetary issues, taking into account industry-specific concerns that engender an international accounting system that reflects rather than resists the erosion of the nation-state.

Unlike Bretton Woods, the constitutional moment of the twenty-first century will not usher in a comprehensive regulatory framework dedicated to advancing a singular norm. Rather, it will mark a bifurcation of the international trade order into two distinct directions: the completion of the comparative advantage enterprise within the umbrella of the WTO and its negotiating rounds, and the enablement of global economic opportunity through establishment and development of new institutions. A constitutional moment (in the form of a conference akin to the Bretton Woods gathering) should formalize and mark the passage to the redirection of trade.[19] At that conference, the Trade Council would be established, and a broad document endorsing the new trade norm adopted. However, rather than a comprehensive regulatory framework such as the GATT, the conference would simply establish an umbrella framework from which future regulation and projects (including rolling, *ad hoc* modest Marshall Plans of sorts to deal with pre-modern areas) will issue.

We have said that security and trade comprise the outer face of the State. But how are they related to one another? In our final chapter, we explain why – *from the point of view of strategy* – it makes sense for the nations of the first world to embrace the nascent norm of global economic opportunity and support the activities we see as important for the Trade Council. Put simply, our view is that a trade system based on the enablement of global economic opportunity will contribute to engendering and extending economic growth in the developing nations, cement a globalized society of post-modern states incorporating the emerging trading powerhouses of the twenty-first century, and thereby directly further the security interests of the developed nations. We acknowledge the debate over the facts regarding the connection between terrorism and poverty, and the question whether trade has any relevance to containing religious fundamentalist forms of Statecraft. But we think that focus is too narrow, and we explain how a wider look at the link between terrorism and global growth reveals how the enablement of global economic opportunity is in the interest of global security.

As we said at the outset of this Introduction, our goal in this book is to present a complete theory of the global trading order. While we are as enamored of theory as any academics, we believe that theory does its best work when it yields concrete proposals for change. There seems to be little doubt that the institutions of global trade are in serious trouble, or worse.[20] Despite this emerging consensus, we believe it important to explain precisely why the Bretton Woods institutions – which worked so well for over a half century – have now become so ineffective. We believe that if we understand why these institutions are now obsolete we can better see what must be done to meet the challenges posed by global trade. In this book, we tell this story in all its detail and we explain how that story leads to the institutional proposals we advance.

2 The Evolving State

Thesis:

The trade order of states follows the constitutional order of states. The current form of the State – the nation-state – is in a process of transformation. To understand the contours of the next trade order of states, we need to identify the causes of the changing constitutional order of states and explore how that constitutional order will engender a new trade order of states.

Our book confronts a number of myths that have pervaded the intellectual conversation of the late twentieth and early twenty-first centuries. These myths all have a common denominator: they are grounded in the claim that history has ended and that with the rise of the modern liberal democracies, we have reached the final stage of development in government.[1] These myths evince a somewhat linear progression, akin to scientific evolution, which culminates in the survival and triumph of the modern liberal democratic model. States, the story goes, went through a succession of oppressive forms of government that did not sufficiently take into account the well-being of the people. Kings, princes, emperors, dictators, and other rulers succeeded one another until Western political thought matured enough to invent "democracy" as the embodiment of the good society. After a bloody struggle against its last, ferocious fascist and communist enemies, democracy defeated the "totalitarian" ideologies, thereby ushering in the end of history.

The "end of history" thesis is widely attributed to Francis Fukuyama, who announced it in 1989.[2] Of course, Fukuyama was not the first to make this bold claim. Hegel had said as much about Napoleon's victory at Jena in 1806.[3] But, unlike Hegel, Fukuyama was not declaring the triumph of the state-nation.[4] Rather, he was declaring the end of the great struggle of the twentieth century, which pitted democracy, fascism, and communism against one another. After the defeat of the Axis Powers in World War II, and following the fall of the Iron Curtain, Fukuyama believed that democracy had triumphed and would, henceforth, be the preferred model for State government.[5]

These political claims, which dominated the world of ideas in the late twentieth century, usually went hand-in-hand with a series of economic assumptions. Since their inception, the economies of the modern liberal democracies were what one may characterize as "tempered market economies." The pure operation of market forces was checked by various welfare programs which, as we describe below, were of the essence of democracy. The political spectrum of Europe and the United States, the cradles of modern democracy, exhibited sharp differences with respect to the extent of government regulation of market forces. Germany's Social-Democratic Party, France's Socialist Party, England's Labor, and like-minded political movements insisted on a deeper correction of unfettered economic activity to achieve redistributive results than more free-market oriented parties (which tended to be associated with the right wing of the political spectrum). Some states (such as the U.S.) believed more in tax-and-spend programs, some adhered to cradle-to-grave protection systems (e.g., Britain), and yet others (e.g., Japan) took an indicative planning approach to achieving the welfare of their people. Regardless of their political affiliation, though, all modern liberal democracies followed an economic system where the well-being of the people (which, as we discuss below, was broadly defined to include the legal apparatus associated with the regulatory state) would be protected through government regulation of the market.

The General Agreement on Tariffs and Trade (GATT) and its system of trade based on comparative advantage were assumed to be a natural complement to the market economies of the modern liberal democracies. As we will discuss in detail throughout this book, modern consciousness was grounded in the assumption that comparative advantage and free trade, working in conjunction with concessions to the domestic need to insulate certain sectors of the national economies, went hand-in-hand with the economic systems of modern liberal democracies. The ultimate global organization of government would include a tempered free market, trading with similarly situated foreign economies. This world outlook had a distinctly Western profile. The end of history, of course, coincided with the victory over the Soviet bloc and, after the defeat of fascism in World War II, the removal of communism as the second and last mortal enemy of democracy. Democracy triumphed and, in time, it would be exported to the newly liberated nations of the Eastern bloc. As to the so-called Third

World, which in time graduated to "less developed" and then to "developing" status, democracy and its political and economic apparatus would also bring about peace, prosperity, and a form of government that would last for the ages.

At the same time as history ended in the marriage of democracy and tempered economies, we have been told that the State is withering away.[6] The evidence, it seems, is everywhere. The states of the European Union have yielded a substantial portion of their authority to Brussels. The inviolability of nation-states' territory, which was enshrined in the United Nations' charter, is giving way to an international system where collective intervention to prevent massive human rights violations is warranted. Networks have now replaced states as the focal point of world governance.[7] States have ceded authority and control of sovereign territory to multinational corporations, whose tentacles span major trading centers, and who jump from one jurisdiction to the next, taking advantage of qualified industrial zones and other privileged export zones, regulatory comparative advantage, and the cheapest available resources. Global or supra-national organizations such as the World Trade Organization (WTO) and the European Commission now control policy questions once thought to be the sole province of sovereign states.

The "end of history" and "death of the State" theses, however, express only partial truths. While it is true that democracy defeated fascism and communism in the ideological struggle for political dominance, history has not ended. The State has not run its course and, like Hegel, Fukuyama was mistaken in his claim for the end of history. Far from dying, the State (and not for the first time) is in a process of change – a metamorphosis. The nature of the State is changing, in a manner that permits the transformation of the notions of control and sovereignty that we have broached.[8] Identifying these changes, gauging their significance, and evaluating their relationship with respect to other features of the relations between states is central to understanding how and why the State continues to evolve. Once we understand how and why the State is evolving, we can explore the relationship between the State, the constitutional order of states, and the trade order.

There can be little doubt that the current form of the State, the nation-state, is undergoing serious and, likely, permanent change. We agree with those who claim that the nation-state is eroding. But we think that is the easy part of the analysis. The more difficult aspect of the analysis is imagining what the nation-state will become and what impact that will have on the global trading order. Our claim is that we are entering a new era of Statecraft. As with prior iterations of the State, the current elements of Statecraft dictate the contours of the internal constitution of states, their external constitutional order, and the policies and regulatory regimes that are enacted in order to effectuate the constitutional theoretical apparatus. We also claim that the victors of war design external systems that accord with their inner Statecraft. In other words, Statecraft is not a uniform proposition across the globe, and the strategic victors will develop an internal system that accords with their internal Statecraft structure.

We believe that as the twenty-first century dawns, a new era of Statecraft is upon us. Our focus in this book is the implications of this Statecraft evolution for the international trading system. In this chapter, we outline the contours of Statecraft, and we introduce some of the trade and commercial concepts that will be explored in depth in subsequent chapters.

STATECRAFT

In this book, we argue that the State goes through successive iterations, and that "Statecraft," a term which we explain below, transforms itself in each era. The story never ends and, in fact, each iteration of the State contains the seeds of its own future transformation. No doubt, changes in Statecraft always look clear in hindsight. Things look less evident when the State is in the throes of a transition from one form of Statecraft to another. This is where we think we stand now.

The conventional wisdom is that "the State" was created in the middle of the fifteenth century. Over the course of the last 500 years, the State has gone through a number of iterations. Importantly, history teaches us that states relate to one another as a society of states in the sense that states share a form or organizing structure. Since the sixteenth century, each particular form of the State comprises what we call a "constitutional order of states." For example, the current form of the State – the nation-state – is the product of unique historical forces that have shaped the configuration of states over the course of the last century. A world comprised of nation-states is a "constitutional" order of states in the sense that the world of states is comprised of nations each exhibiting foundational, common features and shared modes of interaction. The "Statecraft" of modern states (i.e., nation-states) is those features and the modalities of interaction for the society of states.

Statecraft is a term that captures both the inner structure of the State and the constitutional "order" of states, or the international society of states. As we discuss below and in subsequent chapters, the inner and the outer faces of states interact with each other, and produce dynamic patterns of change that, over time, usher in successive epochal manifestations of the State. Following Cooper, we have classified the last three iterations of the State as pre-modern, modern, and post-modern. Our contention is that the nature of Statecraft in each era dictates its inner constitutional order, and the transformative patterns of activity that are bound to bring about the next Statecraft epoch.

In the pre-modern era, for example, the coalescing of the state-nations of Western Europe brought about new patterns of economic activity that destroyed the economic and social orders that had prevailed in the earlier, Kingly states.[9] The ethos of pre-modern Statecraft was to unleash the power of the State to solidify and consolidate itself. The Industrial Revolution, as we will discuss in later chapters, was a natural corollary of the pre-modern solidification process. At the same time, the abandonment of the rigidly regulated feudal system brought about a new phenomenon, economic cycles of boom and bust that left the economic actors of the state-nation vulnerable to wide swings in already unfriendly markets. Yet, the State could not concern itself with providing its subjects a safety net or a minimum level of economic security because its focus was on solidifying itself: this was its ethos. Not only did the State refrain from extending the kind of welfare protection that later became the hallmark of the modern nation-state, it responded to the challenge of solidification by enacting a wide array of regulation intended to consolidate a single, unitary market within its borders, shelter its territories from external economic and strategic threats and, in the process, ensured that there would be no welfare regulation to impede economic expansion.

The mechanics of Statecraft in the pre-modern age planted the seeds of the transformation of the State that would lead to the rise of the modern age. The first element of the modern age, the nation, was a likely outcome of the solidification process of the state-nation.[10] The state-nation building process resulted in the creation of several classes dedicated to accomplishing the solidification of Statecraft in the pre-modern era. The upshot of the inner order of the State was the establishment of industries associated with the State, and the coalescence of its industrial actors into a cohesive nation. The same forces created a national working class that was later absorbed into the middle classes that shored up the modern nation-states. Ultimately, a nation was created and, when the State concluded its solidification process, its legitimating basis became the well-being of the nation on which it rested. The very classes who were purposefully left relatively unregulated during the pre-modern era became the subject of intense regulatory protection in the modern welfare state. Modern liberal democracies began to compete with marxism and fascism as alternative forms of Statecraft, thereby forcing the liberal democracies to institute strong welfare systems to compete for Statecraft dominance.

The major Statecraft elements of the modern era – national sovereignty, welfare, and balance of power – are all the product of mechanisms actuated during the pre-modern era. The modern state was a reaction to the mechanisms put in motion in the pre-modern era in that it established a substantial system of protection for individuals. Further, the welfare state mitigated the hardships engendered by the industrialization process of the state-nation as well as the market imperfections that the state-nation had left untouched.

The State, then, has two dimensions, the inner and the outer. In this chapter and throughout this book we explain how their interaction pushes Statecraft along a cycle of transformation that ushers in each successive era of Statecraft. The outer dimension of the State is exhibited in relations between states. The inner dimension of the State names the relations between the State and a people (for example, the modern nation). Taken together, the inner and the outer dimensions of the State constitute its Statecraft. The outer dimension of the State is comprised of two principal features: strategy and trade. Whether states are at peace or at war with one another is a function of forces that go beyond the immediate interests of any particular state. As we shall explain, the strategic interests of states are driven by the particular form of states as well as issues of ideology and history that are unique to each historical epoch.

Trade, the second aspect of the outer face of the State, is also governed by the particular form of the State as well as issues of history and ideology. The particular ideology of trade (e.g., mercantilism or comparative advantage) follows the constitutional order of states. Mercantilism, for example, is complementary to the state-nation form[11] of the State. Similarly, comparative advantage is a natural complement to the nation-state and its welfare policies. The trade order "follows" the constitutional order of states in that each constitutional order of states is married to a trade order that complements or fits the particular form of the State at any given point in history.

The states that control the establishment of a given trade order tend to be those that dominate the international strategic scene. As we will explain later, in the twentieth century, the victors of what Bobbitt has called the "Long War" established an international order of trade that accords with their view of Statecraft. Part of our enterprise in this book is to identify the changing nature of Statecraft in the early twenty-first century and to articulate the norm and institutions of trade in the post-modern age that the World War II victors can put in place before a new war violently forces the necessary changes.

In this chapter we will consider three successive constitutional orders of the State. These are the state-nation, the nation-state, and the post-modern state. Each form of the State exhibits both an inner and an outer dimension. We believe that the present form of the State – the nation-state – is fading away and will be replaced. Because we believe that the trade order of states follows the constitutional order of states, we are convinced that what we need now is fresh thinking about what the next trade order of states will be. In short, if the nature of the State is changing, and the trade order follows the constitutional order of states, then the current trade order will evolve as well.

THE STATE-NATION

As we discussed above, the State exists for a reason: each iteration of the State legitimates itself in a manner that reflects the particular historical forces of the age. Our contention is that the nature of Statecraft in each era dictates its inner constitutional order, the individuals and groups that interact within each state, the type of industries and technology that will be developed within each era, and the transformative patterns of activity that are bound to bring about the next Statecraft epoch. In this section, we explore the contours of the state-nation, to which we at times refer to as the "pre-modern State," and its historical basis.

The "state-nation" is the product of the seventeenth and eighteenth centuries. It arose during a mixed period of revolutionary progress and oppression. Western Europe and the United States witnessed the French and the American Revolutions, and the birth of a form of government that, in time, would transform and dedicate itself to the welfare of the people. The American Revolution was the first post-colonial movement that threw off the yoke of an oppressive foreign power, and created a state that enjoyed full political and economic self-determination. The French Revolution introduced lofty concepts of liberty, fraternity, equality, and rejected the long-held notion that divine power endorsed the appointment of the King as supreme ruler. At the same time, however, the European powers engaged (during the pre-modern era) in the wholesale conquest and colonization of territories that spanned Africa, Asia, the Americas, the Middle East, and virtually every other region that came to comprise the modern era's "developing world" and the post-modern "emerging economies." In the process, the European powers practiced slavery, discrimination, and other forms of exploitation that became unpalatable as the world entered the modern and post-modern eras.

If there is any singular characteristic to this form of the State it lies in the unique manner in which the State forged out of disparate and (save for geography) largely unrelated feudal states and territories (e.g., dukedoms, territories, and princely states) a unified and unifying whole.

The coalescing process that led to the creation of a unitary State drove the transformation of the nature of Statecraft. The need to cement the disparate parts of the State into one unit gave rise to a State-centric era. Domestically, the State drew on its subjects to strengthen itself. In the process conscription structures were created that enlarged the military power of the State, as well as a legal system that protected property rights and a largely *laissez faire* economic system that contributed to the creation of an industrial and agricultural economic mass that shored up the power of the State and contributed to the solidification process. Outwardly, the State engaged in conquest and a pattern of trade that were intended to solidify its power. It colonized as many territories as its power (relative to state-nation competitors) permitted. It traded based on a system of mercantilism, a largely zero-sum game intended to build up as much gold reserve and as many other resources as possible in the hands of one state.

The hallmark of the state-nation is the use of its particular legitimating thesis to build unity out of diversity in the service of a particular ideal. In the state-nation, the individual serves the goal of making the state more powerful: a "state" is forged out of territories peopled by populations that are ethno-culturally diverse and otherwise lacking in cohesion. The essence of Statecraft in the state-nation is to increase the power of the emerging sovereign. This process has both strategic and trade dimensions: it results in the establishment of a state founded on discrete boundaries, a solid identity associated with the nation, an industrial and commercial base owned and operated by the nation, and the ultimate transformation of the State as a force that unleashes the power of the nation to solidify itself to one that dedicates itself to the welfare of the nation. As we will see, states' failure to pass through this transition process – whether because they were colonized, were not meaningful participants in the international trading system, or otherwise – makes it virtually impossible for them to participate in the modern strategic and trade systems of the nation-state era, presenting them with formidable difficulties as they face the era of the post-modern market state.

PRE-MODERN INNER STATECRAFT: THE SEEDS
OF THE NATION AND WELFARE

The inner face of the solidifying state-nation was characterized by a *laissez faire* regulatory approach to welfare, which transformed itself into an elaborate welfare system during the modern age, commingled with the establishment of a legal system for the protection of market actors. The state-nation was also characterized by an industrial and commercial base that became associated with the nation and, ultimately, allowed it to compete with other nations in a system of comparative advantage. The gradual establishment of conscription and of a system of control and identification of the subjects of the State were also hallmarks of the state-nation, and allowed the nation-states of the modern era to implement welfare programs and the administrative state. As is the case with respect to each era of Statecraft, these hallmarks of pre-modern Statecraft were intended to further the basic purpose of the State in the pre-modern epoch: cementing the merger of diverse territories and populations into a unitary entity, and strengthening the central authority of the State over the emerging entity. In turn, the mechanics of Statecraft shaped the inner order of each discrete state, including the classes of individuals who comprised it, their relationships vis-a-vis one another, and their treatment by the State that ultimately resulted in transformative changes that ushered in the next Statecraft epoch.

The nature of the regulatory apparatus of the State reflected the central features of the state-nation. The inner constitutional order of the state-nation was intended to further the solidification of the State and to unleash of the power of the subjects in realizing that goal. The economic activities of the Industrial Revolution were a natural corollary of Statecraft in this era, in that they created a strong economic base associated with and supporting the State. In turn, the constitutional order of the state-nation was designed to support this structure. The patterns of economic activity of the Industrial Revolution destroyed the economic and social orders that had prevailed in the earlier, Kingly states. The Kingly order was largely feudal, but with all its inequalities it ensured that the peasants would be grounded in land and, while given no opportunity to climb from one class to the next, they would have access to the basic means of subsistence. The Industrial Revolution, together with the regulatory patterns that we discuss below, destroyed this order and created massive classes of workers – the future interlocutors of Karl Marx and communist or socialist movements.

By necessity, the pre-modern State did not engage in the welfare enterprise of the modern world, and its welfare apparatus was characterized by what we would call *laissez faire* policies. The tempered market economy of the modern era was born out of an unregulated market, which first witnessed the rise of a body of law intended to protect property rights in a capitalist economy. The working classes had access to jobs, but those jobs could be taken away from them at will. The State provided them with little, if any, protection against commercial exploitation by capitalist classes with greater bargaining power. At the same time, the abandonment of the rigidly regulated feudal system brought about a new phenomenon, economic cycles of boom and bust that left the economic actors of the state-nation vulnerable to wide swings in already unfriendly markets. To ensure that economies would not collapse completely in bust cycles, the State was forced to enact a wide array of regulation intended to consolidate a single, unitary market within its borders, and to ensure that there would be no welfare regulation to add to the woes of economic uncertainty. Maximum wage legislation was enacted. Labor unions were banned so as to avoid interference with the industrialists' ability to ride out difficult economic times. Taxation raised increasingly high revenues but the percentage of revenues allocated to what we call welfare programs remained very low.

The focus of regulation was, instead, to solidify private property rights and create stable and predictable markets for economic exchange. As illustrated below, legal codes such as the Napoleonic code came into force, grounding property and economic rights in an effective and sophisticated system of law. Conscription raised armies capable of furthering the State's expansionist drive to draw on outside resources to firm itself up. Systems such as the guilds were put into place. As Martin Van Creveld reminds us, no state was more successful in the solidification endeavor than France.[12] The focus of regulation in France's state-nation era was not on the welfare of the people, but on drawing on resources to solidify the State. Napoleon's use of the *levée en masse* or mass conscription allowed him to greatly increase the size of his armies.[13] This, coupled with his ingenious strategic advances, enabled the nation to have an army the size and power of which had never been seen before. Administratively, the government established a centralized bureaucracy with branches accessible far and wide. A legal code was drafted that contributed to the simplification and expansion of law. Notably, there were no exceptions for nobility or other limits on the reach of law. The idea of the rule of law was a central feature of the legal system. Educational reform (especially unification and standardization) was radical, far-reaching, and without precedent. As a result of these developments, the French state-nation protected the private property that strengthened its power, relied on a strong army to defend itself and plunder foreign resources, and put in place an administrative state that controlled the subjects of the state to an unprecedented degree.

Napoleonic economics were designed to strengthen the internal order of the State through a variety of means. Giving loans to businesses and creating tariffs were two ways in which Napoleon bolstered the strength of domestic enterprises. But Napoleon also created a central bank, built roads and bridges, and, most importantly, created the "Code Napoleon." With this codification of French law, Napoleon's Civil Code replaced some 360 local codes of the *Ancien Régime*. The unity and coherence achieved through this unification of disparate and conflicting local laws would not be achieved again.[14] The result was a web of regulation of property rights and transfers, contract rights, family law, and inheritances, interpreted in a relatively uniform manner by the jurists of the state-nation. This regulation provided the dwellers of "Fortress France" with a strong set of juridical protections that stabilized an internal market which French foreign relations law and practice protected against foreign interference.

Substantive reforms were not all that was needed to create a state-nation. With due attention to the cultural aspects of national unity, festivals were initiated, a new national flag (the tricolor) was introduced, and an official anthem (the *Marsellaise*) written for public events. Thus, "France became the first country where the nationalist cause was married to that of the state...."[15] Of course, nationalism – and the conflicts it engendered – were still very much a part of the history of Europe in the first half of the nineteenth century.[16] But the state-nation formation was inevitable: from the mid-nineteenth century on, nationalized states appeared which gathered peoples, armies, and industries (in short, a nation), all in the service of the State. In the end, these patterns of activity of pre-modern Statecraft resulted in the rise of a nation that would later become associated with the French nation-state. In turn, having solidified itself and facing competition from fascist and communist forms of Statecraft, the modern liberal democratic State would unleash its power to provide for the welfare of the nation and create a form of Statecraft most suited, in its outer face, to free trade based on comparative advantage.

THE OUTER FACE OF THE STATE-NATION: OF MERCANTILISM AND POWER

The outer face of the state-nation also accorded with its ethos, as the colonialist and mercantilist enterprises provided a continuous flow of resources that contributed to the strengthening of the internal infrastructure of the emerging State.

Mercantilism prevailed in Europe after the decline of feudalism. The mercantile system was based on national policies of accumulating bullion, establishing colonies and a merchant marine, and developing industry and mining to attain a favorable balance of trade. Mercantilism is a "trade order" – an economic policy of and between states. But it is also an ideology in that it is an element of a certain conception of the State, relations between states, and the obligations of the State to the nation. Mercantilism accords with the state-nation because it is motivated by the solidification needs of the State. "Beggar thy neighbor" policies make eminent sense in a pre-modern world. While (somewhat ironically) they contributed to the formation of a nation that was ready for comparative advantage, mercantilist policies accorded with the state-nation in a way that comparative advantage could not. (We will return later to one of the central premises of our book: comparative advantage is not a universal, timeless theory.) The state-nation building process would ultimately give rise to discrete economic units capable of trading with each other based on comparative advantage.

Mercantilism had an enormous effect on the states that embraced it as an economic theory. The impetus behind mercantilism was states' desire to improve their position in the world relative to other states. Under mercantilist policies and practices, states looked for ways to increase their national wealth and power by heavily regulating inter-state trade.[17] This focus on the solidification and well-being of the State itself as opposed to the well-being of the citizens of the State was an important hallmark of the state-nation. Mercantilism exemplified this attitude. The strict regulations involved in mercantilism engendered indifference on the part of governments to the personal struggles of their citizens while creating quotas or standards for industries that had to be met in order to increase the states' import-export balance or the amount of money in their treasuries. Additionally, the focus on a state's position in the world made states' armies and navies extremely important. A state had to be powerful in order to protect its interests, especially if those interests involved trading with other states.

Mercantilism affected both states' internal (domestic) and external (foreign) policies. Externally, states tried to increase their stores of gold and silver by exploring new areas of the world, trading in certain parts of the world, and colonizing the new territories they found, ultimately creating new trading partners. Internally, states focused on domestic industries and attempted to expand the scope of their commerce – who they could trade with and what types of goods they had available for trade. This expansion in trade increased competition in industries within each state. Under mercantilism, states also encouraged their industries to develop goods for export. This drive to increase production caused factories to grow, attracting people to the cities so they could work in the factories. Mercantilism even affected farming as farmers tried to provide food for all the new city-dwellers. Although states wanted their industries to grow, mercantilism dictated that states rigidly control their economies. States began instituting tariffs on imports to protect their industries against potential foreign trading partners. It became common for different industries to have guilds that prevented an unassociated person from plying that trade. States would also set strict requirements on the way different products could be produced.

The mercantilist drive of the State in the pre-modern era, and its grab for resources through colonialism and other power-seeking enterprises, would end in the modern era (but not before the modern liberal democracies' failure to recognize that this feature of Statecraft had become obsolete caused tremendous economic and strategic loss). As we will see later, the modern State was suited for trade through law and for a rules-based system that would respect the sovereignty of each individual state. Before moving on to the modern era, we pause to consider the technological apparatus that grew of the pre-modern epoch of Statecraft. Here again, the story is one of cyclical evolution based on the nature of the State.

STATECRAFT AND TECHNOLOGICAL ADVANCE

We believe that the nature of Statecraft in any particular era also drives the kind of technological advances that will be pursued. We will expand on this claim throughout this book. In the pre-modern epoch, one of the major industries affected by mercantilism was shipbuilding. States needed more ships, both for navies to protect a state's foreign territories and for merchant ships to facilitate trade. The same pattern of interaction holds true with respect to the creation of specific sectors of industry, services, or other economic activity during every epoch. As a result of increased trade, and because of the State's focus on cementing disparate components to strengthen itself, commercial practices like credit became more prevalent and banks assumed greater importance.[18] Other industries included steel and mining. Transportation and the advent of the railroad were essential means of solidifying the state-nation, and integral parts of the urbanization and industrialization drive that characterized it. Just as shipbuilding was necessary to trade and the strengthening of the state-nation, coal and other mined resources were essential components of the pattern of economic activities that characterized the Statecraft of the state-nation. Further, many important advances were made during this period; however, none of the developments was intended to benefit the individual subjects of states. States focused on themselves and used their citizens as tools to improve and solidify their position in the world.

TRANSFORMATION AND TRANSITION TO MODERN STATECRAFT

The mechanics of Statecraft in the pre-modern age sowed the seeds of the transformation of the State that would lead to the development of the modern age. The first central element of the modern age, the nation, was an inevitable outcome of the solidification process of the state-nation. The state-nation building process resulted in the creation of several classes dedicated to accomplishing the purpose of Statecraft in the pre-modern era. The constitutional order of the state-nation included regulation aimed at empowering the capitalist and industrial classes to build an industrial and agricultural apparatus that would shore up the State. The State encouraged the extension of credit and the establishment of financial institutions. It created a constitutional order that intentionally rejected welfare schemes, so as to leave the industrial classes with as much regulatory space as possible to face the vagaries of the (as yet) unleashed capitalist economies. It put in place legal codes based on a guarantee of State protection of property, contract rights, and other proceeds and necessary components of an industrial, capitalistic economy. The upshot of the inner order of the State was the establishment of industries associated with the State, and the coalescing of its industrial components into a cohesive nation. France, England, and the United States each had their distinct coal mining, shipbuilding, steel making, railroad, and agricultural industries.

The same forces created a national working class, which later was absorbed into the middle classes that shored up the modern nation-states. In turn, the ideological struggles of the twentieth century modern era were born out of this process. When the State finished its consolidation, it had created a working class whose circumstances needed to be transformed. Marxism attempted to create an international proletariat and to undo the nation-building process that occurred in the nineteenth century with respect to the working classes. However, the working classes were essentially national in nature in that they were attached to industries created by capitalist forces that the state-nations fostered and incentivized. Their social and economic situation was dismal. They lacked job protection, health security, and the ability to climb out of their current conditions. Nevertheless, the industrialization process that the state-nation brought about turned them into a distinctly national grouping of individuals. As a result, the working classes were associated with the State that drew on their strength to build its industry; and they would look to the State to rectify the oppressive conditions they endured. The welfare state provided an alternative (national in nature) to communism and fascism as a means of improving workers' conditions.

Marxism and fascism were, in part, answers to the needs of the laboring and industrial classes that the pre-modern age created in the course of strengthening the power of the State. Marxism posited that the only route to improving the workers' condition was a takeover of the means of production. Without such a takeover, the capitalist classes would continue to exploit workers and give them only the means to subsist and to continue to build the industrial base of the State. The unification of the workers of the world would end the cycle of oppression and usher in the end of political history. Fascism offered a different solution. Instead of offering a cross-border unification of classes, it sought to bring about the end of history through a full incorporation of all classes into a racially defined, corporatist nation. The 3,000-year Reich sounded the end of political history, not through the takeover of the means of production by the working classes, but by the ever-lasting domination of the Aryan race. In both scenarios, however, the ideologies spoke to a nation created during the pre-modern era that required a modern Statecraft answer to needs stemming directly from the social circumstances created by pre-modern Statecraft.

It was no wonder, then, that Fukuyama viewed modern liberal democracy as the end of history. The modern liberal democratic form of modern Statecraft answered the same needs that marxism and fascism addressed. Like its competing ideologies, modern liberal democratic forms of government would solve problems that had plagued the pre-modern era and usher in an era of perpetual peace. Modern liberal democracy implicitly recognized that the social conditions it addressed were a function of the pre-modern era of Statecraft. As we explain below, the establishment of welfare was in fact a recognition that the state-nation had to transform itself into a nation-state dedicated to providing an alternative to marxism and fascism. Unlike its two competing ideologies, modern liberal democratic thought provided a natural evolution from pre-modern to modern that did not involve a radical rejection of the foundations of Statecraft. At the end of the day, then, the foundations of Statecraft in the nation-state were laid in the preceding era. History continued and the State reinvented itself.

We now turn to the second iteration of the State that we cover in this chapter, the nation-state, identifying its foundation and explaining its transformation into the post-modern state.

THE NATION-STATE

The nation-state is the product of historical, political, and cultural forces that span two centuries. The Peace of Westphalia in 1648 introduced the idea of a "system" of states. Nationalism, particularly of the kind celebrated by Herder and Fichte in the eighteenth century,[19] added a strong cultural dimension to the idea of a "nation."[20] Sovereignty – control of geography – was central to the idea of a nation-state.[21] Between themselves, states sought equilibrium expressed as the idea of "balance of power." More fundamentally, however, the nation-state was the natural successor of the state-nation. The state-nation had a regulatory apparatus that favored the holders of the means of production, rather than those whose labor drove them. The state-nation by and large viewed the other participants in the international system as competitors, eschewing general policies of negotiation and collaboration.

In the following subsections, we explore the essential hallmarks of Statecraft in the nation-state. In later chapters, we will return to these elements of Statecraft and explain how they affect the global trading system.

STATECRAFT IN THE MODERN ERA: THE NATION AND ITS WELFARE

The transformation of the internal regulatory landscape in the modern liberal democratic state-nations of Europe was the primary manifestation of the passage to the era of the nation-state. The working classes of the pre-modern era became important interlocutors of the State. They joined merchants, industrialists, capital holders, and other groups to form a national base for the State, which the State dedicated itself to fostering and protecting. The regulatory apparatus that came to be known as the "welfare state" was born, initially, as the inner constitutional expression of this Statecraft commitment.

The impetus was, in part, to provide a response to the problems created by the workings of Statecraft in the pre-modern era. First, the welfare state established a safety net to protect its subjects against the uncertainties of the capitalist economies that achieved industrialization. The welfare apparatus varied from one state to the next; however, as we detail in later chapters, their common denominator was unleashing the power of the State to create a set of entitlements for the nation. This would mitigate the impact of the oscillations of economic activities and provide a minimum level of economic benefits to the subjects of the State. Unemployment benefits, aid to families with dependent children, disability benefits, and retirement schemes exemplify the regulatory activities of the nation-state. In addition, minimum wage, minimum income, universal health care, and free education allowed all subjects of the nation, the citizens of the State, to have a minimal level of access to common goods.

Second, the welfare state addressed the externalities created by the industrialization process of the state-nation and the market imperfections that the state-nation had left untouched. Labor regulation began to protect workers' right to unionize, thereby reducing the imbalance in leverage and bargaining power among the various classes that interacted in the pre-modern marketplace. Resource conservation and environmental measures were introduced to compel industries to absorb the costs of some of the externalities their activities created. Health and safety measures were introduced to protect consumers and other citizens of the State. Disclosure and other regulatory burdens were placed on corporations. Employment rules limited employers' ability to terminate their workers, requiring them across Europe to do so only with good reason or to pay generous severance.

Third, the welfare state created an administrative framework to control the nation, and ensure that the welfare regulation that it had put in place would be properly overseen and that the modern State would have control over its nation and territories. Many claims have been made about the origins and historical circumstances that have given rise to the administrative state. Although it is beyond the scope of our project to engage in that conversation, our claim is that the rise of the administrative state was a natural corollary of the nation-state. We posit that Statecraft dictates the contours of the regulatory environment that will prevail in each epoch. Modern Statecraft requires an administrative state because its primary purpose is to guarantee the welfare of the nation and the welfare enterprise- broadly defined to include all of the regulatory activities that we have mentioned – which requires that the State control its subjects, markets, and territory. Control requires a government apparatus that is not present in the pre-modern era: the modern administrative state established such an apparatus. Rather than being the result of accidental historical circumstances, the administrative state was a necessary part of the modern nation-state. In other words, just like comparative advantage, the administrative state was a phenomenon that was particular to a given era of Statecraft.

The nation that was born out of the pre-modern era, then, became the basis of the modern State. While its welfare had been an impediment to the solidification of the state-nation, it became the legitimating drive of the nation-state. In the next subsection, we discuss how sovereignty and balance of power were essential elements of modern Statecraft, and their relationship to the nation and its welfare.

STATECRAFT IN THE NATION-STATE ERA: SOVEREIGNTY AND BALANCE OF POWER

The concept of sovereignty has been the object of persistent scholarly attention. It is not our intention to revisit the debate over the meaning of sovereignty but to identify its basic nature as a hallmark of Statecraft in the modern era. Sovereignty is inextricably tied to the idea of the nation.

The essential goal of the State was to protect the nation against external threats and to provide for its internal welfare. The nation was sovereign and, although it was largely ethnic, it defined itself by its physical borders and the population it inherited through centuries of evolution. The sovereignty needs of the welfare state were entirely dependent on, and defined in relation to, the rise of the nation as the foundation of the State and its welfare as the centerpiece of Statecraft. In the modern age, "sovereignty" meant the ability to define the inner constitutional order of the State free of interference from external forces. As we will discuss, this explains why the GATT and its WTO successor encountered fierce national resistance to the imposition of international trade norms that might displace the regulatory sovereignty of the State over such domestic matters as labor, resource conservation, environmental protection, or health.

The State's dedication to the nation in the modern era also included the State's guarantee of security. Thus, the threat of war between states was solved by the idea of balance of power. The notion of balance of power was linked to the concepts of sovereignty and of the nation as the interlocutor of the State in its quest for legitimacy. In the modern system, nation-states with strong sovereign powers maintained international order by balancing each other's power. Balance of power, rather than the hegemonic domination of an empire or superpower, was the preferred method of achieving order.[22] The modern world viewed states as equal citizens of a global society. The concept of hegemony was antithetical to this world view, however fictional or detached from reality it might have been. Thus, it was the alternative – an order based on balance among equals (or a substantial group of equals) – that came to dominate the Western world in the modern era.

The modern era of strategy – commencing with World War I, continuing through the defeat of fascism, and ending around 1989 with the fall of communism – spanned the better part of the twentieth century. During that period, liberal democracies organized themselves as modern welfare nation-states.[23] A commitment to sovereignty was foundational to the internal and external dimensions of the modern state.[24] Modern states adhered to absolutist notions of sovereignty in their internal policy choices and external policy and military objectives.[25] The notion of sovereignty was linked to the nation as a constitutive feature of the State, to welfare as the legitimating drive of the State, and to the balance of power as a key component of the State's external strategy.

Just as the pre-modern era contained the seeds of its own transformation into modernism, the modern epoch of Statecraft included features that were sure to lead to the demise of the nation-state and the rise of an alternative form of Statecraft. We cannot understand the transition of the State from its current form,[26] that of the nation-state, without appreciating how these two elements of Statecraft evolved into their current configuration and how they are related to one another. We begin with strategy and, then, turn to trade, commerce, and economy.

TRANSFORMATION

Throughout this book we explain how the modern nation-states followed a constitutional order based on interaction among equals. Balance of power, sovereignty, the nation, and its welfare, were concepts that contributed to the division of the World War II victors' world into discrete units that balanced each other to maintain security and traded with one another to achieve prosperity. The post-modern world, on the other hand, is characterized by diffuseness and a fracturing of the borders that shelter each unit and make it an autonomous player in the modern marketplace. In this chapter, we focus on certain aspects of strategy and welfare, and we will continue to sound the theme of post-modern diffuseness and its meaning for the international global order throughout the book. Our goal is to introduce the main hallmarks of the "post-modern" or "market state", and explain how it arises out of the loss of control of the modern state over its nation, borders, security, and welfare needs.

The modern era witnessed a struggle among communism, fascism, and modern liberal democracy over which form of Statecraft would provide the organizational form of the nation-state. World War II ended with the demise of fascism. The fall of the Berlin Wall in 1989 marked the end of communism and, with it, the triumph of democracy.[27] Fukuyama's end of history begins in 1989 with the fall of the Berlin Wall. According to Robert Cooper, 1989 did not mark the end of history, but rather set the stage for the emergence of a new form of the State – the "post-modern" state.[28] Philip Bobbitt similarly rejects Fukuyama's claim, and views 1989 as merely a step in the evolution of the State. He identifies the new form of the State as the "market-state" which, he argues, will succeed the nation-state.[29] These two theorists of the State agree on a number of defining characteristics of the new form of State that, in their view, confirm the continuing evolution of the State.

The year 1989 marked an important point in the development of the State. In *The Breaking of Nations*, Robert Cooper characterizes it as a year that "marks a break in European history."[30] In fact, Cooper attributes so much significance to 1989 that he sees its importance as greater than most previous revolutions and breakups of empires. So, 1989 marked the end of the Cold War, but it also marked the end of the balance of power system that had provided stability in Europe for the better part of half a century. This change was not merely a change in strategy. Rather, it was a dramatic shift in the very idea of security, the fundamental element in strategy.

The modern nation-state has given way to what Cooper describes as the "post-modern state." The essence of this form of the State, in Cooper's view, is its security policy. Relying on neither balance of power nor sovereignty, the system of post-modern states embraces transparency in security and mutual interference in the domestic affairs of one's neighbors.[31] Through the use of treaties such as the Conventional Forces in Europe (CFE) Treaty, states have surrendered one of the core features of statehood – the legitimate monopoly on violence – and given it over to international control. There is a different aspect to the problem of security that poses an even greater threat to the nation-state than that of transparency or mutual interference. As mentioned, the essential security function of the State is to protect against external threats. The State is given power, and enjoys legitimacy, to the degree it uses its power in the service of the nation and to the degree it can deliver on its promise of security. When a state can no longer defend against external security threats, its legitimacy is put in question.

WEAPONS OF MASS DESTRUCTION

The first factor in the transformation of the State from modern to post-modern is the growth of global networked terrorism and the commodification of weapons of mass destruction (WMD). Bobbitt explains:

> For five centuries only a state could destroy another state. And for five centuries, states have developed means of defeating other states. Entire worlds of diplomacy, international law, alliances, and naval, air, and land warfare are all predicated upon conflicts among states. Only states could marshal the resources to threaten the survival of other states; only states could organize societies to defend themselves against such threats. Only states could bring about peace congresses.
>
> We are entering a period, however, when very small numbers of persons, operating with the enormous power of modern computers, biogenetics, air transport, and even small nuclear weapons, can deal lethal blows to any society. Because the origin of these attacks can be effectively disguised, the fundamental bases of the State will change.[32]

What is it about WMD and global networked terrorism that moves Bobbitt to see this development as epochal? Like Cooper, Bobbitt believes that the legitimization of the State is grounded in its continuing ability to deliver on its promise of security and, when it can no longer do so, its legitimating basis must change. This legitimization change is the ground of the claim that while the nation-state is dying, the State lives. Like the threat posed by mobile artillery to the walled cities of fifteenth-century Italy,[33] the ballistic missile, the suitcase bomb, and chemical and biological weapons are engendering a new constitutional order.[34] These weapons of mass destruction make it impossible to defend the nation by defending the perimeters of the nation-state. As a result of this development and the increasing dispersion of this technology, no nation-state can promise to increase the security of the nation by increasing its offensive capabilities: at most it can decrease its vulnerability.

The rise of WMD, and the impact that their proliferation has on State-craft, is unique to the nation-state epoch. The nation-state is the product of a century-long struggle between fascism, communism, and democracy. Bobbitt goes so far as to argue that the twentieth century is best seen as one long struggle (the "Long War") to settle just which form of government would dominate. History has settled this question and democracy is now ascendant. But the triumph of democracy is not the end of history. As Bobbitt and Cooper show, the State faces new threats to security; ones that require new strategies and new legitimating themes. These new threats came about because, in their struggle against fascism and communism, modern liberal democratic states developed nuclear and other weapons of mass destruction. This strategic development joined with the fall of the Berlin Wall and the introduction of market economies behind the Iron Curtain to commodify WMDs. In turn, the increasing availability of such weapons in the marketplace created the loss of control of the modern nation-states over their internal security, and contributed to the passage to the post-modern era.

WELFARE AND ECONOMY

As we discussed earlier, a second legitimating feature of the modern State is welfare.[35] Having grown and become more powerful, the modern states underwent a metamorphosis from state-nation (a State supported by a nation) to nation-state (a State supporting its nation). The primary means of support was the notion of welfare – coupled with a system of protection of minority rights or rights deemed fundamental – as its legitimating objective. Welfare and the maintenance of the domestic order were the principal features of the internal dimension of the State. Europe and the United States differed in their domestic approach to providing welfare to the citizenry. Europe had a stronger set of social entitlements, such as

unemployment benefits, large family allowances, strong employee protection, and early and generous retirement benefits. For several reasons,
some historical and some structural, the United States did not adopt social
entitlement packages to the same extent as Europe.[36] Nevertheless, as in
Europe, the legitimacy of the U.S. government depended in substantial
part on its promotion of the welfare of large middle and working classes.[37]

As we discuss in Chapter 3, welfare has begun a transformation as
a legitimating basis for the State.[38] The decline of welfare is taking two
discrete forms: the strong strain in Continental Europe on the cradle-to-
grave systems established in the twentieth century[39] and, perhaps more
significantly, the failure of the welfare state to take root in the developing countries. With regard to welfare, Europe is witnessing a dual internal
phenomenon. In part, the welfare system is viewed as an inalienable set of
social rights, a core component of the *acquis social* set of progressive measures that should never be reversed. Britain, for example, is increasing its
public spending on welfare.[40] In France, although the election of Nicolas
Sarkozy might reverse the trend, the State is also increasing spending on
public welfare,[41] and any governmental attempt to decrease the level of
benefits in a meaningful way is sure to be met with unrest and protest of
the kind that paralyzed the country at various times in recent years.

At the same time, the State by all accounts is experiencing increasing difficulty in sustaining welfare programs. The aging of the European population, which is further described below, endangers retirement
schemes.[42] The economic burdens placed on employers hinder employment, social mobility, and fluid growth, and such burdens consistently
fall short of generating the income necessary to shore up the system.

One of the central tasks of the State is wealth redistribution. Achieved
principally through taxation, the State extracts wealth from its citizens
and redistributes it in accordance with domestic priorities usually
expressed as "welfare." One of the key aspects of welfare is the national
pension system or social security. From time to time there have been
calls for reformation of pension schemes with claims of underfunding
and looming crisis. In the view of some, the ratios of working to aging
populations in the OECD countries signal (see table on page 33) a future
welfare state funding crisis.

Viewed in isolation, demographic trends indicate that modern welfare
states will face increasing difficulty meeting the needs of retired workers.
But demographic trends are only one piece of the picture of the ability of
modern welfare states to meet ongoing demands for retirement benefits.
For the complete picture, we need to consider two additional factors:
migration and tax competition.

OECD Factbook 2007: Economic, Environmental and Social Statistics – ISBN 92–64–02946-X – © OECD 2007

Population – Elderly population – Ageing societies
Ratio of inactive population aged 65 and over to the total labor force
Percentage

	2000	2005	2010	2015	2020	2025	2030	2035	2040	2045	2050
Australia	23.3	23.4	25.2	28.9	33	37.4	41.9	45.2	48.1	49.7	51.4
Austria	30.7	32.2	34	35.9	38.8	43.8	50	55.2	58.2	60.1	61.9
Belgium	38.4	38.8	39.8	43.9	48.7	54.9	61.3	65.9	68.3	69.4	70.2
Canada	23	22.5	23.5	26.4	30.4	35.3	40.2	43	44.8	46.4	48
Czech Republic	26.3	26.9	29.6	34.8	40.3	44.5	48.7	54	62.6	72.5	79.4
Denmark	26.3	26.9	30.3	35.3	39.8	44.5	49.9	54.5	57.2	57.3	55.3
Finland	29.1	30.9	33.4	40.2	46.2	51.4	55.6	57.5	57.2	57.6	58.6
France	36.4	36.9	38.4	43.9	49.2	54.2	59.3	63.4	66.5	67.7	68.9
Germany	33.3	36.8	38.8	40.2	43.7	49.2	56.6	62.6	64.2	65.3	67
Greece	38.5	40.5	41.3	44	47.1	51.9	57.7	65.5	73.4	80.7	85.1
Hungary	35.9	37	39.1	42	47.7	51.8	53.9	57.8	63.3	70.2	74.1
Iceland	16.2	17.2	17.6	18.9	21.8	25.4	28.9	31.2	32.5	33.3	33.6
Ireland	22.4	21.4	22	24.3	26.9	29.8	33.1	36.9	41.6	47.3	52.1
Italy	42.5	45.6	47.5	51.2	54.8	59.9	68	77.5	86.2	91.2	92.8
Japan	25.3	30.9	37.8	45.4	51.1	54.8	58.8	63.8	70.3	75.9	80.8
Korea	10.8	12.7	15.4	18.4	22.4	29	36.9	45.8	55.7	64.3	72.2
Luxembourg	32.6	32.1	32.1	33.7	36.4	40.7	46	50.6	52.6	52.5	52
Mexico	8	8.9	9.9	11	12.5	14.4	16.8	19.9	23.8	27.9	31.7
Netherlands	26.1	26.7	28.1	32	35.2	39	43	45.6	45.6	43.5	41.5
New Zealand	21.9	20.6	21.2	23.4	26.5	30.8	35.9	40.3	43.9	45.9	47.2
Norway	27.2	26.4	26.8	29.6	32.6	36	39.4	42.8	45.2	45.9	46.4
Poland	24.9	27.6	28.4	33.2	40.5	48.2	53.5	58	63.9	71.5	80.6
Portugal	25.8	26.6	26.6	27.9	29.6	32	35.3	39.1	43.6	48.2	51.4
Slovak Republic	23.6	23.5	25.3	29.3	35.7	42	47.8	53.2	61.3	71.4	80.5
Spain	38.2	37.2	37.3	39.4	42.4	47.3	54.5	63.7	74.7	85.5	90.5
Sweden	31.9	31.8	33.5	36.9	39.5	41.9	44.4	46.3	47	46.7	46.4
Switzerland	25	26.4	28	30.6	33.4	37.3	42.1	46.4	48.9	50.3	51.5
Turkey	12.4	14.7	14	15.1	17.3	20.3	24.3	28.5	33.3	38.2	42.8
United Kingdom	30.8	30.8	31.8	35.2	38.2	41.8	46.5	50.4	52.4	53.2	54.7
United States	21.6	21.1	21.9	24.6	28.3	32.6	36.4	38.7	39.8	40.5	41.3
EU 15 total	34.4	35.8	37.2	40.3	43.8	48.4	54.4	60	63.9	66.4	68
OECD total	24.8	26	27.6	30.5	34	37.9	42.2	46	49.2	51.7	53.8
Slovenia	28.5	30.7	–	–	–	–	–	–	–	–	–

Note: Ratio of the inactive population aged 65 and over to the labor force aged 15 to 64.

In *The Decline of the Welfare State: Demography and Globalization*,[43] Assaf Razin and Efraim Sadka reprise the conventional wisdom that maintenance of welfare schemes in continental Europe at current levels will require sharp rises in taxes.[44] Of course, European states have followed the United States in raising retirement ages and trimming benefits. Still, from the point of demographics alone, this is insufficient to meet the growing population of aging beneficiaries. To make matters worse, low-skill migration will place additional demands on the purses of European welfare states. Low-skill workers are net consumers of welfare benefits. Taken together, the aging population and migration demands on the welfare state will require expansion rather than contraction. Will the welfare state increase its capacity to meet these twin demands? Razin and Sadka argue that just the opposite will occur: the welfare state will decline in size.[45]

To understand the political-economic dynamic that will play out, globalization and tax rates have to be added to the picture. As *The Economist* stated in 1997:

> Globalization is a tax problem for [several] reasons. First, firms have more freedom over where to locate.... This will make it harder for a country to tax [a business] much more heavily than its competitors.... Second, globalization makes it hard to decide where a company should pay tax, regardless of where it is based.... This gives them [the companies] plenty of scope to reduce tax bills by shifting operations around or by crafting transfer-pricing....[46]

The story told by Razin and Sadka is one of increasing fiscal demands on welfare states at a time when globalization will unleash a flurry of strategic behavior by firms as they relocate some or all of their productive capacities in states that compete for their share of rents through competitive tax rates.[47] The conclusion they draw is this: "The combined forces of aging, low-skill migration and globalization seem to be too strong for the welfare state to survive in its present size."[48] We agree that the present form of welfare will change. However, "size" is not the issue.

The difficulty of achieving welfare will arguably lead governments to shift their focus towards the maximization of economic opportunity. Such policies could take many forms. In Japan, for example, the government may focus on subsidizing research and development to give domestic industries the best possible edge.[49] Elsewhere, the emphasis may be on providing education and infrastructure while deregulating markets.[50] Other societies may emphasize commercial structures that give workers ownership stakes, so as to maximize their opportunity for economic advancement.[51] In all events, instead of focusing on guaranteeing the welfare of everyone, the State will gradually shift its foundational approach towards maximizing the economic opportunity available to all.[52] While welfare policies, of course, continue to obtain in Europe and throughout the world, the tide of history seems to be shifting away from welfare as the core element of Statecraft that was axiomatic in the modern world.

As we explain in this and subsequent chapters, these phenomena occur because modern Statecraft was inexorably bound to transform itself through a process that included the dilution of the trading classes that formed its basis into an international trading class, a loss of control by the State over the tools of regulatory control that we described above, and the transformation of the international technological and economic landscape. In this chapter we begin to explain how the nation-state form of the

State has come to gradually dilute and transform itself into a post-modern entity.

LOSS OF CONTROL

The loss of control by the modern State arose as a result of the interaction between the international economic institutions, economic patterns, and general landscape of the modern era, as well as the inner face of the modern State.[53] In this chapter, we describe the principal symptoms of this loss of control, and we begin to advance the explanations for these phenomena, through the lens of our thesis that Statecraft dictates the contours of each epoch and sets in motion mechanisms that lead to the transformation of the State and the ushering in of the subsequent era of Statecraft. Our claim is that the nation-state is in an irreversible process of transformation. To understand this process, and to anticipate what the next form of the State will be, it is necessary to review the specific ways in which the nation-state is losing its control over key features of the regulative sphere. We shall turn our attention first to currency.

Control of money and capital has been a traditional feature of the power of the State. From the power to print money as a means of economic stimulation to the regulation of capital flows within borders, states have traditionally managed to control their domestic economies through direct management of the flow of funds over their borders and through the domestic economy. Traditional economic tools of control over a modern state's internal markets and economies included, prominently, the regulation of money. The supply of money to the market was intricately linked to exports policy. Modern states, through market intervention, could supply or limit currency outflow, and thereby affect the exchange rate of their national currencies vis-a-vis the countries with whom they traded. While modern states were often unable to control inflationary pressures and other market forces, currency policy was a prominent tool in their regulatory control arsenal during the modern era.

By the end of the 1990s, the international flow of capital had reached the point where the very idea of a "domestic financial market" made sense neither from the point of view of currencies nor that of capital flows.[54] The explosion of cross-border activities that we describe in later chapters had contributed to the creation of currency markets, controlled by private interests as well as foreign governmental actors, that made currencies as much of a commodity as securities or raw materials. In capitalist, former communist, and even developing countries, capital observed no borders and currencies saw valuations set by the international markets. In short, currencies became commodities and capital moved from place to place in search of the highest returns. Like goods, capital had gone global.

Loss of control over currencies, however, is not merely a privatization and market phenomenon. It also has taken away from the Western states that won World War II a key tool in their regulatory welfare panoply. For developing countries, loss of control over capital flows and currencies has also not been without problems.[55] In 1997, in what was arguably the most (in)famous example of the real-world consequences of loss of control over currency, the Malaysian ringgit plummeted after the Thai baht succumbed to speculative pressure and was devalued. This was quickly followed by attacks on the currencies of the Philippines, Malaysia, Taiwan, and Korea. Malaysian Prime Minister Mahathir publicly named billionaire speculator George Soros as the culprit behind his country's currency woes. Speaking to a meeting of the International Monetary Fund (IMF) and World Bank, Mahathir argued that societies must be protected from "unscrupulous profiteers" like Soros, lest they do irreparable injury to fragile economies.

As it turned out, Mahathir did more damage than Soros ever could. After Mahathir slapped on currency and capital controls, the Malaysian economy went into a deep recession. Mahathir did not stop at this: he tossed out several key ministers, including his finance minister. It took a few years for the dust to clear, but when it did the Malaysian economy came back strong, forcing Mahathir to sing the praises of global capitalism.[56]

The loss of control of the modern State over currency is part of a larger loss of control stemming from technologies that arose during the modern age. As we explained above, and as we will analyze in greater detail later in this book, the technological advances of a particular epoch are linked to the hallmarks of its Statecraft. The railroad, shipyards, and steel and mining industries of the pre-modern age met the solidification needs of that epoch. During the modern era, as we explain in later chapters, information technology and other means of communicating and collaborating without geographical concentration met the needs of an international economic order based on comparative advantage and liberalized trade among discrete nation-states. In the latter part of the twentieth century currencies became commodities.[57] In the simplest terms, control of currencies was wrested from governments and subjected to the discipline of markets. As they had with other aspects of trade and economy, the combined forces of increased computer power and cheap telecommunications made it all the more easy for currencies and capital to move about the globe in quick fashion. In the late twentieth century, these major technological advances were coupled with increased deregulation and privatization. Whether economic change begot political change, or vice versa, there was no doubt that by the end of the twentieth century, the forces of global capitalism had created the conditions to enable capital to go where it was wanted and stay as long as it was well treated.[58]

This phenomenon is but one part of the increasing diffuseness of means of production that we describe later, and the attendant loss of power of states to control these means of production. When New York legal briefs are outsourced at the click of a button to be drafted by Jamaican lawyers and designs are outsourced by French fashion houses to computer-aided technicians sitting in Tunisia, the domestic authorities *de facto* have lost control over what becomes a geographically fluid process. The power of the modern State (i.e., the nation-state) is gradually declining in various parts of the world, particularly in Europe. To be sure, the nations of the world continue to substantially adhere to territorial and constitutional Statecraft of the kind that emerged in the twentieth century. However, a foundational transformative shift similar to the one that brought about the nation-state in the twentieth century is taking place, with notions of borders and sovereignty gradually losing the central role they played in the modern era.

SOVEREIGNTY

One area where loss of control is most discussed is sovereignty. Many astute observers of international relations have failed to join the chorus calling for the "end of the State." The specific focus of the end of the State argument has been sovereignty and its alleged loss by contemporary welfare states. While there are certainly many facts and events to which one could point for confirmation of the "end of sovereignty" theme, we believe the better view is that this quintessential aspect of the State is not in decline but is, in fact, being relocated.[59]

The relocation of sovereignty from its expression in both power and geography is driven by globalization. One clear example is the advent of the internet and the creation of what might be called "electronic space" and, with it, the evaporation of borders. Consider information. While some states are able to maintain partial control over the flow of information over the internet,[60] there are simply too many instances where the rapid flow of information around the globe has made the control of information by states virtually impossible.

There can be no greater example of sovereignty and the power of the State than law. The State enjoys the power to create and enforce law within its jurisdiction and beyond. In short, the power to produce and enforce law is a singular attribute of sovereignty and, thus, the State. Economic globalization has altered the role of law in one key area, that of private law.

In their book *Dealing In Virtue*, Yves Dezalayn and Bryant Garth, detail the rise of international private law in a way that preempts sovereign enforcement of law in the commercial context. International commercial law arbitration is big business. According to Dezalayn and Garth, an ever-increasing percentage of worldwide transactions are resolved through a network of arbitrators who are members of what can only be described as a "club." No state controls the composition of the community. Membership in select organizations is all that is required.[61] Populated by large English and U.S. law firms, the "law" of international private law is decidedly Anglo-American.

In terms of numbers, there were 120 arbitration centers in 1991 and 1,000 arbitrators by 1990. By 1992, the number of arbitrators had doubled.[62] In effect, the "law" of commercial law has become Anglo-American common law with justice dispensed not through courts, but in offices populated by lawyers trained in England and the United States. Hence, we can say there really is "international law" in the sense that there is law that applies around the globe. But the law is not "global law" because it is the product of one legal system, a system that has now been elevated to a dominant position by virtue of the growth of private arbitration.

To a similar effect are international credit rating agencies that function as gate-keepers in certifying the quality of corporate debt. Like international arbitration, there is "regulation" of business but it is not the State doing the regulating, it is private firms who are applying their own standards and imposing penalties for failure to live up to those standards.

Saskia Sassen describes these developments as "the state reconfigured." As she puts it:

> In many ways the state is involved in this emerging transnational governance system. But it is the state that has itself undergone transformation and participated in legitimating a new doctrine about its role in the economy. Central to this new doctrine is a growing consensus among states to further the growth and strength of the global economy.[63]

In a similar vein, John Ruggie has made the observation that "global markets and transnationalized corporate structures.... are not in the business of replacing states."[64] Echoing Ruggie, Sassen comments: "What matters here is that global capital has made claims on national states which have responded to the production of new forms of legality."[65]

In other words, the State functions not by producing legal regimes but by legitimizing them through acquiescence. Yes, this is deregulation by other means, but it is not loss of control. The State certainly has a hand in the production of these new forms of sovereignty. For example, the State can prohibit commercial arbitration in the way it is conducted and it can also regulate the regulating industries themselves. But Sassen's point, with which we agree, is that sovereignty (i.e., territory) once the hallmark of the State – has been "reconstituted and partly displaced onto other institutional arenas outside the state and outside the framework of nationalized territory."[66]

BALANCE OF POWER

We are witnessing a correlative diminution in the effectiveness and importance of maintaining balance among equals on the international scene.[67] Increasingly, post-modern states accept, to various degrees, control-sharing over domestic matters with supranational or global regimes and institutions.[68] States are experiencing a loss of domestic control because, as we will describe in more detail below, traditional tools for regulating social and economic life have been rendered less effective by increasingly scattered cross-border forces and the rise of environmental, health, and security threats that are too diffuse to be controlled by domestic policy alone.[69] The nation is declining as the basis for the State. Instead of a world subdivided into discrete nation-states and national economies, the international landscape has become diffuse and the main interlocutors of the State and the order of states have become cross-border actors.

In sum, the developments described above have resulted in a trend toward the modern State's loss of its ability to control the domestic arena and to enact policies that would protect the welfare of the nation. To be sure, the world is not completely post-modern; as Cooper notes,[70] post-modern states live alongside modern and even pre-modern states.[71] In addition, there are various pre-modern states in the international scene where the official organs of the State do not even enjoy exclusive use of force within their own borders. Nevertheless, we believe that the trend we are describing provides an accurate account of a transformational move in Statecraft and international relations.

A NEW LEGITIMATING ECONOMIC NORM

In this chapter we have described how trade orders reflect and are reflected by the constitutional order of the society of states. We believe that the reason the current institutions of trade are widely seen as no longer fulfilling their mission is that the nature of Statecraft is changing. In this chapter, we have described the details of each of the key aspects of the nation-state, all in an effort to describe how the nation-state is fading and a new form of the State taking its place.

Throughout this book, we argue that the metamorphosis of the nation-state will be accompanied by a new legitimating economic norm for the State, which will also drive changes to the global trading order. In the trade context, the current norm, which works in harmony with welfare, is best expressed by Ruggie's "embedded liberalism," which we discuss further in subsequent chapters. We believe the nature of the State's commitment to welfare is undergoing change, and with it a change in the global trading order has become inevitable. As we describe in subsequent chapters, the State is moving from a regime of entitlements to one of economic opportunity. We grant that this claim is broad and is likely to be contested and, throughout the balance of this book, we will defend it, to show how it is seeping into the fabric of post-modern Statecraft, and to argue that the global trading order should be revised to shift away from embedded liberalism and its comparative advantage-driven engine, toward the enablement of global economic opportunity.

3 The Changing Nature of Welfare

Thesis:

As the State evolves from a nation-state to a post-modern state, the nature of welfare will change. The regime of law and entitlements that was the uncontested hallmark of the nation-state will evolve into a regime of incentives. The State will deliver on the promise of welfare by providing economic opportunity for its citizens.

Together with law, welfare is one of the two dimensions of the inner face of the State. As we have explained previously, we conceive of "welfare" as more than just entitlements. In achieving legitimacy, the State provides for its people not only in matters of entitlements and social protection, but through legal regimes and regulations. One of the principal justifications for the State is that it delivers order to an otherwise Hobbesian universe. The regulation and facilitation of commercial transactions, for example, is just one of the many ways in which the State's legal regime contributes to the betterment of its subjects. In the modern era, it was uncontested that welfare (in the broad sense that we give to the term) was a pillar of the State. The entitlements system of the modern nation-state, however, is giving way to an incentives-driven framework where government, instead of guaranteeing a set of entitlements to its citizens, will seek to maximize their opportunity to achieve economic security and well-being on their own. Welfare has not withered away, but it no longer occupies the central role that it had in the modern era. The modern supply of entitlements to the nation is gradually giving way to a post-modern Statecraft system where the State will push and prod to give those within its reach greater opportunities to participate in the global marketplace.

As we will explain, welfare as we know it will not disappear completely or all at once. Looking at the developed world today, it is what may be characterized as the "support" (or entitlements) side of welfare that is undergoing the most perceptible and, in our view, greatest change. Although expressed variously in different nations, there is growing evidence that the promise of welfare – understood as a scheme of social protection – is undergoing fundamental change.[1] As we see it, welfare is moving from a system of entitlements to one grounded in incentives. That is, the states of the developed world are trimming their "entitlement spending" and reallocating those resources into activities that are best described as "enabling." When we look at the evidence, we see greater emphasis on the part of states in creating opportunities and less willingness to continue the expansion of welfare, as it is traditionally understood. The State (at least in the developed world) will, of course, continue to engage in support spending, if only to provide security for segments of the population such as the disabled or chronically unemployed persons. We are not suggesting that twentieth-century style welfare has disappeared or will be disappearing overnight. We also do not claim that public spending or State dedication to the well-being of its people has withered away. Rather, we are arguing that the modern *form* of welfare – in particular the adherence to entitlements and to a model of Statecraft where the State unleashes its power to guarantee the welfare of its citizens – is gradually being transformed into a post-modern system where incentives and "enablement of economic opportunity" fill an increasingly larger share of the welfare regulatory space.

What, then, is the remaining role of welfare in the post-modern world? Our answer is that, just like comparative advantage, the modern welfare system is on the cusp of fundamental change as a foundational element in Statecraft. In Chapter 2, we used the concept of welfare as an all-encompassing notion that captured the work of the modern regulatory state. In this chapter, we also use the concept of welfare to capture the policies of a nation-state that foster a broad level of acceptance of modern liberal democracy by the different constituent elements of the nation-state. After World War II, Western Europe, Asia, and the United States grew to be the most powerful players in the international order.[2] In addition to their security and strategic functions, these states redistributed wealth, provided a safety net for their respective nations, and protected economic and other rights for broad segments of the population. The policy choices and the law that sprang from this fundamental element of Statecraft spanned a substantial part of the inner order of the states (including labor laws, unemployment benefits, retirement rules, aid to families, taxation law, subsidies, public investment, and other central components of the domestic legal and regulatory order). Nation-states such as France, the United States, and Japan took different approaches to achieving welfare, but their inner orders shared the same essential hallmarks of legitimacy of the nation-state in relation to the nation. Today, as we show below, welfare is changing its course at the same time as the modern era is nearing its end.

In our examination of the changing nature of welfare in each of these states, we emphasize their gradual evolution away from a system of entitlements to an economic opportunity framework consistent with the diffuse and decentralized nature of the global marketplace. The transformative movement that we identify reflects to a substantial extent the metamorphosis of the twentieth-century global trading order into the diffuse, cross-border marketplace that characterizes the phenomenon of globalization. The French state encourages private interests to fund economic projects for laid off employees where 30 years ago the state would either have used its power to avoid the layoffs or to create substitute jobs itself. Japan's state fosters the creation of small and medium enterprises to counter the rising joblessness in that country, where 30 years ago the fundamental legitimating drive of that state was to protect an intricate system of government-industry partnership designed to maintain full employment. The United States retreats from its already minimal welfare system to free up private economic interests and stimulate economic growth.

In all cases, the State pushes and prods, and encourages the spread of economic opportunity, leaving it to the individual to avail him- or herself of the possibility that is created. Rather than using its full power to retain control of the national marketplace and ensure a minimal level of security for its citizens, the State creates conditions that are most appropriate for the individual to achieve economic opportunity. As we will detail later in this book, this change arises in part from the transformation of the international landscape from an aggregation of discrete economic units associated with the nation-state, relying on each nation-state to supply welfare guarantees to its nation, to a diffuse and interloped set of cross-border industries. In such a world, we will show, the modern version of welfare – while eminently suited to the modern era – was bound to evolve into a program of economic opportunity adapted to a diffuse and fluid market.

The story we tell is one of gradual evolution rather than radical and sudden transformation. Welfare has been a foundational tenet of modern Statecraft. The GATT system evolved as the modern global trading order because, as we detail later, it was a natural international companion to the domestic supply of welfare. Our theory posits that each era of Statecraft contains the seeds of its own transformation. We will explain how the modern system of trade contributed to the creation of the globalization phenomenon, which in turn changed the nature of the State and its ability or desire to deliver welfare in the twentieth-century form. These changes, in turn, planted the seeds of the new animating norm of Statecraft: the enablement of economic opportunity.

The regulatory movement of the modern era was primarily top-down, featuring a high degree of sovereign control by nation-states over national economies and the associated supply of welfare. The ethos of the global trading order in that era was aimed at generating free movement of goods and services so as, in part, to facilitate the welfare mission of the State, all the while preserving its sovereign nature and ability to discharge that task. In the nascent post-modern epoch, the State faces diffuse economic conditions. The economic landscape that the State must regulate today is more suited to the post-modern pushing and prodding of a system of enablement of economic opportunity than to welfare in the modern era. We illustrate this story of transformation and gradual metamorphosis in the context of the French, Japanese, and American states.

FRANCE: TRANSFORMATION OF THE WELFARE STATE

We begin with an analysis of one of the leading post-war examples of a welfare state, that of France. True, our claims about the changing nature of the State and its promise of the delivery of "welfare" is intended to reach all the states of the European Union, albeit with nuanees and varying degrees of applicability. We begin with France to detail our argument not only because it is emblematic of certain trends in the development of the State, but because in many ways France poses a stellar example of how the State has maintained a strong commitment to bolstering its economy while altering the means by which this is accomplished. As this diagram shows, despite pressures to cut back on social spending, French state spending has remained strong.

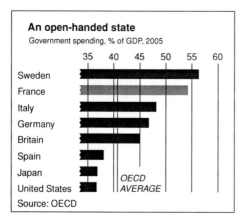

There is an aspect to this story that has not been told and that is how the French state has managed to increase its commitment to economic welfare while embracing approaches to the task that are more geared

toward generating economic opportunity than maintaining the traditional system of entitlements and guarantees.

Before World War II, the French state took a *laissez-faire* approach
to economic policy. Many firms and companies were small to medium-
sized, family-owned, or closely held firms that paid little attention to efficiency or global competitiveness. Neither culture nor economics required
anything different. After the war laid waste to vast portions of the country, a series of French governments became more involved in the structure and management of the economy. The model for this was called
dirigisme.

French *dirigisme* involved government intervention in a number of
facets of the economy, in particular infrastructure and transportation.
Following a policy of state-led development, from 1945–1975, economic
growth averaged 4.5 percent. *Dirigisme* was the explicit policy of the
center-right governments of Charles de Gaulle and Georges Pompidou.

The year 1981 saw the election of Socialist François Mitterrand. Mitterrand promised even greater state intervention in the economy than
his predecessors. He made good on his promise by nationalizing various
industries and banks. A currency crisis in 1983 effectively ended the era
of *dirigisme*.[3] At the time, state revenues totaled 42.6 percent of GDP. By
1999, that figure would rise to 46 percent. The short version of the story is
that the French state has continued to grow in size. But, as we will show,
that is not the interesting part of the story.

To the untrained eye, the 1990s were an era of retrenchment for the
dirigiste model of government in France. There is some truth to the claim
that the French government got out of the business of running the economy. But the whole truth is more complicated.[4] While the French state
did get out of the business of owning and running many sectors of the
economy, the state increased its industrial presence in other ways. When
the details are examined, it becomes clear that the French state substituted direct involvement with market-based incentives. We shall examine
one recent scheme that illustrates nicely the unique and surprisingly creative lengths to which the French state is willing to go to preserve not
only welfare, but also a certain approach to work and life that is uniquely
French in character.

Much of French political life can be explained through the lens of jobs
and the degree to which French unions have been successful in extract-
ing concessions from the government as the latter imposes measures to
shore up the economy. For example, after electing a left administration,
in 1983, that had won on a campaign promising to strengthen *dirigisme*,
the government was forced to retreat from its promise and, after three
years of cautious retreat, the right returned to power and the process of
fundamental change was fully underway.

In their trenchant analysis of the French state evolution from *dirigisme* to the embrace of market-oriented reforms, Jonah Levy, Mari Miura, and Gene Park[5] identify four changes in the French state's approach to the economy that confirm a fundamental shift in its approach to the economy. The first concerns macroeconomic policy. In the postwar period, the government stimulated the economy through deficit spending and monetary policy that led to inflation. Successive devaluations were the remedy for inflation until 1983 when the French franc was informally pegged to the Deutschmark. By running a rate of inflation lower than its trading partners, together with austerity budgets and real interest rates of between 5 and 8 percent, France was able to keep inflation low and achieve a trade surplus.

The second set of reforms concerned France's public enterprises. The year 1982 saw the nationalization of leading industrial conglomerates and nearly 40 banks. When combined with the nationalizations carried out by DeGaulle, 13 of France's 20 largest firms and nearly all of its banks were controlled by the state. Of course, large public subsidies were the norm. These subsidies were spent to both expand employment and invest in ways deemed "strategic" by the government. Nineteen eighty-three saw a complete abandonment of this fundamental aspect of *dirigisme*. Not only were nationalized firms released from the planning targets imposed by the government, they were instructed to shift their focus to profitability. When the right returned to power in 1986, privatization began in earnest. Once complete, the French government was in charge of energy production, transportation, and little else.

Perhaps the most important shift in policy was the end of state efforts to manage industry and the freeing of firms to raise capital on their own. Gone were the days of government bailouts and industry subsidies. Bankruptcies separated weak from strong firms and, helped by the release of price controls, strong firms were now able to reap the rewards of their new-found freedom from state control. Finally, the de-indexing of wages and the lifting of restrictions on layoffs completed the dismantling of *dirigisme*; and yet, it would be a mistake to conclude that the French state had somehow faded away. In other words, paradoxical though it may seem, the end of *dirigisme* saw not a shrinking of the French state but its growth. This paradox needs to be explained.

In both its *dirigiste* and post-*dirigiste* manifestations, French labor policy has been all about jobs: creating them, preserving them, and minimizing the pain of losing them. Early retirement schemes,[6] which cost approximately 1 million francs per retiree, were expected to be temporary. But to this day, the creation of new jobs in France has been sluggish, at best. Despite a variety of efforts from both right and left governments, the number of French workers employed in a public labor scheme is up two and half times in the post-*dirigiste* period.[7] Not even Sweden outspends France on labor market intervention. On social protection, France is a leader. The OECD reports that French welfare spending was 28.5 percent of GDP in 2001, up from 21.1 percent in 1980.[8]

Against this background, it is important to understand that despite popular perceptions (and some hard realities), French governments are grappling with the rising demands of pension and health care systems at a time when unemployment remains above 10 percent. Eschewing the interventionist *dirigiste* approach to the economy, which placed the firm in the hands of the French state, French bureaucrats now see small- and medium-sized firms (SMEs) as the solution to both problems of employment and the long-term health of the social system, that is, welfare. In fact, the bureaucrats have receded into the background. The job of the state is not to pick winners and losers, and manage them. Rather, the state is now in the business of creating "a supportive environment"[9] for private managers. They are doing this by encouraging new ventures, underwriting plant and equipment modernization, improving and providing IT support, and worker training. Thus, the French state is creating what is aptly termed "an enabling environment."[10]

An example of creative bureaucratic thinking illustrates the degree of creativity within the corporate realm as the state works with the private sector to meet the demands of unions, employees, and the state. In August of 2006, as all of France was enjoying the annual vacation month, the *Wall Street Journal* ran a story[11] about a scheme at France Télécom that crystallized the new French method for reducing unemployment through market incentives while doing so in a way that avoided the wrath of France's powerful unions. The story told how the world's fifth-largest telecommunications company was funding about one thousand small, entrepreneurial ventures from cafes to magicians to wineries. Was France Télécom branching out into other business ventures? Hardly. What it was doing was trying to stay competitive and move into new areas of telecommunications, all as it suffered under the restrictive reins of French labor law. As the article described the situation, "[t]wo-thirds of France Télécom workers have civil-service status that guarantees them a job for life, and the rest are protected by strict French labor laws."[12] So, how does the scheme work?

Let's look at the question to which this scheme is the answer. Large companies like France Télécom[13] cannot reduce their workforces with layoffs – French labor law makes it onerous to do so. So, when technology changes, a company like France Télécom has to take workers whose skills are now useless and place them in jobs that require little or no skill. For example, technicians with skills in an obsolete technology now become managers of call centers. Without the flexibility to hire and fire based on the changing demands of the marketplace, firms are forced to maintain bloated employment rolls that weigh heavily on profitability and undercut the flow of investor capital.

The challenge is how to move employees off the payroll without running afoul of French labor laws. The task facing France Télécom was to find ways of taking employees with civil service status and moving them to hospitals, teaching, and government jobs. With encouragement from the French government, France Télécom agreed to pay the employees' salary for four months and to compensate them if they switched to lower paying work outside the firm. But the managers were not satisfied with the 2,600 workers who left; they needed more. The next step was inspiring entrepreneurs.

The entrepreneurs came from the ranks of France Télécom employees: any employee with a business plan could apply for funding from France Télécom. The company set up offices around the country where employees could get assistance developing their ideas and formulating a detailed plan. If accepted (and only 10 percent of proposals were rejected), the employee received funding from the company to buy equipment, draft a proper business plan, and apply for bank funding. If the venture failed in the first three years, the employee could return to the company.

When we began our discussion of post-war France, we said that the paradox of French state intervention in the economy was one of increasing levels of spending and the renunciation of the *dirigiste* model. The discussion of the scheme at France Télécom provides a representative example of a fundamental change in the nature of state intervention in the French economy. France exemplifies the increasing use by states of market-centered approaches to economy and welfare. In France, "welfare" comprises job security, unemployment insurance, retirement, and medical care. The lesson is that the French state has not dismantled the influence of the state in the economy. Rather, it has retooled its interventionist strategies, all in an effort to create economic opportunity for the population.

The international trade system of the modern era relied on comparative advantage and the concentration of national enterprises in fields where they have a comparative advantage. As we will explain, the modern trade configuration ultimately resulted in the creation of a fluid system where firms compete in an increasingly globalized marketplace and are owned by cross-border interloped interests. In these circumstances, it is inevitable that firms will engage in constant adjustment to remain competitive, including in particular job restructurings and layoffs. The modern trade system delegated to the State the responsibility for retraining workers and shepherding them to new jobs when their industries shed excess salary weight. Our thesis is that, in the post-modern era, the State is losing the tools to accomplish this task, and its legitimating drive is shifting toward enabling economic opportunity. The France Télécom scheme provides a post-modern example of the use of private funds and a system of incentives to achieve a result that increases economic opportunity for workers in the global marketplace. The partnership is largely a reaction to and reflection of the transformation of the modern State caused by the international patterns of activity. In other words, history does not end but continues as the State and its subjects explore new possibilities and adjust to a new epoch. Our task in this book is to identify how the global trading order should also adjust itself, in a timely fashion, to the new Statecraft reality and move forward together with the historical forces that are calling for its transformation, in light (among other factors) of the domestic transformation of welfare that we describe.

JAPAN AND INDICATIVE PLANNING

Japan is a prototypical statist political economy. That said, of the three contemporary states we use to illustrate our thesis regarding the changing nature of the state, Japan poses the most difficult challenge. The reason is that Japan – the second largest economy in the world – has never constructed a European welfare state. Nevertheless, Japan's policies qualify as welfare policies within the meaning of our definition of welfare as coextensive with modern unleashing of the power of the State to shore up the nation.[14] For a variety of reasons, some having to do with the particular nature of structural reforms after World War II, Japan prescinded from producing the kind of welfare state seen in the European Union. Having decided against engendering a European-style welfare state, successive Japanese governments find themselves trying to address the problems of the welfare state through the singular device of employment.[15] The emphasis on job preservation, coupled with Japan's unique but ultimately unsuccessful approach to managing the relationship between industry and the state, now poses serious long-term problems for the country.[16]

One area in which Japan has made significant strides is that of corporate governance (in particular the undoing of interlocking corporate ownership (*keiretsu*) and government support of so-called "zombie" firms and failed banks). As we shall discuss, these changes have led to national distress as Japan unlocked close relationships between government and industry. Nevertheless, these changes are important and necessary for the long-term economic health of Japan.

Interestingly, and despite many differences, the states of France and Japan share four core features: (1) meritocratic elite schools that recruited and trained the nation's best-and-brightest youth for high-level positions in state administration; (2) multi-year planning processes that established the priorities and parameters of the nation's economic development; (3) a variety of policy instruments that permitted state authorities to influence and channel resources to key sectors or even individual firms (strategic use of trade policy, subsidized credit, research aid, price-rigging, etc.); and (4) a political foundation of conservative hegemony that allowed planners to slight the needs of labor favoring investment over consumption.[17]

The end of World War II saw the former Japanese Empire reduced in size to the four primary islands of Honshu, Hokkaido, Kyushu, and Shikoku. The country was forced to relinquish its hold on Korea, Taiwan, Japanese Sakhalin, the Pescadores, and the Kuriles. The Ryukyu island chain was placed under U.S. administration. The year 1945 saw Japan looking at 30 percent of its industrial capacity destroyed, 80 percent of its shipping lost, and rice production standing at about 32 percent the pre-war average. By war's end, the country's industrial capacity operated at just 10 percent of its regular pre-war level. Japanese cities had faced the flaming maelstrom of United States air power. Tokyo had lost over 57 percent of its dwellings and Osaka nearly 60 percent. Perhaps most pressing was the prospect of mass starvation, as the nation faced terrible shortages of available food stocks. Disaster was only averted by the U.S. occupation forces that began importing food in 1946.

The issuance of excessive currency brought about significant economic inflation. The cost of living in Japan began to rise by about 10 percent each month between 1945 and 1947. The U.S. occupation authorities, administered under the Supreme Commander of the Allied Powers (SCAP), responded by imposing price controls and fixing the yen to the dollar at 360/1 in 1949. SCAP continued to drive economic policy in Japan until the occupation terminated in April 1952.

As part of SCAP's efforts toward the democratization of Japan, the administration engaged in a multifaceted plan involving land reform and "zaibatsu busting." SCAP was given the authority to dissolve any company it regarded as monopolistic, and many of the great zaibatsu were broken up during this period. However, by 1948 American authorities began to see such an aggressive anti-trust program as hindering economic recovery, and the process of anti-monopolization was significantly reduced. The land reform program, on the other hand, focusing on the prohibition of absentee landlordism, was more successful, and the program eventually led to massive reduction in farming tenancy as opposed to land ownership.

At the beginning of 1950, industrial production in Japan stood at 83.6 percent of what it had been in 1937, the year Japan embarked on the second Sino-Japanese war. However, with the advent of the Korean War, industrial production jumped to 114.4 percent of this 1937 figure. By 1950, the United States had already funneled around $2 billion into the Japanese economy. By the mid-1950s, the United States spent an additional $4 billion for the purchase of supplies and equipment for the United States military. Japan also became the center for U.S. military rest and recreation during this period. By 1953, real consumption surpassed the pre-World War II average. The economy was further strengthened by the fact that the government of Japan only spent 1 to 2 percent of GNP on military spending. Instead, the government invested in public funds used to develop national industries. State funds were also made available to the private banks. The relaxation of anti-monopoly laws further contributed to economic growth. As such, firms began to form loose associations known as *keiretsu* that reflected the pre-war *zaibatsu* in form. The *keiretsu*, designed to reduce market risk, formed along horizontal and vertical lines – the horizontal making hostile takeovers rare and the vertical ensuring the existence of reliable industrial supply bases.

Protectionism ran rampant during this period. By the end of the 1950s, only 20 percent of imports into Japan were free of either bans or quotas.[18] The Ministry of International Trade and Industry (MITI) greatly restricted "foreign exchange allocations and imposed a value added tax of 40 percent on imported automobiles."[19] The result was the dramatic growth of protected industries. Between 1951 and 1961, "the ratio of imported cars to domestic declined from 44.6 percent to .7 percent."[20] The years between 1953 and 1960 saw unprecedented growth in Japan as the economy grew at an average rate of 9.3 percent every year. By 1965, the Japanese economy was four times the level of what it was before the outbreak of World War II. By 1969, Japan was the third largest steel producer, and produced almost 50 percent of the world's merchant ships. By 1970, the Japanese GNP had reached $202 billion, the third largest in the world.

The unprecedented double-digit growth experienced by Japan since the end of World War II was suddenly interrupted by the outbreak of the 1973 Yom Kippur War. In that year, Japan quickly found itself faced with a deficit in international payments as oil prices quadrupled. The resulting rise in energy prices led to an economic recession and, by 1974, consumer prices increased by 25 percent. The response by the Japanese government was to put in place a long-term plan to reduce dependence on oil, and MITI took the lead. The government supported research into alternative energy sources, promoting the accelerated construction of nuclear power plants and offsetting the additional expense of oil costs by increasing exports. The result was a drop in dependence on Middle Eastern oil from 85 percent of Japan's total petroleum supply in 1970 to 73 percent in 1980. Further, between 1974 and 1987, crude steel production dropped from 117.1 million tons per year to 98.5 million tons, and pig iron production dropped from 90.4 million tons to 73.4 in that same period.[21] By 1983 over 25 percent of Japan's electricity was generated by nuclear energy. By 1975, it had become clear that Japan quickly recovered from the "oil shock" of 1973, and the economy was once again steadily growing. Between 1975 through 1980, the average annual rate of GNP grew between 4 to 5 percent each year.

Just as the country had done after World War II, Japan entered another period of growth. In 1983, industrial production increased to over 40 percent as compared to 1974. By 1981, Japan controlled 70 percent of the world market in computer chips. By 1989, Japan produced a quarter of all passenger cars manufactured globally. In 1991, Japan had the world's highest GNP per capita.

Academics, economists, and historians offer multiple explanations for this second resurgence. Briefly, the primary reasons seem to be these: (1) a shift on the part of business leaders and government agencies, such as MITI, from emphasizing the expansion of heavy industry to fostering the development of high technology businesses; (2) a business focus on quality control management theory; (3) a strong cultural work ethic; (4) close cooperation between big business and government agencies; (5) close cooperation between the *keiretsu* as expressed in interlocking directorates and strong personal ties between members/employees; (6) the existence of protective tariffs; (7) income saving on the part of Japanese workers; and (8) a shift to internal financing on the part of large businesses away from financing through the banking system.

This last point requires elaboration. The oil crisis of 1971 caused the government to draw upon national savings and bond issuance. This in turn led to a loosening of financial controls and to a period of financial deregulation. In 1980, foreign exchange controls were completely abolished, and security companies were able to borrow in the call market. In response, the Bank of Japan began to steadily decrease its discount rate, from 9 percent in 1980 to 2.5 percent in 1987. The result was an aggressive expansion of lending practices on the part of banks. The availability of easily borrowed money contributed to escalating corporate profits that also corresponded with rapidly rising real estate prices associated with general asset inflation. Real estate prices in Japan's major urban centers in 1991 averaged five times more than they did in 1970. Subsequently, Japanese companies began looking overseas to expand real estate holdings and investments, and speculation became widespread. Japanese companies also began to look at overseas labor markets for the manufacturing sector. What was seen by many to be unstoppable Japanese growth began to be viewed by others as the expansion of an asset bubble.

Simply put, in the 1980s the Japanese yen increased in value against the U.S. dollar. The result was that Japanese exporters began to be threatened by cheaper overseas manufacturing costs. The Bank of Japan responded to this by lowering short-term interest rates to around 2.5 percent. Investors began to over-borrow, and the supply of money increased. It followed that Japanese stock and real estate markets rapidly expanded into what came to be known as the "bubble economy."[22] Beginning to fear growing labor shortages and inflation, the Bank of Japan took steps to tighten monetary policy by raising short-term interest rates five times between May 1989 and August 1990. This tightening process contributed to the "piercing" of the asset bubble.

In April 1990, the bubble burst. In that month share prices on the Nikkei stock market dropped by 40 percent. Real estate prices, inflated from speculative trading, did not instantly synchronize with the drop in stock prices. However, the real estate market could not continue to maintain the widening gap with falling stock prices and, over the next few years, the real property market also declined in value. Real economic growth during 1991 remained at 5.1 percent despite the drop in the Nikkei exchange.[23] Nonetheless, by the end of 1991, output growth also declined. In fact, from 1991 to 1999, real output growth averaged around 1 percent as compared with 4 percent achieved in the 1980s.[24]

By mid-1991, the Japanese economy entered an actual depression. Land prices in Tokyo dropped to about 60 percent of their peak. Companies were forced to restrict expansionist activities and real wages froze.[25] By 1993, average real disposable household incomes began to drop. In response to the depressed conditions, Japanese companies attempted to expand their export operations, but the yen continued to increase in value, and by 1994 it reached 100 yen to the U.S. dollar, which in turn hurt such operations. The depression continued throughout the 1990s. Contributing to the economic malaise was the massive earthquake that hit the Kansai region and the industrial city of Kobe.

By 2004, Japan's GDP per capita had fallen to 71 percent of that of the United States. From 1996 through 2002, the per capita GDP grew at just .02 percent. Industrial production completely stagnated from 1991 well into the mid-2000s, whereas it had increased on average 8.5 percent per year between 1953 and 1991.[26] By 2003, the Japanese economy again began to grow, reaching a growth rate of around 2.0 percent through 2004 and 2.8 percent for 2005. However, this rate was still substantially lower than it had been during any significant period since World War II or as compared to other industrial economies such as the United States or the European Union.

The explanation of how an economy that at one time seemed unstoppable could enter into an unusually long period of stagnant economic growth is the subject of persistent scholarly debate. One particularly insightful analysis points to the following factors:

1. High Tax Rates: In Japan top margin income tax rates come into effect at lower income levels as compared to other industrialized nations. The result is a lower return on risk-taking ventures.
2. Hidden Barriers to Imports: Japan has continued to maintain numerous import barriers. The result is a stifling of foreign competition and a growth in domestic inefficiencies.
3. Favoritism: Japan has a history of favoritism in regulatory decisions as it relates to irregular payments given to government officials. Such cronyism has made it more difficult for newcomers to establish themselves in government and business roles. The result is the establishment of a network that contributes to existing economic interests that have thus far proven themselves slow to respond to the changing nature of the world economy.
4. Price Controls: Japan's history of price controls may have initially contributed to the countries post-war economic recovery. However, the current result of price controls has been the discouragement of price competition and inhibition of "signaling mechanism(s) that restructure the economy away from declining sectors toward growing ones, from inefficient businesses towards well managed ones."
5. Japan's Banking System: More than 40 percent of company shares are held by bank-related institutions. Members of the *keiretsu* own 20 to 30 percent of their group's bank. The result is that banks lend to primarily entrenched companies that they have had long-term relationships with as opposed to funding new ventures.[27]

The authors gloss these facts with the observation that "economic rigidities . . . have robbed Japan's economy of its ability to adapt by replacing old firms and jobs with new ones."[28] Further, they note that restrictive polices may appear to work for a time, but they eventually drag on the economy once they have been in place long enough to "bind."[29] The overall result has been that Japan found itself in a position where it needed to be more dynamic, yet found "its economy too high cost to compete with the Chinese and too inflexible to keep pace with the nimble Americans."[30]

The story of Japan is in large measure connected to the political party that has ruled Japan for decades, the Liberal Democratic Party (LDP).

Notwithstanding occasional bows in the direction of their opponents, the LDP has largely been responsible for Japan's failure to develop a welfare state. Fearful of overspending that would hinder future development, the 1970s and 1980s saw Japanese bureaucrats focus on the preservation of jobs to the exclusion of almost every other principal social concern. Japan has surely had its share of reformers and reformist prime ministers. Nevertheless, reformers have never been able to mount the kind of coercion necessary to steer the state into an expansionary mode.

Four factors are responsible for the LDP's failure to expand the welfare state. The Japanese developmental model, authored in the Ministry of Finance, relied upon a deflationary fiscal policy together with low taxation, both of which were thought to stimulate private capital accumulation. Second, the LDP was ideologically opposed to an expansionist welfare state. Believing that welfare states created dependence – which dependence would ultimately weaken the productive drive of Japanese workers – the LDP grounded its anti-welfare state attitude in an ideology of self-reliance. The oil crisis of the 1970s saw industrial restructuring in European states which took the form of early retirement provisions. In Japan, corporations turned to the government to provide subsidies for early retirement and reemployment. Finally, the 1960s saw a Japan free of the internal strife that plagued the European nations and the United States. May 1968 never occurred in Japan. Instead, unions and employers agreed on measures to secure employment, thereby freeing the government from the need to provide a safety net from fallout from industrial restructuring.

Despite its long-standing antipathy to the creation of a fully developed welfare state, the Japanese government of the early 1970s expanded public spending in both the general account and public works. Declaring "the First Year of the Welfare Era," Prime Minister Tanaka embarked on an expansive fiscal policy which created inflation at the same moment as the first oil crisis. By 1974, the welfare era was all but at an end and the LDP was scrambling for a new way to facilitate growth in the public sector.

With the bursting of the economic bubble in 1991, and the deep and prolonged recession that followed, Japanese political leaders were forced to come to the recognition that their failure to engender a European welfare state had effected a complete stifling of productivity and growth in the economy. In a word, the Japanese rejected a welfare state in favor of employment protection. The vision is one of full employment as an alternative to a welfare state. This alternative has come at great cost. The ties between Japanese companies and the government, the refusal of the government to put pressure on banks to foreclose on nonconforming loans, and a total lack of effective stimulative interventions in the economy left

Japan ranked first at the end of the 1990s in employment security but with
a labor market that was effectively providing unemployment insurance
for Japanese workers. All of this came to an end when unemployment
rates jumped to 5.4 percent in 2002.[31] With unemployment on the rise
and no government program in place to combat the problem, the problem of job security came to the fore. Inexorably, deregulation of the labor
market began.

There can be little doubt that the decision to forego a social safety net
system has engendered slow corporate adjustment and impeded reform
of the labor market. In the face of union and government pressure, companies cannot lay off workers, and workers have no means of replacing
their lost income. The overall effect of this is the obvious hindering of corporate restructuring, profitability, and the flexibility necessary to meet the
demands of globalization. In short, with the lack of a safety net, Japanese
employers become the government for purposes of unemployment insurance. In the face of this situation, how is the Japanese state changing?

Perhaps the greatest threat to the solvency of the Japanese state is
the remarkable life expectancy of its citizens. Japan has the highest life
expectancy rate in the world.[32] With a median age of just over 41 years,
a large percentage of the Japanese population can expect to grow older
at a rate that outpaces any other country in the world. But this is not
the real problem. The long-term difficulty for the Japanese state is its low
fertility rate of 1.32. With a replacement rate of 2.1, the long-term demographic train wreck is easy to envision. Of course European states have
their own problems with declining birth rates,[33] but the problem is solved
through immigration. Historically, Japan has been hostile to immigration
and that is an attitude that has to change.[34]

The so-called "sanctuary" economy can no longer be sustained. Something has to give. Either changes in attitudes about immigration, structural changes in employment (e.g., eliminating job security), or extraordinary or unforeseen economic growth is necessary to solve the looming
problem of an overly large aging population. No solutions seem to be on
the horizon.

Although it is true that the so-called "lost decade" of the 1990s forced
the Japanese to come to terms with the pathologies of their corporate
structure, it is argued that the root causes of the problem pre-existed
this decade.[35] Undoing the fundamental features of the Japanese political economy that were regarded as responsible for the economic miracle –
keiretsu ties, full employment, and a bank system that caused no harm – all
of these have been undone. Their undoing represents the single greatest
change to the nature of the Japanese state since the end of the war. Additionally, these changes have engendered a sharp rise in the unemployment

rate, bankruptcies, and the removal of government backing for firms that cannot compete in an open market.

In its efforts to restructure itself, the Japanese state has pursued a three-prong strategy of structural reform. First, the government has accelerated the deregulation process in earnest. Second, through accounting and other reforms the government has increased the transparency of the economy. Finally, since 1999, the government has passed a series of measures in support of restructuring. Specifically, these measures have encouraged the creation of small- and medium-sized firms.[36] In commenting on reforms passed by the Japanese government in 1999, the IMF identified the following as most significant: (1) the Industrial Revitalization Law; (2) the revisions of the commercial code; (3) the bankruptcy reform (civil rehabilitation laws); (4) the reform of accounting standards; and (5) the reform of labor laws (temporary work and work dispatching).[37]

The workforce reductions in a variety of industries have returned the return on equity of half of these firms to historic levels (4–5 percent). These reductions have been across-the-board and in a variety of industries from the automotive industry to Sony Corporation to the banking industry. Additionally, substantial decreases in cost, shareholding arrangements, and the weakening of supplier-manufacturer ties have engendered substantial restructuring. Of course, there has been a marked increase in bankruptcies (23 percent in 2000).[38]

There can be little doubt that globalization has effected change in the Japanese state's approach to political economy. The relentless critiques of the shortcomings of the Japanese economy by foreign capital investors were addressed and, accordingly, Japanese share prices rebounded.[39] Do effects such as these signal a fundamental change in the nature of the Japanese state?

We mentioned earlier that full employment has been the principal goal of all Japanese governments since the end of World War II. The reason for this policy emphasis is simple: Japan has never had a European-style welfare state. Full-employment is Japan's answer to the welfare legitimacy question. But the collapse of the bubble economy in 1990 put the Japanese approach to welfare in serious question. Since that time there have, indeed, been reforms. In both job creation and finance, Japanese politicians and regulators have effected modest but discernible responses to a faltering economy.

The first response of the government to rising unemployment in the 1990s was to increase spending on public works projects. During the decade from 1992 to 2002, the government launched nine large-scale public spending programs, with public works and housing construction accounting for the bulk of the spending.[40] As budget deficits soared, the government scaled back public works spending. Nevertheless, long-term debt reached 157.3 percent of GDP in 2003.[41]

Budget deficits proved to be no match for the Japanese will to retain full employment. Consistently ranked by the OECD at or near the top in terms of worker security, and in the face of calls for reform of the policy of full employment, there have been no fundamental changes in the position of the government when it comes to full-time workers.

Part-time workers are another story. There, market reforms have been adopted by the government with noticeable effect. From 1998 to 2002, the number of temporary workers doubled from 306,000 to 721,000.[42] The greatest impact of temporary workers have been felt on the youth of Japan, as temporary workers effectively block entry of Japanese youth into the full-time employment ranks.[43]

But does this review of the political economy of the Japanese state prove that the nature of the Japanese state is changing with respect to welfare? True, the political economy of today is rather different than it was in 1990.[44] Yet, we must ask the question "has the nature of the Japanese state's intervention in the economy really changed its nature such that we could say that Japan confirms our thesis about the changing nature of the State?" Levy, Miura, and Park[45] maintain that through restructuring industry, loosening *keiretsu* ties, expanded flexibility of labor markets and making wholesale regulatory reforms, the Japanese state has evolved away from a statist to a developmental model. They are not alone in this judgment. Nevertheless, we cannot deny the conclusion that meeting ongoing and fresh challenges may prove difficult for the government because, as one commentator put it, "Japan clearly lacks a political system with the capacity to formulate and deliver bold reforms."[46] Despite this gloomy forecast, there is some hope that bold reforms may be more possible than previously thought. To take just one example, Japan is now implementing privatization of its postal system[47] – something thought to be all but impossible. As the OECD put it, "(o)pening government-dominated markets to the private sector would enhance competition, which appears weak in Japan according to a number of indicators."[48] While slow to evince the trend, Japan appears more ready than ever to move from a statist, modern state to a post-modern state.

In the Japanese case as well, then, the statist control of the national economy and supply of welfare entitlements to the nation is developing into a looser system where the welfare goals of the State are achieved through the enablement of economic opportunity rather than strong control of the national economic actors aimed at achieving job security and modern welfare guarantees. As we detail in subsequent chapters, states are losing important tools of regulation in the post-modern marketplace. The commodification of currencies and the fluidity of a global job market where an increasing number of tasks may be spread across the globe as the pace of technological advances are just two examples. The Japanese story reflects this transformative shift. Further, it shows how such shifts impact the domestic system, thereby engendering fundamental changes in the nature of welfare.

THE UNITED STATES AND THE NEW POLITICS OF SELF-RELIANCE

Of all the developed nations of the world, the United States has devoted less to social welfare (at least as traditionally understood) than any of the other first-world nations.[49] To take just one example, European nations have long subsidized families with direct support for increased birth rates as well as state-supported childcare. The United States does not provide any support for childcare without a ground in poverty. In terms of social protection, the American approach is *laissez-faire* or, as critics would have it, punitive.

The story of welfare in America often starts with Franklin D. Roosevelt's "New Deal." As the global economic depression wrecked havoc on the American economy, policymakers confronted a range of short- and long-term economic challenges. Finding work for the mass of unemployed Americans was the first of many tasks. Through a variety of public works programs and with the help of deficit spending, Roosevelt managed to bring the economy (especially manufacturing) back from the brink in 1932 to steady recovery and ultimate prosperity.

If any single contribution stands out it is the Social Security Act of 1935. For the first time in the nation's history, a true "welfare system" was created, providing retirement funding, unemployment insurance, and welfare benefits for the poor. Demonstrating prescience, Roosevelt insisted that the social security system be funded through payroll taxes rather than as a budget item. In this way, the system would not be buffeted by the changing winds of politics, thereby ensuring its long-term stability. While there is now debate over the long-term viability of the system,[50] there can be little doubt that social security will continue to be an integral feature of the American approach to welfare.

The other great American welfare program is Medicare. As everyone knows, there is no universal health coverage in the United States. Medical insurance is purchased from a variety of private providers and is normally part of a package of employer-provided benefits. Signed into law in 1965 by President Lyndon B. Johnson, Medicare was structured as an amendment to the Social Security legislation of the Roosevelt era. The scope of Medicare is limited to the elderly and those with special needs. Like Social Security, funding for Medicare comes from payroll taxes. Covering everything from prescription drugs to long-term care, Medicare is a complicated scheme and the subject of endless political debate. The only systematic effort to reform Medicare (and health insurance generally) came during the first term of Bill Clinton's administration. The reform effort was deemed a failure.

This brief picture of the American approach to welfare provides a backdrop against which to explore our claim that the nation-states of the world are shifting their approach to welfare and embracing a new norm, that of the enablement of global economic opportunity. Having surveyed developments in France and Japan, we are cognizant of the fact that evidence for our claim is not decisive. But we do not claim our description of the changing nature of the State is definitive or that the transformation process has completed its course. The evolution of the State, as we describe in later chapters, arises out of the interaction between the global trading order and the inner workings of Statecraft. The metamorphosis that we have identified is, we claim, now underway. We think it undeniable that the ironclad guarantee of welfare that legitimated the State in the twentieth-century modern era is, in the early twenty-first century, no longer an uncontroverted element of Statecraft. The globalized international order, whether it be called the "flat world" (like Friedman), the "society of market states" (Bobbitt), or "post-modern" (Cooper), has changed the way in which the State provides for the well-being of its subjects as well as the very concept of the nation. These phenomena, coupled with the internal changes to welfare that we are describing in this chapter, constitute organic shifts in the nature of Statecraft. Regardless of the extent to which welfare in France, Japan, or the United States has been transformed, the crucial point is that the historical tide of Statecraft moves, on a global structural level, away from the system of entitlements that is a hallmark of the modern era.

We are firm in our conviction that the nature of the State is changing, and nowhere is this change more pronounced than in the United States. We see the evidence for this claim in a variety of places. One place to gauge a shift in state attitudes is in the public pronouncements of its heads of state. To that end, consider these remarks by recent presidents. We start with remarks by President Clinton:

> The mission of this administration from day one has been to increase economic opportunity and maintain national security; to empower the individuals of this country to assume personal responsibility for their own futures.[51]

I do believe that the most important thing we can be doing today as a nation to create opportunity for our people is to give them the tools they need to succeed. In a global economy, the government cannot give anybody a guaranteed success story, but you can give people the tools to make the most of their own lives.[52]

The preeminent mission of our new government is to give all Americans an opportunity, not a guarantee but a real opportunity to build better lives.[53]

President Clinton's successor, George W. Bush, has made similar statements:

Government doesn't create jobs, but it can encourage an environment in which jobs are created.[54]

I like to remind people: Government doesn't create wealth; government creates an environment in which the entrepreneurial spirit can flourish, in which people can realize their dreams, in which small businesses can grow to be big businesses, in which the newly arrived can have a chance to realize the great promise of our country.[55]

If the remarks of American presidents are not enough to convince that a change is in the air, consider this passage from a leading columnist for the *New York Times*:

Since lifetime employment is a form of fat a flat world simply cannot sustain any longer, compassionate flatism seeks to focus its energy on how government and business can enhance every worker's *lifetime employability*. Lifetime employment depends on preserving a lot of fat. Lifetime employability requires replacing that fat with muscle. The social contract that progressives should try to enforce between government and workers, and companies and workers, is one in which government and companies say, "We cannot guarantee you any lifetime employment. But we can guarantee you that the government and companies will focus on giving you the tools to make you more lifetime employable." The whole mind-set of a flat world is one in which the individual worker is going to become more and more responsible for managing his or her own career, risks, and economic security, and the job of government and business is to help workers build the necessary muscles to do that.[56]

These remarks by Thomas Friedman capture the change we see in the bargain between the State and its subjects. In the realm of welfare, the fundamental pact of the nation-state and its people was that the State would provide for the care and sustenance of the nation. In a state such as Germany, that promise was met by a managerial economy: it was the task of government to broker deals between labor and employers. Government was a facilitator and, in some cases, a manager. In Japan, full, lifetime employment was the result of a pact between government and industry whereby government conceived of its welfare task as management of the economy through a variety of non-market and anti-market mechanisms. We believe that the nature of the welfare pledge is changing. There are two places to see this. The first is in the ways in which states are using incentives to solve problems traditionally addressed through law and regulation. The second is in the states' relations to their nations. Here, the nature of welfare is changing, and doing so in a manner consistent with the global, emerging norm of enhancement of economic opportunity.

In addition to speeches by American presidents, what other evidence do we have that the nature of the welfare promise is changing in the United States? The most obvious example is one of the hallmarks of Bill Clinton's tenure in the White House, that of the program "welfare-to-work." Welfare-to-work is a new type of social welfare program in that the State retrains the unemployed instead of delivering support in the form of maintenance. In addition to retraining, the recipient is required to seek work.[57] Finally, the period of time benefits are received is shortened. While these programs are criticized for their failure to impart truly useful skills, there can be little doubt that these programs signal a shift in how the State conceives of its welfare obligation to the nation. Stated simply, the State is substituting skills for sustenance. As it sees itself, the State is empowering the disadvantaged of the nation to provide for themselves. The "opportunity" given by the State is that of providing the means (i.e., the skills) necessary to take advantage of economic opportunity, no matter where it might be found.

In the midst of the dislocations wrought by globalization, there is increasing evidence of rising volatility in incomes and a shift in all things "risky" from the government to individuals. These are the principal contentions of Jacob Hacker in his recent book *The Great Risk Shift*.[58] Hacker's rhetorical stance is that of the defender of Everyman against the "high" moralism of what he calls the "Personal Responsibility Crusade." As Hacker puts it, "[t]he core assertion embodied in the Personal Responsibility Crusade is that Americans are best off dealing with economic risks on their own, without the overweening interference or expense of wider systems of risk sharing."[59]

With respect to Hacker's first point, that of volatility in wages, there is no doubt of the volatility nor of its effects on workers. Polls indicate a sizeable increase in worker anxiety over possible job loss.[60] But are the dislocations merely perceived or do they in fact exist? Again, Hacker is correct. Are such shifts to be regretted? In a review of Hacker's book, Brink Lindsey[61] pointed to research suggesting that when compared with the quiescent past, vastly improved conditions of material wealth as well as improved access to consumer credit and home equity loans cushion the up and down effects of the global economy. Additionally, recent empirical evidence suggests that notwithstanding their anxiety, job turbulence may in fact lead to *better* jobs for workers.[62]

What of Hacker's second claim, that the American government is shifting risk from itself to the nation? Hacker offers three examples in support of his claim: 401(k) plans, Health Savings Accounts, and proposals to replace traditional social security benefits with personal retirement accounts. How do each of these plans shift risk from the government to the individual?

The first thing to notice is that Hacker's claims are consistent with a principal theme of our book; that is, that the nature of welfare is changing from a regime of entitlement to one of economic opportunity. The risk shift Hacker sees in the three programs mentioned are clear examples of the State putting an individual's economic future in his or her own hands and not those of the State. As Hacker puts it, the shift is one from "shared risk" to one of individual responsibility. Let us discuss one of Hacker's examples to see this claim in detail.

Named after a section of the Internal Revenue Code, the 401(k) plan is an employer-sponsored plan that permits an employee to contribute to a retirement plan where the employee's contributions are matched by the employer up to a given percentage of salary. Most plans are "participant-directed," meaning that the employee is free to choose the investment vehicle most appropriate for his or her age and circumstances. Contributions are free from federal tax and there is no tax on earnings until withdrawal.

Hacker's complaint about 401(k)s is that they "put all the major risks and responsibilities – market risk, outliving one's savings, deciding how much to contribute and how to invest those contributions – onto workers themselves."[63] While we have some reservations about the cogency of Hacker's claims regarding the risks of 401(k)s,[64] our argument does not require us to take issue with Hacker's substantive claims about 401(k) plans. We think he is right (in fact, it is difficult to see any way to deny) that having workers decide where and when to invest their retirement dollars is, indeed, shifting the thinking regarding retirement from the State to the individual. We take no position on the question whether this shift is a good thing or not. Our claim is that the shift is inexorable and part of a larger shift in the State's commitment to welfare. No matter what we think of the substance of Hacker's analysis of 401(k)s, Medicare, or Health Savings Accounts, there is little doubt that the individuals who comprise a nation will have to think for themselves because the State is no longer doing the thinking for them. The State will provide opportunities, but it is up to the individual to make the most of those opportunities. The stakes are high.

This is by no means the only, or even most prominent, example of the American shift to the enablement of economic opportunity as a legitimating element of Statecraft. The American story has always been unique among the twentieth-century welfare states. The American welfare state has seen a belated development vis-a-vis its European counterparts. It has been less generous and all-encompassing than, say, the French system or the British cradle-to-grave regulatory scheme. It has relied more on passive macro-economic measures, such as tax cuts, than on the massive public spending of the European welfare states.[65] The reasons for these differences, including the Federalist system, the early twentieth-century Supreme Court rejection of federal attempts to push forward a more European-like welfare agenda, and others which are beyond the scope of this book. What is important to us is that having engaged in less welfare regulation than the other World War II victors, the United States has also departed further from the tenets of modern welfare. The purer embrace of enablement of economic opportunity that we have witnessed in America further confirms our claim that the modern welfare system is giving way to an organic norm of enablement of economic opportunity.

FROM ENTITLEMENTS TO ECONOMIC OPPORTUNITY

In the three examples discussed in this chapter, the nation-state welfare model – whether European entitlements, Japanese indicative planning, or the lean-and-mean American approach – is waning and no longer accomplishing the purpose for which it was established. A transformative shift may be identified, where the State relinquishes control over the social and economic matters that it regulated in the modern era. In earlier chapters, we have identified how this shift was a result of the interaction between domestic Statecraft and the international society of states. Welfare, however, will not disappear overnight. Rather, as we argue below, it will become one element of the enablement of global economic opportunity, rather than the center of the legitimating drive of the State.

The regulatory prong of welfare will continue to operate in the postmodern system of cross-border, incentives-based collaboration among states. Environmental regulation, labor protection, intellectual property regulatory schemes, competition laws, corporate codes, and all of the other components of regulatory welfare identified in Chapter 2, are integral aspects of the enablement of global economic opportunity. Their erosion as exclusive tools of nation-states correlates with the transformation of the international order of states from an aggregation of discrete nation-states to a diffuse collectivity. The problem here is not that regulatory welfare has become obsolete, but that the structure of the international order of states requires that its implementation be realigned to a post-modern, cross-border system that will supersede and subsume the national welfare systems of the modern era.

What we have called "redistributionist welfare" in Chapter 2 will also remain in place, but these welfare schemes will tend to become but one element of the panoply of policy tools of the global enablement of economic opportunity. We have explained in detail the reasons why redistributionist welfare is on the wane. These include strain on resources, loss of control, and the failure of the policies of entitlements to stimulate economic activity. The rise of the post-modern market state to replace the modern nation-state, however, will not occur overnight. A sudden dismantlement of the welfare system would actually destroy economic opportunity. Unlike mercantilism, which had to be destroyed overnight, the introduction of the enablement of global economic opportunity can be superimposed and gradually replace the modern system.

In Western Europe, for example, the interventionist policies of the State are a necessary component of economic stability. Minimum salaries, unemployment benefits, retirement schemes, aid to families with dependent children, housing allowances, and other elements of regulatory benefits cannot disappear overnight without sending the economies that they regulate back to pre-modern pockets of disaffection. Millions of people rely in those countries on entitlements from the State, and their sudden disappearance would be the functional equivalent of, say, massive plant closures in a purely market-based economy.

The trend, however, is for the replacement of this system of entitlements with a system of economic opportunity. The system of entitlements is reaching its physical limit, even in the West, and is failing to reach the remaining pockets of pre-modernism in the West, including for example the exclusion of the Parisian or Londonian suburbs. The modern liberal democracies will, inevitably, continue their march toward enabling economic opportunity as a substitute for redistributionist welfare entitlements. The transition should be encouraged not by force but, in line with the hallmarks of Statecraft in the post-modern era, with a system of incentives. The violent demonstrations that accompany each attempt by the French government to retreat from redistributionist welfare policies show the difficulties in prodding the transformative shift by force.

However, as we have explained, the metamorphosis is inevitable, and the modern liberal democracies will only gain by pushing the changes along. In order to do so, a system of choice that will work together with the international system we advocate should be put in place. In Paris' excluded suburbs, for example, the ghetto dwellers would be given a choice between opting into the redistributionist welfare French system, or waiving welfare rights and opting into a system intended to engender the enablement of global economic opportunity.[66] The system of loans for the poor that we describe in Chapter 6 could be modified to accord with the French system, and small enterprises from the suburbs given both loans and preferential access to certain markets. The participating enterprises would not be covered by redistributionist welfare rules. They would, for example, not be required to give their workers the kind of protections against termination that apply throughout France. They would not have to permit their employees to work only 35 hours per week or to benefit from the many weeks of vacation that the French system guarantees.

Such domestic changes will work hand-in-hand with the post-modern system of international trade that we have advocated to preserve the State and liberal democracies in the post-modern age. In an epoch when the State no longer legitimizes itself by guaranteeing its nation's welfare solely through entitlements, it must take active steps to further the new ethos in order to maintain its legitimacy. The best way to accomplish this goal would be to make available economic opportunity packages domestically, all the while participating in the global enterprise of spreading economic opportunity.

What we advocate, then, is a fundamental rethinking of trade policy by the world's principal commercial actors. This rethinking should be both inward and outward, looking both to domestic welfare policy and trade policy. As we have explained, no less than the future of the liberal democracies is at stake. They will either become post-modern liberal democracies, or remain mired in the modern stage of their evolution. In Chapter 4, we analyze the relationship between the Bretton Woods Order and modern Statecraft. We will then explain how modern Statecraft has evolved into post-modern Statecraft, as we begin to advance our theory of how the global trading order should follow suit.

4 Disaster and Redemption: 1930s and Bretton Woods

Thesis:

The trade order established at Bretton Woods was the product of forces unique to the postwar era. The norm of comparative advantage was a natural complement to the nation-state constitutional order of the society of states. Bretton Woods illustrates how a trade norm complements and enhances domestic Statecraft. In the case of Bretton Woods, it also demonstrates how the marriage of a trade norm to a particular iteration of the State sows the seeds of metamorphosis in the nature of the State.

World War II left the European nations and Japan in ruins. Before the war's end,[1] it was clear that vast reconstruction would be the only way to revive the economies of Europe and Asia. However, reconstruction would not be sufficient, for it was plain that investment in both infrastructure and, in the case of the Axis powers, the development of democratic institutions, would need to be accompanied by monetary policy reform of a global nature. The system established at Bretton Woods[2] had three principal structural dimensions: (1) the ordering of international trade through an International Trade Organization; (2) the fostering of international development under the umbrella of the International Bank for Reconstruction and Development; and (3) the administration of monetary and financial matters through the International Monetary Fund. The International Trade Organization did not pass congressional muster, and the larger enterprise was reduced to the GATT, a core component aimed principally at removing barriers to trade and adopting exceptions to trade liberalization rules to shelter domestic policies thought at the time to be essential to the operation of the modern liberal democratic welfare state.[3]

As we will show, these institutions were the product of a set of ideas that were not only integrated, but went far deeper than the immediate concerns of the post-war environment. What we call "The Bretton Woods Order" was both a reaction to the disastrous mercantilist policies that hampered democracies as the outbreak of war was imminent, as well as the logical expression of an integrated set of ideas regarding sovereignty, free trade, and Statecraft. In the fullness of time, democracy would triumph as the preferred model for Statecraft. However, as we shall explain, the seeds of the demise of the Bretton Woods Order were sown long before any crack would appear in the Berlin Wall. Rather than ushering in the end of trade history, the Bretton Woods Order set in motion international regulatory mechanisms that accorded with the constitutional order of the modern liberal democracies. As the post-modern era arrived, these institutions would lose their effectiveness. One of our main tasks in this book is to explore the reason for the decline of the institutions of international trade.

When the United States, Britain, and France met at Bretton Woods, their aspiration was to produce nothing less than a new global economic order. That order would bring financial stability (e.g., stable exchange rates) and promote economic growth through free trade. Successful post-war reconstruction of Europe and Japan was far from certain. In the wake of war, German postwar GDP was a third of what it had been a decade before. In Italy and Japan, postwar levels were about the same as they were in 1910, and Austria hovered around its 1870 level.[4] By contrast, the United States was an economic powerhouse. With the dollar effectively established as the world's reserve currency, and Europe in dire need of American goods to rebuild its shattered cities, the United States enjoyed a period of sustained economic prosperity.[5] As we explain in this chapter, the victors of World War II (and the defeated powers they chose to bring into their camp) adopted an international trade system that mirrored the essential components of modern Statecraft in the liberal democratic world. Balance of powers would be achieved by supporting the economies of the defeated powers through the Marshall Plan.[6] The regulatory modern State, which legitimated itself through the supply of welfare to the nation, would draw additional resources from the global system, all the while sheltering its internal body of policies from international intrusion. The sovereignty feature of the modern states, defined in relation to the welfare policies that legitimated the State in those countries, would join with the welfare and redistributionist policies of the day to form a harmonious link between domestic Statecraft and the international economic order of modern states.

In the early part of the 1970s, President Richard Nixon retreated from the original Bretton Woods Order when he took the United States off the gold standard. This decision effectively freed all currencies – but especially the dollar – to float in the foreign exchange markets. Eventually, currencies would become commodities as the now globalized market wrested control of currency from nations. Despite this development, other pillars of the Bretton Woods Order remained in place, and the structure that Bretton Woods established is credited as a postwar success, effectively bringing about economic stability and growth in Europe and Japan and contributing to the ultimate success of democracy in its struggle against fascism and communism.[7]

The institutions of international trade established after World War II evolved over the next 60 years in accordance with the modern principles of Statecraft exhibited by the victors of World War II. These institutions, including the original International Trade Organization and its successor General Agreement on Tariffs and Trade (the "GATT"), would prove to be a boon both to United States and the nation-states of Europe and Asia. From the standpoint of global efficiency, putting aside redistributionist concerns within the nation-states, the contribution to global growth of a system that rejected mercantilism was an unmitigated success. Liberalization of trade allowed the modern liberal democracies to perform in a fundamentally sounder way than before World War II. In this chapter, we explain the relationship between the State, the health of the political architecture that it puts in place, and its strategic and trade expressions, using the GATT and Bretton Woods to illustrate our theoretical claims.

THE STATE AND TRADE

Our argument is that there is a triangular link among the inner face of the State, and its outer expression in strategy and trade. The nature of the international system that serves the interests of individual states depends on the nature of their Statecraft. For the nation-states of Europe, Asia, and the United States, the Bretton Woods Order made sense. The modern liberal democracies that won World War II had an incentive to adopt comparative advantage as well as other pillars of the GATT and the other international trade regulatory regimes. The defeated powers, under the prevailing strategic doctrines, were invited to join the victors and to pursue a set of common interests. As with every other epochal constitutional moment, we argue, the dominant strategic players in this era of Statecraft faced choices with respect to the establishment of the international trading system that mirrored their struggles on the strategic plane. The trade system that was adopted dovetailed with the inner face of Statecraft of the Western victors, and the post-fascist democracies that joined them.

In this chapter, we explain what we mean by the link between the inner face of Statecraft, and its outer strategic and trade expressions.

The organic relationships that we define are, we claim, "constitutional" in nature. The hallmarks of Statecraft encompass foundational sets of norms and rules of law that characterize a particular era and define its normative and institutional architecture. In the modern age, the welfare nation-states followed a model of Statecraft that featured a redistributionist and general regulatory role, in addition to numerous other areas of activity consistent with control over a discrete nation, for whose well-being the power of the State is unleashed. The international strategic interests of the modern liberal democracies included a need to form a more cohesive bloc than before World War II. The opportunity to liberalize trade made sense for the victors and their allies. The modern liberal democratic constitutional ethos could become "embedded" in the international trade order, and each nation could be governed by a state dedicated to its welfare and draw increased sustenance from its interactions with other national groupings in the global trading order. As we detail later, the system created by the liberal democratic victors ultimately eroded the nation and its welfare as the basis of the State: the post-modern State that would then arise could no longer be embedded in the Bretton Woods Order.

We posit that once the constitutional mechanisms are understood, and the interactive patterns that transform them over time are brought to light, the victors of war have the opportunity to achieve their strategic interests in the trade field. Although we believe that, as a matter of descriptive history, the pre-modern and modern periods show that the victors of war may adopt systems that exclude large groups of states from enjoying the benefits of trade, we will argue in later chapters that this is not necessarily the case and that trade need not be a zero sum game. In Chapter 5 and beyond, we will explain how frictions in the international trade order arose mainly in relation to distributive and fairness issues involving the relationship between pre-modern states and modern states, and to the rise of post-modern states and of an international trade order that produced globalization and radically transformed the economic landscape in which the modern states operated. While the trading order also came into conflict with the participating states' ability to effectuate welfare programs, the victors of World War II ultimately resolved these tensions by law and diplomacy in a relatively satisfactory fashion, and the major unresolved questions that lingered through the modern period resulted from the difficulties that the modern liberal democracies had in their relations to pre-modern states and in the metamorphosis of the world markets into a post-modern diffuse mass. In this chapter, through the lens of the twentieth century, we argue that the foundational notions of the international trading system do not reflect the outcome of a material dialectic among states (such as the historical recognition of the damage that arose from the failure to follow a comparative advantage model) but arise from the interwoven architecture of the State, the international trade order of states, and the parallel yet connected evolution of both.

We argue that transformations in domestic Statecraft drive the evolution of the international trade order and, in turn, transformative shifts on the international commercial plane tend to change the domestic configuration of the State. This relationship of interdependence and connectedness is dynamic and manifests itself on a foundational level. The domestic constitutional architecture of the State, such as its choice of a particular route to the nation's welfare through policies of indicative planning or cradle-to-grave social protection, has profound repercussions for the ordering of the international trade system.[8] At the same time, shifts in the foundational rules of the international trade system and in patterns of international economic activity, such as the rise of a new set of international economic actors and transformations in currency markets, affect the ability of the State to maintain its domestic Statecraft and tend to transform the internal order of the State.[9] Like Jacob's Ladder,[10] the State and the order of states are animated by a constant interaction going from bottom to top, and vice versa, in a dynamic motion that shapes both spheres and, in turn, propels them forward through various stages of history. Just as Fukuyama and Hegel were lured into thinking that strategic and political history had ended, trade theorists might misinterpret an historical transformation portending the end of trade history.

Trade policy, then, never reaches a universal and timeless state of being. Rather, it must be adjusted to reflect internal political and ideological goals and the evolving international scene. To be sure, structural shifts do not happen overnight. However, there comes a point when a constitutional moment is needed. At that moment, states must come together and recognize that Statecraft and the order of the society of states have undergone a metamorphosis of sufficient magnitude to warrant a new set of constitutional rules.[11] In this book, we argue that such a constitutional moment has become necessary and is now overdue.

The constitutional moment is a rite of passage, in that it marks an international awareness that change has occurred, and embraces new foundational norms and institutions for a new era. The failure of states to recognize the constitutional moment will not only prejudice them economically, but also possibly hamper the achievement of their non-trade strategic foreign policy objectives. Ending history, then, is not only an academic and intellectual mistake; it is a dangerous illusion comparable to the belief that World War II invaders could be repelled by a Maginot Line.[12] The human difficulty in stepping out of deeply rooted paradigms to look at the future is bound to generate defeat in the present. We have selected the twentieth century to illustrate our theory, focusing on the GATT/WTO system. The twentieth-century trade story, as classically told, is one of failure and redemption. In this instance, beginning the inquiry with an exploration of redemption, and telling the story with the voice of an economist, makes the contours of failure clearer. Once we give the economist's account, we will narrate the story of those whom Keynes called the "poets of Bretton Woods," thereby painting a complete picture of the historical manifestations of our theoretical construct.

POST-WAR REDEMPTION: COMPARATIVE ADVANTAGE
AND THE TRADE ORDER OF STATES

Redemption happened after World War II, with the incorporation into the GATT of the theories of absolute and comparative advantage developed by Adam Smith and David Ricardo.[13] Their theory was simple: states would maximize their wealth by unilaterally eliminating import restrictions.[14] However, there was no mention of the use of law to erect an international system that would institutionalize their economic insights.[15] The GATT did that.[16] At its trade core, the GATT established three "disciplines" that reduced states' ability to impose trade barriers that protect the domestic economy: (1) tariff bindings; (2) an anti-discrimination norm applicable to internal taxation and regulation; and (3) a prohibition of quotas and like measures.[17] The United States and the United Kingdom clashed over the principle of non-discrimination. The United States insisted on it as an indispensable component of a system of trade among modern liberal democracies and those who wish to join the free world, to be contrasted with (among other things) the preferential system of trade that Imperial Japan and Nazi Germany sought to impose in their respective spheres of influence. The United States view prevailed, and it was reflected in the overall constitutional architecture of the GATT and the trade legal disciplines that comprised it.

The first trade-liberalizing discipline created a framework for the GATT Contracting Parties to "bind" the tariffs that they imposed on foreign products, the primary protectionist barrier of the first half of the twentieth century, to maximum permitted ceilings to be negotiated down in relation to various categories of products and (in time) services over successive GATT "rounds"[18]. In turn, each state committed, under the Most Favored Nation Clause of the GATT, to extend to all trading partners the lowest tariff concession chosen by the state with respect to any partner. This structure generated eight completed rounds of trade negotiations (Doha being underway as of this writing), and a drastic reduction of the global tariff barriers to trade that prevailed before Bretton Woods.[19] The second discipline required the Contracting Parties to respect a nondiscrimination norm that guaranteed all imported products the same treatment as "like" domestic products with respect to internal taxation and regulation.[20] This "national treatment" discipline, among other things, prevented the circumvention of a tariff binding through imposition of a discriminatory burden in the form of, for example, an internal sales tax.[21] The concept of discrimination was, of course, laden with ambiguity and has generated substantial controversy. Interpretive difficulties arise because the discrimination principle allows international challenges to national policies ostensibly unrelated to trade, but that nevertheless disparately impact foreign products owing to differences in the regulatory levels of protection in various states – one of the facets of the "linkage" issue.[22] However, putting aside these interpretive issues, the national treatment component of the GATT is an indispensable element of any treaty of integration that includes a tariff reduction scheme. Without a national treatment discipline, a member state of such a treaty could impose discriminatory taxation or regulation on foreign products so as to avoid its tariff obligations.[23]

The third discipline prohibits the imposition of quantitative restrictions to trade and their functional equivalents.[24] The purpose of this discipline, and the interpretive questions that it has generated, parallels the national treatment story. Here, too, the founders of the GATT evidently sought to deprive states of a tool for circumvention of the tariff discipline.[25] In sum, then, the GATT gave multilateral, institutional expression to the classic economic theories of Ricardo and Smith.

The orthodox economic account of the GATT speaks of redemption, because it contrasts the GATT with the economic failures that preceded World War II. The crux of the story is that, before World War II, the major trading partners failed to recognize that commerce should be based on comparative advantage and that states should remove artificial barriers to trade (principally tariffs). Instead, the animating principle of trade remained driven by protectionist impulses that led to trade wars and international commercial collapse at the very time when the Great Depression and the rise of fascism endangered the economic and strategic health of the liberal democracies. The failure to move beyond protectionism compounded the harm caused by the democracies' choice – expressed in the Treaty of Versailles – to oppress Germany instead of bringing it into Europe's fold as a partner.[26] Bretton Woods is the constitutional moment of this story in that it reflects the understanding of the historical mistakes made by the liberal democracies. The Book of Mistakes had to be rewritten into the Book of Redemption. Economic collapse caused by trade wars would not only be unthinkable, but made impossible by a trading system that adopted comparative advantage as its fundamental value.[27]

STATECRAFT AND TRADE

All serious students of trade have learned that the economic ideology of trade provides only a partial and, perhaps, even misleading account of the original intent of the framers of the GATT and the reasons for its general acceptance by the Contracting Parties. In order to understand the GATT, one must understand the internal foundational frameworks and constitutional rules of the major players who brought about its formation.[28] These constitutional rules help explain why the major economic powers that formed the GATT chose the legal structure they did and how they mustered the political willingness to accept the trade disciplines imposed under the GATT. Our constitutional account complements the purely economic story. We believe that the internal configuration of the states that formed the GATT needed to work in harmony with any international system put in place. States did not simply have an economic epiphany. They chose the framework underlying the GATT because it allowed them to maintain their domestic architecture as they entered into an international framework that expanded the global economic pie.[29] The main players' commitment to an interventionist welfare state ensured that the economic project would be married to a political redistributive enterprise.[30]

Our thesis is consistent with strategic developments in the twentieth century. We agree with Bobbitt that the wars of the twentieth century are best seen as one long struggle over the dominant model for Statecraft. Communism, fascism, and democracy held out their respective promises (and possibilities) of welfare and security. Each state was a nation-state and, as such, was a participant in the balance of power scheme that brought world order. Having defeated fascism, the post-war democratic states went head-to-head with communism for the final phase of the twentieth century. This struggle was not only strategic, as a matter of war and peace, but it was a matter of "welfare" as well. The United States and its newly democratic allies opposed communism both in the theater of war and the economic theater. Democracy vanquished communism not (only) on the battlefield, but in managing to raise standards of living and establishing a welfare system that integrated into the national economic whole the working classes that were the target of communism's ideological war. The welfare state was thus an ideological alternative to the central state/command economic model of communism. The post-war trade norm of comparative advantage was a central element in the ideological and political arsenal of democracy. In fact, we would go so far as to say that the economic success of the West, a success engendered partially by the norm of comparative advantage and its marriage to a society of democratic nation-states, was arguably as important to the ultimate victory of democracy over communism than mutual assured destruction or any other strategic policy.[31]

Although this account goes deeper than the economic tale, it still speaks of the end of history. It starts with constitutional rules, which were fundamental to modern liberal democracies after World War II. These rules included the broad legal and policy schemes that embodied a given nation-state's policy choices with respect to redistributive justice and the relationship between various economic segments of society or issues affecting the nation and the State's relation to its subjects. In Europe, these schemes took the shape of public enterprise, unemployment compensation, housing aid, assistance to large families, and other policies intended to transfer wealth from high-income segments of society to lower income workers and thus protect discrete classes deemed to be disadvantaged in the market. In the United States, the emphasis was more exclusively on tax and transfer policies. Japan, for its part, relied heavily on centralized planning of industrial activity and subsidies of research and development that would shore up enterprises housing a large part of the domestic workforce.[32]

In all cases, the State regulated across a wide array of subject matters. It established property and economic rights available generally to the nation. It provided for labor protection rules that shored up the working classes of the nation. It regulated resource conservation, consumer rights, sales of securities, competition, and myriad other areas relevant to the economic and social life of the nation.[33] Of course, the victors of World War II had differing approaches to the relevant regulatory areas. From minute regulation, such as pesticide levels or technical machinery specifications, to broad constitutional areas such as expropriation, free speech, or the rights of discrete minorities, the states adopted disparate approaches to specific subject matter areas. Despite their different viewpoints, all major players shared a basic philosophy of domestic Statecraft that went hand-in-hand with liberalized trade which, although including a regulatory harmonization drive, respected the sovereign power to enact those modern regulations.[34] The Bretton Woods system, in other words, married international economic policies (and an international order of states dedicated to wealth maximization) to a legal framework that protected the nation-states' power to control their domestic economies.[35]

The harmonious functioning of domestic constitutional rules and international law did go hand-in-hand with historical tendencies that made comparative advantage a better foundational norm for the international trading system than the domestically driven mercantilist policies that preceded World War II. The founders of the GATT believed that mercantilism, as embodied in statutes like the Hawley-Smoot Tariff Act of 1930,[36] had contributed to the economic disaster of the 1930s and to the advent of fascism as a contender for a model of Statecraft.[37] Thus, they committed the liberal democracies to a set of rules that would not only make such disasters legally impossible, but would in no way threaten their perception of economic sovereignty. The GATT created a world trade system that accorded with these states' internal laws and politics.[38] These were expressions of the constitutional nature of modern Statecraft. The application of mercantilist policies to a modern epoch was bound to produce economically disastrous results because it did not accord with the nature of Statecraft of the time. The State was expanding within the frame of a new era, and it not only had to transform its inner nature, but its outer trade expression as well: it had to articulate a modern structure that would accord with the inner face of Statecraft and its expression in the strategic realm.

Our theory posits that the relationship between the domestic constitutional realm and the international trade order of states goes beyond the marriage of a good economic idea with a legal system that makes it politically feasible. We depart from the notion that Bretton Woods joined comparative advantage with a theory of modern liberal democracy as the highest expression of the State, thus achieving the ultimate trade order of states. Rather, we submit that Bretton Woods ushered in a crucial and historically appropriate constitutional moment that acknowledged both the then-current evolutionary stage of the State and the new order of states generated by the metamorphosis in Statecraft. From its inception, then, the Bretton Woods system set in motion the seeds of a transformation that would ultimately necessitate another constitutional moment for the trade order of states.

Our starting point coincides with the analysis of Bretton Woods as a joint political and economic enterprise in that we agree that the Keynesian welfare state was particularly well suited to the GATT framework as well as its introduction of comparative advantage and anti-protectionist rules. Keynes was right to call the lawyers, and the political theory that they wrote into the GATT, the "poets of Bretton Woods."[39] Ruggie's brilliant insights, captured by "embedded liberalism," also provide an accurate snapshot of the political history of the time. The GATT, as explained above, sheltered welfare policies and left its constituent states free to act as experimental laboratories for improvement of their peoples' welfare.[40] All in all, it is true that the GATT established a framework that insulated

domestic politics and redistribution choices from international intervention, and to that extent accorded with the ethos of the welfare state.

However, in our account, Bretton Woods came (and, as discussed
below, it came too late) to crystallize in a constitutional moment transformations that had previously taken place and to paint one more constitutional portrait of the State and its trade manifestation. Bretton Woods
was another episode in the continuous evolutionary cycle of Statecraft
and of its formative interaction with the global trading order. Recognizing
Bretton Woods as such mandates inquiry into what the next constitutional
stage should be, and when the rite of passage should be actuated. That
inquiry is our task in subsequent chapters. For the moment, let us explain
further the Bretton Woods that was (and the Bretton Woods that should
have come earlier) in light of our Statecraft thesis.

CONSTITUTIONAL CYCLES, THE STATE, AND BRETTON WOODS

As discussed in Chapter 2, the State may be understood as an enduring
entity that evolves through successive constitutional cycles. During each
cycle, the State exhibits relatively stable, yet slowly shifting, constitutional features on both the domestic and international planes. At the same
time, often as a result of the operation of these constitutional features,
new realities arise that force states to adjust their fundamental constitutional elements, and gradually usher in yet another cycle. Though at these
moments theorists like Hegel or Fukuyama are inclined to predict "the
end of history," they are not in fact glimpsing the beginning of a Kantian
era of "perpetual peace"[41] nor an end to the evolution of Statecraft. Rather,
those voices keenly reflect a sentiment of transformation, widely felt, that
should prompt an inquiry into whether a new constitutional cycle is at
hand.

The State that Bretton Woods encountered arose from a period of
solidification of the "nation" as its basis. At least in Europe, twentieth-
century states were founded upon nations that had come together under a
state for the purpose of amassing resources and fighting wars that would
further their goals of solidification.[42] On the international scene, these
states maintained complex colonizing enterprises with strong commercial
motivations that by all accounts generated substantial economic benefits
for the colonizers.[43] This influenced the political and economic power of
those nation-states that dominated the international scene. At the same
time, the domestic process of building a nation generated a population
comprised of various segments collectively affiliated with a single state;
these segments included a large working class, a bourgeoisie, and upper

classes or nobility.[44] The State was then forced to contend with the newly constituted nation.

The focus of our inquiry is not the organizational nature of the State as a modern liberal democracy, but rather the solidification process that it experienced, the attendant birth of a nation as its support, the supply of welfare to the nation as its legitimating drive, and the evolution in Statecraft that arose out of these phenomena. It is against this backdrop that the competing theories of marxism, fascism, and modern liberal democracy struggled with one another for control of the State. Under each scenario envisaged by the models, whether a triumph of the workers, an eternal Reich, or Fukuyama's "end of history," Statecraft history runs its course and ends in a particular form of organization in relation to the nation.[45] In each case, the nation is the basis of the State, and the welfare of that nation is the State's legitimating *raison d'etre*. Hence, a shared objective is achieved by different routes.

The significance of the nature of Statecraft for Bretton Woods lies in the natural harmony between comparative advantage and a nation-state's Statecraft. We agree with scholars such as Ruggie that from a political standpoint, Bretton Woods worked harmoniously with the internal ethos of modern liberal democracies.[46] We agree with Keynes that, without the delicate poetry of Bretton Woods, the modern liberal democracies might not have accepted the GATT as they did.[47] We accept the economists' account of comparative advantage as a better norm for the twentieth-century trading world than mercantilism.[48] However, our story focuses on Statecraft as an integrated set of ideas and concepts and the manifestation of those ideas in the domestic and international realms. We submit that by 1917, the modern liberal democracies had sufficient evidence of the need for a trade constitutional moment in the realm of pure ideas and their manifestation in the economic reality of the society of states. Thus, Bretton Woods could have occurred then as the next stage in the evolution of Statecraft and ordering of states.

By 1917, the evolution of the State to the form of the nation-state, and the internal economic order it generated, had resulted in an industrialized world subdivided into discrete economies co-extensive and associated with the nation. The nation owned virtually all means of production within the territory governed by its state, the welfare of that nation provided the State with its legitimating drive, and states had the means and the incentive to regulate and control the domestic realm. The very elements that changed the nature of Statecraft, from a state supported by the nation (the state-nation) to a state unleashing its power to shore up the nation (the nation-state), were reflected in the domestic reality. The core assets of each state lay in the hands of the nation – one of the key assumptions of Bretton Woods that is gradually waning as a result of the transformative mechanisms put in motion by Bretton Woods itself.[49] Industrial, agricultural, and other types of output could consistently be identified with the nation. The trading world could be subdivided into blocs, each of which was comprised of an aggregate of goods, capital, assets, currency, and other resources that in a real sense belonged to the nation. Nevertheless, the State had a sufficient degree of control over this "national" economy, and a concrete bloc of resources associated with its nation, to implement welfare policies of the type contemplated by the economic and political bargain of Bretton Woods and to legitimize itself vis-à-vis the nation. Given the condition of Statecraft in 1917, the foundational norms of the trade order of states had to change, thus signaling that the time for a constitutional moment had already arrived by the time of Bretton Woods.

The last pieces of the Statecraft puzzle lie in the concept of balance of power and in the connection between strategy, war, and the trade order of states. The modern world, as described by Robert Cooper, puts balance of power at the center of strategic Statecraft.[50] A multi-polar world of solidified nation-states rests on a balance of power among its constituent entities. In the trade world, this phenomenon is replicated, and here again the Bretton Woods moment may be understood as recognizing the phenomenon, albeit too late. Bretton Woods joined the theory of comparative advantage with substantial foreign investment in sovereign, democratic blocs in Western Europe (and Japan) as part of the Marshall Plan. The new trade system respected borders and sovereignty, and it allowed states to advance national welfare through internal policies. The Marshall Plan's infusion of capital into Europe created trading partners whose economic strengths would enable them to maintain the requisite balance of powers.[51] In turn, the GATT organized itself around succeeding rounds of negotiation that gradually reduced barriers to (and otherwise liberalized) trade. At the end of the day, the structural nature of the system accorded with the constitutional nature and organic link between domestic Statecraft and the outer face of the State.

In our view, the victors of war have the opportunity to identify these constitutional mechanisms and to craft a system that accords with their strategic interests. The Bretton Woods Order allowed the victors of World War II to shore up their interests as they prepared for the final stage of the Long War, the defeat of communism as an alternative form of Statecraft. The corollary of our argument is twofold: the international society of states is crafted by the strategic powers of the day. More often than not, the victors of war dominate the strategic scene, and they have the capacity to acquire the conceptual tools to fashion a system that serves their strategic interests. The international trade system, then, represents not only embedded Statecraft, but the Statecraft of a particular time and place. The strategic international order dictates the trade order's structural and constitutional contours, in that it produces the players that shape it based on their inner Statecraft. The constitutional nature of the State transforms itself as a new international order of states arises and causes foundational shifts for the constituent states. The concept of the end of history remains irrelevant in all eras, as the history of the State passes from one epoch to the next and contains within itself the seeds of future transformations of Statecraft.

In the following chapters, we detail the foundational changes engendered by the Bretton Woods Order. We describe how the post-modern State arose in substantial part out of the diffuse mechanisms that Bretton Woods set in motion, and we identify the new animating norm that we argue should be used to ground the post-modern international economic order, which we term the "enablement of global economic opportunity." We view the structure from the standpoint of the victors of World War II, including powers that arose after the war, such as China and India. We describe the institutions that we believe should be charged with implementing the norm, and we craft an incentives-based, cross-border regulatory structure that will supplement and ultimately succeed comparative advantage as the post-modern foundational principle of trade in the globalized markets of the twenty-first century.

5 The Transformation of the Bretton Woods World and the Rise of a New Economic Order

Thesis:

The trade order of Bretton Woods was the expression of unique world-historical events that wed a trade order to a constitutional order of states. This order was established by the victors of World War II, who chose an international trade order that accorded with the nature of their State-craft. Today, the nation-state is fading and its trade order – comparative advantage – is also under increasing pressure. Additionally, economic activity capacity is globally dispersed. The cross-border enterprise is the hallmark of the new global trade order as states move from a norm of comparative advantage to enablement of economic opportunity. To complete the next constitutional cycle, a post-modern Statecraft constitutional structure must be at the core of future global trade policy.

Bretton Woods inherited and shaped a world subdivided into national economies coextensive with the nation-states that established the trade order of the GATT. As described in Chapter 4, the theoretical foundation of the system respected sovereignty, left it to internal domestic policy to control the redistribution of wealth and to provide for the well-being of the subjects of the nation-state, and removed protectionist trade restrictions as a tool of governmental regulation. The structural changes implemented by Bretton Woods accorded with the face of modern State-craft. Pre-modern Statecraft involved an inward-looking movement of solidification of the State, drawing on its labor pool, its colonization conquests, and the industrial resources that were created as a byproduct of the pre-modern enterprise. For the state-nation, mercantilism made sense. Just as a merchant wants to beat the competition in a zero-sum game aimed at solidifying her enterprise, the pre-modern states used mercantilist, beggar-thy-neighbor policies to bolster and solidify the State at the expense of their neighbors.

The conventional wisdom is that modern liberal democracies should have understood that comparative advantage provided a better system of trade than mercantilism, and thereby averted trade wars that weakened them at the worst possible historical moment.[1] This type of argument usually goes hand-in-hand with the claim that the modern liberal democracies should not have oppressed Germany at Versailles, but rather brought it into the fold of Europe. As Robert Schuman poignantly declared in 1950, "a united Europe was not achieved and we had war." Had Schuman opined on the pre-World War II failure to integrate the economies of the modern liberal democracies, he surely would have added that "comparative advantage and open borders were not achieved, and we had a trade war." The story of failure and redemption is classic. After World War II, learning from their tragic mistakes, the nations of Europe united and the trading states of the democratic world coalesced into a system that recognized what they took to be universal and timeless principles: comparative advantage, economic integration, and political cooperation.

What these accounts fail to recognize is that the establishment of comparative advantage as the foundational principle of the system, as well as the integration of Europe, are intricately linked to the evolution of Statecraft and the constitutional order of states. An "end of history" sense permeates discussions of comparative advantage and integration. In these narratives, the political and economic history of the world is viewed as an upward slope of progress ending with democracies trading among themselves without protectionist barriers, but with a sufficient liberal democratic regulatory apparatus to protect the welfare of citizens and prevent the rise of unbridled international capitalism. Put simply: We, the enlightened liberal democrats, prevailed against communists by extending welfare to the people and ushering in capitalism with a human face. We then overcame our nationalistic urge to view trade as a zero-sum game and ultimately recognized that comparative advantage would enable and empower our welfare systems to operate more effectively. We continued down the road of international partnership and, in more enlightened places like Europe, we transcended our attachment to national borders and created integrated areas that made it virtually impossible for member states to engage in war against one another, all the while dramatically increasing standards of living and economic performance.[2]

The concept of *acquis social* in France best captures this view of the world. The *acquis social* is the result of a painstaking climb up a ladder of progressive measures that will come under threat at some point in their history and must be defended against reactionary backlash.[3] The very concept of "reactionaries" in French culture is commonly understood to describe those who hinder social progress. Social progress, in turn, refers to the welfare culture of the French nation-state. The 35-hour workweek, the 13th month of salary paid at the end of the year, the relatively low retirement age, the special retirement benefits extended to the labor force in sectors that historically faced difficult working conditions, the labor protections afforded employees and their entitlements upon termination, all belong to a basket of *acquis* that the French citizenry will take to the streets in order to protect. Even abortion rights, and the 1974 Weil Law, come within the social basket of progressive measures that are intended to build, block by block, the good polity and associated good life for the nation. The paradigm is not one of cycles and epochs, with the State and its subjects needing to reinvent themselves in each era, but of a gradual progression that culminates in an end-of-history type of State, one to be defended and protected against assaults from those who would turn the clock back.[4]

This approach to political history has a distinctly European flavor, and evidently was written from the standpoint of the modern liberal democratic victors of the long ideological war of the twentieth century. Yet the end of history must, by definition, be a universal phenomenon, and Fukuyama and the other would-be history terminators held by necessity that the rest of the world would ultimately catch up to the West and conclude their historical course at the same finish line. This is what the trade and political leaders of the West have been attempting to accomplish. Doha seeks to bring poorer countries into the fold of liberalized world trade.[5] The Free Trade of the Americas Agreement aims to bring about an integrated area in the Americas that will act as a counterpart to the European Union.[6] Europe, for its part, continues to expand eastward. It grew from six member states to incorporate 27 countries, including significant former members of the Warsaw alliance such as Poland, Bulgaria, and Romania. In the end, so the story goes, from Turkey (assuming that the West sheds the taboo of a Muslim nation joining Europe) to Moscow we will have a united European bloc, trading freely in a single market, exchanging goods and services with a liberalized and fortified North and South American set of economies, while the nations of Africa and Asia will meaningfully integrate themselves into the world economy.[7]

This "end of history" narrative, however, is fundamentally flawed. The problem is that this account fails to recognize that our present situation is in large part a manifestation of the current evolutionary iteration of the State. As we have argued, each epochal manifestation of the State sets in motion changes that ultimately transform the international landscape. In turn, the State will evolve again in response to the metamorphosis of the international legal field in which it operates, and this new cycle will then necessitate a revision of the international legal order. As explained later, a constitutional moment ushering in a revision of the institutions and animating principles of the system is necessary. Failure to recognize that a constitutional shift is needed will inevitably create profound economic and political problems. Today, we find ourselves at such a juncture because the international economic landscape has evolved from a set of discrete economic units (states) trading with one another (and speaking vertically to an international system aimed at liberalizing trade while respecting sovereignty and balance of powers) to what may be termed a "horizontalizing system" where trade actors cut across borders to form international industries that have more in common with each other than with the other players in the states in which they operate. This is the essence of the post-modern trading world and, as we detail in subsequent chapters, there is a dearth of appropriate institutions and norms to regulate this transformed global economy. A foundational restructuring of the global trading order is therefore needed.

In this chapter, we begin by explaining how, looking at the Bretton Woods Order right after World War II through the lens of modern Statecraft, a theoretician of trade could have articulated the principal legal and structural issues that would face the system over the ensuing decades. For instance, even though it was deflected by the poets of Bretton Woods in the bargain of embedded liberalism, "linkage" was bound to become a core question facing the Bretton Woods generation because of the central place occupied by sovereignty and control over the nation's welfare in the Statecraft model of the twentieth century. We then explain how, as a matter of predictive history, a theoretician armed with the Statecraft lens could have foreseen that the Bretton Woods Order would generate a transformed international economic landscape. We then describe the new world, and explain why the tools of modern Statecraft are insufficient to regulate the post-modern world, focusing primarily on the failure of Doha. In subsequent chapters, we will advance our solution to the current international legal vacuum. Our goal is to explain, in the realm of political architecture, that the salient features of the day may be predicted by understanding the epochal hallmarks of Statecraft and the transformation of a regime and its graduation to a new era may also be appraised and anticipated when analyzed through the lens of Statecraft. By understanding what mattered in the heyday of Bretton Woods, we gain insights into how to frame the important issues of the day in the current post-modern world. By analyzing how Statecraft drives changes to the global trading order, we learn how to revise the current international systems to accord and work in harmony with the architecture of the State today.

BRETTON WOODS, LINKAGE, AND STATECRAFT: THE VICTORY OF REGULATORY COMPARATIVE ADVANTAGE

The core issues that faced the Bretton Woods system are directly related to the essentials of Statecraft. The successive generations of challenges arising under the GATT related principally to the erosion of domestic sovereign control over welfare policies caused by the liberalization of trade in goods.[8] In turn, the centrality of welfare in modern Statecraft made it inevitable that the "linkage" issue would be one of the essential problems of the day and that, in time, it would lead to the erosion of welfare policies, the regulatory enmeshment of the trading world, and the erosion of the international economic landscape that accords with Bretton Woods. This result obtains for three distinct reasons. First, the free trade *telos* of the GATT was bound to displace gradually conflicting domestic policies.[9] Second, while the GATT at its core sought to give consumers access to cheaper and more abundant goods, and to increase the global pie for domestic redistribution, it was also bound to result in interloping ownership of means of production across borders as manufacturers, distributors, retailers, and other actors in the market inevitably moved across borders to acquire stakes in productive firms.[10] Third, as described in the next section of this chapter, just as the modern and pre-modern eras necessitated a revolution in transportation, steel, coal, and other industrial essentials, the shift to the post-modern era (the embryo of which was contained in the GATT) necessitated a revolution in communications that contributed to the entrenchment of post-modern economic activity and the creation of a "flat world."

In our analysis, then, nothing happens by chance. Globalization does not simply happen to coincide with the communications revolution. Rather, the establishment of comparative advantage as the normative foundation of global trade created a global web of economic actors, thereby making it necessary for them to communicate rapidly and efficiently in a single market. Globalization did not merely coincide with phenomena such as the commodification of currencies or privatization of public debt. Rather, the combination of interloping economic activity and communications advances created a market where information and knowledge traveled rapidly to identify the most advantageous currency, investment, or economic activity. The very phenomena that transformed the international field in which Bretton Woods was conceived, then, arose in the wake of the structural mechanisms put in place by

Bretton Woods itself. In other words, Bretton Woods contained the seeds of its own demise. Like every other epochal trading order, it was a manifestation of the nature of Statecraft in a specific era, the century of the modern nation-state. Had observers been armed with the proper tools of analysis they could have engaged in predictive history and foreseen the metamorphosis that ultimately would make it necessary to overhaul the trading order and usher in the post-modern ethos of trade.

We begin with an analysis of the fundamental issues that faced the Bretton Woods system and explain how those issues are directly linked to the state of Statecraft during the Bretton Woods era. After this discussion, we proceed to an analysis of the transformation of the global trading order and Statecraft that Bretton Woods gradually engendered.

LINKAGE

The "linkage issue" is at the center of current trade debates. Traditionally characterized as a conflict between trade values and domestic policies on the environment, health, resource conservation, consumer safety, and other sensitive areas of domestic regulation, the linkage issue has been the subject of significant conflict, led to a major overhaul of the system's dispute resolution mechanisms, and caused violent protests in Seattle, Genoa, and other trade talk venues.[11] Linkage has come to embody a clash of absolutes: critics of free trade depict it as a conflict between market-based capitalists bent on using trade rules to achieve global *laissez faire*. Advocates of domestic regulation strive to temper jungle capitalism by adding a human face. If you stand on the side of trade, the clash is seen as one between proponents of efficiency and a global system that maximizes resources versus stubborn adherents to liberal policies that have run their course.

Both views reflect only partial truths. The significance of linkage, and the proper structural analysis of the issue, is related to Statecraft in the Bretton Woods era. Linkage was inevitable because of the core values underlying Bretton Woods. Over time, every constitutional system develops a foundational set of values that frame the constitutional conflicts that come to preoccupy its courts and policy makers.[12] For the GATT and the modern era, the core set of values involved free movement of goods and services on the one hand, and respect for control over welfare policies on the other. None of these systems would produce the rules and analyses that it did, or frame the constitutional issues that became central to its existence, unless it had an outside point of reference.[13]

The point of reference for the GATT was the conflict between the core values of free movement of goods and the protection of sovereignty and control over domestic welfare policies. As we explained in the previous chapter, Bretton Woods embodied a legitimate set of international norms because it fulfilled the *telos* of the international system, all the while respecting the principal elements of modern Statecraft: sovereignty, welfare (a state exercising its sovereign power for the benefit of the nation), and balance of power. In these circumstances, it was inevitable that the friction between the international system and the regulatory power to foster the nation's welfare would be the significant issue of the day, and the source of the *malaise* that ultimately gripped the GATT. If the GATT did not value sovereignty and domestic regulation as an essential element of Statecraft (which would be the case if, for example, the participating states all believed in anarchy or complete *laissez faire*) there would be no linkage issue because there would be nothing to link. It was also significant that the GATT's perception as a "rich man's club" (and a predominantly white one at that) would arise because of the blatant imbalances of power that followed decolonization. Rising to the challenges of the present will require more than the tools of modern Statecraft. The economic and political order that gave rise to the GATT is no longer the world in which we find ourselves,[14] which is why we need to overhaul the vocabulary and concepts with which we confront the present context of trade. Before we get there, however, let us delve more deeply into linkage and its motives.

At its inception, the GATT recognized that the import of products from one country to another necessarily entailed the import of social and economic regulation applicable to the country of export. For example, if French consumers purchase oranges harvested in Morocco under a regulation that tolerates a higher level of pesticides, the Moroccan regulation is essentially imported into France together with that country's oranges.[15] Taken to an extreme, this could lead to a complete displacement of the French standard. Imagine that France has on its books legislation that regulates the level of pesticides for domestically grown oranges. This piece of legislation would become essentially a dead letter if the Moroccan oranges, harvested there under different regulations, became the only oranges available on the market. In such a scenario, the French consumer would effectively become subject to Moroccan pesticide standards.

The GATT recognized the friction that would arise in cases where disparate regulatory levels obtain in the jurisdiction of import and export. The GATT explicitly provided that, as long as a measure is not a means of engaging in covert protectionism or arbitrarily treating foreign products, each Contracting State has the right to enact measures necessary to protect human, animal or plant life, health, conserve resources, or further other regulatory goals. In our hypothetical, France may be able to enact domestic legislation prohibiting the marketing (not just the growth or harvesting) of all oranges grown using more than a specified level of pesticides. Such a measure relates to the protection of human health, and may possibly be sheltered from GATT invalidation in virtue of its domestic purpose.[16]

However, as explained above, the GATT's commitment to free trade and the integration of markets was certain, as it did, to create a "linkage issue" which would gradually erode the domestic jurisdictions' ability to control welfare policies. The "linkage" issue has classically been cast as a conflict between domestic regulation and its underlying purposes on the one hand, and the animating values of free trade and *laissez faire* of the GATT on the other. In our hypothetical, the conflict involves a domestic value related to consumer protection, health, and public safety, pitted against the international trading system's interest in promoting what might be termed "regulatory comparative advantage." Morocco may have a comparative advantage in natural resources and labor supply. But it also has a comparative advantage in the level of regulation it imposes on its producers. It is presumably cheaper to produce oranges that are less safe for the consumer, than to comply with consumer protection regulation that imposes a relatively higher standard on the producer. The classic question of trade decision making has always been understood as how best to reconcile those competing claims.

Regardless of how one understands the trade jurisprudence that has evolved around these issues, there is undeniable encroachment on sovereignty understood in relation to modern Statecraft, specifically the right to regulate social and domestic issues in an unfettered fashion.[17] The GATT panels and other tribunals applying international trade law have routinely followed certain principles of "non-discrimination" and "proportionality."[18] It is true that the structure of the GATT is intended to create a negative integration space where each country can freely choose its level of domestic protection free from interference by its neighbors. However, the very requirements of non-discrimination and proportionality undermine the theoretical foundations of the system and have created the tension between trade and domestic law that occupy most trade scholars.[19] If a measure must be non-discriminatory, then there must be a way to root out discrimination. One obvious legal tool is to inquire into whether the measure is the least trade restrictive way of accomplishing the goal at hand. If it can be said that the measure is not the least trade restrictive way, then the natural inference is that the measure is discriminatory by virtue of its disparate impact. Why would France adopt a tough measure against Moroccan products if there is a better way to protect French consumers? The most reasonable and logical explanation would be that France sought to counter Moroccan regulatory comparative advantage with regulatory protectionism, the very evil that the GATT is intended to combat.

In our oranges hypothetical, Morocco would probably ask France (in a hypothetical dispute before the WTO) to use label laws rather than a flat-out ban on the marketing of oranges with a high level of pesticides. The French consumer would arguably be protected against the safety threat because of warnings attached to the product. The consumer's freedom of choice would join with the system's interest in the free flow of goods, and coalesce into a regulatory framework where foreign products would not face discrimination. France would further its interest in protecting consumers, but it would not impose on them and on its trading partner a regulatory level of protection that is overly trade restrictive. Abstracting the purpose of the regulation to protecting the consumer through informed choice, the system could arguably respect the negative integration framework of the GATT, yet invalidate the French measure.

France, on the other hand, will have a strong interest in compelling Morocco to adopt regulatory levels comparable to those of France, or be shut out of the market. In order to enforce its regulatory preferences, France would likely have to adopt an import embargo. The embargo could require that oranges marketed into French territory be produced in countries that impose the same or substantially similar standards as the French standard. Alternatively, the system might evaluate each producer's operations and determine if it complies with U.S. standards. The first route is preferable from the French standpoint because it will avoid a costly administrative inquiry or, alternatively, spot enforcement that generates a risk of failure to detect offenders. In all cases, France could be viewed either as defending its sovereignty and the integrity of its market or depriving foreign producers of their regulatory comparative advantage, or both.

Evaluating the legitimacy of the French policy in light of free trade principles is the kind of analysis that trade tribunals, whether at the WTO, European Union, or NAFTA levels, are engaged in.[20] The cases implicate deep questions with respect to the nature of government intervention in markets. Undoubtedly, the advocates of free trade are sympathetic to fostering *laissez faire* policies and more suspicious of government regulation than critics of free trade. They would rely more on disclosure and consumer choice than on arguably paternalistic impositions on the market of a single, centrally defined set of values. Underlying their view is, in part, the implicit recognition that regulation is another manifestation of comparative advantage, and that countries should be allowed to trade on what we term their "regulatory comparative advantage." Observers holding a less sympathetic view of free trade would take the opposite side, and give more regulatory leeway to domestic regulation in the country of import. They would tend to view the issue as one of fairness, rather than of utility, and regard trade based on comparative advantage in, say, cheaper labor, lower safety standards or lesser environmental protection, as "unfair trade."[21]

The Shrimp and Turtle controversy that became the emblem of globalization protesters also illustrates the clash between competing values and the question whether a market-based resolution of such tension is at all possible. Although it is different from the Moroccan hypothetical in that it involves a U.S. attempt to impose an embargo on shrimp caught by countries that do not require shrimping boats to use turtle excluder devices (TEDs), rather than a regulation of general applicability that happens to have a disparate impact on foreign goods, the case involves a clash of values mixed with the possibility of protectionist intent. U.S. regulation provided that all shrimping boats should employ the TED method of protection of sea turtles, and the United States sought to make sure that foreign shrimpers operated under the same rules. The WTO tribunals that ruled on the case initially declared the U.S. measure illegal under international trade law because it was not sufficiently narrowly tailored to achieve its intended environmental and resource conservation purposes. They reasoned in essence that the United States could have evaluated each importer on an individual basis, rather than by its citizenship in a country that does not adhere to environmental rules similar to those of the United States. They further took the position that the United States could have sought collaboration with the exporting countries to facilitate achievement of the environmental goals that the GATT accepts as legitimate. This conflict is exemplary of the linkage issue in that sea turtles "do not carry passports" and the United States' failure to impose protective standards deprived it of tools to safeguard the species against harm caused by domestic consumption of shrimp.[22]

For environmental advocates, the Shrimp and Turtle case represents an unacceptable encroachment upon the domestic sovereign power of the United States to regulate in the most environmentally effective fashion. By depriving the United States of its ability to coerce change in a foreign regulatory environment, the GATT essentially diluted the enforcement power of U.S. law. It is cumbersome to certify companies on an individual basis, and even more elusive to make sure that any certification or licensing requirements are maintained in the country of export. It is hard to imagine that countries such as Thailand or Malaysia, that thrive on regulatory comparative advantage, will agree through collaborative talks to raise their domestic regulatory schemes to levels sought by the United States.[23]

For advocates of free trade, on the other hand, the case represents little more than the application of international legal principles to prod and push a participating state to cleanse its domestic policies of protectionist impulses. In the final analysis, they would argue, the United States attempted to deprive the exporters of shrimp of their regulatory comparative advantage, and to force harmonization through economic coercion.[24] This is the very protectionism the GATT intended to prohibit. If shrimp can be caught cheaper in Asia, as a result of natural conditions or more lenient regulation, then free trade dictates these more efficient producers should take over a larger market share. Whether or not sea turtles are affected on a global, cross-border level does not factor into a trade equation effectuating a system whose *telos* is the free movement of goods.[25]

However one looks at the GATT, then, there is inevitable friction between international norms and domestic Statecraft. Those who understand the GATT's jurisprudence as balancing trade interests against domestic interests will conclude that the very exercise of balancing encroaches on domestic sovereignty. The trade tribunals essentially determine if the asserted domestic interest serves a sufficiently important domestic policy, and is narrowly enough tailored, to justify a deviation from international trade. Much like a constitutional court will define a set of higher values, such as equal treatment of similarly situated persons, free speech, or freedom from arbitrary government action (and then might determine whether there is a sufficiently important countervailing interest to justify its encroachment in various situations), a GATT tribunal will point to the free movement of goods and services as the *telos* of the system, and judge whether encroachment on this value is justified. Thus, in Shrimp and Turtle, the GATT may be understood as seeking to balance environmental and trade concerns. The tribunals *de facto* eliminated methods of achieving the environmental goals that they judged to be overly burdensome on trade, without (in their judgment) eviscerating the core implementation of U.S. environmental policy.

The same result obtains if one considers the GATT jurisprudence as seeking to eliminate discrimination. It is a rare case when the motive behind legislation can unambiguously be said to be protectionist. In the Shrimp/Turtle case, it is unclear whether the United States intended to deprive Indonesia of its regulatory comparative advantage when it barred the import of shrimp caught by boats that do not operate with sea turtle excluder devices. The legislation was, at least in part, the result of pressure from domestic economic interests. Shrimpers faced essentially the same problem as the domestic orange growers in our hypothetical. Indonesian shrimping boats faced a lesser regulatory burden in bringing their

goods to markets. American shrimpers, then, had to compete with oper-
ators dealing with a different set of rules, which were being imported
into the United States together with the products at issue. The United
States' attempt to impose its legislation on another country, then, could
be viewed as a protectionist measure to deprive foreigners of their regulatory comparative advantage.[26]

On the other hand, the measure clearly had an environmental component. Organizations concerned for sea turtles evidently favored tight
legislation of the kind adopted by the United States. Just as imposing one
pesticide standard would have leveled the safety playing field in France, so
too did the United States' attempt to impose one shrimping standard on all
products reaching the United States protect its interest in resource conservation in a uniform and more efficient fashion. As mentioned, sea turtles
do not carry passports or recognize United Nations endorsed boundaries.
If the United States did not attempt to export its regulation, its consumption of shrimp would have directly and substantially contributed to the
depletion of sea turtles.

Whether we view free trade jurisprudence as a balancing exercise or
as an anti-discrimination exercise, the inquiry focuses on the extent to
which the country of import could have adopted a less restrictive measure. If balancing, the less restrictive measure would be more likely to
outweigh the countervailing domestic measures. If seeking to eliminate
discrimination, the measure would defeat the inference that failure to
regulate at the narrowest level evinces protectionist intent. In both cases,
the free trade system pushed up against the boundaries of domestic regulation. This inward movement corresponds to the free trade of goods and
services movement underlying the system. At bottom, free movement is
on the offensive, and the trade analysis focuses on the extent to which it
would push back the boundaries of domestic legislation.

The result is that it has become very difficult for countries participating
in the GATT to resist the advance of regulatory comparative advantage
and the cross-border spread in multiple directions of regulatory standards emanating from a multitude of domestic sources. The constitutional scrutiny that has been applied over the past half century to countervailing domestic measures has routinely concluded that the Contracting
Parties, in particular developing countries, should have the ability to
trade on their regulatory comparative advantage. Countries of import
are banned from requiring that regulatory levels akin to domestic legislation be put in place abroad as a condition to opening up borders to trade.
The proportionality requirement forces them to select narrower modes of
regulation, and to lean in favor of policies that best accommodate the economic underpinnings of free trade. This result was inevitable if the GATT's

fundamental purpose, allowing for liberalized trade in goods, was to be accomplished. By definition, countries of export had to take advantage of laxer regulatory environments in order to meaningfully participate in the global trading system. To enjoy a regulatory comparative advantage, it is not enough to have greater access to natural resources, cheap labor, or other means of production. Comparative advantage is, in fact, a reflection of the total state of a particular economy; and regulation and law shape comparative advantage as much as the natural state of a particular country's resources.

We submit that the decades of linkage jurisprudence and trade disputes are intrinsically linked to the fundamentals of Statecraft engendered during the Bretton Woods era. The system had a built-in tension: it advocated regulatory comparative advantage at the same time as it protected regulatory sovereignty. Indonesia was encouraged to sell its shrimp in the U.S. market, and to benefit from its laxer environmental and resource conservation rules. The United States, on the other hand, was told that it would continue to control its domestic regulatory sphere, despite the opening of barriers to trade. Yet, in the GATT, the world had to have open borders, and in a world of open borders, regulation travels with goods. The world becomes a pastiche of interloping standards, measured by the extent to which goods from a particular country have a share of a given market. Domestic jurisdictions cannot keep goods out without destroying Bretton Woods. The international system cannot encourage free movement without threatening free regulation and full control over the economy. Ultimately, then, the bargain of embedded liberalism would flounder. Free trade without infringement on sovereignty is impossible. Sovereignty cannot be infringed without destroying the global system that makes embedded liberalism possible, and we cannot maintain the GATT and Bretton Woods in its current form once we destroy the international landscape that made it possible.

BEYOND LINKAGE: ERODING THE NATION-STATE BASIS OF BRETTON WOODS – FROM UNITY TO DISPERSION AND THE RISE OF THE INTERLOPED ECONOMY

It was not only possible to predict linkage would grow to be a core issue in trade disputes but also to foresee that the trading world would – giving effect to Bretton Woods – cease to be divided into the regulatory units that occupied the global economic space in 1945. Bretton Woods' adoption and institutionalization of comparative advantage led to the radical transformation of the economic landscape, after World War II, causing the shift away from mercantilism as the only possible policy option. The trading world transformed itself, in substantial part as a result of the system created by the GATT and related treaties, from a set of discrete economic units governed by a unified body of welfare norms to an interloped economy. The integration of the world's economies involved several inter-related phenomena: diffuse and cross-border ownership of firms, intertwined sets of regulations traveling with the goods to which they apply, the rise of regional economic blocs, sophisticated communication, computer systems allowing efficient outsourcing of jobs, dependency on foreign sources to maintain currency value, and debt and equity ownership.

Regulatory entanglement was an inevitable product of the age of comparative advantage. The structure of the system could not generate a different outcome. Comparative advantage implicates various factors. A country may have natural resources in demand by the international markets. It may have developed expertise at a particular technology either as a result of government intervention or market factors. Yet another country may have abundant and relatively inexpensive labor. In all cases, however, regulatory comparative advantage provided one of the strongest bases for a state to assert an edge in the global marketplace. As explained above, while the GATT system included a mechanism to preserve domestic regulation, it had to result in the invasion of that body of law by imported norms, and yield what might be viewed as diffuse, fluctuating, and evolving regulation that escapes the control of any single state. Regulatory comparative advantage destroyed the legal unity of the discrete economic units that comprised the modern world. In turn, the advent of regulatory comparative advantage was bound, as a structural matter, to result in the destruction of the unified economic landscape that characterized the modern trading world. Having fortified itself and created the necessary conditions to apply comparative advantage (as further described in Chapter 6), the world was bound to engage in a process of *de facto* regulatory harmonization. By accepting that goods embodying disparate regulatory levels would travel across borders, the trade system endorsed a state of affairs whereby law, the inner face of the State, would travel with the goods. In turn, the pressure on domestic regulation caused by the import of goods produced under different regulatory schemes was bound to generate a need for *de jure* regulatory harmonization. The solidified nation-state, centered on its welfare regulation after the end of the state-nation process, would inevitably be affected by this process.

THE DISPERSED AND INTERLOPED ECONOMY

With Bretton Woods, it was also inevitable that the subdivision of the world into economic units coextensive with nation-states would be eroded. The GATT and the WTO opened up borders to trade in goods and services. This openness lies at the heart of comparative advantage. In such a marketplace, goods and services are exchanged across borders by consumers, distributors, and manufacturers. Manufacturers will purchase components necessary for their output, and distributors will purchase products for domestic resale (in particular from jurisdictions that enjoy a regulatory comparative advantage). Importers will inevitably seek to acquire equity or other stakes in their suppliers, so as to increase profit margins. Conversely, exporters will seek to participate in the profits of the importing companies. Joint ventures and other cross-border partnerships will flourish. The upshot is that the trading world that grew out of the Bretton Woods system gradually "flattened" the economic units that formed the core of that system (the nation-states).

This outward expansion of market activities and of market integration is directly related to the adoption of comparative advantage as the animating norm of the system. In the mercantilist era, the inward solidification process led to the creation of a national industrial context that set the stage for comparative advantage. In the comparative advantage era, the gradual relocation of factors of production to the countries with the most comparative advantage created relationships that were bound to yield a diffuse world.

The textiles industry provides a clear example of the phenomenon. The principal players in the industry include manufacturers, designers, brand owners, distributors, and retailers. At the beginning of the comparative advantage era, all of these actors were associated with one nation and national industries were identified with and geographically located within nation-states.[27] In Paris, for example, the *Sentier* was thriving as the headquarters of mass production and mid-tier brands, and the Rue St Honore as the center of haute couture and high-end products. The model was national in character. The *Sentier* merchants presented the face of their companies to retailers and wholesalers. Designers worked in the back office to produce the models for each season. Manufacturers were also located in the neighborhood, together with producers of cloth, buttons, zippers, hardware, fabric, and other raw and intermediate materials needed to make the goods at issue.[28] The same held true on Rue St Honore, albeit on a somewhat less concentrated level. The French fashion houses manufactured their goods in France, just like the Italian houses manufactured in Italy. Their showrooms and trade shows took place in Paris. The factories with which they worked were located in regions of France traditionally devoted to the production of textiles, leather, and other fashion goods.

Free trade gradually changed the rules of the game. Although the reduction of textiles and leather tariffs was by no means a smooth or complete process, and other barriers to trade faced the industry, comparative advantage resulted in the gradual shift of manufacturing to the Far East.[29] The phenomenon was manifold. First, companies having sufficient volume to outsource production shifted away from domestic manufacturers to Tunisia, Portugal, or other North African and Southern European countries. They then moved to the Far East countries affording at the time the most comparative advantage by way of cheaper labor and less restrictive regulation, taking into account other factors such as expertise and skills, customs duties, transportation costs, and other considerations relevant to the ultimate pricing of the product. The domestic industry in France went through a first stage of transformation with the gradual elimination of domestic production. Companies remaining in France did so in order to make a statement, in the face of the compelling economic logic of moving manufacturing abroad. At the same time, comparative advantage brought about the gradual displacement of companies that could not afford to compete with those products or the manufacture by French companies abroad or the sale in France by foreign companies. Comparative advantage essentially ushered in an era where only those economic actors most able to take advantage of global markets would flourish.

The New York Garment District experienced a similar transformation. Manufacturers traditionally worked in the Garment District or in Queens or Brooklyn-based factories. Buyers from department stores attended market weeks or showroom events to place their orders. Sales agents traveled the country to drum up orders from the other customers, who did not have the resources or the need to make their way to New York. In the end, a localized industry, associated with the U.S. nation, conducted its business in a self-contained, autonomous fashion. Today, the world has changed drastically. Production agents (in China, India, and other Asian countries) specialize in procuring goods for New York-based brand owners. Chinese manufacturers have begun to sell goods *en masse* to U.S. distributors and department stores. U.S. brand owners are acquiring interests in Chinese factories so as to control production, and to share in the profits generated by their entry into the global market. Chinese manufacturers are acquiring equity stakes in their customers and increasingly looking to bring home the entire sourcing line, from design to production.[30] Chinese consumers are joining the global trading classes, and U.S. mass merchants such as Wal-Mart are fighting off Carrefour and other European *grandes surfaces* for this new market.[31]

In other words, the French and U.S. fashion industry can best be seen as an internationalized, cross-border enterprise largely dissociated from the nations and states in which their respective components sit and comprised of partnerships between domestic creators and sellers, and foreign manufacturing companies. The next stage of the commercial evolution came naturally, with French and American economic actors in the textiles industry reaching out to take advantage of the comparative advantage enjoyed by foreign manufacturers. First, sellers and distributors began to take equity stakes in their manufacturers. As volume increased, manufacturers found it necessary to expand their operations. Establishing a new factory requires cash and a commitment from the buyer to agree to long-term supply contracts. The buyer, in return for its commitment or a possible capital infusion, will want to participate in the profits generated by the manufacturer. A joint venture will be created, whereby manufacturer and distributors essentially integrate their enterprises vertically across borders.

For the brand owner, the incentive lies not only in the opportunity to participate in profit distribution, but in controlling the production and quality of its product. Outsourcing production involves a loss of control over, among other things, back door sales from factories and quality. A factory operator in China will sell the goods to the brand owner, who will price them differently based on the territory in which they are sold (wholesale distributors in Japan, for instance, will purchase the goods at a higher price than those operating in Korea). The pricing structure will be created so as to maximize profits. By way of illustration, Japanese tourists are known for shopping in Korea.[32] They search for better deals on high-end products displayed in Japan. A brand owner might price its products very high in Tokyo, and significantly lower in Korea. For a Chinese goods maker, an arbitrage opportunity will arise to sell goods to Japan "through the back door" at a price lower than that charged by the brand owner. Under classic parallel exports rule, such a sale would not breach the trademark rights of the brand owner, and in all events it will be difficult to detect. The solution, for the brand owner, will be to acquire a stake in its manufacturer.

At the next stage of evolution, manufacturing companies will, in the normal course of their business growth, seek to expand their activities beyond production of goods. They may invest a part of their profits to acquire stakes in their customers. The design expertise that first remained in the country of import will slowly shift to the country of export. In turn, this creates an incentive for Western companies to partner up with Chinese manufacturers/wholesalers, pooling resources such as privileged access to American buyers working in large department stores or chains, to create profitable joint ventures. The expansion of economic activity also creates a market in the country of export, which producers in the country of import increasingly view as attractive outlets for their products. For example, Wal-Mart and the French mass merchant Carrefour have engaged in fierce competition for the Chinese market.[33] This rush to take advantage of the demand created in countries of export often involves partnerships and alliances with local economic interests, and further contributes to the creation of an interloped global economic world.

At bottom, interloping ownership, the spread of production units across nation-state borders, and the cross fertilization of enterprises have contributed to the replacement of national products with global, diffuse goods. This phenomenon, we submit, was the inevitable outcome of the GATT and Bretton Woods and its logic of comparative advantage. The world transformed itself from a compact of economic units associated with the states that comprised the trading world, into a global trading mass linked across borders by commercial and corporate ties. As further developed in the next chapters, the subjects of regulation escaped the control of the domestic regulators in that they created global enterprises with tentacles reaching across borders. This phenomenon joined with the import of disparate regulatory systems, together with goods and services, to create a global market regulated in a kaleidoscopic fashion by overlapping and interloping sets of rules, and a regulatory vacuum that the comparative advantage framework of Bretton Woods was not structurally fit to fill.

Bretton Woods foresaw this development, but only to the extent of the conflict between domestic regulation and free trade norms. It created, first, an incomplete set of norms that was intended to shelter domestic regulation. In 1994, it added a more effective dispute resolution system to develop constitutional jurisprudence and fill the normative vacuum. However, its model remained focused on the interaction among states as discrete economic units, and it did not plan for the structural change that would inevitably accompany the elimination of barriers to trade. From discrete economic units looking outward after their inward solidification period, the new set of commercial actors included the global trading class that Bretton Woods created, but no institution or regulating norm was put in place.

Succinctly stated, Bretton Woods created a global market and left it to national authorities (unprepared to coordinate and take collective action) to regulate the market. The malaise that we are experiencing today is, as further described in the next chapters, rooted in this loss of control. Ricardo and Keynes would probably tell us that, ultimately, the Chinese and the Indians will acquire sufficient buying power and open their markets to bring in our goods and sustain our industries. Wal-Mart will penetrate and conquer the Chinese market and what we lose in the Garment District we will gain in Shanghai. They may be partially right, but a fundamental error lies in a failure to recognize that comparative advantage is simply one aspect of one phase of a larger evolutionary cycle. This error leads to an even greater mistake: we are now entering a world that requires new ideas and principles to govern it. Keynes' poets of trade are failing us because they are not rewriting the Bretton Woods script for the post-modern world.

We now turn to the next transformative change, the communications revolution, and its impact on the rise of outsourcing as an organizational principle of economic activity.

THE COMMUNICATIONS REVOLUTION

The transformation of patterns of economic activity brought about by Bretton Woods has been accelerated and intensified by the revolution in global communications. The steel mill, textiles plant, and agricultural field of the twentieth century have been replaced by computer workstations that can be run from virtually anywhere in the world. Microchips can now be manufactured in Silicon Valley from computer software using codes written in India that, in the aggregate, can be compared to a factory in terms of complexity. Transcription services can be outsourced via access service provider software to the Philippines. A U.S. appellate brief can be researched and written in Jamaica and filed by a licensed attorney in Camden, New Jersey.[34] Increased trade and competition were bound to generate innovation, and the resulting communications breakthroughs furthered the establishment of a global marketplace where the phenomenon of discrete national economies has eroded.

We submit that the communications revolution was at least in part a result of the Bretton Woods system, and it further contributed to the creation of a flat global market without sufficient central regulatory controls. The elimination of barriers to trade created an outward movement that brought together into one interactive market the solidified economies created in the post-modern era. The strengthening of the State in the pre-modern era resulted in the creation of industries such as steel, transportation, or coal, necessary to solidify the home base. By contrast, comparative advantage brought about the rise of a system of communications designed to maximize and facilitate interaction among global enterprises. For example, the manufacture of products in China for a French brand owner involves a complex interaction of design and modeling that is almost entirely computerized. The quality and design control exercised in France needs to be communicated on a timely basis to the factory managers in charge of ensuring that the end product complies with the style guides and specifications created by the brand owner. The economic opportunities generated by the opening up of borders to trade created, in turn, a need for computerized facilitation of cross-border economic interaction.

The rise of the outsourced transcription services industry also illustrates how the international trade system engendered a revolution in communications. Transcription services are amenable to performance by typists in countries such as the Philippines, at a much lower rate than a comparable workforce in the West. A medical conference in New York can be taped and transferred to Manila for same-day transcription by a crew of typists. The transcripts can be made available at the end of the conference to the participants by an American company outsourcing its services to those Filipino workers at a much lower price than would obtain had the company used U.S. labor. In turn, participants in the industry have developed and fine tuned means of communication that, with relative ease, make possible the transmission of the relevant data to and from the location of the production facility.

Our claim is that Bretton Woods contained within itself the seeds of the communications revolution, which in turn contributed to the flattening of the world into a global marketplace and the creation of a global trading class. This phenomenon joined with the globalization of economic forces and the erosion of control over welfare policies, thereby eroding the power of twentieth-century nation-states to exert the type of control over their economic units that characterized modern Statecraft. In other words, it is not the case that globalization arose as a result of an accidental revolution in communications. In the pre-modern world, the solidification of the State required a revolution in means of transportation. The colonialization enterprise required means of transportation to bring goods from the colonies to the metropolis. In the era of Bretton Woods, the "horizontalization process" resulted in the need for new forms of communication that ultimately led to a communications revolution.

This revolution further contributed to blurring the state lines that divided the trading classes in the modern world, and to the creation of a cross-border trading mass shoring up the flat world. As we detail throughout this book, the cross-border, diffuse trading class escapes the control of individual states, and makes it easier for companies and individuals operating in any single jurisdiction to avail themselves of the regulatory environment of another. For example, by sending design to Romania or manufacturing to Tunisia, a French fashion house has essentially removed two crucial divisions from the scope of the French regulatory control. The communications revolution, working hand-in-hand with the rise of the interloped enterprise, both arose out of the system created by Bretton Woods and foundationally changed Statecraft to require Bretton Woods to be supplemented by another set of norms and institutions.

We now turn to another hallmark of the changed international landscape that resulted from the Bretton Woods order, the commodification of policy tools that were traditionally used by nation-states to implement modern era welfare.

ELUSIVE POLICY TOOLS

The explosion of economic activity in the transformed world has also brought about a gradual commodification of the fundamental policy tools of economic regulation and wealth transfer, which are increasingly influenced by international, diffuse markets and correlatively escaping control by domestic regulators. Monetary policy, for example, is increasingly escaping control by states.[35] Public debt is increasingly held by foreign actors and affected more by the interplay of commercial interests than by domestic policy choices. In turn, as explained below, this phenomenon is directly related to the transformative changes that we described in the first sections of this chapter. A simplified and simplistic example is the relationship between the United States and Japan. The United States has for a long time been a main purchaser of Japanese goods, and Japan a main purchaser of U.S. debt. While it is true that the United States has a continuing ability to self-finance its debt, over time this phenomenon may extend to new actors on the international scene, including prominently China, with a resulting decrease in domestic control.[36]

These phenomena, also engendered by the Bretton Woods-driven transformation of the international economic landscape, have further engendered the erosion of modern Statecraft and contributed to the gradual shift toward a post-modern Statecraft. A nation coextensive with national boundaries and a national economy and output is slowly fading away as the interlocutor of the State: it is being replaced by a diffuse array of economic actors and activities that fall outside of their traditional control. States are losing their grip over some economic tools used for regulation of economic and social life. At the same time, the states' ability to muster domestic resources to sustain their welfare on a domestic level is being challenged. The upshot is that the welfare of a nation, delivered by a State with strong hallmarks of sovereignty, is fading away as an essential component of Statecraft and a legitimating drive for states. This pillar of the Bretton Woods world is bound to continue to gradually recess and become a more peripheral component of Statecraft as the twenty-first century unfolds.

FROM TRADING STATES TO TRADING INDIVIDUALS: THE DECLINE OF BALANCE OF POWER

Concurrently with these phenomena, the balance of power that characterized the modern world, which was centered on the modern liberal democracies of Europe, the United States, and Japan, is eroding. As a result of the global marketplace wrought by Bretton Woods, the twenty-first century has inherited a multi-polar economic world resting on a global middle class spread across the North and the South, Brazil, India, China, and South Korea, to cite a few, who have increasingly become world economic centers. Developing countries have achieved growing importance in the world markets and gradually eroded the dominant market share of the developed countries. The old Second World, made up of communist countries, is being replaced by a new Second World comprised of economies that often surpass the First World on growth and competitiveness scales. Lying within and alongside the first (post-modern) and second (modern) economies are pre-modern collectives of people that lack the education, infrastructure, and other conditions to benefit from the liberalization of trade that the WTO brought about. These collectives may be Brazilian shantytowns, Afghan mountain towns, or the "excluded" neighborhoods that surround Paris. The bottom line, though, is that the main interlocutors of trade are no longer national middle classes represented by their states. Rather the trading world is comprised of a diffuse trading class, numbering some 800 million people and spreading out in a multipolar economic configuration, that is surrounded by those who have yet to become meaningful participants in the global marketplace.

The configuration of the international trade system parallels the contemporaneous strategic challenges of the day. The modern strategic and trade order rested on balance of powers because its interlocutors were states. The trading states needed to have enough of a share of the international pie to justify their participation in the system. The legitimating ethos of the State was welfare, and the acquisition of additional resources to redistribute internally furthered this legitimacy drive. Legitimacy, then, meant being a meaningful participant in the international trading system. If a state did not acquire sufficient resources, then power would not be balanced enough to justify its participation in the trade order. This aligned with the reification of states, on the strategic plane, into single units entitled to defend themselves against external aggression and to achieve security for their citizens as a fundamental purpose. Without sufficient power on the commercial or strategic front, states would not be able to legitimate themselves. This was the essence of the modern world.

In today's post-modern era, the collectivity of states is attempting to replicate the modern era. As we explain below, Doha is attempting to turn developing states into meaningful players in global markets so as to create the context for their legitimate participation in international commercial relations. Likewise, the United Nations is insisting on a model premised on each state's ability to defend its borders against existential threats from the outside. However, the new interlocutor of the world strategic and commercial systems is the global trading class that Bretton Woods has created, and this compact of individuals cutting through borders is gradually replacing the State as a major actor in international relations. As we explain in the next chapters, states remain important participants in the trading and strategic systems. Nevertheless, in the strategic realm, the struggles of the day (against global networked terrorism and the proliferation of weapons of mass destruction in the hands of terrorists and rogue states often driven by totalitarian theocratic ideologies) pit a collective, global trading class against diffuse forces. The United Nations' state-centric structure is not sufficient to create an adequate strategy for this trading class. On the commercial plane, the same trading class has coalesced and generated problems that the GATT and the institutions of Bretton Woods are not capable of solving.

In a way, we are repeating the nation-state building process that has characterized the pre-modern, state-nation era, except that we are doing it on a global scale. Back then, we had to manage the diffuseness of power within a nation, and ensure that the working classes did not cause the implosion of the nation. Welfare accomplished that role, and Bretton Woods embedded the welfare system into the global trading order. Today, the transformative changes that we have identified require that we embed a new norm into a global trading order that must be structured and implemented so as to solidify the billion strong middle class and ensure that the pre-modern populations do not cause its implosion. This is as true in the strategic realm as it is in the realm of trade. This is the central focus of the vision that we advance in the following chapters. In concluding this chapter, we explain why our theoretical construct has real life impact on the policy, institutions, and discourse of trade, using the Doha debate to illustrate our claim.

THE DOHA CASE STUDY: WHY THEORY MATTERS AND WHY WE MUST CHANGE

The metamorphosis of the Bretton Woods world means that the trade system's conceptual tool for understanding itself (an aggregation of nation-states governed by the sovereignty, welfare, and balance of power principles of the twentieth century) is eroding. We believe that a new constitutional moment is needed to usher in a new trade norm and trade institutions that will complement the Bretton Woods norm of comparative advantage and accord with the post-modern evolution of key actors of the trading world. In Chapter 6, we outline the contours of the new norm, which we describe as the "enablement of global economic opportunity," of the post-modern institutions needed to implement the norm, and of the constitutional moment we envision. We now turn to Doha and show why the failures of world leaders to understand the theoretical norms that animate trade and Statecraft have profound practical consequences.

The world trade system has reached an impasse and, at the same time, it is experiencing a *malaise* as deep and dangerous as the breakdown of the 1930s. Now, as then, the root cause of the trade crisis is the failure to transform the international system to reflect the inner order of the State. As happened in the 1930s, the inability of the principal trading states to adjust to the international landscape has a deep effect on the international political landscape, hampering those states in their fight against the strategic threats of the day. Now as then, the policymakers and pundits continue to urge more of the same.[37] Today, they ask for more comparative advantage, back then they asked for more protectionism and mercantilism.

The Doha round of negotiations provides an illustration of the practical effect of our failure to adjust. Doha was supposed to spread the gospel of comparative advantage to the developing world. In doing so, the GATT process would erode the very concept of "developing world," prodding the world markets toward greater integration. Doha promised to end the GATT's status as a rich man's club by defeating the forces of Western protectionism in key fields such as textiles, agriculture, and steel. The history of the GATT since World War II saw the progressive spread of comparative advantage in fields where countries thought of as "developing" could compete using cheap labor, access to natural resources, or lax regulation. Some states, such as India, Benin, or Indonesia, had acquired independence from European colonizers. Others, like China, departed from a more rigid central regulation of the economy, for complex reasons that included the fall of the Eastern bloc and the defeat of communism, to compete in global markets. In all cases, those states acquired comparative advantage in sectors of the economy that significantly affected the welfare of the Western allies, and they amassed substantial means of production and international goodwill in those fields.

Doha sought to firm up the integration of these new economic powers in the global economy and, at the same time, to pave the way for the integration of additional states. The geopolitical map of the economic world that Doha inherited was comprised of significant blocs of non-Western countries. In Central and South America, states such as Brazil, Argentina, or Mexico had become important actors on the global scene when Doha convened, and potential key partners to the United States in a Free Trade of the Americas Agreement. In Asia, in addition to Korea, China, and India as obvious flag bearers of economic performance, populous states such as Indonesia became important international economic players. In the former Soviet bloc, formerly communist states such as

Poland have grown to be economic havens and enter the European Union as already important Member States.[38] In Africa and the Middle East, the situation is more nuanced. Some African countries achieved a measure of success in fields where their natural resources are in demand, and in various industries that evolved after independence, but by and large the African states suffer from fundamental functional difficulties, including urban blight and poverty, health calamities, and borders inherited from the colonial nation-state era that for many years have pitted differing ethnic groups against one another in existential wars over control of the State.[39] In the Middle East, the centrality of oil as a power source has created a massive concentration of wealth. However, at the same time, wealth is unevenly distributed, and the more rapid population growth rate has created countries (such as Egypt or Jordan) where comfortable middle classes are minorities living amidst a large, disadvantaged population.

For Doha, a principal tool for bringing the poorer countries into the fold, and grounding the achievements of the rapidly developing states, was the removal of what has been perceived as the last barriers to trade by the first-world nations.[40] These barriers were primarily applied in the form of tariffs, production subsidies, or the abuse of safeguard measures or of measures ostensibly aimed at furthering domestic interests such as environmental regulation or health. Doha was obviously right to focus on barriers to trade as a key issue. While the integration of global markets that took place during the GATT years is undeniable, the political power of domestic lobbies (e.g., the agricultural lobby) continued to influence domestic policy so much so that today key Western markets are still somewhat obstructed for non-Western actors.

In the United States, for example, the steel industry benefited for the past 30 years from obviously protectionist measures, which the WTO Dispute Settlement Body found illegal. Virtually every administration since President Ford's, for instance, applied safeguard tariffs to industries facing competitors from emerging economies (e.g., steel) on the ground that a sudden shift in production patterns warranted an intervention to moderate the economic impact of the outflow of market activities. However, the facts showed beyond a doubt that the American steel industry had lost its competitive edge to Korean steel mills because those mills used more efficient methods of production with cheaper labor. Most U.S. companies had been in bankruptcy for substantial periods of time. The claim that any shift in market activities was sudden enough to legally justify a market intervention was a clear pretext to cave in to domestic pressures. Likewise, in the agricultural field, the United States and Europe have extended domestic subsidies that severely distort competition and hamper market access by states such as Benin. While not illegal under the GATT (in most instances), those subsidies fundamentally violated the spirit of comparative advantage.

Doha promised to eliminate the barriers to trade that the Western advocates of comparative advantage still conceded to the natural pull of domestic protectionism. The American South would sacrifice a large portion of its cotton culture so that, in Benin, a competitive cotton industry could continue to grow and gain a place in the global market that its comparative performance warrants under free market rules.[41] European textile workers, in culturally significant urban concentrations such as Paris' *Sentier* or New York's Garment District, would accept the economic brunt of the dislocation of market activities from those centers to China, India, Brazil, or Indonesia. Ultimately, the global pie would have been more evenly distributed among the nation-states that comprise the trading bloc.

The Doha ethos accorded with the underlying theoretical rationale for the GATT. The treaties, as we have detailed in Chapter 4, were intended to liberalize trade all the while respecting the modern liberal democratic Statecraft of the World War II victors. The countries traditionally associated with the West, including principally Western Europe, the United States, and Japan, used the trading system to increase their wealth and redistribute it internally through top down welfare policies of the type that we have described. The system reified the nation-states as unitary actors, each of whom should receive a portion of the global resources that somehow legitimizes its membership in, and the rules governing, the international trade system. Doha, and the remaining GATT rules giving developing countries certain preferential rights to impose tariffs to protect growing domestic industries, was in essence an effort to end discrimination against the developing world, and to promote some mild affirmative effort to integrate these states.

The failure of Doha coincides with a widespread criticism of and protests against free trade that leads to doubts about the legitimacy and effectiveness of the institutions of world trade.[42] An exploration of the extent to which these phenomena are related sheds some light on the root causes of Doha's fundamental structural shortfalls. Doha failed fundamentally because the negotiating parties could not agree on how far the West would go to remove protection of certain markets. On a deeper level, Doha asked the world to go further down the path of integration without addressing directly the root cause of the crisis of legitimacy. Much as voters rejected the European Constitution partially because they challenged the very notion of free capitalist markets, so did the Doha participants refuse to embrace the ethos of more free trade and to push the system further along the road of integration.

The root cause of the failure of Doha, we submit, is the insistence on completing an economic enterprise launched and constituted by the World War II victors, using tools that while still relevant ignore the constitutional structure of post-modern Statecraft, without focusing as well on implementing norms and institutions that are necessary to align the global trading order with domestic Statecraft. Doha essentially operated as if each state participating in the round of negotiations has a welfare system of Statecraft that permits it to operate consistent with the GATT ethos. However, the theoretical framework of Doha, despite its professed insistence on fairness rather than mere maximization of global resources, could not achieve its stated goal because welfare, sovereignty, and balance of power are fading as constitutional elements of Statecraft.

With respect to the non-Western countries, such a system of welfare simply does not exist. Countries like India acquired independence in the latter part of the welfare state era. They never went through the pre-modern and modern political and social processes that gave European countries like France the welfare system presupposed by the GATT. The sheer magnitude of their populations may have made it impossible for the Southern states to achieve a meaningful welfare system of Statecraft. In all events, though, by the time they had the political independence necessary to devise their institutions, the Southern states found themselves in a world where Statecraft had already evolved to a new stage of development: the post-modern State. The ethos of Statecraft, rather than insisting on welfare, had moved to the enablement of economic opportunity. Instead of recognizing that these states operate in a post-modern world and will not undergo the welfare state transformative stage for which the GATT was devised, Doha insists on treating them like younger siblings who would thrive in the family enterprise if only given a meaningful job and benefits. The siblings, however, did not go through the training that made their elders succeed, not because they are unable to do so but because the curriculum had changed.

In these circumstances, Doha fails the South because its *mea culpa* is premised only on a confession of being a rich man's club unwilling to extend its tools of resource formation to the poor man. Doha's real sin, however, is the lack of recognition that the very countries that it sought to integrate into world markets are not similarly situated. No matter how many resources are shifted to African or other less developed states, the domestic political and economic system is such that world trade would be unlikely to benefit anyone beyond the trading classes that already exist. The same holds true for countries like Brazil, Indonesia, or China. While free trade creates extraordinary opportunities, the benefits of world trade do not extend to countries lacking a modern welfare system or an infrastructure that enables the nation to reap the benefits of comparative advantage. As a result, the spread of the free trade gospel has become erratic and fortuitous. Further, the global trade system is losing its legitimacy because it does not operate in synch with an ethos that accords with the inner face of the State.[43]

This phenomenon joins the Western reluctance to accept the decline of welfare, and the association of the GATT's free trade system with the erosion of a system that has been viewed in many quarters as compassionate and socially beneficial. The loud protests that accompany every attempt in countries like France to shrink the welfare apparatus so as to compete better, illustrate the crisis of confidence that is felt in the Western street.[44] The protesters at Genoa or Seattle do not object to the right of African or South American nations to compete fairly. If anything, the protest resounds among political actors who, a generation ago, were by and large "third worldists" (*tiers-mondistes*). The true bone of contention is the subtle but unarticulated recognition that the modern world, and its insistence on guaranteeing the economic security of the population, is graduating (because of the interaction between domestic and international statecraft that we discussed) to post-modernism. The Western street rightly perceives free trade and the amorphous mass of market based policies associated with it as a root cause of the erosion of welfare as a pillar of Statecraft. Just as Doha speaks a foreign language to Southern states that do not regard welfare as a form of Statecraft, it asks Western countries to engage in more comparative advantage when the core concerns relate to how the world system should be adjusted to regulate in a flat world.

Instead of presenting an alternative vision of trade that integrates and responds to the Western discomfort with its changing nature, Doha blindly insists on a rusty trade ethos. The Doha mentality can be likened to the pre-World War II trade culture of mercantilism that missed the necessity of adjusting the world trade system to a transformed domestic Statecraft. While more comparative advantage is obviously better than more mercantilism, now as then the trade system does not accord with the geopolitical landscape of the day. Before World War II, the strategic order of the day was a solidification of the economic bloc of liberal democratic states to contain fascism and communism. Today, as countries as diverse as Spain, the United States, or Indonesia, prepare for a post-modern fight against stateless forces of global networked terrorism, the world system is relying on an obsolete state-centric model that ignores crucial post-modern masses that simply will never operate according to the GATT rules and experiencing a loss of confidence among the Western victors that bring the system to crisis. The next chapters explain why a constitutional moment is sorely needed, today, to bring the world trade system in harmony with the geopolitical map of the world in which Doha operates. Finally, we outline the contours of the new norms and institutional structures that should be implemented, we analyze their legitimacy in light of established international trade principles, and we explore the extent to which they accord with the strategc interests of the post-modern liberal democracies.

6 The End of Bretton Woods and the Beginning of a New Global Trading Order

Thesis:

Statecraft evolves through successive stages, each characterized by foundational norms that shape the constitutional structure of states and of the international system in which they participate. The norms drive the design of the institutions that are best suited for states sharing hallmarks of a given Statecraft era, and the victors of epochal wars have the opportunity to shape institutions that best suit their form of Statecraft. A new trading and welfare norm is emerging in the era of post-modern Statecraft: the enablement of global economic opportunity. This era of Statecraft requires new institutions to govern trade in a diffuse and globalized world.

Our claim is that today's trade partners must devise new international economic institutions, operating in accordance with a novel animating norm. This transformation of the constitutional structure of international trade, we believe, is necessary because Statecraft has entered a new epochal iteration. Over hundreds of years, trade has married itself to both law and strategy in each successive evolution of the State. Today, as it did at Bretton Woods, the world needs a constitutional moment that will generate new institutions and actuate a new norm. This is what must be done in order to give global commercial actors the best chance of meeting the challenges of the post-modern world. In this chapter we describe the trade institutions of the post-modern age, drawing analytical inspiration from the institutional history of the prior eras of Statecraft. In the next two chapters, we explore the contours of the new norm and analyze its legitimacy in relation to the domestic and international legal systems.

Statecraft evolves through successive stages, characterized by foundational norms that shape the constitutional structure of states and of the international system in which they live. The norms drive the design of the institutions that are best suited for states sharing hallmarks of a given Statecraft era, and the victors of war have the opportunity to shape institutions that best suit their form of Statecraft. We have already explained how the domestic and international spheres interact with each other, and how this interconnected relationship ultimately yields epochal transformations. In each stage, the institutional questions remain the same. Do we need any inter-state institutions in the first place? If so, which states should participate, and what would they seek to accomplish? What decisions would lie within their power? How would they go about making decisions? Would any tribunal be needed to enforce, restrain, or interpret the measures coming out of these institutions? How do we measure the legitimacy of these institutions, and of the duties they are empowered to discharge?

Our thesis is that the nature of Statecraft drives the identification of the international norm appropriate to each epoch, as well as the design of the institutions that should be put in place to implement such a norm. The answers to the epochal international institutional issues, in other words, lie within the nature of the State. In order to devise the institutions of the post-modern world, we look back at the trials and errors of the last two eras of Statecraft, pre-modern and modern, and ask how the world of commerce organized itself across borders in prior eras. This analysis allows us, in the second part of this chapter, to derive from the post-modern hallmarks of Statecraft, those trade institutions that should be put in place.

THE PRE-MODERN ERA: GUNBOAT DIPLOMACY AND LOW-GRADE COOPERATION

The animating norm of the pre-modern era was predominantly mercantilism. We have explained why mercantilism made sense for the pre-modern world. The State embarked on an enterprise intended to solidify itself and ground its power. The people physically located within the boundaries of states engaged in work that resulted in the creation of a cohesive state economy which, ultimately, anchored the nation as the basis of the State.[1] The supply of welfare to the subjects of the State was not yet a foundational norm of that system, because the State had to solidify itself, and a nation had to develop, before that constitutional mechanism could come into play. The inner face of the State was reflected in the international behavior of states. The fundamental purpose of foreign policy in the pre-modern era was to acquire power vis-a-vis other states.[2] This animating drive, consistent with the Statecraft element of self-solidification, permeated the behavior of states in the strategic realm. States introduced conscription laws that raised large numbers of citizens to fuel the State's drive to solidify itself through foreign conquests and wars.[3] The pre-modern State vied for control of resources, assets, and people, in an aggressive, highly competitive colonization enterprise. The pre-modern State developed industries that supported its strategic drive and anchored the domestic economy that would come to be associated with the nation.

In both war and trade, states played a zero-sum game against one another, mingled with treaty, truce, or alliance-making.[4] The pre-modern hallmarks of Statecraft were power, unilateralism, and conquest. This foundational structure of the State also yielded the international geopolitical map of the day, in both the strategic and trade realms. Pre-modern Statecraft produced a global map where European powers dominated the commercial world and competed with one another. State-nations associated with Britain, France, Russia, Germany, Italy, Belgium, the Netherlands, Spain, Portugal, Hungary, Austria, and various other territories, won the military conflicts of the day. Their dominance in the strategic realm, while shared to a certain extent with non-European states such as the waning Ottoman Empire, mirrored their respective stakes in the global order.

Thus, the European states dominated the modern strategic and commercial scenes. Their pre-modern enterprise involved colonization and the consequential denial of meaningful development to large portions of the world population – a phenomenon that lies at the root of many issues facing the post-modern order of states. Colonization, regardless of the extent to which it was driven by ideologies of racial superiority, made sense as a foreign endeavor in a world where states competed to marshal the greatest store of resources.[5] By acquiring vast territories and assets, the competing states fostered the solidification process of the pre-modern world. In this context, as we have explained, the most logical and meaningful choice was a mercantilist trade policy.[6] In turn, in such a world, international institutions were not needed, and indeed there were virtually none in the trading world.

The norm of mercantilism does not require that there be any process for producing international agreements, norms, or ventures. The norm is implemented almost entirely by the use of unilateral, power-based means by the states interacting in the international sphere. The creation of resources, to the extent that it involves the international commercial order of states, principally involves conquest and commercial domination. While states engage in selective diplomacy when finding themselves in certain situations of interdependence and where collective action drives a particular outcome, their animating principle by-and-large remains amassing resources through a zero-sum game. This makes sense in an epoch where the constitutional structure of the State embodies the principle of self-solidification. As the State gathers power, it has less use for collaborative enterprises and more of an incentive to view the international order as, principally, a source of opportunities for amassing assets and resources. International collaboration may still be sought in circumstances where states are interdependent and their objectives can best be achieved through collective action, but the overarching structure of the system does not include a permanent international norm of general application that would require implementation through institutions. Unlike comparative advantage, which requires a trade liberalizing institutional structure, there is no need for global trade institutions of any significance in a society of states where the players seek to achieve both strategic and commercial goals through the use of power. To be sure, then, states engaged in diplomacy in the commercial field, treaties were signed, and they had various incentives to negotiate with one another in situations of interdependence even in an era where power and unilateralism animated relations between the dominant actors. However, it may fairly be concluded that, rather than being the norm, the international treaties of the pre-modern era were instances of international collaboration that were ancillary to the dominant unilateral trade ethos of the era; mercantilism, and competition for colonies.

The lack of international institutions, then, averted thorny questions of participation, democracy deficit, transparency, and governance. Such concerns would not become pressing agenda items until Statecraft graduated to the modern era, institutions became necessary and their constitution and operations were brought to the forefront.

THE GATT: A MODERN TREATY

The introduction of comparative advantage as the animating norm of international trade necessitated the establishment of trade institutions. The principal institutions, which survived throughout the modern period, had the natural goal of removing barriers to trade and encouraging nations to specialize in what they do best. In designing these institutions, however, the founders of the GATT used tools derived from the Statecraft of the modern era. As we explained in Chapter 4, the GATT respected national sovereignty to the fullest extent possible, not only in its adherence to comparative advantage as a foundational norm of the system,[7] but in its choice of the institutions that were devised to implement the norm. No international norm that displaces a domestic norm could be adopted without the consent of the national government. No international institutions had jurisdiction to adjudicate disputes and render judgments fully binding on the national governments.[8] The pursuit of the *telos* of the treaty – reduction of barriers to trade – was done only with the consent of each participant, to be withheld at its discretion.

This result was achieved by the negotiating round structure that Bretton Woods set in motion. The GATT organized itself around successive rounds of negotiations intended to reduce tariffs.[9] During each round, the Contracting Parties generally took up a particular set of barriers to trade and sought to negotiate their reduction. The Parties negotiated Schedules indicating their tariff "bindings," or the maximum allowable tariff that each Party would impose on other GATT members.[10] Although certain states spearheaded negotiations and often set the tone for similarly situated countries, the treaty did not allow the Parties to impose tariff reductions on one another. If a nation-state deemed a particular set of products to be important to its national economy, it had the right to impose a tariff with respect to that product category and reject any concessions requested by its trading partner.[11]

As we described in Chapters 4 and 5, the treaty also imposed various "disciplines" intended to make sure that the only barriers to trade would be tariffs transparently set forth on a Schedule and subject to reductions pursuant to the rounds of negotiation. The GATT, however, did not initially give any tribunals the power and jurisdiction to determine whether a national norm violated the international norm. Unlike the European Community, which very early on empowered the European Court of Justice to adjudicate conflicts between national norms and international law, the GATT (after it established a system of arbitral panels in 1952) did not even allow for a panel ruling to become binding unless all Contracting Parties, including the losing party in a particular dispute, accepted the judgment. This structure accorded with the nature of the GATT as a modern treaty. The GATT respected the sovereign right of the modern states that joined the treaty to unimpeded regulation within their borders. While the linkage issue was inevitable, and pressure at the border on the regulatory autonomy of each state would come with comparative advantage, the GATT theoretically did not enact any norm that could displace domestic regulation. Its institutions, then, were consistent with the subdivision of the world into autonomous economies associated with a nation, who could not impose any rule on one another without consent.

This structure was, as we explained, the legal embodiment of the modern notion of sovereignty, which in turn was an essential element of twentieth-century Statecraft. This foundational architecture would have been eroded if the Contracting Parties did not have the right to reject tariff concessions. Unlike the European Community, where ultimately majorities and qualified majorities acquired the right to impose their will on minority members, the GATT did not allow its members to impose legislation of general applicability on one another.[12] This accorded with the modern notion that states, like individuals in a democracy, should have an equal voice in their particular organization. Just as U.N. members have one vote per State, the GATT members were given autonomy to decide whether the tariff reductions that formed the core of the GATT enterprise would apply to them.[13] Further, the Bretton Woods institutions reflected its concern for modern balance of power, and the modern association of the nation with the State. In keeping with the one nation/one vote paradigm, the GATT included within its purview all nation-states that agreed to join the treaty, and gave them each one vote. The GATT ultimately grew to an organization that included more than 150 countries.[14] Each country was committed to free trade, with the possibility of selectively protecting a national industry.

At the same time, the GATT's institutional structure recognized that certain countries (called, alternatively, the "South," the "Third World," "less developed," or "developing" countries) did not have enough power to participate meaningfully in the system. In order (at least in part) to extend the reach of the GATT, and achieve universal membership consistent with the end of history mentality, the GATT founders sheltered developing nations from its early rounds of negotiations.[15] This institutional structure also included some concessions and preferential treatment, which had the ancillary effect of giving a boost to the emerging economies. This did not, however, address the structural problems that were caused by their failure to traverse a modern period that would make them ready for trade. Indeed, in the end, the GATT system substantially accomplished its goal – advancing the modern liberal democratic victors' position – but encountered serious difficulties in trying to integrate the less developed world into the globalized markets that it ushered in.

Similar sovereignty concerns applied to dispute resolution. Domestic sovereignty in the modern age meant that no sovereign nation could be dragged into an international court with the power to impose its will on a member. The International Court of Justice, for example, could not assert jurisdiction over any nation-state belonging to the U.N. unless the state accepted the jurisdiction and signed a submission defining the scope of the court's power to render a decision. The GATT followed the same model. Starting in 1952, the GATT established a system of panels to render decisions regarding disputes between countries.[16] These panels had jurisdiction, among other things, to determine the extent to which a country could avail itself of regulatory comparative advantage. For example, a panel was charged with deciding whether Mexico's tuna industry could be banned from exporting to the United States because it did not follow dolphin protection rules akin to those in place in North America.[17] Other panels decided whether Japan could protect disfavored minorities by excluding leather imports that threatened their livelihood.[18]

However, in all instances, a panel's decision would not become binding unless and until all members, including the losing party, accepted it. This ensured that nation-states would not be compelled by a supranational body to adopt an interpretation of the GATT which infringed on their national sovereignty. If the United States was told that it could not deprive Mexico of its regulatory comparative advantage, the United States could reject the GATT decisions and protect its domestic sovereign right to exclude tuna caught in violation of dolphin protection rules. This arrangement stayed in place until 1994, when the Marrakesh Agreement ushered in a new dispute resolution system. The Marrakesh deal installed a system of panels, and an appellate body, that had much greater power to impose an international will on domestic jurisdictions than the panel system of 1945. Marrakesh reversed the practice of making a ruling binding only if all Contracting Parties accepted it. Instead, it revised the adjudicatory framework of international trade to provide that the ruling would become binding on the parties unless all states objected to it. The newly created Appellate Body began to render decisions with the look and feel of a domestic appellate court imposing a norm on the parties over whom it has jurisdiction.[19]

This change in the dispute resolution system joined with the final efforts to remove lingering tariffs, and it can best be understood as a late modern era system of dispute resolution that, although squarely protective of the states' sovereignty concerns, included some embryonic postmodern features. After 50 years of negotiation, the GATT parties finally lowered tariffs from an average of 40 percent to an average of about 4 percent.[20] Ultimately, there would be no tariffs, and no non-tariff barriers to trade because an international court would (relatively) aggressively oversee their removal. The conventional explanation for the 1994 Marrakesh Agreement, and its emphasis on dispute resolution with teeth, is that an international body had to impose its will on countries seeking to escape their free trade obligations. In order to further the *telos* of a system in advanced stages of its evolution, an effective dispute resolution had to be put in place.

Although it included a judicial system that could impose its will on recalcitrant states, the Marrakesh Agreement still limited its reach to state-to-state proceedings. International legal observers have long noted the reluctance of states to sue one another, whether due to resource limitations or to the fear that one's lawsuit exposes one's breaches to retaliation by other states. Despite Marrakesh, and despite the fact that private actors often influenced deeply whether their state representatives would bring a proceeding and how they would conduct it, the GATT still looked modern. Unlike Europe, it never acquired direct effect, or gave to the true enforcers of international law (individuals and private economic interests acting as private attorneys general), any standing to remedy breaches of the treaty. The post-modern habit of accepting supranational authority that the European and United States trade actors had acquired trickled down to the GATT. The emerging economies that sought to assert their regulatory comparative advantage and challenge European and U.S. efforts to keep out their products had a shared interest in enhancing the effectiveness of the dispute resolution system. Despite its newly acquired post-modern patina, then, the post-Marrakesh GATT judicial institutions remained firmly grounded in a modern framework.

Because of its structure, the GATT raised little, if any, democratic participation or legitimacy questions in the decision making rounds. Each state bargained in the shadow of its veto rights. Until Marrakesh, there was no dispute resolution body with the capacity to impose its rules on the domestic states. In the next subsections of this chapter, drawing on the lessons learned from the past, we outline the contours of the post-modern trade institutions of the twenty-first century.

INSTITUTIONALIZING THE ENABLEMENT OF GLOBAL ECONOMIC OPPORTUNITY

Today, as in the Bretton Woods era, the world must embrace a new constitutional norm for the trading system. In Bretton Woods, the trading partners ushered in comparative advantage, a norm that accorded with the hallmarks of modern Statecraft. At the time, as we have explained, the principal trading partners had graduated to the modern era of Statecraft: they needed to institutionalize comparative advantage in order to bring the world trade system in line with the modern constitutional principles of sovereignty, balance of power, nation-state, and welfare. Today, the decline of welfare, the "flattening" of the world, and the other hallmarks of post-modern Statecraft we identified, require that the world install institutions designed to give life to the global enablement of economic opportunity, a norm that we have elucidated earlier in this book and which we explore in further detail in Chapter 7.

DESIGNING POST-MODERN INSTITUTIONS: THE INTERLOCUTORS

The design of these post-modern trade institutions will involve more intricate issues than those addressed by the trade institutions of the modern and pre-modern eras. In order to design and define the membership of the new trade institutions, we first need to explore the geopolitical configuration of the international economic world that yielded the GATT. The key GATT participants were initially modern states, with pre-modern and post-modern states having little if any relevance for the trade institutions. After the GATT and its affiliate international institutions were formed, the modern liberal democratic world consolidated itself by inviting into its fold the nation-states defeated in World War II. The Marshall Plan gave to states that later became mainstays of European democracy the economic means to compete in the newly liberalized markets. The investment was an unmitigated success. Germany joined France as the twin engine of integrated Europe. To this day, Germany, while deprived of the power to maintain a meaningful army, is an essential actor on the international political and economic scene. Having completely retreated from the aggressive tenets of nazism, Germany symbolizes a moderate European voice that tempers that of other Western actors such as the United States.[21]

The victors also helped Japan to rebound from World War II, and Japan came to occupy an essential role in the modern international economic order. The role of Japan as an anchor of Asia, unsurpassed until the rise of China in the early post-modern age, was felt profoundly throughout various sectors of the global economy. Japan's participation in the world economy was, in many respects, a model outcome of comparative advantage. Under its indicative planning form of modern Statecraft, Japan developed a global edge in automobile, electronics, computers, and a wide array of other industries. At the same time, Japan's success created a strong trading class eager to buy European and American goods in equally diverse industries including high-tech sectors as well as luxury goods, wine, and food.[22]

As these states moved through the modern era to graduate to post-modern Statecraft, other states that were either colonized or less developed after World War II achieved various degrees of success in the marketplace. Africa faced extraordinary challenges when it emerged from colonization. Most of the African states that gained their independence in the 1950s and 1960s derived their national identity from the territories that the Europeans arbitrarily carved out when dividing Africa. Nigeria and the Nigerian identity, for example, were created as a result of the legitimization of the State through its constitutional tie to a nation. Nigeria, like many West African former colonies, included within its borders three very distinct ethnic groups, including a Muslim population in the Northern parts of the country and a Christian and Animist population in more sub-Saharan regions. The nation that formed the basis of the Nigerian nation-state was a wholly artificial creation of the colonizing power. The Nigerians "activated" their identity in order to obtain their independence, and ethnic strife broke out almost immediately after independence was achieved.[23] In other words, when claiming self-determination, Nigeria and the vast majority of African states used the then-prevailing modern Statecraft concepts and vocabulary. However, because their nation did not develop out of a process of pre-modern solidification, but rather out of a colonial history during which European powers drew on local resources to solidify their assets, the nation-states of Africa in fact were, and continue to be, pre-modern states with little if any chance of graduating by themselves to modern – let alone post-modern – Statecraft (except for small pockets of trading classes that have begun to coalesce within these states).[24]

States like Nigeria that still bear the hallmarks of pre-modern age Statecraft, span a massive amount of territory. These pre-modern states include, in addition to most of Africa, large segments of countries like Afghanistan, Pakistan, Egypt, and other Asian and South American states that never went through the pre-modern solidification process that yielded the economic infrastructure necessary to enter the modern age. These states are characterized by a very low per capita income, reliance on volatile commodities and other natural resources for commerce in the global markets, and the relatively low number of citizens that are actively engaged in industrial, services, or other commercial activities that characterize the modern age.[25]

Alongside the pre-modern states are what we call partial graduates of the pre-modern era. These include Brazil, Argentina, Hong Kong, Taiwan, Indonesia, South Africa,[26] and most prominently China[27] and India.[28] They share characteristics of the modern world, and yet they contain pockets of pre-modern population that are so large that they cannot be considered fully modern. This group comprises many countries formerly known as "less developed," such as Brazil or India, that have developed an industrial and other economic base typical of the modern world. These countries have a comparative advantage in a wide array of products that are characteristic of the modern era: textiles, steel, electronics, and automobiles. The trading classes that were formed as a result of their entry into the modern age have the same characteristics as the trading classes of the modern states of Europe and the United States.[29] At the same time, their pre-modern population, alongside the modern population, is much like that of the pre-modern African nations. The favellas of Rio, or the suburban sprawl of Jakarta, do not differ meaningfully from pre-modern Africa.[30] The pre-modern dwellers of modern states such as Brazil or Indonesia do not have access to the industrial infrastructure that came with modern evolution. They do not have the education, skills, or other fundamental hallmarks of an opportunity to pursue a meaningful living in the marketplace.[31] Indeed, they do not even have access to a competitive marketplace.[32]

The international configuration of the post-modern age, then, is characterized by a diffuse overlap of pre-modern, modern, and post-modern pockets. The GATT structure – a product of the modern age – only works as intended with respect to the modern trading classes. Chinese factories in Shenzhen, for example, have access to European and United States markets through comparative advantage and liberalized trade. American and European consumers and manufacturers benefit from cheaper goods, and the creation of a Chinese trading class is gradually generating a massive new market for manufacturing and other goods that in time should greatly benefit not only Chinese but also Western concerns.

The India outsourcing phenomenon is an example of the successful working of comparative advantage. Here as well, Indian workers provide to Western consumers various services that would cost significantly more in the West. At the same time, India is becoming an economic powerhouse with a large trading class that, in time, will also turn *en masse* to European and American goods to satisfy its needs.[33] Likewise, trade among the victors of World War II continues to increase as a result of GATT policy.[34] American goods have become a mainstay of European consumerism. European and Japanese companies continue to gain access to the large and avid U.S. markets, and the respective economies of these nations are now, more than ever, interdependent and poised for continued growth. No new institutions are needed to regulate these phenomena. They are purely the result of the introduction by the GATT of institutionalized comparative advantage.

New trade institutions, however, are needed to handle the vacuum created by the rise of post-modern trading classes, and the failure of the GATT system to integrate meaningfully the pre-modern segments of the world population in the world economic system. In both instances, the GATT did not include within its framework the kind of institutions needed to deal with these phenomena.[35] Let us start with the pre-modern question. As we explained, when extended to states that did not undergo the pre-modern or modern stages of development, comparative advantage was bound to achieve an economic result vastly different from the European or American outcomes. In an African country that was used a means for the solidification process of the European pre-modern age, the economic infrastructure needed to play the comparative advantage game is simply non-existent. Unlike Europe, where during the pre-modern era the nation solidified itself around a middle class (which came to form the basis of the State), the African state inherited a nation that came to life artificially and without solidification as a result of decolonization. Even those countries, like China, India, Brazil, or South Africa, where a meaningful trading class developed, the pre-modern population is so large that those states cannot meaningfully be compared to the United States, Japan, or Europe.[36]

The GATT's reliance on the domestic state to reallocate resources and generate welfare is, as we have described, meaningless in the context of these states. Because they missed evolutionary stages of Statecraft, they are simply incapable of following the modern GATT model, and the first task of the international trade institutions of the post-modern age is to fill this vacuum.[37] In turn, this can only be done through a post-modern institution that, as described below, will push and prod for the enablement of global economic opportunity in the pre-modern world, rather than relying on an obsolete model that calls on participating states to grow their internal wealth through trade grounded in comparative advantage.

THE TRADE COUNCIL

We advocate the establishment by the modern liberal democracies of a Trade Council, whose first task will be to accomplish the goals just described. Unlike the GATT, the Trade Council must have a selective membership, and it must operate in partnership with states, regional organizations, and industry participants. The history of trade gives us some guidance as to how to build the Trade Council. First, the Trade Council must be charged in a constitutional moment with a clearly defined task that departs from the structural framework of the past, and a shift in the historical development of trade put in motion. However, as has always been the case, the planners and participants must then adjust the institution as its history evolves in what are sure to be fits and starts. The establishment of Europe illustrates this principle. In 1950, when Robert Schuman laid out his vision of Europe, he rejected a power-based version of the continent. "A united Europe was not achieved," he famously announced, and "we had war."[38] The task at hand was to make war "not merely unthinkable but also impossible" by binding France and Germany to a newly created partnership. Europe, however, was not to be made all at once. It would arise, as Schuman predicted with uncanny accuracy, out of the fitful interaction of the new European institutions and the Member States and their individuals. Fifty-five years and countless crises and adjustments to the original treaties later, Europe is well on its way to achieving the post-modern united European states that Schuman envisioned.

Like Europe, the Trade Council must be comprised of a select set of states that span the territories it will reach. Again, like Europe, the Trade Council will not accomplish its goal overnight. Rather, it will build the type of problem-solving programs that we describe in this book, and in the future will by necessity adjust its workings to accommodate the outcome in the field of the economic processes that it puts in motion. Understanding how the Trade Council will deal with this wide array of problems goes hand-in-hand with defining its make-up. The first task of the Trade Council will be to spread economic opportunity to those areas of the pre-modern world that have strategic value to the victors of World War II in connection with the new existential struggles of the day. This does not mean that other areas of the world mired in poverty will be abandoned forever because they do not have strategic importance to the world. On the contrary, a proactive spread of economic opportunity throughout the world may avert future strategic problems, as we discuss in Chapter 8. However, as the Trade Council gets underway and begins to shift trade from maximizing the global pie for domestic redistribution to active intervention, it will of necessity follow a problem-solving methodology rather than a comprehensive governance scheme based on the modern liberal democratic model. This, as detailed later in this chapter, is the route not only to accomplishing the transformed ethos of international trade but also to resolve the initial democracy issues that the new institutions of trade will face.

MEMBERSHIP

In keeping with the diffuse nature of the international marketplace, we believe the new trade organization should be comprised of a shifting representation of states and their governments that is dictated by the industries at issue. The organization could have permanent trading partners – the body that we refer to as "the Trade Council" – and then delegate to responsible persons, as determined by expertise in a given subject matter area, who would work jointly with industry representatives and (as explained below) other international organizations. The initial trading members would be drawn from the victors of World War II, who have graduated to post-modern Statecraft, and from representatives of the pre-modern and modern world that are their new partners in the strategic struggles of the twenty-first century.

These states would initially include representatives from every continent. For Europe, the task will be rather simple. The European Union, acting as a compact, will by all means be a permanent member of the Trade Council. If Turkey is folded into the European Union, it will not have a separate seat. However, given its strategic importance at the gates of Iraq, Iran, Kurdistan, and the Crescent, Turkey would have its own seat should the European Union not accept this Muslim nation into the predominantly secular compact. Going eastward, Russia obviously must have a seat, owing to its central position of power with respect to the former Soviet Republics. In the Americas, the United States, as a key economic player and leader of the post-modern world, is also without question slated to have a seat. In Latin and Central America, until the advent of a free trade bloc akin to that of Europe, the representative states should consist of the new economic powers: Brazil, Mexico, and Argentina are prominent candidates.

In Asia, the new economic powerhouses must be members of the Trade Council. Thus, China and India will join. In addition, states like Indonesia or Malaysia, which have strategic significance and are battlegrounds in the twenty-first-century diffuse wars, should also be brought into the fold of world trade with a prominent role. The Southeast Asian "tiger states" must also participate, and it would be best if they joined as an alliance. Japan, of course, will also have a seat on the Trade Council. Africa and the Middle East, as the most pre-modern of regions, will generate the thorniest questions of membership. The task would be made easier if a coalition of states agreed to send a delegate to the Trade Council. For example, the Arab League may be a representative.[39] For this somewhat ineffective and declining body, this could be a boost that revives the dream of a pan-Arab nation, in the context of positive economic development rather than nationalistic struggles. The same analysis holds true for Africa. A union of African states would be the most logical regional arrangement of states to sit on the Trade Council in that (as described later) it would be best placed to coordinate with domestic states the type of programs that we advocate. However, if a workable coalition cannot be put together, the state participants will include Egypt, Jordan, Pakistan, South Africa, Nigeria, Ethiopia, and Tunisia, states that are either indispensable to strategic stability or have come to acquire a unique commercial role on the international economic scene.

The Trade Council will also include representatives of the industries that are affected by the incentives-driven programs which, as explained below and in subsequent chapters, we envision the Council to advance. The government representatives could, as is the case in the European Union, be delegates of the executive or other branches of government that regulate the relevant sector. Health officials could join trade ministers, for example, in projects affecting the pharmaceutical industries, along with industry representatives. As we will detail, the Trade Council will also work in collaboration with other international organizations, including by way of example organizations dealing with intellectual property, environmental or labor standards, corruption, or other criminal activities.

The task of the Trade Council will be *ad hoc* and geared toward problem-solving, incentives driven projects designed for the diffuse post-modern era. Some of these projects will be industry specific, and others will require more widespread intervention to spread and globally enable economic activity. Just as Bretton Woods started with a structural adjustment of the international economic landscape in the form of the Marshall Plan to create the conditions necessary for free trade, the Trade Council will have its formative constitutional moment and proceed to prod the international economic landscape in the direction of economic opportunity, through a "gradual new Marshall Plan."

THE TRADE COUNCIL IN THE PRE-MODERN WORLD:
A GRADUAL NEW MARSHALL PLAN

With respect to the pre-modern world, the Trade Council will establish programs designed to create the conditions necessary for the enablement of global economic opportunity. The type of economic development that this new trade institution will foster will be in line with the diffuseness of the twenty-first century world. The twentieth century's Marshall Plan was intended to shore up nation-states so that a trading world with a relative balance of powers could be put in place. We believe that twenty-first century trade will also require a Marshall Plan–like investment to complement trade, though one that is of a gradual and *ad hoc* nature in line with the pushing and prodding of economic activity that characterizes the trade norm we advocate.

This task will be accomplished, first, by collaboration between the Trade Council and regional and other developmental banks. For example, as described below, banks that specialize in small loans for low-income households in developing countries should be a special focus of the Trade Council. These institutions enable economic opportunity in a wide variety of sectors ranging from tourism to local crafts, to spread to the remotest regions of the globe. This aspect of the Trade Council's activities is crucial to its governance function. As we detailed earlier, the shift from modern to post-modern Statecraft produced a governance vacuum. The states of the world do not have the ability to effectively assure a sufficient portion of their population that they will have access to meaningful welfare and, thus, cannot control basic policy tools that characterize the modern era. We will return to this function later in this chapter.

The second function of the Trade Council will be to provide a forum for addressing discrete global issues that arise out of the transformation of the international economic order of states. As we have detailed, the erosion of the nation-based boundaries of the modern age has caused a significant vacuum in governance. The passage to the post-modern global economic epoch has witnessed market forces coming to control sensitive areas of economic life, such as currency fluctuations, that once lay within the virtually exclusive purview of nation-state regulators. Market forces, however, ultimately reach a stage where coordinated regulatory action is needed in order to achieve the fundamental stability that benefits all actors. This is a classic scenario where the modern State would intervene to regulate the nation, yet the cross-border diffuseness of many large issues makes it very difficult for individual nation-states to control issues that have become globalized and transcend what once were national boundaries. This is where the Trade Council will act, in the manner that we describe.

To illustrate this phenomenon, consider the relationship of interdependence among actors from China, the United States, the European Union, and other powerful states such as Japan, in relation to the value of the dollar relative to other currencies. Chinese actors hold the largest amount of foreign currency reserves in the world. China's central bank has recently announced that China's reserves amount to $987 billion,[40] and they are growing by $18 billion on a monthly basis.[41] Other Chinese financial institutions and actors also hold an astonishing amount of U.S. dollars. This surplus is a direct result of China's resounding success in the liberalized global markets. The entry of China into the GATT, and its sheer economic force, have made that state's manufacturers, merchants, consumers, government authorities, and other economic actors, prime players in world markets. China's trade surplus now exceeds $100 billion,[42] and its work force and enterprises are firmly grounded in key global industries, such as textiles and electronics.

This is a GATT success story which, at the same time as it reflects a positive evolution in the global economy, is creating a new generation of problems and challenges that the current domestic and international institutions and norms are incapable of addressing. We have described how the GATT gave rise to the age of a global horizontal set of trading classes, following the creation and solidification of industry in the premodern era and its close association with the nation in the modern economic age. In the post-modern world of global industry, China is rapidly becoming a preferred industrial zone for enterprises operating in various discrete sectors. In cities like Shenzhen, hundreds of thousands of workers manufacture products distributed in key world markets. Western consumers, including prominently American ones, benefit from access to efficiently priced goods that far outweigh in price/quality ratio those manufactured in many other parts of the globe.

While the normative and institutional framework created by the GATT allowed China to achieve this outcome, the GATT and international trade generally do not have any institutions or norms capable of addressing sensitive problems associated with the fundamental changes generated by entry into the post-modern age. Other institutions, like the International Monetary Fund, are designed to promote cooperation with a view to achieving financial stability, but they do not have the institutional capacity to merge trade and financial concerns in incentives-driven legislation of the type that we advocate.[43] Likewise, domestic states are by themselves incapable of addressing these issues. The relationship between expanded trade and dollar value is a prime example of this scenario. With its extraordinary trade surplus, China and its financial institutions invest substantially in the United States. China has invested its foreign currency reserves principally in long-term Treasury bonds and other government securities of the United States. As of this writing, China holds approximately $700 billion in U.S. currency, about half of which has been invested in U.S. long-term bonds.[44] On the one hand, this creates a symbiotic relationship with the U.S. economy that does not necessitate any government intervention. The influx of foreign capital allows the United States to maintain relatively low long-term interest rates. Among other effects, this has allowed the U.S. economy to experience a housing boom that has stimulated consumption, in particular consumption of foreign goods such as Chinese manufactured products. In turn, China's success generates more dollars that are again invested back in the United States. When all is said and done, it can be argued, everyone benefits from this two-way success.[45]

However, history often shows that, when left unaddressed, the seeds of economic disaster grow in times of unmitigated success. The economic collapse of the 1930s was born out of the roaring 1920s, when the world optimistically and brazenly burned the spoils of its pre-modern consolidation, and failed to usher in a decidedly modern age of comparative advantage and liberalized commerce. Our example illustrates the type of existential dangers that world economic players have not yet prepared themselves to deal with. Elementary principles of economic theory dictate that a country like China, which holds substantial foreign currency reserves, must revalue its currency (the Yuan) upwards so as to avoid inflationary pressures. Yet, China has pegged the Yuan's value to the dollar, so as to keep it artificially low and boost its exports. This policy choice stems from China's reliance on exports to maintain its growth and to sustain the new trading classes flocking *en masse* to the industrial centers of the country.

In the long run, however, this situation confronts the trading world with a set of dilemmas that reach all of the principal economic actors of the world. China has an incentive to shift its reliance on export-oriented growth to domestically driven consumption, so as to avoid a financial collapse that is sure to come if it maintains its current Yuan/dollar policy. At the same time, China cannot afford to harm the economy of the United States by withdrawing wholesale from its dollar holdings. Such a course of action would necessarily bring about an unsustainable raise in interest rates, which would result in a substantial U.S. recession. The recession would, at least initially, cut down on U.S. imports of Chinese goods and destroy several industrial centers in China. Concurrently, the Yuan's increased value would make China's exports to other countries, including in particular the European Union, much more expensive than they currently are, and further contribute to the collapse of the Chinese nation's newly-acquired power.

Europe would suffer a fate far worse than deprivation of cheap Yuan-priced goods. The collapse of the dollar would immediately bring down the prices of American products. The higher interest rate would, ironically, create an American economy that resembles today's Chinese economy. The lower dollar, and the associated boost in exports, would gradually replace the domestic demand (stifled by high interest rates) as growth catalysts. In turn, Europe would see its market flooded with American goods, and it would lose much of its traditional American export outlets. Japan would also be an unmitigated loser in this scenario. As America exports more and buys less, Japan would not only lose its American customers but it would also face a European market which, confronted by a surge of cheap exports, would likely shut its doors to foreign goods, catching Japanese goods in its new protectionist net.

The IMF and the OECD see this as a central problem of the world economy.[46] Unless it is addressed – we are told – the prospects for future world economic growth might be derailed. Yet, no single state can address the problem, and no international norm or institution exists to tackle it in a meaningful and holistic fashion. This is because the modern instruments of regulation are escaping the control of the nation-states that ruled the modern world. The United States and other Western states, in their modern incarnation, had a strong degree of control over their currencies and the associated export and import drives. Currency exchange levels could be maintained or adjusted by central bank tightening or loosening of money creation. Central banks would routinely engage in such intervention, based on the state of the domestic economy. In turn, the principle of balance of power would dictate the extent to which a state would intervene in the domestic economy. A nation-state would not devalue its currency to such an extent as to destabilize its relationship with a main trading partner. In the post-modern world, however, the sheer volume of currency trading and the relationship of interdependence that we described mean that states can no longer, by themselves, maintain

monetary stability. The Trade Council, through a coordinated program of incentives, would provide the forum for achieving currency
stability.[47]

Likewise, international institutions such as the IMF, while charged
with ensuring financial stability, do not have the breadth of reach within
the post-modern world that we envisage for the Trade Council. As
described in the next chapter, we believe that the Trade Council should
operate based on a system of incentives that joins the international and
domestic realms and cuts across the traditional vertical and horizontal
boundaries of the modern world. While the IMF might be a partner with
the Trade Council, it could not implement the incentives-based program
that we advocate.

The Trade Council will also seek to fill the vacuum of the GATT and its
institutions with respect to the enormous population mass that we have
called "vulnerable middle classes" and excluded classes. The fascinating
part of this phenomenon is that it appears in states that have taken a decidedly post-modern turn such as European states or the United States, as
well as in states that are emerging on virtually every continent from pre-
modern to post-modern Statecraft, like Brazil, India, China, and certain
former Soviet republics. A staggering number of individuals find themselves in a state of economic insecurity for a wide array of reasons, all
of which are connected to the transformation of the world in the modern age. French or American economic blocs, such as textiles industry
players, find themselves on the decline as a result of a shift of the locus
of their industrial activity to states that emerged from the pre-modern to
the modern era such as China and India. In those states, in turn, some
of the new middle classes find themselves vulnerable to a sudden shift of
industrial activity from their jurisdictions to other emerging economies,
like African states, that can surge from pre-modern to modern on account
of a sharper comparative advantage.[48]

This cross-border creation of similarly-situated classes of individuals
is a hallmark of the post-modern world. The phenomenon is not limited to the vulnerable middle class. Across the globe, a successful class
of entrepreneurs, executives, professionals, merchants, teachers, doctors,
and a wide array of other individuals, are (to various degrees) actively
engaged in the global market of the post-modern world. They experience collectively a relatively high degree of economic security, and they
have skills or resources that enable them to share meaningfully in global
wealth. A Mexico City corporate lawyer, a Dallas executive, and a Hong
Kong factory owner share remarkably similar experiences in the early
post-modern age, and their global interests coalesce around relatively
similar strategic objectives tending toward stability.

Alongside these groupings of individuals lies yet another group: a vast number of masses who experience the harsh conditions of pre-modern Statecraft and patterns of economic activity. These classes of individuals span the entire globe, crisscrossing formal borders that no longer embody a discrete nation. They form the most troublesome aggregation of individuals in the post-modern world and share the hallmarks of a form of pre-modernism that has not traversed the modern era and, yet, live alongside and within economic systems that have been profoundly influenced by such epochal transformation.

One group includes entire states that emerged from colonization with artificially created "nations," difficulties in establishing central authority, and no industrial base to compete in the modern world. These states are succeeding to various degrees in the post-modern global markets. However, in all cases, they contain vast pockets of population whose economic conditions, measured by conventional criteria, fall far behind those of the global middle classes. These post-modern disfavored classes may be found, first, in most states of Sub-Saharan Africa. Africa has suffered more than any other continent from colonization, and its history renders it incapable, unless it musters global support, to meaningfully enter the post-modern age. African states never built nations. The nation-states of Africa, born of the independent local movements that coalesced around an identity against the foreign powers, were fraught with ethnic and religious struggles. Unlike Europe, which grew a middle class that formed the foundation of the nation in the pre-modern era, African states inherited boundaries drawn by the colonizers in the course of their enterprise. The goal of the European nations that invaded Africa, based on their Statecraft of the time, was to draw and amass as much resources as possible to solidify the State's basis. When the modern age began to emphasize nationhood, the African states naturally came to view the identity that the colonizers defined for them as the nation that should form the basis of their independence.

The "end of history" sentiment that Fukuyama identified worked hand-in-hand with the national activation of an artificial identity. If modern liberal democracies were the preferred form of government, then this form of Statecraft should be extended to the new African states. The nation that, in modern Statecraft, formed the basis of modern liberal democracies would be the African nation, and the newly-independent states would come within the family of nations. Even for states that chose marxist forms of government, national identity remains a bedrock of Statecraft. While the form of service to the nation took the form of communism rather than modern liberal democratic welfare, the country as inherited from colonial boundaries was the fundamental unit to which Statecraft applied.

The African nation-states, however, proved to be "prison states" for the various ethnic groups that were lumped together in a unit that emerged from colonialism without undergoing a pre-modern stage of Statecraft. The Biafran massacres illustrate the extent to which the failure to recognize the natural evolution of Statecraft can generate disasters of unfathomable proportion. Nigeria, like most West African states, included a number of ethnic groups characterized not only by disparate tribal allegiances but by different colonial religious experiences. The North, traditionally influenced by North Africa, tended to embrace Islam. The South, especially the capital port cities, tended to be Christian bastions – the result of the missionary work of the colonizers. While animist and other home-grown religions continued to play an important role, the ethnic tensions that colonization brought about joined with the underdeveloped infrastructure of the post-colonization African states to form a pre-modern collectivity facing post-modern powerhouses in the global markets.

In these circumstances, the export of modern age democracy to create a political structure that could foster economic development was bound to be a failure. As insightful observers of African politics (e.g., Ronen) noted, losing an election in Africa had a vastly different meaning than in Europe. In the United States, however strongly one might feel about the victory of a Republican or Democratic candidate, the vast majority of citizens will not experience a drastic change in access to resources or the pursuit of happiness depending on whether the "Left" or the "Right" wins. In Africa, on the other hand, the victory of a coalition of ethnic groups meant, in the early days, that the meager resources would be allocated to the victors. The defeated lost a war more than an election, and faced existential questions of survival if they failed to accede to power. The massacre of hungry Biafrans illustrates this sad historical fact, and the speed with which Nigeria reconciled provides further testimony to the fact that the structure of Statecraft, rather than inherent ethnic tensions, was the cause of the failure of early independent Africa to enjoy meaningful entry into the modern age, and to participate today in the post-modern economic era.

Colonization and the failure of many states to pass through the modern and pre-modern eras also left its mark in other areas of the world. While emerging as major economic powers and surpassing Africa in technology, gross domestic product, export of goods, market penetration, and all other indicators of economic performance, states such as India have enormous populations in pre-modern conditions. The same holds true for Brazil, Indonesia, China, and other states that, while including a powerful middle class that joins with European, American, and Asian states to form the post-modern middle class, still are home to a disproportionately high level of individuals that we call the "excluded."[49] To be sure, globalization has decreased poverty and resulted in an unprecedented spread of wealth to masses that previously did not have any opportunity to access it. However, this progress has been accompanied by uncertainty and vulnerability that require global, concerted action.

Indeed, the phenomenon is global. The common denominator of the African states and the Favellas of Rio, or the untouchables of India, is their lack of access to meaningful economic opportunity. No matter how much work or goodwill these individuals muster, only a small percentage of them will enter the post-modern trading class in the foreseeable future. In turn, this essential characteristic is shared with European suburban dwellers, in particular the Arab immigrants of Paris, Berlin, or London. In Paris, for example, "93" has become the symbol of a developing country in the midst of a post-modern economy. 93 is the number of the *"departement"* (district) abutting Paris to the West, where the riots of 2004 and 2005 originated. The film of the same name as the department that shocked France right before the riots reflects the situation of the individuals of 93. In that film, the security situation deteriorates to such an extent, as a result of the utter lack of economic opportunity, the French government decides to declare martial law in the area and *de facto* cut it off from France. This image reflects the reality in the field: in 93, the kind of access to capital, jobs or economic opportunity that characterizes nearby Paris simply does not exist. Although the 93 dwellers may have access to government benefits that the citizens of, say, Angola, do not, their lack of economic opportunity is equivalent to that of Angolan citizens.

In turn, no single State faces the problems of the excluded classes alone. The African states, even if they mustered the political will to put ethnic strife behind them, do not have the resources to create the infrastructure or access to capital necessary to lift a meaningful number of the excluded from poverty. The excluded classes of India and China find themselves in roughly the same situation. As to 93 in France, the already stretched welfare state can continue to pump money into safety net programs, but the lack of economic opportunity will inevitably continue to sap the morale of the ghetto dwellers, ultimately resulting in more self destructiveness and further descent into social strife.

THE WORKINGS OF THE TRADE COUNCIL

As an international organization, the Trade Council will step into the regulatory vacuum of the post-modern era and implement programs intended to spread economic opportunity to the excluded classes and to the vulnerable middle classes. As discussed in the next chapter, economic opportunity for the excluded classes means: (1) access to capital, (2) establishment of infrastructure, and (3) elimination of structural impediments to modern era economic growth. Let us start with capital. In Chapter 7, we will discuss in depth how cross-border infusion of capital in the modern era followed the basic principles of modern Statecraft. Enterprises would move to developing countries to take advantage of comparative advantage in labor, regulation or other factors of production. The host states were charged with what we call the "extraction of welfare benefits" from foreign enterprises. They initially did so through programs intended to ensure that the foreign concerns conducted sufficient business with local enterprises to justify their use of cheaper labor or regulatory conditions, made technology or other intellectual property available to the local economy, took on domestic partners, or reinvested profits locally. Ultimately, however, just as European-style welfare did not work, relying on foreign enterprises to bring in capital and economic development was also bound to fail.

First, post-modern diffuseness meant that states could not impose welfare requirements without creating risk that foreign investors would shift production to other states. If a domestic jurisdiction imposed too many requirements on foreign investors, then the investors would simply pack up and move to the next jurisdiction. Second, the rules of customary international law advocated by the victors of World War II operated to reinforce this pattern. International investment rules included, most prominently, a requirement of non-discrimination and minimum level of international legal protection.[50] Developing countries resisted the imposition of this body of international law for the economic security of foreigners, but their need for foreign investment meant that, ultimately, they had to cave in and accept a body of norms that gave foreign investors the ability to transfer a minimal amount of benefits to the domestic economy.

The Trade Council will radically shift the paradigm for infusing capital into the pre-modern pockets of the post-modern world. Instead of relying on the regulation of foreign private enterprises by the domestic host states, the Trade Council will adopt a two-prong approach to making capital available to the excluded classes. First, the Trade Council will put into place a new Marshall Plan. This plan will include a financial institutional framework for making financial instruments adapted to the circumstances of a given region available to small entrepreneurs. Unlike the Marshall Plan, which featured a one time massive investment into the destroyed economies of war torn Europe, the New Marshall Plan will include gradual extension, on a microeconomic level, of capital resources to entrepreneurs.

The Trade Council will act as an umbrella organization, presiding over a network of institutions that could be used to make financing available, and for establishing the related infrastructure that we describe. These institutions will include, first, regional banks that will be funded by the member states of the Trade Council. The Grameen Bank, which along with its founder Muhammed Yunus won the 2006 Nobel Peace Prize, illustrates the type of the institutions that should partner up with the Trade Council to set the new Marshall Plan into motion.[51]

In 2006, Muhammad Yunus and the Grameen Bank were jointly awarded the Nobel Peace Prize "for their efforts to create economic and social development from below." A Bangladeshi banker and economist, Yunus is the founder of the Grameen Bank.[52] Started in 1976, the Grameen bank began as a research project at the University of Chittagong. Yunus' aim was to test his method for offering credit and banking services to the poor. Previously, the poor were denied banking services on the ground that their poverty was not bankable and, hence, not profitable. But as Yunus believes that "poverty in the world is an artificial creation,"[53] he also believes that offering credit to "these millions of small people with their millions of small pursuits can add up to create the biggest development wonder."[54] The banking system was first introduced to the villages surrounding the university, and the method's success soon allowed Grameen Bank to spread throughout Bangladesh. Grameen was eventually granted independence from the university and continues to expand today.

Grameen's unconventionality lies in its ability to promote peace indirectly while striving to eradicate poverty. Defying traditional collateral-based banking, mutual trust and accountability are placed in the hands of the masses. The banking system is based on the idea that all people have "endless potential," which cannot be measured by material possessions. Thus, the poor have profitable skills that are under-utilized because of the lack of money available to buy the basic components necessary for business and trade. Using primarily Yunus' concept of micro-credit, the bank lends small sums of money to the poor; and, repayment can be arbitrary and drawn out over long periods of time. For example, an individual borrowing 100 taka (US $1.50) can pay only 2 taka (US $0.034) a week. Thus, beggars are not encouraged to quit begging; they are encouraged to derive income by buying and selling low-cost items. The bank system further assumes that if credit is accessible to these individuals, they will be able to identify and engage in viable money-generating projects.

In operation, a bank branch is established with a branch manager and several center managers that cover an area of 15 to 22 rural villages.

To familiarize themselves with the respective localities and to explain the bank's functions and operations, the managers first visit the villages. Eventually, in order to facilitate banking for the population, Grameen managers come directly to people's doorsteps. Every week 20,223 staff meet 6.83 million borrowers at their homes to deliver services.[55] Repayment to the bank is ensured under the micro-credit system. In order to obtain a loan, a group of five prospective individuals must apply together. At first, only two of the five are eligible for, and receive, the loan. Grameen then scrutinizes the group for a month to see if they conform to the bank's rules. If the first two group members abide by the rules and repay the loan with interest in a period of six weeks, then the remaining group members become eligible for a loan. If one individual fails to repay the allotted sum, further credit is denied to the entire group. Yet, liability to repay that sum to the bank is not passed on to the group. This way, more than monetary incentives are introduced to the group dynamic; trust, responsibility, and dependability prove to be key components.

However, because Grameen bank functions as a social service more than a bank, if an individual faces difficulty, the bank helps the person regain strength and overcome difficulty. As most banks continuously collect interest, at Grameen Bank the interest never exceeds the loan, regardless of the amount of time lapsed. No interest is charged after the interest amount equals the loaned amount. Further, no signed legal instrument binds the lender and the borrower, so no court of law will be introduced to enforce provisions of any contract. Grameen Bank also goes to great lengths to assist the families of borrowers.[56] Grameen allots resources to the education of children by offering routine scholarships and student loans. Housing, sanitation programs, access to clean drinking water, and emergency relief programs are also provided. Grameen also assists in individual creation of pension funds and savings accounts. Finally, a free insurance program ensures that in case of death of a borrower, liability will not be transferred to the family.

For the poorest of beggars, or those who would turn to crime or other illegal activities as means of income if Grameen Bank were not an option, an alternative program called Struggling Members Programme exists.[57] This special program reaches out to 87,000 members, many of whom are disabled, blind, retarded, or old and sick. Stipulations for this program are different from those for regular Grameen members; in fact, struggling members essentially make up their own rules. All loans are interest-free, loans can be made for very long term, and can be repaid in very small increments. The objective of this program is to help people find dignity within themselves, so they and their own can have the opportunity to eventually become regular Grameen Bank members.

Since Grameen Bank's inception, Tk 301.72 billion (US $5.89 billion) has been loaned, and Tk 269.06 billion (US $5.23 billion) has been repaid, with a loan recovery rate of 99 percent. Of these figures, Tk 32.66 billion (US $486.74 million) in loans remains outstanding. In 2005, the total revenue generated by Grameen was Tk 7.39 billion (US $112.40 million), while total expenditure for 2005 was Tk 6.39 billion (US $97.19 million). The total profit for 2005 was Tk 1000 million (US $15.21 million), of which 100 percent went to the Rehabilitation Fund, created for disaster relief. In 1995, Grameen Bank made the decision to no longer accept donor funds. Since that time, none has been accepted, and Grameen Bank remains a stable and successful socioeconomic establishment.

The positive impact that Grameen Bank has had and continues to have has been well documented by agencies such as the World Bank, the International Food Research Policy Institute (IFPRI), and the Bangladesh Institute of Development Studies (BIDS). According to these organizations, more than half of Grameen borrowers in Bangladesh, – about 50 million people – have risen out of acute poverty. These borrowers now have their children in schools, families that can eat three meals a day, a sanitary toilet, rainproof housing, clean drinking water, and the ability to repay a loan.[58]

The Trade Council will seek to fund a network of Grameen Banks, drawing the necessary resources from the states that comprise it, working in partnership with the states that will benefit from the establishment of this network of financial institutions. This is where strategy meets economics. The extension of economic opportunity, as we explain in Chapter 7, is not a top-down principle to be applied on a comprehensive level by a central authority, in the manner of nation-state welfare. Rather, it will be extended, pushing and prodding through various regions of the world, and the Trade Council will need to prioritize limited resources and identify the regions of the world where financial institutions should be established.

This task will, of necessity, follow the strategic order of the day. Just as the GATT solidified the economies of the victors of World War II, the new international trade institutions will, before a disaster strikes, work to solidify the economies of the pre-modern pockets of the post-modern era and contribute to the existential struggles of the twenty-first century. If these priorities had to be set today, for example, the first candidates for the New Marshall Plan would be Egypt, Jordan, Tunisia, Ethiopia, and Pakistan. Egypt and Jordan stand at the border of war-torn Iraq, fundamentalist Iran, and fractured Sudan. Their economic well-being is essential to the strategic interests of the World War II victors (i.e., containing Islamic fundamentalism). Ethiopia is located in the Horn of Africa, at the fault line of a clash between fundamentalist and moderate Islam, and African Christianity. Here again, the extension of economic opportunity will not only contribute to global economic development but also foster a buffer zone against the extension of radical Islam.

Tunisia, too, is at a crossroads. Over the past 20 years, the country has become a rapidly growing manufacturing base for European companies,[59] especially those coming from French speaking states. Tunisia benefits from its proximity to Europe. It is governed by a secular government, and is at the moment strongly committed to fighting radical Islam and global networked terrorism. Its labor pool is prepared to provide manufacturing services at a cheaper price. All in all, Tunisia can be viewed as a small China, located at the gates of Europe. Yet Tunisia is threatened with the same kind of terrorist and religious strife that has plagued neighboring Algeria. Strong Islamist cells operate in the country and, as the recent bombings of tourist spots demonstrate, they have the means and intent to disrupt the Tunisian economy. Their objective is to install a government that will take Tunisia out of the moderate camp and ground it in the fundamental Islamist lineup. This is a primary candidate for the Trade Council to intervene and to extend to that nation the gradually unfolding New Marshall Plan.

THE TRADE COUNCIL AND INCENTIVES

The Trade Council will also work with private interests and domestic states to create a system of domestic incentives for companies to establish what may be conceptualized as "social contracts" in the pre-modern and modern pockets of the post-modern world. In Chapter 7, we discuss at length the concept of the social contract in the context of the agreements entered into between large multinational corporations and the domestic economies of less developed states. These social contracts will be entered into with respect to both the excluded classes and the vulnerable middle classes. Their goal will be to incentivize foreign enterprises to achieve the same type of performance requirements that host jurisdictions tried to impose on them. Where regulation failed, incentives might win.

The incentives-based partnership among the Trade Council, states, and private enterprises will include the use of tax and other regulatory incentives by the home states of the foreign investor. This package of incentives would be made available to enterprises that achieve the performance goals defined by the Trade Council. By way of example, the Trade Council may set as one of its goals the expansion of the free trade zones recently established in Jordan and Egypt. These zones feature the establishment of industrial facilities for European and American companies, which can then export their products to the home country with an extremely low tariff treatment. These zones extend economic opportunity to areas of the world that, as discussed above, are of extreme strategic importance.

The passage into the post-modern epoch, however, renders the system of tariffs insufficient to incentivize companies to move to free trade zones that are strategically located. Post-modern diffuseness, together with the virtual elimination of tariffs during the modern era, has two consequences for projects like the free trade zones. First, manufacturing shifts rapidly to states that offer the most welcoming regulatory and labor climate. Second, the virtual elimination of tariffs renders the very concept of "free trade zones" much less powerful than it was in the modern era. When tariffs averaged 50 percent of the landed cost of a product, establishing a free trade zone carried a strong likelihood of attracting a meaningful amount of business. With tariffs averaging less than 5 percent, however, enterprises are much more interested in locating a jurisdiction that provides skilled labor at a relatively low wage, such as China or India, rather than flocking to states that offer slightly lower tariffs, but that cannot compete with the regulatory comparative advantage of the powerhouses of the post-modern age.

In addition, without the system of incentives that we are advocating, free trade zones suffer from the same ailments as the international investment system of the modern age. Even if enterprises establish factories in the free trade zones, the host states do not gain much economic development beyond the temporary employment of workers at relatively low wages. Enterprises will not accept a system that forces them to confer on the domestic economy benefits that go beyond those attendant to the operation of a factory in the most cost-effective way. The failure to impose performance requirements through binding rules in the modern era will inevitably repeat itself in a post-modern age where enterprises have a wide array of choices. In an era where the comparative benefits of free trade are less significant than ever, private enterprises are bound to vote with their feet to a much greater extent than before and to leave their host jurisdictions if they attempt to impose unwanted regulation and resource redistribution on them.

Instead of relying on domestic regulation, the post-modern system must motivate enterprises to move to strategically desirable locations through a system of incentives established by the home jurisdiction of the investor enterprise. This system of incentives may include tax breaks, subsidies, and other benefits that may be used by the "exporting jurisdiction" to entice its enterprises to move to free trade zones. In other words, if the United States wants its companies to move to the Egyptian free trade zone, and to have a meaningful impact in relation to the enablement of global economic opportunity, it must also act domestically rather than rely solely on the mechanics of tariff reduction and the Egyptian government's ability to regulate. The strategic interests of the United States in such a system are clear, and in keeping with post-modern Statecraft the structural framework will include a partnership among an international organization, domestic states, and private concerns.

The social contract, in this instance, could involve a promise by the enterprise to use local suppliers to manufacture a meaningful part of its product. It could also include a commitment to acquire stakes in local companies, and to give them privileged status as suppliers to the home market of the investor enterprise. Likewise, the investor enterprise could commit to take on a specified amount of higher-level employees. Instead of primarily using local workers for unskilled jobs and "Western" workers for skilled undertakings, the enterprise could train and equip the local workforce with the skills necessary to establish businesses of their own and compete in the post-modern global market.

This structure would go hand-in-hand with the network of banks that we advocate. Entrepreneurship and economic opportunity might arise among the excluded classes on account of the system of incentives created by the Trade Council and its partners. An Egyptian company manufacturing zippers or other garment hardware might, for example, acquire the skills and network necessary to distribute its products directly and compete meaningfully in the United States. That enterprise could apply for a loan from a regional bank working with the Trade Council to build the infrastructure necessary to produce its goods in greater quantity and enter in the post-modern global markets. The enablement of global economic opportunity would come from the junction of two separate, eminently post-modern, incentives-driven programs under the aegis of the Trade Council.

The social contract would also extend to solving the problem of the vulnerable middle classes. The social contract, in this context, would provide incentives to companies in return for action that fosters the economic opportunities for the vulnerable middle classes. Take, for example, the workers of Shenzhen. These individuals exemplify the Chinese economic miracle. Hundreds of thousands of jobs are being created by foreign enterprises flocking to the city to establish manufacturing operations. Local companies are being acquired by foreign investors, buying stakes abroad, or servicing the myriad concerns that seek to install their manufacturing operations in Shenzhen. At the end of the day, the city stands as a shining example of the successful integration of a powerful nation into the post-modern global markets, and of a seemingly bright future for an entire new section of the global middle class.

However, the Chinese boom may be as fragile as the shifting sands of economic opportunity in the post-modern age. In a state like Somalia or

Egypt, the establishment of a free trade zone, with incentives to move, would significantly disrupt the operations of a city like Shenzhen. When industries such as electronics or textiles moved from the United States or Europe to Shenzhen, the American and European economies had reached the modern age that resulted in the creation of a wide array of substitute industries, including a solid services sector and a highly competitive high technology industry. Even with these fallbacks, the shift of industry from, say, West Virginia or Michigan to China, has caused serious social problems and protests in a country like the United States.

In China, unlike the United States, the economy has jumped straight into the post-modern age. While the internal Chinese market is obviously growing at a tremendous pace and will in all events provide alternative demands in the event of a massive withdrawal of foreign manufacturing concerns, China does not have an economic basis born of the modern nation-state era of the same type as the United States. This is by no means an exclusively Chinese problem. In the *maquiladoras* of Mexico, the problem is the same, on an even grander scale. Automobile, electronics, and other industries that moved to the other side of the border could shift just as rapidly to, say, the Far East or further south in the Americas, and leave behind an economic vacuum that will engulf millions of workers. Compared to the protests coming from West Virginia, the economic catastrophe that would arise out of the loss of Shenzhen or a *maquiladora* will reach enormous proportions. The workers and factories that lose their edge will have virtually no new economic opportunity and vast, strategically important regions that have just seen their expectations rise will experience a hopeless spiral into pre-modern poverty.

The problem lies in the fragility and vulnerability of these markets and, as we have explained, twentieth-century welfare policies will not solve it. The social contract that would apply to the vulnerable middle classes of China or Mexico would incentivize enterprises to take steps to firm up and grow economic opportunities for those individuals. One category of measures could involve a commitment to continue to do business with the vulnerable middle classes for a fixed period of time. American companies who take on long-term supply contracts with Shenzhen factories, for example, would receive incentive benefits in return for their commitments. Another important area of intervention would involve the establishment of alternate enterprises to shore up the economy and opportunities in the region at issue. The middle classes of Shenzen, Tunisia, or the *maquiladoras* all face deep uncertainty associated with the diffuseness of the post-modern world. The *economic* insecurity that they experience arises out of the revolutionized communications in the post-modern era, and the rapidity with which global economic factors can shift the locus of

their activities. Newly acquired gains and market footholds could be lost
to new competition from the large pockets of pre-modern classes that the
post-modern world will seek to integrate.

The introduction of alternative sectors of economic activity to these
vast classes of individual players should be an essential goal of the new
global trade order, and a focus of the Trade Council's activities. Here again,
a post-modern system of incentives, rather than regulation, would be put
in place through an alliance of shifting members, depending on the location and nature of the measure. In the case of the *maquiladoras*, for example, the principal actors are the United States and Mexico. In the case of
China, European, Asian, and American interests are involved. A project in
Pakistan, or in Somalia, would attract permanent members of the Trade
Council as well as varied regional interests.

In all scenarios, companies from the member states would be given
incentives to enter into transactions that foster new sectors of activity in
a strategically selected location. Large multinational concerns would face
economic conditions in which it makes sense for them to engage in activities that create more economic opportunity for the middle classes of the
areas in which they invest. If General Motors manufactures component
parts in Mexico, its factoring subsidiary may establish an outsourced loan
processing unit in the *maquiladora*. Even if the component part business
dwindles when GM moves its manufacturing operations to Guatemala as
a result of the signature of a broader free trade agreement, the outsourced
factoring center would continue to provide economic opportunity for the
maquiladoras.

The social contract and incentives package would also apply to the
vulnerable middle classes of Europe or the United States. The outflow
of manufacturing jobs to the emerging actors of the post-modern world,
and the difficulty inherent in competing with companies that can avail
themselves of global manufacturing and distribution markets, has made
it very difficult for significant sectors of the previously flourishing middle classes from having access to economic opportunity. Together with
domestic states, the Trade Council would work on programs intended
to extend economic opportunity back to those middle classes. The work
necessary would also involve coordination among private interests and
domestic states, but it would be of a different nature than that described
above with respect to the vulnerable middle classes of the emerging
economies.

By way of example, let us return to the French garment industry.
For the enterprise that lost its market share because larger competitors
shifted production to China, a number of economic opportunities might
be extended. It is not enough to rely, as the GATT does, on a domestic
state's ability to provide retraining programs for workers who will convert

to new sectors of activity, or to extend welfare benefits to those workers who cannot transition to new careers. Those programs can be very beneficial, but they are insufficient to engender economic opportunity. With respect to these middle classes, the Trade Council would create programs that would give them preferred access to markets in the emerging economies as well as subsidized access to manufacturing facilities located in those countries. China and France, for example, could work with the Trade Council to ensure that a large French retailer such as Carrefour has access to the Chinese market. In turn, a specified number of sinking French enterprises would be granted access to Chinese factories, and their goods would be granted preferred access to the Carrefour outlets of Shanghai or Beijing.

These enterprises would not, by themselves, have the resources to ship manufacturing to China. However, a combination of subsidies, government-managed pooling of resources with other similarly situated companies, and contracts with retailers procured with the assistance of government forces would ensure that the enterprises are brought back within the fold of the post-modern global market. This would be a win-win situation for all involved. China would get more manufacturing business. France would shore up its traditional small and medium-sized enterprises. Carrefour would gain a much-desired foothold in Chinese retail markets. Chinese consumers would gain access to French goods that they would otherwise not see in local markets. Lastly, of course, the French companies that would otherwise be collateral damage of the post-modern age would gain a new lease on life.

At bottom, we propose that the Trade Council act globally with respect to the issues that we have identified in the same manner as the Ministry of Industry and Trade traditionally acted with respect to the Japanese economy. The post-modern scenario that we envisage is one of enablement of global economic opportunity, to be achieved in fits and starts like every other goal of international trade law, through a shifting partnership of international associations acting under the aegis of an efficient, flexible, and selective association of states. As we discuss in the next chapter, this structure not only ensures that trade will shift its emphasis to foster the post-modern principles of international economic law and institutions, but it will take care of virtually all questions of legitimacy, democratic participation, and transparency.

THE TRADE COUNCIL, INFRASTRUCTURES, AND GLOBAL THREATS

The next area of activities for the Trade Council relates to the establishment of infrastructures for the pre-modern pockets of the post-modern world, and of collaboration with other post-modern organizations, to address the externalities generated by the passage from the modern to post-modern age. Let us start with the second category of work, which will also be relevant to our discussion of infrastructures. As discussed previously, the globalization of economic activities has resulted in a large number of externalities, which no single state has the capacity to regulate and which no international organization focused on a specific subject-matter areas can properly address. Environmental protection and resource conservation are classic examples of this phenomenon. As is well-known, the explosion of economic activities in the post-modern age has created thorny questions of environmental protection. The externalities created by globalized and intensified industrial activities span several discrete subject matter areas, awareness of which reaches around the globe. Global warming, acid rain, destruction of rain forests, multiplication of the number of endangered species, are all examples of the type of environmental dangers that were born out of the modern era and have become post-modern mainstays.

The modern age relied on domestic Statecraft and its panoply of welfare policy tools to take care of these problems. Regulating industry's impact on the environment was a central function of the welfare nation-state. Examples of such regulation abound. The United States Clean Air Act, the European directives on the impact of packaging and waste on the environment or on the disposal of toxic waste, or the Japanese Basic Environmental Law, all illustrate the modern State's attempt to provide environmental protection for its citizens. In the post-modern world, however, these regulations will not suffice to address the issues at hand. Reducing global warming and deforestation, for example, will not be achieved without international intervention and a package of incentives.[60] The issues are too vast and require too much coordination among global players to be addressed unilaterally. More fundamentally, the interests of the relevant players are diametrically opposed.

For countries such as Brazil or Indonesia, a certain level of environmental sacrifice is viewed as necessary for growth. If the Indonesian shrimping industry destroys sea turtles in order to achieve economic growth, the people of Indonesia might be better off in the short run. If the Amazon forest is slowly destroyed to support the booming Brazilian miracle, the Brazilians might very reasonably conclude that their higher standard of living is worth the environmental damage they have wrought. For American or European interests, however, this is a double loss. First, companies from these countries will face competition that they might view as unfair because it proceeds from a regulatory comparative advantage. Second, the citizens of these countries will feel the impact of environmental damage that does virtually nothing to shore up their own economy.

History has shown dialogue among such competing interests will not yield agreement. Western interests will continue to push for stricter environmental protection, pointing to the long-term disasters as a compelling reason for consensual regulation. The emerging economies will respond with cries of hypocrisy, correctly pointing out that the pre-modern age featured wholesale environmental destruction by Western economic interests.[61] The West drew its pre-modern strength from practices that it condemns today, the argument goes, and it cannot be heard to keep down emerging economies in the name of principles that it undermined when its own economic interests were at stake.

The impossibility of this dialogue is the main reason why environmental organizations do not achieve concrete progress on the international plane. The Trade Council would replace this dialogue of the deaf with a system of incentives linked to the programs that we describe earlier in this chapter. States that agree to comply with defined environmental objectives could be given preferential treatment in the web of incentives given to Western companies to do business abroad. For example, if Indonesia adopted a sea turtle protection system that complies with the Western standards, a more substantial package of incentives could be given by a coalition of Western states to induce their companies to manufacture in Indonesia. The same structure could be used to induce Brazil to cease destroying the Amazon forest.

The incentives-based approach to tackling these global problems would go hand-in-hand with international efforts to build infrastructure necessary to assist the pre-modern regions of the post-modern age to compete more meaningfully in global markets. The New Marshall Plan that we advocate would include, in addition to the financial instruments system described earlier, investment in the infrastructure of strategically designated states. In turn, these states would be asked to comply with internationally defined goals in order to avail themselves of the economic packages. The Trade Council would coordinate among the Western states, which would pool resources to fund the projects, the host states, and regional organizations such as the Organization of African States.

The objectives would include environmental responsibility, as well as compliance with other efforts to mitigate the externalities of the modern era. In addition, the objectives would include the correction of the structural distortion that arose from the modern age, and in particular from the colonizing enterprise. As a condition to acceding to the New Marshall Plan, states would be asked to relax the formal boundaries inherited from the colonial age. For instance, trade among neighboring tribal groupings that were separated by an artificial border could be fostered through the creation of special cross-border trading zones. If Nigeria and its neighbors are to receive aid, they would be asked to agree to these trading zones, so as to ensure that the infrastructure thereby created actually expands economic opportunity, rather than being another failed attempt to be explained by a poor institutional structure.

Building new and updating existing infrastructure will inevitably cause more capital to flow into these regions. However, challenges to this progress must not be overlooked. One of the most threatening of such challenges is likely to be the longstanding tradition of government corruption. In the next section, we analyze different sources of the problem, highlighting regions and industries most susceptible to fraud, and discuss how a post-modern solution to the corruption issue could be achieved. The how and why of this problem is studied so as to ensure that the progress of structural enhancement and foreign investment is not compromised in the future.

CORRUPTION

According to the World Bank, corruption is defined as "the abuse of public office for private gains." When a government office is abused, public interests are compromised, and economic goals travel further out of reach.[62] Yet multiple forms of corruption exist in all countries today. In a 2006 report, Bill Rodgers cited several incidents of corruption around the globe. In Peru, one-time intelligence chief Vladimiro Montesinos was caught bribing a congressman in 2000. The scandal resulted in termination of the 10 year rule of the autocratic President Alberto Fujimori. In the U.S., Congressman Randy "Duke" Cunningham was found accepting more than two million dollars in bribes. He was forced to resign and sentenced to jail. According to Rodgers, "[o]il rich countries such as Venezuela and Nigeria are especially susceptible to corruption" in large part because of the concentration of highly valuable resources in the hands of a central elite or ruling figure.[63]

Yet, although corruption exists in many countries, Irene Hors cited a study by the OECD Development Centre and the UN Development Programme, which examined Benin, Bolivia, Morocco, Pakistan, and the Philippines, and found corruption to be closely correlated to the nature of the government involved.[64] Hors explored the link between political and economic power. Patrimonialism in Morocco is a government form that ensures that political power equates to economic privilege. Next, Hors found a more indirect connection between political and economic power, as in the Philippines, where political power, such as a dominant position in a patronage-based system, can be bought and sold.[65]

However, the poorest nations around the world are known to endure the most adverse effects of corruption. In many of these underdeveloped societies, people have come to consider corruption as an integral part of culture. Hors stated that "underdevelopment is conducive to corruption." She reasoned that low wages paid to the civil service encourages petty corruption. Further, the disproportion between the supply and demand for public services gives rise to opportunities for corruption. And because most individuals invest in careers in the public sector because of the lack of jobs in the private sector, people are more likely to become involved in corrupt practices. Hors finally explained that insufficient education in underdeveloped countries maintains citizens ignorant of their rights, impeding them from political input.[66]

A Harvard study by Shang-Jin Wei concluded that countries with a high incidence of corruption have proportionally lower economic performance, and also that corruption ultimately has adverse effects on economic development.[67] Firstly, the paper offered an example of how bureaucratic corruption and extortion can ruin small business by under-the-table dealings and refusal to pay bills. This bureaucratic corruption harmed domestic investment. Offering a quantitative example, Wei demonstrated that if a poor and corrupt country like the Philippines could decrease its corruption levels to those of Singapore's, the domestic investment/GDP would rise by 6.6 percentage points. Next, after researching direct investment from 14 major source countries to 41 source countries, Wei proved that host-country corruption discouraged foreign investment. And quantitatively, if India could decrease its corruption to Singaporean levels, the positive effect on foreign investment would be equivalent to reducing its marginal corporate tax rate by 22 percentage points. Wei added that considering China's size and proximity to major source countries, China, as a host country, is an underachiever, and corruption in the country is very much to blame. Wei next suggested that the economic growth rate is harmed by corruption. He said that if Bangladesh could reduce its corruption to Singapore's levels, GDP growth rate would be higher, which in turn would lead to a 50 percent increase in per capita income. With respect to size and composition of government expenditure, several important effects were found. First, corruption increases public investment at the expense of private investment. Second, corruption steers public expenditure away from necessary public operations and maintenance. Third, essential health and education funds are denied public expenditure. Fourth, productivity of public investment in a country's infrastructure is reduced. Finally, tax revenue may be reduced because corruption undermines the government's ability to collect taxes. Thus, corruption has negative effects on nearly every element of a country's sustainability. The net effect is an increase in poverty.

Effective combating of graft and corruption will require collaboration between the Trade Council and other institutions. These ailments of the post-modern age are also an inheritance from the modern era. In states where power is the only way to acquire wealth, corruption is viewed as a legitimate entitlement of the power struggle. In order to enable global economic opportunity, however, corruption must be fought, and fought vigorously. In this respect, the Trade Council will collaborate with the International Criminal Court, in devising special statutes that would apply to given investments and projects. Violators would be prosecuted internationally, and the continued implementation of any project would be made conditional on compliance with the achievement of corruption objectives.

Finally, then, the Trade Council would preside over a networked web of organizations capable of tackling the diffuse nature of post-modern problems. In Chapter 7, we continue to explore the contours of the enablement of global economic opportunity. However, just like Schuman had a vision but could not imagine the precise hurdles and obstacles that would lead to its implementation, the founders of the Trade Council will have to start by shifting the trade paradigm and moving it in a new direction, all the while adjusting their program in response to the salient problems of the day. As a flexible and diffuse post-modern organization, the Trade Council will have the capacity to respond to these questions. Put succinctly, the structure we advocate would create a possibility of dealing with the problems of the day, rather than reflexively perpetuating a system that blindly adheres to the last iteration of Statecraft.

7 The Enablement of Global Economic Opportunity

Thesis:

The trade system requires a new animating norm: the enablement of global economic opportunity. The modern liberal democratic victors of World War II should effect a fundamental shift toward global economic opportunity, replacing a regime of regulation with one driven by incentives.

In Chapter 6, we began to develop the substance of the new animating norm of the international trading system: the enablement of global economic opportunity. Additionally, we began to define the contours of the norm when discussing the institutions that we think should be charged with its implementation. In this chapter, we develop in greater depth our conception of the enablement of global economic opportunity as an animating "constitutional principle."[1] In the first part of the chapter, we start with an evaluation of the norm in light of a construct for judging the legitimacy of international norms. In the second part, we present various scenarios that illustrate how it might be applied by the framers of the international trade system. We conclude with an explanation of why the interests of the principal strategic and economic players of the early post-modern world would be well-served by a reform of the WTO organization that could institutionalize the norm and give it constitutional preeminence comparable to that of comparative advantage.

LEGITIMACY AND REALIZABILITY

The question of the legitimacy of international legal norms has been a preoccupation of academics and commentators alike.[2] Our goal in this book is not to produce a new and overriding theory of the legitimacy of international law. Rather, based on the history of Statecraft and its relationship to the international trading system, we have identified a set of factors by which we believe each iteration of the international trading system should be judged. These indicia of legitimacy are derived from the particular elements of Statecraft in the epoch under scrutiny. We start by articulating these elements from a theoretical standpoint, illustrating our discussion with lessons drawn from the pre-modern and modern eras. We then move on to applying these lessons to post-modern Statecraft.

International legal thinkers have long linked legitimacy not only to its formal acceptance by the representatives of sovereign states, but by the degree to which a given set of international norms is accepted by the individual subjects of those states. Scholars such as Joseph Weiler have analyzed "social legitimacy" and the factors that may be used to determine, *ex ante*, whether a given norm will achieve that sort of acceptance by the individuals whose lives it affects.[3] They have gone beyond the simplistic model that merely replicates the political concerns of modern liberal democracies, and for example calls for reduction of the "democracy deficit" that plagues institutions like those of the European Union and of the GATT by generating greater parliamentary participation.[4] Weiler, for example, points out that each time a set of states integrates into a larger economic area, the transfer of control from the states to a supra-national authority creates legitimacy problems that a supra-national parliament cannot solve in their entirety.[5] This reason is a legitimacy problem that arises out of the possibility of a group of nationalities outvoting another. If France, Greece, England, and Portugal merge into a greater area, and a binding decision is made by a vote of representatives coming from three out of the four states, the citizens of the minority state may perceive legitimacy questions with the decision regardless of who these representatives are. Whether supra-national members of a parliament vote in favor of a measure that binds the minority state, or whether representatives of the executive branches of each country or professional bureaucrats acting on behalf of the supra-national institutions make that decision, the legitimacy question remains: how to justify the imposition on its citizens of a norm that was not accepted by the minority state?

No one has analyzed this question with greater subtlety than Weiler. In a seminal article on the transformation of the European Union, Weiler famously articulated the relationship between "Voice" and "Exit" in international law.[6] He argued that classic international legal systems leave their contracting states with the opportunity to escape the rules of the system on a selective basis. This selective exit framework stems largely from the structural inability of the other contracting states to enforce all rules on a consistent basis. For example, domestic law in Western liberal democracies is enforced by a system of courts, agencies and law enforcement that the public has accepted as an integral part of the legal and social fabric. United States citizens accept that the Federal courts may order a sitting president to turn over confidential papers or be tried for sexual harassment, whether or not they agree with the substance of the decision, because they accept the Supreme Court and the other national courts as the ultimate arbiters of the law of their system. In the modern world of international law that Weiler examined, there is no strong system of enforcement. Diplomatic pressure, international courts or panels that act with the consent of the states, and military force, are the typical "enforcers" of the modern world.[7]

To illustrate this principle, consider the wide array of international conventions spanning subject matter as varied as torture, rights to sea bed mining, labor, or environmentally harmful emissions.[8] The modern world saw a flurry of legislative activity, reminiscent of the work of a modern liberal democratic parliament which ultimately gave birth to a large body of international norms. In all cases, however, enforcement of the norms was left purposefully weak. If a state that joined a convention forbidding automobile emissions exceeding a specified level, other states usually had very little recourse to enjoin a violation and, in point of fact, did not wish to acquire more enforcement means. In the best of cases, the treaty would include an international court or panel charged with enforcing the norms only on a state-to-state level. However, in a typical case, the court would acquire jurisdiction only with the consent of the parties involved: its decisions would not have directly binding effect in the domestic jurisdiction. Finally, there would be little, if any, retribution for a failure to obey. In addition, states participating in the framework would not have the resources to pursue all violations and, by necessity, would target only the most egregious breaches of the international norm for prosecution. To compound the weakness of international law, the very states that suffered prejudice from a breach of international law would, at the same time, be violating the international legal rules themselves. This would act as a self-deterrent against complaining about less than egregious offenses – states knew full well that the very reflex of tolerance for violations that protected their neighbors would no longer be applied to them if they deviated from the overall framework of selective exit.[9]

This system obtained in the international frameworks for which international tribunals and panels were provided. In many a treaty or convention, however, the system did not even contemplate an arbiter of disputes or enforcer of violations. International law was left to the inter-state realm of adjudication. These relational patterns brought about the selective application of international law at a level that the participating states could tolerate. In other words, the treaty would become a general framework for an ongoing discussion of the level of compliance with its norms, based on the extent to which the states could accept the international rule at the time. As Weiler pointed out, this overall weakness of international law actually encouraged states to agree to internationally binding norms without insisting on a framework that made their application dependent in all cases on the continued good will of the domestic authorities and citizens.[10] If the framework could be selectively exited, the participants could safely agree to join, with the knowledge that they had enough legal wiggle room to reject the international norms at a later time, based on the domestic considerations of the time.

As we have explained, the GATT, at least until the 1994 Marrakesh Agreement, fit the profile of a classic international organization. The tariff-reducing enterprise of the modern international trade system would not proceed without the consent of the contracting states. The seminal norm, liberalized trade based on the legal implementation of comparative advantage, accorded with the modern liberal democratic ethos of Statecraft. Each round of negotiations, with its focus on a particular set of products, would involve a dialogue among states aimed at establishing their tolerable level of compliance with that norm. The removal of non-tariff barriers to trade was, at least as a theoretical construct, driven by a desire to "tariffy" all regulatory barriers to the free movement of goods for the sake of transparency,[11] which would in turn make it feasible to negotiate consensual tariff reductions, and to create an efficient system of trade that would not require any change to the domestic regulatory choices of the modern nation-states. The dispute resolution system, with its emphasis on panels that had no binding authority unless the losing party accepted their jurisdiction and decision, confirmed the classic nature of the GATT in the Weiler construct of international law.[12]

The European Union, on the other hand, did not fit the classic model and, in the work of its Court of Justice, created a new constitutional order. Its Court of Justice worked in conjunction with national courts to render binding decisions. Individuals were given access to those courts – bypassing the traditional inhibitions against state enforcement of international norms – to act as "private attorneys general" and give full effect to international law. The European Court of Justice adopted an aggressive constitutional agenda, giving direct effect and supremacy to European law without explicit textual support from the organic treaty. On top of the new legal/constitutional order, the Court gave expansive treatment to the economic constitution of Europe, and went on to strike down regulatory measures that hindered the free movement of goods, services, and other factors of production without a strong countervailing domestic justification. On the legislative side, Europe was initially scheduled to move from unanimous to majority voting.[13] Under this system, as Weiler noted, European states would have the capacity to adopt norms that bind other participants in the cross border system, without the consent of any elected representatives of those states. In Weiler's construct, it was the combination of the majority voting transition and the unexpectedly strong weight given to European law by the Court that brought about the Luxembourg Crisis that almost toppled Europe in the mid-1960s, and that was resolved only when the Luxembourg Accords *de facto* revised the original treaty provisions to give each state a right of veto over legislation that conflicted with its essential national interests. The European Court had unsettled the balance between Voice and Exit by essentially removing Exit, and the Member States saved the European Union by insisting on the strongest possible Voice in making law. Thirty years later, after the European legislative institutions matured and the public accepted the reach and limits of Europe, the Single European Act shifted Europe to majority voting without any meaningful public outcry. Voice and Exit were also balanced in the new era.[14]

We posit that the legitimacy of international law has to be drawn from the hallmarks of Statecraft in a particular era. The tensions that Weiler identified, and the construct that he developed to explain them, arose because the conflict occurred in the modern era. Sovereignty and the ability to control domestic welfare policies were essential to the ethos of modern Statecraft. Had he been president of a post-modern state, Charles De Gaulle would in all likelihood not have reacted the way he did in the Luxembourg Crisis. The threat to national sovereignty that arose from the supranational imposition of a binding norm drew its significance from modern Statecraft. Like comparative advantage, the analysis of Voice and Exit as it relates to the application of supranational norms to a domestic jurisdiction is a function of the time and place in which it is applied. In 1950s and 1960s Europe, at the heart of the modern era, nation-states were experiencing the peak of their national identity. They could not tolerate the intrusion in their internal affairs of other nation-states, especially those that they just fought in World War II. Yet, the modern world was following a modern liberal democratic model committed to a universal rule of law and the international order of states was adopting a stream of legislative pronouncements that, under that theoretical model, should apply to all nations.

Weiler's Voice/Exit equilibrium is, then, an axiom that balances the need for international rules of law ostensibly applicable to all in a neutral fashion, with the nation-states' need to maintain in its discretion the type of modern sovereignty that formed the essence of modern Statecraft. By allowing for selective exit, or requiring an absolute veto right over new legislation, the nation-states of the modern era managed to achieve this balance.

BEYOND LEGITIMACY: POST-MODERN STATECRAFT

The European Union and its tensions arose not only because of sovereignty concerns specific to the modern era, but because the European treaty framework represented an early graduation into the post-modern era which, as we will discuss, foreshadowed the global graduation from modern to post-modern. In the modern era, the domestic state was the principal ontological unit of analysis. Under the GATT, domestic states were charged with the redistribution of increased benefits arising from the institutionalization of comparative advantage. Most international treaties extended obligations on states, the very entities that had selective exit capacity. In the modern system, then, the domestic state had the sole and exclusive power to regulate, subject only to norms of international law that could be avoided when domestic regulation required.

The European Union's enterprise, however, required that states engaged in integration agree on a continuous basis to legislation that applies to the entire territory. Weiler correctly pointed out that, whenever states integrate into a larger area, they face the issues associated with the possible imposition of a norm that will be imposed on all constituent states by the majority. This issue replicates the political concerns for minority rights in modern liberal democracies. Weiler and other commentators have also observed that demanding more parliamentary democracy is somewhat beside the point. As pointed out earlier, whether decision-makers are parliamentarians or, as in Europe, representatives of the executive branches of the member states, the problem of imposing a norm selected by the majority on the whole remains the same. (The conventional answer to the democracy deficit question, which focuses on the extension of parliamentary democracy, is akin to stating that African Americans' rights would be protected in the absence of a judicially enforced constitutional right to equal protection simply by requiring that they achieve more minority representation in the legislature charged with making the rules that apply to them.) More adequate solutions, such as the "subsidiarity principle" that was later introduced in Europe, focus on the removal from the supranational jurisdiction of the power to act with respect to certain issues that belong exclusively to the domestic realm.[15] (This is akin to saying, in the case of a minority, that a legislature may not encroach on certain constitutionally protected rights.)

This is a post-modern problem because, unlike the GATT and comparative advantage, the European Union enterprise required the establishment of a government charged with adopting and implementing rules of law that no individual state could put in place by itself. As we explained, modern Statecraft tolerated very little intrusion into domestic regulation, and the GATT's system of comparative advantage was designed to delegate to the domestic states the power to regulate and control the market. In effect, however, the European Union experienced an accelerated version of the globalized diffuseness phenomenon that we have described in Chapter 5. The European Union created a single market, and dramatically opened up trade and movement to all member states. In other words, the European Union achieved post-modern status much faster than the rest of the world. "Fortress Europe" adhered in the modern age to a modern outlook vis-a-vis the outside world, but within its borders it was a resolutely post-modern entity.

This created a need for affirmative legislation of the type that we argue is required in today's post-modern world. Monetary policies needed to be coordinated and, ultimately, were unified into a single currency, the Euro. Social conditions needed to be harmonized so that a somewhat unitary entity could be created; budgets, deficits, and other economic tools were harmonized. The post-modern European Union would not survive if, say, Portugal or other largely pre-modern Southern European countries did not establish a modern market substantially equivalent to the modern markets of France or Germany, such that a coherent modern whole could be merged into a post-modern entity. Immigration rules were required to accommodate the cross-border flow of people that come with post-modern Statecraft.[16] Antitrust, environmental, intellectual property, and commercial codes required harmonization. All of these subject matter areas required the adoption of a new form of government – eminently post-modern in nature – in that it had to supplant the modern nation-state and adopt legislation for the entire integrated area, regardless of the discrete nationhood basis of each constituent entity.

The European enterprise, then, required more than sensitivity to sovereign, nation-based Statecraft, and strong Voice to counterbalance the elimination of Exit. Our construct further explains the crises and transformative patterns of Europe. The European Union entered the post-modern age and faced the question that the global markets must address today, at the peak of the era of modern Statecraft. The apparent inconsistency that came to be encapsulated in the term "Fortress Europe" is best explained through this lens. Fortress Europe was, on the inside, a decidedly post-modern entity. To the outside world, however, it reverted to its natural modern Statecraft reflex: a sovereign fortress, bent on protecting its regulatory power to provide for the welfare of its nation. The remarkable and unique nature of Europe, in other words, is that it went through a post-modern transformation in the midst of the modern age. This is the root of the European *malaise* and of the crises experienced by the Union. Its markets became interloped, its enterprises and people traversed borders, the discreteness of its national economies became blurred, and it experienced a myriad of other post-modern symptoms, all in an epoch when the norm called for a modern constitutional structure centered around the nation, its sovereignty, its welfare and its ability to co-exist with others in a world guided in large part by balance of power.

It was not until 1992, and the dawn of the post-modern age, that the Luxembourg Accords, and the attendant veto right of each member state, were eliminated. At that time, Europe was ready to be the first true post-modern success. The citizenship of the continent had reached a fluid, diffuse state, freely moving from one entity to the next. Legislation was passed by groups of lawmakers that, although formally affiliated to individual member states, did not form the type of oppressive, nationality-based groupings that De Gaulle feared when he provoked the Luxembourg Crisis. The European markets became truly unified, featuring a single currency, the erosion of regulatory disparities that hindered commerce, highly interloped ownership of companies and factors of production, and removal of borders. The post-modern enterprise, which took root in the modern age, suddenly exploded into a full blown post-modern, market polity. Weiler, then, was right that the Luxembourg compromise saved Europe; the (humble) addition that we make is that the salvation came because the compromise allowed the European powers to bide their time for 30 years, until the post-modern epoch would make it possible for them to establish a true post-modern polity, with post-modern institutions capable of filling the governance vacuum engendered by the graduation to post-modernism.

GLOBAL ECONOMIC OPPORTUNITY IN EUROPE

We learn from the European experience that the enablement of global economic opportunity is an eminently post-modern enterprise. A substantial part of the European legislative enterprise can be viewed as enabling economic opportunity in Europe. The new legislation was made necessary by the sudden integration of European markets, in relation to free movement of goods, services, capital, and people. Over a period of 50 years, the GATT reduced the average tariff on goods and services from more than

50 percent to around 5 percent.[17] In Europe, the elimination of the tariffs occurred virtually overnight. In addition, the European Court took an aggressively early stance on what constituted non-tariff barriers to trade.[18] Until it was reversed in 1990, the Court's jurisprudence required that regulatory measures hindering trade, ranging from labeling laws to pornography standards, be justified by and narrowly tailored to further a sufficiently significant state interest. Where alternative, less trade-burdensome methods of regulating the relevant issue were reasonably available (such as labeling to disclose changes in product content) the Court invalidated the legislation at issue.[19]

Europe's harmonization process is in part a natural response to the vigorous economic constitutional jurisprudence of the Court, which is designed to further the principle of enablement of economic opportunity. When the Court ruled, for example, that Dutch pesticides law could not be applied to ban the marketing of apples or other produce coming from member states that adopted a less stringent set of regulatory norms, it enabled producers from member states, where the pesticides level was lower than in the Netherlands, to compete in the Dutch markets. The consequences of the Court's decision, however, were not limited to the easing of companies' ability to enter the newly opened markets. In the context of the European Union, it also prompted the lawmaking institutions of the Union to establish common rules applicable to all undertakings doing business in the Union. The unique circumstances of the European Union, as a supranational post-modern entity, created an incentive for the member states to harmonize. The regulation at issue affected the social fabric of the welfare apparatus of the nation. The member states shared a common, modern drive to legitimize the State by enabling the welfare of the nation. It followed that the modern constitutional structure of the member states joined with the post-modern need for regulation to generate supranational norms that furthered the post-modern animating principle of the enablement of economic opportunity.

In addition to harmonization, the member states adopted a broad basket of rules and regulations that emphasize economic opportunity. The member states took drastic steps to coordinate their financial and economic regulations. They ultimately adopted a Euro zone that spans the European continent. They created a central registration system for trademarks and patents.[20] They adopted a merger regulation that gave the European regulators oversight over the large mergers and acquisitions that the pan-Europeanization of business was sure to bring about. They controlled member states' ability to enforce intellectual property rights that unduly burdened intra-European trade.[21] They established a

European central bank.[22] They adopted environmental, privacy, labor, immigration, and many other rules that leveled the playing field for economic actors. They instituted mechanisms of mutual recognition of contributions to retirement or other social protection funds. This web of cross-border regulation made it possible for post-modern economic conditions, including interloping ownership of enterprises, movement of people across borders, rapid and widespread movement of goods, services, and capital, to arise.

This regulatory drive was the direct result of the post-modernization of Europe. The centers of regulation – Paris, London, Berlin, and the other member states' capitals – lost the ability to address the economic and social issues of post-modern Europe when they created a single market. Harmonization, the creation of European rules and institutions to facilitate and regulate intellectual property usage, concentration of business as a result of mergers and acquisitions, the coordination of fundamental economic policies, and a myriad of other regulations that came out of the European Union, came to meet the post-modern need to fill a regulatory vacuum that inevitably accompanies the liberalization of trade and the establishment of pan-national markets.

At the same time, Europe addressed the issues that arose with the post-modern integration of markets in a modern age, and the protection of welfare as the legitimating principle of the nation-states that merged into Europe. First, the welfare drive of each European state now had to be coordinated with the other member states of the Union. As we explained above, the web of harmonizing regulations included measures that profoundly affected the individual member states' ability to provide welfare to their nations. European legislation was needed to ensure that an appropriate common regulatory threshold would be established to address these issues. Next, national welfare measures needed to be sheltered from displacement by European norms. By way of example, national subsidies of key sectors like the farming and agricultural sector needed to be sheltered against the European drive to ensure free market competition, purified of artificial production support by government.[23]

In this instance, the European institutions chose to substitute a pan-European system that would accomplish a substantially equivalent result. They devoted an enormous amount of resources to accomplishing this goal. The European subsidies, funded by member state contributions, essentially replaced the national web of support to farmers and other agricultural workers. The modern age created a special place for certain industries and economic sectors, in particular farming, textiles, coal, steel, and other industries that had driven the pre-modern epoch into the modern age. The provision of welfare to these sectors was an essential goal of the European drive to preserve modern Statecraft while entering the post-modern era, and the intricate system of European subsidies was put into place to establish this post-modern super-structure in support of a modern objective.

In other instances, the European Union accommodated modern needs by using the same type of regulatory devices as the GATT. In the area of taxation, for example, the European treaties and institutions put into place a framework that protected national rights to implement welfare policies through tax laws. The European treaties prohibited discriminatory taxation, just as the GATT outlawed this form of regulatory protectionism. French wine, for example, could not benefit from better tax treatment than British beer so that the French wine industry would continue to enjoy special status.[24] However, to the extent that the member states did not engage in protectionist tactics, they had the absolute right to use tax policy in any way they saw fit. This essential element of the welfare system that we described earlier was sheltered from interference by the European polity, so as to accommodate the modern Statecraft needs of the individual components of the post-modern European entity.

The travails that Europe endured to accomplish this legislative task provide insight into the kind of issues that would face any institution charged with promulgating legislation to engender global economic opportunity in the post-modern age. Additionally, it gives us a context for presenting our analysis of the legitimacy of the norm that we are advocating. Through 40 years of trial and error, Europe went a long way toward resolving for itself the question of how to legislate for a supranational entity that integrates constituent nation-states. The rules-based, Kantian entity that Europe created stumbled and almost failed when it encountered the Kantian dilemma of how to achieve collective agreement through rules all the while avoiding the tyranny of a massive, global government. The reasons for Europe's success are, here again, linked to the modern status of the constituent states that merged into a post-modern entity, and to the post-modern nature of the enterprise.[25]

When Europe created its institutions, it sought at first to replicate the modern nation-state model of a central government imposing top-down rules on the entire entity. As we explained above, this model encountered serious difficulties. We have argued that the difficulties occurred because the modern constituent states of Europe could not, at the time, accept relinquishment of their national sovereign power to regulate welfare. By the time the Single European Act of 1992 and subsequent foundational legislation (such as the common currency) came about, however, several phenomena joined to create the conditions for post-modern legislation. The post-modern age had arrived full-fledged. The erosion of the welfare form of Statecraft that we discussed in Chapter 2 had engendered a more pressing need to create post-modern legislation designed to enable European economic opportunity. Europe had already *de facto* created a set of institutions able to legislate consistently and comprehensively with increased acceptance (and correlated social legitimacy) from the "European street." Through a complex set of interactions, these institutions demonstrated sensitivity to the modern need to preserve welfare, all the while managing to produce legislation to fill the regularity vacuum created by the post-modernization of Europe.

In other words, through a regulatory and integration enterprise that was made necessary by the post-modernization of Europe, the European Union managed to create a larger, nation-state like entity. The trouble that it encountered was based on the member states' reluctance to give up control over their welfare policies, but the Luxembourg Accords, and the complex patterns of interaction that the European and national institutions experienced, made it possible for the member states to maintain sufficient control over their regulatory borders until the post-modern age changed the rules of the game and made it more palatable for the European nations to relinquish the kind of sovereign control that was associated with the modern era Statecraft. Thus, by the time the post-modern age arrived, Europe had already experienced the trial-and-error process and wrestled with the democracy and transparency concerns that come with the legal implementation of the enablement of economic opportunity.

Most significantly, aside from protecting the welfare policies during the modern age, the European reflex for managing post-modern regulation was to select a limited set of regulatory issues – all linked to the enablement of economic opportunity – to be dealt with by the European polity. This system allowed Europe to reduce the pressure to find a method of European government that would achieve acceptance and legitimacy in Europe. The principal tool used to achieve this goal was the constitutional requirement of subsidiarity that the Treaty of Maastricht – an eminently post-modern policy instrument – introduced to Europe. Subsidiarity essentially created the first post-modern system of Federalism. It provided that all issues should be left to the sovereign regulation of the modern states or, if possible, more regional governments, except for issues that could only be dealt with by collective, European action. The best way to think about this legal regime is to compare it with the institutionalization of comparative advantage at Bretton Woods.

When the victors of World War II institutionalized comparative advantage into the GATT, in theory they protected the contracting states from intrusion by the supranational system beyond that which the modern drive to liberalize trade would tolerate. The legal tools employed to accomplish this system included, primarily, the structure described in Chapter 4: a consensual reduction in tariffs, coupled with the elimination of non-tariff barriers to trade in a way that did not infringe on the modern sovereign legitimating drive to provide welfare to the nation. Subsidiarity, likewise, made sure that the only limitation on constituent states' sovereign right to regulate occurs in subject matter areas where collective regulation is indispensable. In turn, the subject matter areas that fall within this category are defined by post-modern factors: the need to coordinate economic conditions, the harmonization of legal rules and regulatory frameworks, and the creation of central merger rules are, for example, made necessary by the post-modernization of Europe, which created a diffuse, collective market in need of regulation.

Unlike modern welfare, which required a comprehensive governmental plan to generate the necessary regulation to protect the nation, the enablement of global economic opportunity necessitates that regulation address discrete problems. These problems, in the European context, included principally the harmonization and coordination action that we have described above. By the time the post-modern age of regulation arrived, Europe had created an essentially modern liberal democratic way of accomplishing the regulatory task. This modern structure, superimposed on the post-modern, limited nature of the regulatory task, allowed Europe to achieve a remarkable, and, as we will discuss, unique degree of success. That is to say, the post-modern nature of Europe created a need to implement legislatively the enablement of economic opportunity in a limited set of fields. The modern nature of Europe, in turn, created what we may call a "habit of governance." The institutions established with a view to, initially, creating a regulatory framework that could protect the modern nation-states that comprised the whole, were trained to govern and, in due course, to produce massive post-modern legislation.

The European experience teaches us that the enablement of global economic opportunity, as a norm appropriate for the post-modern world, can be achieved with full formal and social legitimacy. Unlike Europe, the areas of the world to which the enablement of global economic opportunity must be spread span disparate, heterogeneous states. The European states managed to create a modern-like habit of governance, over almost half a century, in large part because they shared a common history, relatively similar institutions, and a strongly held desire to achieve peace through integration.[26] The current difficulties that states like Turkey are facing with respect to admission to the European club underscore this point.[27] For the post-modern enterprise of Europe to achieve such a striking success, the economies and political systems of the constituent states had to start off with fundamental common features.[28]

By contrast, the post-modern world is comprised of a kaleido-scopic mix of modern, pre-modern, and post-modern classes and states, criss-crossing the current boundaries of the world to form a mass that simply cannot be targeted through a world government replicating the institutions of Europe. We learn from Europe that the post-modern insti-tutionalization of the enablement of global economic opportunity is a task that requires problem-solving legislation, focused on discrete issues and problems. This facilitates the task in that, unlike a modern nation-state that must comprehensively regulate to provide for cradle-to-grave welfare, the post-modern enterprise may pick and choose among various potential regulatory projects and make progress based on an established level of priorities, without failing in the accomplishment of its task. We have described at length how these priorities should be established.

We will now explore three examples of post-modern legislation, drawn from real case studies, and explain why their implementation by the Trade Council would engender no legitimacy concerns.

POST-MODERN LEGISLATION: ILLUSTRATIVE CASES

In the modern age, each nation-state utilized and exploited natural resources as it pleased. No supranational rules or laws existed to gov-ern the exploitation of these resources, nor did any specific ownership rights for the resources exist. Recently, an eminently post-modern treaty – the Rio Convention on Biological Diversity – brought about an impor-tant change. The convention recognized and substantiated each coun-try's sovereign right over its own natural resources. However, the treaty created a policy, the essence of which is that if one country extracts resources from another country, any benefits derived as a result of the project must be shared between the parties.[29] This framework created a post-modern, incentives-based framework for creating economic oppor-tunity. It replaced antiquated modern regulation, such as the perfor-mance requirements that we detail in Chapter 5, with a structure that would allow companies to realize profits all the while enabling economic opportunity.

The type of projects that this regulatory framework has the potential to generate can be illustrated by a contract signed by the American pharma-ceutical giant, Merck, with the National Institute of Biodiversity of Costa Rica (INBio), which granted Merck the right to exploit Costa Rica's plant resources.[30] Specifically, INBio agreed to gather and prepare the 10,000 potentially medicinally effective plants that Merck requested. Merck then paid INBio $1.1 million up front to repopulate the specific plant species from the extraction area. Merck also agreed to make payment royalties of about 3 percent to INBio if any drug is manufactured and sold from the Costa Rican plant extractions. Also, Merck continues to pay a premium for the preservation of a section of the rain forest, as they expect to classify and utilize further resources.[31]

Another post-modern framework involves debt-for-nature swaps. Developed in 1984 by the World Wildlife Fund (WWF), a debt-for-nature swap is a mechanism for enhancing conservation efforts in developing and third-world countries, all the while enabling economic opportunity for foreign interests and domestic actors.[32] The concept arose from the observation that most of the world's biodiversity is concentrated in the countries with the greatest financial difficulties and foreign debts. To understand the mechanism of a debt-for-nature swap, it is first necessary to understand that Third World debts are bought and sold in the world market like wheat and oil. Consider a scenario where a bank loans a country a million dollars in exchange for a note promising repayment within a particular time period and at a certain interest rate. The country misses interest payments and asks for a time extension on the loan. Deciding not to run the risk that the country will be unable to repay the loan, the bank may decide to sell the initial loan note for a considerably smaller amount of cash.

The idea underlying debt-for-nature swapping is that conservation organizations can obtain some of the devalued debt and trade it for rain forest protection. An early version of this type of agreement was signed in 1987 by the Government of Bolivia and Conservation International (CI).[33] Under the contract, CI acquired $650,000 of Bolivia's debt for $100,000. In exchange, the Government of Bolivia provided the Beni Biosphere Reserve with maximum legal protection, and also created three more protected areas nearby. The Bolivian Government further agreed to provide $250,000 to local Beni Reserve management activities. As these exchanges serve interests of both indebted countries and conservationists, debt-for-nature swapping has become increasingly popular, especially in the Philippines, Ecuador, and Sudan.[34]

Such an incentives-based framework cuts through the knot of irreconcilable arguments regarding regulatory comparative advantage. We have explained in Chapter 5 that the performance requirements were an unworkable form of regulation that matched the modern theoretical mould, but would not accomplish any tangible result in the post-modern world. The foreign companies' ability to shift production rapidly in the diffuse post-modern world would make it virtually impossible for individual states to impose performance requirements. An incentives-based scheme, on the other hand, would lead to a race to the top of the economic opportunity ladder instead of a race to the bottom of the regulatory well.

In turn, the limited and consensual nature of the projects would eliminate most issues of democracy deficit (except, as discussed below, insofar as it relates to the establishment of priorities). The programs described above would, in the scenarios that we explore in greater depth below, be supplemented by a system of domestic incentives coordinated by the Trade Council. Merck, for example, would be further incentivized by a construct of U.S. regulation aimed at encouraging the company to enter into contracts of the type that it signed with InBio, in areas of the post-modern world that serve U.S. and other Western interests. The domestic framework could include tax breaks or, as we discuss, special intellectual property or regulatory benefits. The limited nature of the project, and its reliance on incentives that promote voluntary compliance by all interested parties, would eliminate the governance concerns that would otherwise arise if a world government, or any regulatory body, attempted to achieve the result by mandatory legislation of the type that prevailed in the modern world.

The post-modern, Trade Council, feature of the Merck example is not so much the decentralized, privately-arrived-at market-based logic that drove it. Rather, its relevance lies in the fact that, given a proper system of incentives, such beneficial projects could be brokered through a post-modern institution like the Trade Council. In other words, the enablement of economic opportunity would focus, as it did in Europe, on the resolution of distinctly post-modern issues, as was the case in Europe. However, unlike Europe, where a habit of governance was developed out of the mixture of modern and post-modern historical circumstances and developments, the enablement of global economic opportunity would proceed on an *ad hoc*, case-by-case basis that does not require the Trade Council to consider thorny questions associated with voting rights, imposition of norms on potentially unwilling participants, and the other matters arising out of the diffuseness of the global market in the post-modern order of states. By promoting incentives that come from the domestic and international realms, and that cut across the traditional horizontal and vertical boundaries that limit the enablement of such projects in a modern paradigm, the Trade Council will create a system where private actors are purposely encouraged, by design rather than market happenstance, to enter into these types of agreement.

This conclusion would also obtain in the case of post-modern frameworks dealing with coordination among states. For example, in 1997, the United States and Turkey entered into a pipeline agreement to accommodate the U.S. need to build pipelines in the Caspian Sea to suit American interests.[35] The U.S. promised to give Turkey $823,000 to help plan Turkey's part of the pipeline. At the time, the Caspian Sea was estimated to hold 100–200 billion barrels of oil reserves. Iran, Russia, and the United States all had great interest in the area, yet all had sufficient domestic and import energy sources. Turkey did not have a source for energy. With the world's seventeenth largest economy and 65 million people to provide with energy, Turkey was really at an all-time high demand for energy.[36] So when the United States offered to participate and contribute to the Baku-Tbilisi-Ceyhan pipeline, its investment could potentially bolster its domestic economy and that of a strategic ally in the region. In the end, the outcome was abundant gain for the American and other Western shareholders with heavy investments in BP, an energy company and the pipeline operator. It bolstered the Turkish economy and a key ally, and it helped resolve an American energy concern.[37] Here again, the Trade Council could consciously foster economic opportunity enhancing projects where, left unattended, the happenstance of market and international politics might not accomplish the desired result.

ENABLEMENT OF GLOBAL ECONOMIC OPPORTUNITY: SCENARIOS FOR GROWTH

In the modern era, the vulnerability of emerging classes was addressed by welfare systems. The Shenzhen phenomenon is not new. It happened throughout nineteenth- and twentieth-century Europe, after the Industrial Revolution. France, for example, shifted from a rural to an industrial society. The process came with the concentration of cities, which served as industrial centers. In the event, the family networks that characterized rural life were broken. In addition, the relative security of rural organizations also disappeared. The inequalities that separated landowners from workers in the rural areas were, of course, oppressive to the peasants. However, the system in place provided for some basic security and an economic system that, barring droughts or other disasters, afforded workers basic sustenance.[38]

Until the rise of the welfare state, workers in industrial cities faced conditions that caused them heightened insecurity. The labor market heavily favored employers. There were few, if any, labor rules to foster job security or workplace conditions. Employers (or "capitalists") had the ability to set wages at a level that would ensure subsistence, but no ability to set aside enough resources to gamble with a job loss. A worker who, say, weaved textiles in a factory or extracted coal from a mine, could be told to work for 18 hours a day. He could be paid a wage that, while sufficient to survive, would not enable him to save enough money to endure job loss or open a small business. Labor unions were not protected by law. Occupational safety was only a byproduct of the employer's interest in keeping the worker able to perform his functions. There was no social safety net to help out of work employees to stay afloat.

These social conditions were the subject of classic novels by the likes of Zola, Dickens, and Sinclair. The utter dependency of the workers on their capitalist employers, the abuse and oppression of entire pre-modern segments of society, and the lack of hope and attendant social instability, accompanied the pre-modern process of solidification. Marx himself wrote against this background. His prediction that the workers of the world would ultimately throw off the yoke of capitalism stemmed from the perceived inability of the vulnerable classes to achieve economic security in the pre-modern system. The zero-sum game involved capitalist interests, pitted against working class interests. The survival of the capitalist class depended on the oppression of the working class. The meaningful survival of the working class could not be achieved, unless the capitalist class was defeated. In this world, religion was the opium of the people, but the practical solution for the working class was to take over ownership of the very means of production that oppressed them.

In came the welfare state. The legitimating drive of the State, to supply welfare to the people, wrestled head on with the marxist view of how to solve the woes of pre-modern society. It addressed the vulnerable elements of the working class, and unleashed the power of the solidified State to fortify the class against oppression and exploitation. The State provided a safety net for workers who lost their jobs or who could not integrate meaningfully into the labor force. In France, this took the form of unemployment benefits, aid to families with children, or housing allowances. In a related regulatory venture, the State required employers to honor the seniority of their employees, and mandated a generous compensation package in the event of termination without good reason. In doing so, the State essentially dismantled the economic system of worker dependency. Even in the absence of new economic opportunities, the individual subjects were entitled to benefits that would give them a minimum standard of living.[39]

This was by no means an exclusively European enterprise. In post-World War II Japan, the welfare state essentially set up a culture of lifetime employment. Instead of protecting the workers by establishing a safety net in the event of job loss, the Japanese state created a system whereby job loss was virtually impossible. The State engaged in indicative planning, so as to provide employers with a firm and secure base from which to operate. The establishment of a strong industrial sector, with the assistance of state organs such as the famed MITI, created the context for extending welfare to the Japanese nation. The workers of the large, state-assisted enterprises, coalesced to form a strong middle class that became the basis of the nation. The State helped employers achieve economic stability and positive performance. At the same time, it used its regulatory apparatus to compel these enterprises to create a culture of lifetime employment that achieved welfare goals functionally equivalent to those of the European modern liberal democracies.[40]

The welfare state of the modern era established minimum working conditions that stripped the capitalist class of its ability to impose a wide array of employment practices on workers that lacked bargaining power. The introduction of the minimum wage and of mandated overtime pay deprived employers of the ability to maintain their workers at bare subsistence levels. Occupational safety rules, mandatory vacation time, the right to bargain collectively, establishment of employment tribunals and other employment rules gave workers a standard of living that, essentially, blunted the force of the marxist critique. Instead of capturing the means of production, the workers were presented with a societal bargain where they would become part of the nation. To that extent, the legitimating drive of the State had a self-preserving quality. In competing with fascism and communism for capture of the mantle of Statecraft, the modern liberal democracies had to provide workers and the rest of the nation with an alternative vision of the State, one that would move beyond the Dickensian deprivations of pre-modern life. The welfare nation-state accomplished this goal.

The establishment of the welfare nation-state resulted in the merger of the pre-modern capitalist classes and working classes which, together, merged into a middle class that became the basis of the nation. The nation declared its allegiance to the State. The State unleashed its welfare power to serve the nation. The pre-modern world graduated to the modern liberal democratic world, and gave to the pre-modern vulnerable classes a social safety net, a standard of living, and a national identity that solidified the modern welfare nation-states into the bloc that eventually bested communism and fascism for control of the State.

Today, the post-modern world includes a uniquely similar pattern of migration of and emergence from the pre-modern world as the Western liberal democracies have not witnessed in more than 100 years. However, as we explained in Chapter 5, the world cannot administer the modern welfare potion to solve the problems of the pre-modern pockets of the post-modern world. China's Shenzhen, India's Mumbai (Bombay), or Mexico's maquiladoras, for example, while shining examples of progress, also find themselves in a similar position as Lille, Manchester, or Milan in the early twentieth century. In the maquiladoras, for example, a largely rural population mass has migrated from Southern Mexico to the border towns, to take advantage of jobs created by the relocation of American industrial enterprises to these towns. In Shenzen, large masses of Chinese farmers have moved to a city that has rapidly become a textiles and garment industrial center. In India's high-tech sector, the situation is somewhat different but the pattern similar. Skilled workers who previously were looking outside of the country to put their skills to use can now find employment in various outsourced industries, and are also flocking toward newly created industrial centers that have the same hallmarks of vulnerability as the industrial centers of the late pre-modern/early-modern world. The welfare solution cannot work because these pre-modern economic zones are graduating to modern status in the midst of an emerging post-modern era, without having undertaken the structural changes that accompanied the passage from pre-modern to post-modern in the European or American liberal democracies. In earlier chapters, we went through a detailed explanation of why the modern solution is now obsolete. In this chapter, we develop and present scenarios that would provide a post-modern solution to the relevant questions.

Let us start with the maquiladoras.[41] These economic zones are children of the trade regime of the modern era. The reduction of tariffs and other barriers to trade between Mexico and the United States gave U.S. companies a strong economic incentive to move their manufacturing operations to the border towns. On January 1, 1994, the North American Free Trade Agreement (NAFTA) between Canada, Mexico, and the United States, came into effect. One of the aims of the treaty was to create more jobs and to increase wages throughout North America, in part to stem the flow of illegal immigration from the South toward the United States. New relaxed rules on foreign investment and export duties made opening large factories by U.S., Japanese, and European companies far easier than in the past. The maquiladoras were established throughout northern Mexico, in cities like Tijuana, Juarez, and Matamoras.

In the maquiladora factories, component parts and products are manufactured or assembled for export to the United States. Workers make anything from leather gloves and toys to televisions and computers. BMW, Honeywell, Chrysler, Fisher Price, Sony, and Xerox are among the many household names that benefit from the availability of low-wage labor and other business-favorable circumstances. The number of maquiladoras has doubled from 2,000 in the mid-1990s to nearly 4,000 several years later, and the number of workers has doubled from 500,000 to over one million.[42] (The chart below illustrates the growth of employment in the maquiladoras.) Low skilled workers earn between $3.50 and $5 a day. These minimal wages provide people with a meager living in these border towns where the cost of living is 30 percent higher than in the rest of the country. Thus, many of the workers are forced to live in shantytowns.

Oftentimes, none of benefits of the maquiladoras – water and electricity – reach the shantytowns, which remain impoverished and disease ridden.[43] These are the very conditions that European and American workers experienced at the onset of the pre-modern age. Yet, as described below, there is no welfare state or other regulatory authority that can address the problem of the vulnerable classes of the maquiladoras.

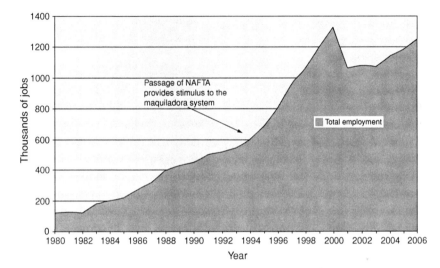

Chart: Maquiladora Employment, 1980–2000[44]

This regulatory vacuum also extends to the kind of monetary and fiscal policies that we described in Chapter 5, and which we explained escape the reach of any single state. In December 1994, for example, the peso was devalued. As a result of the devaluation of the peso, the price of groceries and basic services increased significantly for maquiladora workers. The price of a whole chicken, for example, jumped from 4 pesos to 10 pesos. Yet, the same devaluation factor that hurt the workers helped the maquiladoras. For companies that pay wages in pesos and sell products for dollars, profits grew substantially. However, as described below, there is no regulatory mechanism to provide incentives for the companies that take advantage of the maquiladoras to share their profits with the vulnerable classes that inhabit them.

The story of Honeywell illustrates the workings of the maquiladoras, their current failure, and their possible redemption. Honeywell established a substantial manufacturing presence in the maquiladoras. Honeywell has operations that cover a broad range of industrial products, including aerospace products and services; control technologies for buildings, homes and industry; turbocharging systems, automotive products;

specialty chemicals, fibers; polymers and electronic materials.[45] NAFTA made it possible for Honeywell to move these manufacturing operations to Mexico with little or no downside. The virtual elimination of tariffs in the sectors in which Honeywell operates provided an eminently modern incentive for the company to shift production to the maquiladoras. For Honeywell and like-minded companies, the relocation of manufacturing facilities was based on the very kind of economic analysis that the GATT (and the provisions of NAFTA that replicated the GATT) contemplated and fostered, but which resulted in the vulnerability of the Mexican emerging trading class.

From the Mexican labor pool, Honeywell could hire unskilled and semi-skilled workers at very low wages. An automobile components assembly line would, for example, be staffed by Mexican workers charged with repetitive and menial tasks, lower level supervision, and semi-skilled technical work. The management and skilled workforce would likely be comprised of American higher level employees and executives, delegated to the maquiladora. The intellectual property used to build the company's product line would also be distinctly American. Components needed for the assembly line could be shipped from the nearby United States, without paying any tariff. The finished products would also be shipped without tariffs, in this case back to the United States distribution and consumer markets. For Honeywell, the benefit is clear. The maquiladora essentially allows the company to substitute a lower paid Mexican workforce for its unskilled, unionized American workforce. This saving in production costs far outweighs any additional shipping or transportation costs that may be attendant to shifting production to the maquiladora. Honeywell has no obligation to contribute any benefits to the Mexican economy other than what serves the economic interests of the company.

For the Mexican host, as we explained, the analysis is more problematic. On the one hand, it is evident that the maquiladoras' industrial activities are making jobs available to Mexican workers that would otherwise be wholly out of reach. The migration from the poorer, Southern states of Mexico to the maquiladora illustrates the benefits reaped by Mexican workers. The availability of a job, albeit at a wage that would make any American worker cringe, fundamentally transforms the life of the Mexican worker. The influx of American higher echelon workers, and their need to procure domestic services, also benefits the domestic economy. The same result obtains with respect to the services that are required by the industrial plants, or the goods they might need. It is true that, by and large, these goods will be procured through long-term supply arrangements with American suppliers. However, the local plant will inevitably turn, in the mid- and long-term, to domestic suppliers that may provide parts and services together with the kind of warranty, after-sale, or other benefits attendant to geographical proximity. For the American employees living in Mexico's maquiladoras, local services will also become a necessary part of daily life. From car mechanics to newspaper deliverers, through internet service providers and television technicians, living in a maquiladora, albeit so close to the homeland's border, will entail a fair amount of engagement with local businesses.[46]

For the Mexican economy, however, this natural outflow of business is not enough to eliminate the vulnerability of the emerging middle classes that grow in the maquiladora and, just like the modern world erred dramatically by continuing to apply pre-modern mercantilist policies when comparative advantage beckoned, the post-modern decision makers continue to insist blindly on modern solutions to post-modern problems such as those of the maquiladoras. Today's international order of states faces structural questions associated with the passage from one era of Statecraft to the next. These questions echo those that the modern society of states faced 100 years ago. Then, as now, the existing international and domestic Statecraft structures were simply inadequate tools for resolving the new foundational issues of the day. The pre-modern policies of mercantilism were obsolete and prejudicial in a rising modern age of nations and welfare Statecraft (with the important exception of colonial possessions). Until decolonization (which we believe should have occurred as early as the emergence of the concept of a nation) the modern liberal democracies had no strategic or trading interest in relinquishing territories. The African, Asian and other colonized people were still a long way from being recognized by the colonizers as potentially independent groups of individuals. For France to give up Lebanon or Cameroon, or England to give up Kenya or Palestine, would accomplish no more than ceding to a competitor an entity that, for the strategic reasons we describe below, came to be viewed as an extension (in the case of France) or a dominion (in the case of Great Britain) of the nation.

FROM STATECRAFT TO A TRADE ORDER

In the early modern era, the fragmentation of the world into discrete economic units associated with a nation formed as a result of specific historical circumstances, and made institutionalized comparative advantage the natural choice for the international order of states. The institutional and structural concerns that we have explored in depth joined with the strategic considerations of the day. The world further subdivided itself into blocs, born out of historical, geographical and political circumstances, which competed with one another for the soul of the State. After World

War II, the states that ultimately emerged as the victors of the Long War recognized that the liberalization of trade rules and the establishment of mechanisms fundamentally adapted to their inner face suited their strategic interest, a conclusion that an analysis of Statecraft could have yielded some years and several global catastrophes earlier. The defeated fascist nations were included in the camp of the victors, to strengthen them against the new communist Statecraft threat.

Today, the victors of World War II face a fundamentally different geopolitical strategic map and international economic context. As we discuss further in this chapter, their interests align with new powers, including China, India, Brazil, and other emerging states. Comparative advantage and the modern rules do not do enough to address fundamental issues related to the economic security of the local populations that, ultimately, free trade is supposed to integrate. More fundamentally, more troubling, and more urgent is that unless complemented by international programs and rules designed to institutionalize the enablement of global economic opportunity, the continued application of comparative advantage from the era of modern Statecraft threatens to result in prejudice to the inter-state relations of a similar kind as those caused by the stubborn application of mercantilist policies, not tempered by liberalized trade.

Yet the trading world continues to diagnose and seek to cure post-modern ailments using modern tools. The maquiladoras example illustrates this failure to recognize the post-modern nature of central problems facing the trading world. Instead of turning to the post-modern solutions we advocate, the United States and Canada have insisted that the solution to the maquiladora problem lies in the extension of modern welfare state principles to Mexico. They insist that the vulnerable middle classes of Mexico will achieve modern salvation if only Mexico complied with the commitments, forced upon it by Canada and the United States, to apply the modern welfare state apparatus to the maquiladoras. In order to understand the story, we must go back to the early 1990s, and to the negotiations surrounding the NAFTA.

NAFTA AND POST-MODERN STATECRAFT

When NAFTA was being negotiated, the American trade unions joined with anti-trade forces such as Ross Perot to oppose the trade liberalization that the treaty was sure to achieve. The opponents of NAFTA concentrated their opposition campaigns on the impact on American jobs that they believed the maquiladoras would have. Perot's "Great Sucking Sound" became the slogan of the anti-NAFTA forces. The sucking sound was, of course, the sound of unionized and other American jobs flowing down to the maquiladoras.[47] The NAFTA, its opponents claimed, would result in a race to the bottom that trade critics vociferously denounced. Mexico would attract American companies with a regulatory form of comparative advantage of the worst type: practices hostile to labor rights such as resistance to unions, abysmal occupational safety regulations, lax environmental and resource conservation rules and, to top it, all wages that would make it impossible for any American worker to survive in any American city. For labor and human rights advocates, the harm to the American labor classes joined with the failure to develop the Mexican working classes. If American investors moved to Mexico to take advantage of abysmal labor, environmental, or other regulatory schemes typical of the modern state, they would merely engage in "social dumping" and never contribute to the meaningful growth of Mexico's workers and their entry into what we call "the modern economic age."[48]

When President Clinton took office, he faced considerable opposition from trade unions and the left wing of the Democratic Party to the NAFTA and, in order to placate the critics, he agreed to a framework that was intended to extend Western welfare to the Mexican free trade zones that would result from the implementation of the treaty. As we discuss in Chapter 8, our book is neither a political manifesto nor an endorsement of any particular political persuasion. Furthermore, while the failure to recognize the current epochal transformation is not the exclusive province of any political orientation, the American and European Left have generally tended to adhere more closely than the right-wing modern liberal democratic parties to the ideological tenets of the modern world, and to reject efforts at instilling post-modern economic values in the markets.

As mentioned earlier, we believe in what may be characterized as "managed epochal transformation," and that in today's transitional era welfare as the modern world knew it may actually be a component of the enablement of global economic opportunity. Our point here, however, is that ideological insistence on continuing welfare as practiced in the modern age of Statecraft prompted the Clinton Administration to put into place a treaty provision which, while it initially saved NAFTA from the isolationist and labor daggers that were bound to kill it, was bound to hurt and possibly destroy the vulnerable trading classes that a liberalized flow of goods and services created.

President Clinton's response to his labor wing and to Ross Perot was, in essence, to impose welfare requirements on Mexico. If the problem lay in Mexico's failure to regulate, the thinking went, then we should force them to increase their regulatory thresholds as a condition to joining the NAFTA. This reflex was eminently modern. To the modern mind, all issues of "fair trade" are analyzed in light of the subdivision of the world into discrete economic units of comparable, balanced economic and regulatory levels. Fair trade issues arise when nation-states that have not joined the "end of history" bandwagon enter the fray. These nation-states create imbalances in the system because they offer working conditions that drag the rest of the world down (hence the race to the "bottom" which bottom would not exist were it not for the modern "top"). In order to remedy this imbalance, we need to lift up these modern states and reach the "end of history."

That is exactly what President Clinton set out to do. He asked his staff to study Mexican regulations and report on the areas where they lacked a welfare system of the type found in the modern world. The response was surprising, yet typical of developing countries. The problem lay not so much in the law on the books, but with the law in action. President Clinton was informed that Mexican law provides a comprehensive welfare scheme which, in theory, provides for a wide net of social protection for Mexican workers and the environment. If applied, this scheme would avert a race to the bottom. Mexican law indeed protects the right of workers to organize. It requires employers to provide for occupational safety rules similar to those that govern European or American enterprises. It codifies a comprehensive set of environmental laws that prevent enterprises from engaging in most of the practices that European and American environmental schemes prohibit. It protects employees against termination without just cause, and gives them monetary compensation if they are laid off. It establishes a minimum wage, and stringent requirements regarding compensation for overtime work. It defines discrimination broadly enough to protect vulnerable classes, such as pregnant women or older workers.[49]

The problem with Mexican law, President Clinton was told, is simply that it is not enforced. The law on the books diverges widely from the law in action.[50] The solution, then, was to narrow the gap and to require the Mexicans to enforce their laws. That is precisely what the Side Agreements on the Labor and the Environments set out to accomplish. The centerpiece of these agreements was an absolute mandate for each of the NAFTA member states to enforce their labor and environmental laws, especially minimum employment standards, including minimum wage, occupational safety rules such as prevention of occupational injuries and illnesses, right to organize, compensation for workplace related injuries, elimination of employment discrimination, equal pay for equal work, and compensation for wrongful termination.[51]

The Side Agreements established National Administrative Offices (NAOs), charged with examining complaints by private parties that a member state did not enforce its own laws. Each NAO has the power to issue a report detailing the offense, which in theory might compel the offending state to bring its enforcement system into compliance. Certain violations may, after the NAO process is exhausted, be litigated in arbitral proceedings between the two states. In the face of stiff opposition, President Clinton was able to push the NAFTA past the labor unions and the isolationists by pointing to these Side Agreements. Under his vision, Mexico would be lifted up toward the modern end of history, rather than dragging the United States and Canada back toward a pre-modern age of jungle capitalism.

The Side Agreements, then, were intended to compel Mexico to apply its welfare standards and to redistribute wealth to the Mexican workers that would flock to the maquiladoras. Just like the GATT increased wealth, and the modern nation-states applied their welfare systems to fortify their middle classes, Mexico would derive resources from the NAFTA and be compelled to spread it to its rising middle class through an international requirement that the domestic welfare system be given effect. At the same time, the NAFTA prohibited discrimination against foreign companies, and in particular the performance requirements that developing countries such as Mexico had sought to impose.[52]

The Side Agreements, however, fell short of achieving their intended results. The international treaties did not lead to meaningful and lasting change in the Mexican authorities' willingness to apply their laws. Companies like Honeywell moved to the maquiladoras to take advantage of the very regulatory comparative advantage that the Side Agreements sought to mitigate. United States corporations hired workers for very low wages, with virtually no regulatory burdens in relation to labor or environmental matters. Where Mexican law gave workers rights such as severance, the employers worked out a system of waiver where, in consideration for some very low compensation, the employee released rights to the legal welfare entitlements. Unions had very little luck making inroads in the maquiladoras. Employers discouraged unionization and sent a clear signal to their employees that non-union workers, the kind of employees that the maquiladoras had to offer, would be given hiring preferences. The cases brought against United States investors and local authorities to compel enforcement of the local laws were unsuccessful. In a case against a subsidiary of Sony, for example, the local NAO found wholesale violation of Mexican laws regarding the right to organize and to be free from retaliation for belonging to a union. The case was a textbook example of retaliatory measures that employers may deploy to deter their employees from organizing. Union leaders were dismissed. Workers attempting to attend union meetings were also fired immediately upon taking steps to foster the union movement. The Sony affiliate forced low paid workers to sign waivers of lawsuit, in return for severance packages that, in most cases, did not exceed a one time payment of less than $100.[53]

While the NAO's public report unearthed and published the wholesale violation of labor rights, the lack of enforcement power of the NAO meant that it could not compel enforcement of labor laws. Instead, both local authorities and Sony ignored the NAO. A local Mexican judge ruled that the waivers at issue were lawful, and his injunction to Sony to otherwise apply the law was left unheeded. Under NAFTA, the NAO's public report was the main tool to achieve compliance with the labor scheme. If it failed to compel voluntary compliance by local authorities, the next enforcement stages, ministerial consultations and arbitral panel determinations, were highly unlikely events. Arbitral panels were stripped by the treaty of jurisdiction over the most egregious violations. They could not, for example, render binding decisions on failure to enforce domestic law relating to the right to organize. Ministerial consultations, while a more effective tool to compel enforcement than the lower level NAO, were dependent on the political will of the United States Department of Labor or its Canadian counterpart. This case was typical of the way the Side Agreements operated in the field, and mirrored the failure to remedy similar wholesale violations by household names such as Sprint, General Electric, or Honeywell. In the end, then, the Side Agreements remained a dead letter, just like the domestic laws that they were supposed to revive.[54]

The critics of NAFTA blame the failure of enforcement for the failure of the Side Agreements to achieve welfare results that would work hand-in-hand with the trade liberalizing effect of the treaty. At worst, they claim, President Clinton fooled the labor and other critics of the treaty by crafting a classically ineffective piece of international legislation to induce them to withdraw their opposition to a dangerous international trade liberalizing scheme. Like other conventions and international treaties, they argue, the Side Agreements were bound to be a dead letter because they did not include a sufficiently effective dispute resolution mechanism. This enforcement deficit made it inevitable that resources would not be made available to local authorities to deploy modern enforcement schemes. At best, the Side Agreements simply failed because they were structurally deficient, and they should be amended to give aggrieved unions and individuals more effective rights to struggle against violations of the labor and environmental aspects of the NAFTA.[55]

This criticism of the NAFTA entirely misses the mark, and in point of fact the ambiguous nature of the Side Agreements on Labor and the Environment actually saved the NAFTA and made it possible for the newly integrated area to move on to the post-modern stage of its development. Just as mercantilism failed for the early twentieth-century European and American modern nation-states, the modern welfare state is not compatible with post-modern zones like the maquiladoras. Unlike early twentieth-century European nations, Mexico, or other emerging post-modern economies like Brazil, China, India, or Indonesia, do not have cohesive national industries, closely associated with the geographic boundaries of the nation. Instead of facing a late pre-modern consolidation of industry into a trading class corresponding with the nation, these countries have witnessed a post-modern economic movement that yielded a widely disparate and heterogeneous mix of industrial pockets, often controlled or owned by cross-border, supranational interests, around which the vulnerable middle classes gravitate.[56]

In twentieth-century Lille, the French government faced a capitalist, industrial class that feared the rise of a communist revolution among its workers. The state-nation epoch had created a commonality of identity among these classes, and the ruling classes, based on the concept of the nation. The terrain was ripe for a bargain that would include a highly intricate and interdependent welfare system of the type that we described in earlier chapters. Companies would be required to retain workers beyond what pure economic interests might require, to provide them with minimum levels of job security and quality of life, and to contribute to a vast social safety net system. Health and retirement benefits, aid to families with children, housing allowances, minimum guaranteed income, and the entire panoply of welfare measures arose to give the solidified nation a buffer against the communist model of Statecraft, and its insistence on the takeover of the means of production by the workers as the only way of resolving the problems of the pre-modern world.

The national nature of the regulated industries, and the incredibly complex and interconnected web of national regulations that surrounded their operations, does not exist in post-modern Mexico, China, or India.[57] The enterprises that moved to the maquiladoras did so as a result of a post-modern international system that encourages companies to shift production to the most economically advantageous locale. Honeywell is not a Mexican enterprise, and if Mexico attempts to impose on Honeywell a welfare structure that includes top-down mandatory regulation, the post-modern markets will signal to Honeywell that maquiladora operations should be moved to, say, Nicaragua or Guatemala. In addition, the treaty's distinctly modern prohibition of performance requirements leaves the Mexican economy without a way to compel additional infusion of resources necessary to enable economic opportunity. NAFTA prohibits Mexican agencies of government from intervening to facilitate arrangements that would provide incentives for companies like Honeywell voluntarily to transfer resources. Honeywell, for example, cannot be required to use a certain amount of domestic content or local suppliers to support its core business. Compulsory licenses, technology transfer, and other measures intended to convey know-how, technologies, methods, programs, and other business assets that are protected by intellectual property laws are prohibited under NAFTA's anti-discrimination principles. The prohibition of performance requirements also calcifies the labor allocation structures that tend to make less skilled labor available to the Mexican vulnerable classes. The anti-discrimination principle *de jure* bans affirmative action in favor of these classes.

Ultimately, there is a fundamental contradiction between the modern Statecraft concept of comparative advantage, as it applies in the post-modern world, and the modern notion of welfare. For the twentieth-century nation-states, opening up borders to trade meant giving national industries access to foreign market outlets, and national consumers access to cheaper foreign goods. At the end of the process, a post-modern world of interloped ownership of the means of production would arise, which would make the welfare regulatory apparatus increasingly irrelevant in that it lost its capacity to regulate. In today's post-modern world, comparative advantage results in the transplantation of industries to zones like the maquiladoras. This economic phenomenon is post-modern, in that it results in the movement of actual means of production more than the movement of goods or services. It occurs not at a time when the nation rose and the State legitimated itself by assuring welfare of the nation, but at a time when the post-modern diffuseness of the means of production, traditional policy tools, and the subjects of regulation, make it impossible for a state to create, apply, or achieve any meaningful results with traditional approaches to welfare (e.g., regulation).

Instead, what is needed is a decidedly post-modern approach to problems such as that of the maquiladoras. Ironically, the failure of the Side Agreements to achieve their intended result could give public policymakers the chance to focus on a post-modern solution that fits the state of the relevant economic actors, and may propel NAFTA toward post-modern redemption. The first issue is the establishment of an infrastructure that will firm up and solidify the economic conditions of the vulnerable middle classes. The burden, instead of being placed on the Mexican state, should be shouldered by the Trade Council, acting in conjunction with the governments of the United States, Mexico and Canada, and representatives of industry and other interested groups. Here is a scenario of how, in the Honeywell example, the enablement of global economic opportunity would apply to the Mexican border towns. The Honeywell Package would include a series of domestic incentives extended by the governments of the United States and Mexico, in return for a suspension of the Side Agreements on Labor and the Environment as they apply to that company. The domestic package of incentives could include, of course, tax incentives – as we already suggested. However, a successful package will include a much more sophisticated bundle of incentives including, in Honeywell's case, intellectual property and other regulatory incentives.

Let us start with intellectual property. Like most companies establishing operations in the maquiladoras, Honeywell owns a substantial number of patents and other intellectual property. Intellectual property law includes a uniform bundle of incentives designed to reward creation, protect inventors and creators from seeing the fruit of their labor appropriated by persons who did not invest any resource or intelligence into their development, and, at the same time, protecting the public's interest in limiting monopolies.

The operation of these intellectual property laws can be illustrated by the following example. Honeywell's aerospace products department might, in the ordinary course of business, invest enormous amounts in research and development. By way of illustration, imagine the aerospace department pursuing the development of a new kind of polymer-based product to be used in connection with space shuttles, satellites or other aerospace products. The investment in the research and development would likely range in the hundreds of millions of dollars. Of course, the pricing of the product would take into account the amounts necessary to give Honeywell a return on its investment. After the product is developed, a competitor would have the technological capacity to reverse engineer the Honeywell product and, for a relatively low cost, reproduce the technology that cost Honeywell a large investment to develop. The competitor would, of course, be able to price Honeywell out of the market and to appropriate the fruits of Honeywell's investment. Unless the law gave Honeywell a means to protect its invention, the company would likely not expend its resources on the development of the new product.

In come the patent and other intellectual property laws. They give Honeywell a bundle of rights, at the core of which is a monopoly over the right to manufacture, market, and distribute products based on the patent. As long as Honeywell is able to comply with the intellectual property requirements for patent grants (such as the requirement that the invention not be obvious and be novel) then the law grants companies like Honeywell the exclusive right to make products that incorporate the invention. For many years, the bundle of rights varied from one country to the next. Today, harmonization of global markets has led international organizations to enter into treaties that unify the bundle of intellectual property rights associated with a patent. The term of the patent is 20 years throughout most of the trading states of the world. The type of inventions that can be patented is defined in a remarkably similar fashion. The limits on the scope of the patent, too, have been harmonized.

The worldwide intellectual property systems balance the public's interest in narrowing the scope of monopoly against this "reward/incentive" function of intellectual property. Monopolies, by definition, result in higher prices to consumers. Honeywell, if it does not face competition in the market, will establish the price of its aerospace product so as to maximize profits and recoup its investment. A higher price, even with a lower volume, might result in higher profits than a more widespread distribution of products at a lower price. The consumers who would have purchased the products under free competition conditions represent the "deadweight loss" associated with the monopolies. Yet, intellectual property driven monopolies are good for the markets and the economy, and the regulatory response is to delineate the contours of the monopoly to accomplish the reward/incentive function of intellectual property with the least possible monopoly burden.[58] For example, the 20-year term of a patent reflects the judgment that, in most instances, the inventor will have enough time during this exclusivity period to recoup its investment. Rules regarding the patentability of certain inventions, such as natural products, reflect the State's attempts to limit monopolies to inventions that not only contribute to the public interest in new products but also require either creative sparks or investment aimed at producing an obscure product.

In the system of incentives aimed at enabling global economic opportunity that we advocate, the bundle of rights afforded domestically and internationally to a company like Honeywell would be adjusted based on Honeywell's contribution to the solidification of the vulnerable trading classes of the post-modern world. Mexico will not pass through the modern welfare state epoch that Europe and the United States experienced. The modern solution to the post-modern maquiladoras, then, will not achieve its intended result. If public and foreign policy makers continue to insist on a modern solution, they will only cause the slow death of the maquiladoras, and thereby undermine the strategic objectives of the victors of World War II, as we describe in detail in Chapter 8. Instead of this policy failure, the post-modern system of incentives and diffuse collaboration in the enablement of global economic opportunity will put international trade regulation on a workable growth track.

In our example, the intellectual property laws of the United States and Canada would be adjusted to take into account not only the public's interest in rewarding and incentivizing inventors, but the contribution of a company like Honeywell to post-modern trading zones like the maquiladoras. The contribution aspect of the social contract could involve a transfer of intellectual property to a domestic Mexican interest. Honeywell could, for example, transfer rights to practice a patent for home-building products to a local competitor. The bundle of rights transferred would be delineated by the social contract. The Mexican company could be given rights to practice the patent and sell the covered products in a particular territory, which probably would involve a Spanish-speaking market in Latin or South America. Alternatively, the Mexican company could become a partner in a joint venture with Honeywell intended to exploit the patent in that territory.

The transfer of technology would give the Mexican competitor more economic opportunities to expand its sales, workforce and other operations. It would contribute to the establishment of economic opportunity in the maquiladoras that is not dependent on the continued presence of Honeywell in the country. In other words, it would achieve the same kind of "performance" targets that NAFTA prohibits Mexico from imposing on foreign investors as a matter of "requirements." Using the post-modern system that we describe, it would accomplish what the modern system of welfare requirements cannot bring about. The Mexican state cannot impose on the post-modern economic actors that operate within its borders the type of redistributionist rules that the nation-states of the twentieth century, legitimating themselves through the provision of welfare to the nation, maintained during the modern epoch. Mexico does not have an infrastructure of the kind that the pre-modern and modern eras of Statecraft brought to the modern liberal democracies of Europe or North America. The enablement of global economic opportunity, in the case of the maquiladoras as in the case of Shenzhen's factories, provides an alternative that works in harmony with the changing nature of the State from modern to post-modern.

The enablement of global economic opportunity is particularly suited to solve the salient issues of the post-modern trading world. In Chapter 8, we present our argument that the trade component of the post-modern system must be adjusted to focus on the enablement of global economic opportunity because, in addition to the trade and economic considerations that we have already analyzed, the strategic objectives of the day dictate that the system be transformed. We argue that, just as strategic epochs are ushered in through organic conferences or treaties, the trade system should formalize its passage to a new era through a constitutional statement incorporated in basic treaties. These are the reasons why we believe that states like the United States, which have emerged victorious or been invited to the family of victors after World War II, should adopt a norm that, essentially, requires them to further give up on sovereign power, as that concept is understood in modern Statecraft. Honeywell should be given economic incentives because firming up the maquiladoras is in the best strategic interests of the United States.

AN EMERGING NEW NORM: THE TRADE COUNCIL AND ECONOMIC DEVELOPMENT

The core argument of this chapter is that the enablement of global economic opportunity will develop into the basic welfare norm of the post-modern system of trade.[59] This is true, we maintain, not merely because it is strategically desirable, but because it would import into the global trading system an animating principle that will fill the regulatory space where comparative advantage reaches its limit. Comparative advantage is, of course, a norm that is here to stay. There will be more battles waged over the Doha issues and, in particular, the continued extension of comparative advantage to industrial, agricultural, and other sectors that the World War II victors will not relinquish willingly.[60] The deepening of comparative advantage will, in fact, create additional economic opportunity for post-modern trading classes operating in emerging economies, and ultimately create new markets for industrial products of the West (e.g., farming equipment for new agricultural concerns). Comparative advantage will also continue its diffuseness-generating enterprise and push the international order of states deeper into the post-modern era. This is where the enablement of global economic opportunity will intervene. The norm supports the post-modern State's legitimating drive to create economic opportunity. Just like comparative advantage assisted the modern State in providing welfare, enabling global economic opportunity will work in the same direction as the post-modern State and contribute to the removal of the obstacles that post-modern states, especially those of the South, face in creating economic systems that provide trade actors with meaningful access to the post-modern global market.

In our Honeywell scenario, a system of incentives would focus both on amending U.S. and Canadian intellectual property laws and on changing the international intellectual property treaties to accommodate the changes in national systems. In the United States, additional monopoly rights (or additional intellectual property rights) might be given to Honeywell with respect to other patented products. For example, Honeywell is likely to have a substantial number of patents nearing expiration. In exchange for Honeywell's contribution to the maquiladoras under its social contract, the U.S. and Canadian patent offices may extend the patent term for these inventions beyond the standard 20-year duration.

The package of benefits would not necessarily be limited to an extension of the patent term. Domestic patent law could, for example, be amended to make granted patents non-challengeable for a stated period of time. Under intellectual property practice, the governmental patent office often grants a patent, which is later challenged by a private party in a court proceeding. The judicial proceeding will consider the question whether the governmental agency acted in accordance with patent law requirements when it granted the patent. The court will, in most cases, scrutinize legal elements of a patent such as non-obviousness much more closely than the patent office. In return for Honeywell's commitment under a social contract with the host area in Mexico, the United States or Canada could shelter from judicial patents granted by the relevant government agency.

The Trade Council would coordinate the international aspects of the patent scheme, as well as the domestic details. The World Intellectual Property Organization and the TRIPS treaty signed under the GATT's auspices both require contracting states to transpose uniform patentability requirements into domestic law. Patents must have a 20-year term. They must be made available for any invention that is not obvious, novel and useful. Contracting states may not deny patents to discrete classes of products, such as pharmaceuticals, that they seek to make available at a cheaper cost.[61] In coordination with the domestic jurisdiction and the international organizations, the Trade Council will ensure that the package of incentives will encourage companies like Honeywell to enter into social contracts that comply with existing law.

This regulatory framework will accord with intellectual property in the post-modern world. In the modern era, intellectual property rights gave their holders the ability to compete with other national industries. Expanding the scope of intellectual property rights would give the beneficiaries a competitive edge against other national companies. In today's post-modern world, ownership of intellectual property holding companies is diffuse and spans across borders. Intellectual property is also transferred rapidly, by way of license or assignments, to cross-border concerns. The grant of incentives to companies like Honeywell, who commit to contribute to the establishment of post-modern infrastructure, would give them an edge in the international, post-modern global market. The system of incentives, then, would impose burdens on global actors that are correlated to the benefits granted to the recipients of the incentives.

To that extent, the intellectual property-based incentives would be more equitable than, say, a direct tax.

In addition, the Trade Council would coordinate among the principal state actors involved in monetary and other regulatory issues affecting the maquiladoras, non-governmental organizations, and industry concerns, so as to fill the regulatory vacuum that applies to these issues. Here again, the legislative work of the Trade Council would involve managing the diffuseness of the post-modern world. Monetary and immigration policies, for example, would be appropriate targets for regulation. We have explained that the devaluation of the peso hurt the vulnerable classes of the maquiladoras to a much greater extent than the rest of the Mexican population. There is a built-in tension in the Mexican government's incentive to devalue the peso, and on its impact on the post-modern maquiladoras. For Mexico (other than the maquiladoras), a devaluation of the peso of the type that we described earlier in this chapter might stimulate economic growth. For the maquiladoras, it is sure to increase costs of living for Mexican middle classes beyond a tolerable level.[62]

Again, the problem is post-modern. The transplantation of American industry to the maquiladoras makes these zones essentially hybrids of the American and Mexican markets. Peso fluctuations have a disparate impact on these zones, because their economic activities bear hallmarks of both the United States and the Mexican markets. The cost of living is higher in the maquiladoras than in other Mexican zones because they have been industrialized by companies like Honeywell or Sony. The wages paid to the Mexican workers, on the other hand, are closer to the prevailing Mexican wage because the regulatory comparative advantage that led to the establishment of the maquiladoras invites the industrial concerns to establish operations that take advantage of the lower wages of the local workforce.

Acting in concert with American and Mexican authorities, the Trade Council could craft a package that would peg the dollar and the peso to a fixed rate of exchange for purposes of the maquiladoras only. We believe that economic indicators traditionally associated with nation-states, such as balance of payments or exchange rates, have lost their usefulness in the post-modern world. Instead, we argue, economic indicators should be adjusted to recognize that the post-modern global market cuts across borders and includes different zones that are no longer associated with the boundaries of the nation. A special dollar/peso zone would accord with the post-modern structure of the global market. It would maintain the incentive that NAFTA extends to American and Canadian industries, while giving the Mexican worker (greater) purchasing power commensurate with the hybrid economic conditions of the maquiladoras.

In order to incentivize Mexico to agree to such a special currency zone, the Trade Council could add an immigration component to the package. One of the main purposes of the NAFTA was to foster wage growth in Mexico to stem the illegal flow of immigrants into the United States. This was a modern solution to the problem of illegal immigration. By increasing the pie available for redistribution in Mexico, the United States is contributing to the solidification of the Mexican economy. In turn, a solidified economy would stem the tide of illegal immigration because Mexican workers would have increased opportunity at home. This solution, however, could not work because, as we explained above, the Mexican state does not have the capacity to implement or impose welfare solutions in the post-modern epoch.

In return for a commitment to stabilize the peso, then, the package would permit a limited inflow of Mexican immigrants and a correlated change in U.S. law. There are today an estimated 10 million illegal immigrants living in the United States, and this figure continues to grow rapidly on a daily basis.[63] An estimated 3 million people illegally cross the border each year, the vast majority of whom are Mexican.[64] Indeed, as shown below, almost 60 percent of the illegal immigrants living in the United States come from Mexico.

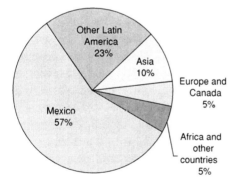

Undocumented Population in the United States by Country and Region of Origin, 2002. *Source:* Urban Institute, Washington, DC, 2004.

While the demand for low-skilled labor continues to increase in the United States, the supply of workers suitable for these jobs declines. Thus, illegal immigrants flow into the country in search of these low-wage jobs. Though the wages offered to these workers are low and often sub-standard compared with those given to legal workers, the wages are nevertheless greater than those offered in Mexico, even the maquiladoras. Yet an illegal and undocumented workforce creates economic and political difficulty for both Americans and Mexicans.[65] For the United States, the formation of an illegal workforce brings with it all the accompaniments of a black market, including smuggling, fraudulent documents, deceptively low wages, and abuse.[66] On the other hand, the illegal Mexicans live in a world largely devoid of rights and protections and become vulnerable to the abuse of employers and border smugglers. Therefore, although the United States has encouraged more trade, investment, and political ties with Mexico, it has ineffectively labored to stop illegal immigration across the border.

In efforts to acknowledge and accommodate illegal Mexican immigration to the United States, lawmakers have introduced several policies through the years. In 1986, The Immigration Reform and Control Act was passed by Congress.[67] The law contained three provisions aimed at regaining "control of our borders." First, in order to reduce the demand for illegal labor, the law required all U.S. companies to check all employee documentation, and fined those companies known to hire illegal immigrants. Next, to cease the supply of illegal workers, the law ordered increased spending on the Border Patrol. Finally, to address the problem of the millions of illegal alien workers already in the United States, the law granted permanent legal status to 2.8 million people who had been in the country since January 1, 1982.

Then, in 2001, after meeting with Mexican President Vincente Fox, George Bush said he would ask Congress to legalize Mexican aliens if they would take the jobs that American workers declined.[68] He also proposed the abolition of some of the laws that bar American companies from employing illegal Mexican workers. In a joint news conference give by President Bush and Mexican President Vincente Fox, President Bush stated: "The truth of the matter is that if somebody is willing to do jobs others in America aren't willing to do, we ought to welcome that person to the country and we ought to make that a legal part of our economy."[69] Further, he said, "We ought not to penalize an employer who's trying to get a job done, who hires somebody who's willing to do that kind of work."[70] Bush claimed that he would attempt to expedite congressional approval of guest-worker status for those illegal Mexicans ready to work. However, he was ultimately unable to achieve the grant of legal status to any of the illegal Mexicans already living in the United States.

Recently, Congress again rejected Bush's attempt to accomplish immigration progress and, after a bitter and high visibility struggle, it discarded the president's proposal to legalize the status of illegal aliens. Under the Trade Council, a managed program linked to Mexican measures to solidify the status of the maquiladora workers would be introduced. This postmodern program could, for example, establish a registered guest worker program in exchange for the Mexican measures regarding the peso that we described above, or other measures that would fortify the maquiladoras. As discussed in the next chapter, such a framework would shift the integrated areas of North and South America toward a course of action that in fact achieves the goal of creating meaningful economic opportunity. It would create a model that could be replicated in the Free Trade of the Americas Agreement, and that would apply policy tools of the current epoch rather than gradually obsolete measures of the waning modern era.

Such measures would prod the trading world along post-modern, managed integration of the type that we are advocating. The failure to put in place an architecture that makes this possible would leave the world with discrete problems and no institutionally available response. In Chapter 8, we explain why it is in the best interests of the United States and other World War II victors to adhere to the post-modern system of trade we describe. Further, we present a system for measuring the effectiveness of post-modern measures. We conclude by explaining the continuing role of welfare in the age of global economic opportunity.

8 Trade and Security

Thesis:

Trade and Strategy – the two dimensions of the outer face of the State – are linked through a global trading order that functions in the context of post-modern Statecraft. In the twentieth century, the victors of war have created a system of trade that accords with their inner constitutional order. In the twenty-first century, these states need to join with emerged and emerging states to foster and develop the interloped and interdependent cross-border relationships born out of the Long War of the twentieth century.

We have argued that the international trade order should be designed to accord with the nature of Statecraft in each epoch, and that the victors of war in the twentieth century have established a system that accords with their internal constitutional order. The existence of a link between trade and security in the modern era is controversial. Nevertheless, we have claimed that an international trade system that accords with modern Statecraft should have been put in place in the twentieth century regardless of its immediate actual contribution to the democracies' security needs. When, in 1950, Robert Schuman made the declaration that unity was required to make war "not only unthinkable but materially impossible," he squarely endorsed the premise that integration of the important resources of the day, coal and steel, would contribute to collective security. The "United States of Europe" that he foresaw arising after a long and tortuous road would bind their constituent states in a partnership that would prevent war. The partnership was not achieved before World War II, Schuman posited, and as a direct result Europe faced the devastation wrought by another globalized conflict. Our claim has been that, regardless of the extent to which Schuman was right and the democracies' failure to institutionalize comparative advantage before World War II contributed to their weakening and failure to co-opt fascist states into the modern liberal democratic camp, the establishment of a trade structure that complements the epochal Statecraft of the modern era was an indispensable component of the security policy of the modern liberal democracies.[1]

In this chapter, we argue that in the post-modern age the strategic interests of the victors of World War II should motivate them to adopt a trading system based on the norm we advocate, that of the enablement of global economic opportunity. Our claim is that the Western victors of World War II should adopt an economic norm that extends economic opportunity beyond the natural expansion of business activities resulting from market-based considerations of private actors. We discuss the obvious objection to this argument, which is to ask why that should be the case? Why should the United States give patent, food and drug approval or taxation incentives to American companies entering into social contracts with the maquiladoras? Why should immigration rules be relaxed in the West in return for commitments to achieve some form of infrastructural growth? In other words, why should the post-modern age include a foundational, animating drive to extend economic opportunity across the globe? Would it not be preferable to let the markets operate unfettered and tolerate the regulatory vacuum that accompanies the post-modern globalization of diffuse markets (i.e., those that escape regulation by any single jurisdiction)?

Our answer to these questions is both strategic and economic. Our claim is that, just as in the modern era, the structure of the international order of states must reflect the inner face of the State. We are entering a new age, the post-modern age, where the international economic landscape that the GATT created gradually morphed into a twenty-first century order that necessitates a rethinking of the norms and institutions of global trade. In Chapters 5, 6, and 7 we have argued that, left unaddressed, the failure to transform trade for the post-modern age will result in the collapse of vulnerable middle classes and engender a failure to fortify the post-modern trading classes. The decline of the State as the central ontological unit of trade analysis, the erosion of welfare in the West and its failure to launch in the South (as well as the post-modernization of the global market) provide structural reasons why global trade institutions should become post-modern. This answer, which we have explored in depth in previous chapters, is not sufficient because it does not explain how the structural change that we advocate will be beneficial to the strategic interests of the World War II victors. That is the question we address in this chapter.

VICTORS AND STATECRAFT

For the World War II victors, the Bretton Woods Order made sense from a strategic standpoint. Their task after the war was to avoid the mistakes that had preceded and engendered the conflict. They found themselves in the middle of the Long War with the foundational task of defeating the Soviet bloc's competing view of Statecraft. Bretton Woods, the Marshall Plan, and the general trade-constitutional shift that followed World War II accorded with this fundamental goal.[2] The welfare state, or *"État Providence"* as it was known in France, gave the nation an alternative to communism.[3] The concept of the "providing" State captures the role that welfare played in establishing a viable constitutional alternative to communism. The State would regulate markets so as to give the nation a minimum safety net of social protective measures, at the same time as it provided it with security. Economic and strategic security emanated from a State dedicated to the well-being of its nation. These securities found their expression not only in the establishment of a collective Western military force capable of protecting its member nations from communist invasion, but in an economic system designed to give the nation the means of decent livelihood that would make it unnecessary for the working classes to wrest the means of production from their capitalist oppressors.

This system could not work in conjunction with the pre-modern policies of mercantilism and economic punishment of the defeated fascist powers. A repeat of the Treaty of Versailles may have led to the rise of communist states in France, Germany, and other European nation-states that became the bulwark of the Western modern liberal democratic world. The Communist Party of France, for example, earned more than 40 percent of the popular vote in the first post-War election.[4] The sympathetic sentiment stemmed of course from the fact that the Communist Resistance had provided the main ideologically grounded opposition to the nazi and fascist movements. However, without the means of providing welfare to the nation, the modern liberal democratic State would have been unlikely to curb the advance of communism as the preferred model for Statecraft. Likewise, without a reconstruction of Germany and an invitation to the former fascist nation-states to join what we have come to call the "free world," modern liberal democratic Statecraft would have been as hampered in its existential struggle against communism as it had been in its fight against fascism.

Then came Bretton Woods. The Bretton Woods project not only embedded liberalism into the international economic order of states, thereby providing a structurally workable trade system: it worked hand-in-hand to give the modern liberal democratic nation-states the economic means to deliver welfare and build a strategic bloc capable of containing the Soviet communist vision of Statecraft. The international economic order of states created by Bretton Woods came with the investment infusion of the Marshall Plan. The Marshall Plan created partners of sufficient strength to trade based on comparative advantage. Comparative advantage-driven trade led to specialization that drastically increased the aggregate economic pie available to the World War II victors. The increased economic pie could be redistributed through an intricate system of welfare dedicated to the well-being of the nation. In the end, the Western victors could achieve a well-balanced alliance of sufficient collective strength to repel the Soviet bloc with a successful welfare redistributionist State that gave its nation a workable and preferable alternative to communist Statecraft. The proof, indeed, was in the pudding. While the Soviet bloc crumbled internally, and Western communist parties disappeared, the modern liberal democratic victors fared so well as to motivate insightful observers like Fukuyama to embrace the illusion that history had, indeed, come to a (happy) ending.

Bretton Woods, in the conceptual sense that we are ascribing to this historical event, was therefore the only course that would achieve the structural, economic and strategic objectives of the Western modern liberal democratic victors. The alternative, continued mercantilism, would have resulted in a repeat of the disasters that preceded World War II. The global pie would have shrunk. Instead of creating a Western bloc, the World War II victors would have become fragmented and separated. The compact of discrete economic units associated with the nation would not have entered into the economic alliance that was the indispensable complement to its strategic alliance. Each nation-state would have struggled with its delivery of welfare to the nation, and some might have embraced the communist model. Thus, instead of a cohesive and successful bloc, the Western model might have paled in the face of the unified communist Statecraft creed, and the history of the Long War might have been written by Soviet historians instead of ours.

Succinctly, welfare was the legitimating drive of the modern nation-state: it served as an animating norm that provided an alternative to communism. In the communist version of Statecraft, the State unleashed its powers for the benefit of the nation, bringing it closer to taking over the means of production and achieving the utopian political and social system that Marx envisioned. In modern liberal democracies, the State also unleashed its powers for the benefit of the nation, enabling it to attain a standard of living that would make it unnecessary to achieve the good life through a communist revolution. Bretton Woods embedded welfare for the nation into the international trade order, by giving the State the economic and structural means of accomplishing this goal within the framework of a coherent bloc that, on the military/strategic front, would repel the advance of communism.

The upshot of this analysis is that the victors of war have the opportunity to establish a structurally sound trade system, one that serves their economic and strategic interests. However, the system does not guarantee that the strategic interests of this association of states will win the day. Instead, it puts in place a structure that is best designed to further these interests and to increase the possibility of strategic victory for a discrete group of countries. As we have argued, comparative advantage was a principle that worked for a specific era of Statecraft. Even more fundamentally, comparative advantage was a principle that worked for a subset of economic actors in that era. As we have explained repeatedly, comparative advantage did not work for the poor masses of sub-Saharan Africa, or the excluded classes of Brazil or Indonesia. Not only did history not end with comparative advantage and modern liberal democratic Statecraft, but the transition it experienced served the interests of the victors of war only: it failed to provide a structural framework adequate for the vast majority of the global population.[5]

THE CAUSES OF TERRORISM

Our claim is that in today's post-modern age, failure to adjust international trade institutions will have disastrous results for the Western liberal democracies and their relationship to the emerging global powers. We have argued earlier in the book that, today, the world finds itself in a situation similar to that which it faced after World War II. A new era is upon us, and new concepts must be developed to envision a new global trading order. Just as Bretton Woods did, we are looking at the structural adjustments that are necessary from the standpoint of the modern liberal democracies that won World War II, and seeking to ascertain their strategic and economic interests in doing so. Yet, unlike Bretton Woods, we are rethinking the current trade norm before the next globalized conflict. Instead, we are evaluating the existential threats of the current era, the changes in Statecraft that have arisen since the modern age, and the transformation of the international economic landscape, all as we are introducing the norm that we believe is necessary to change the international economic order before war makes that choice inevitable. In other words, we are engaged in the same kind of exercise the modern liberal democracies might have conducted, had they looked at the trade system in 1917 instead of adopting the Treaty of Versailles then and waiting for the end of World War II to adjust the landscape of trade in the modern era of Statecraft. This process, we claim, will result in the establishment of a new global trading order that is best designed to protect the interests of modern liberal democracies.

Our argument is based on the premise that the principal existential threats of the present epoch emanate from global networked terrorism and state-sponsored religious fundamentalism. Global networked terrorism aims at eroding the foundation of post-modern states. Fundamentalist states, such as Iran, provide an ideological alternative to modern liberal democratic systems, and in time we believe that they will increasingly further their strategic interests by acting through proxy organizations that share their ideology but are more elusive targets for retaliation or deterrence by enemy states. In both cases, the stakes are existential and, we argue, necessitate a shift to a post-modern trade order.[6] The first question that we must answer is whether the enablement of global economic opportunity would contribute to the modern liberal democratic fight against global networked terrorism or the containment of religious fundamentalism.

Terrorism comes in different forms. It can be carried out by separatist movements, indigenous revolutionary groups of the right and left, or by international groups seeking to strike at their own government's interests from abroad or to influence the target country's policy choices.[7] Although "terrorism" is subject to various interpretations, "a central feature of each is the inclusion of terrorists' goal of inducing fear in a target audience that transcends the physical harm caused to immediate victims."[8] The terrorists' primary purpose is often to alter a current state of political balance.[9] Many countries of different political regimes at differing levels of economic welfare have been terrorized. Consequently, the roots of terrorism have been explored by countless researchers and politicians. Various viewpoints have been developed as a result of this debate, many of them exploring the links between economy and security.

At one end of the spectrum of the debate are the views commonly expressed by politicians, journalists, scholars, and officials responsible for administering aid to foreign countries. These people tend to believe that poverty and minimal education are the primary causes of terrorism. For example, the former president of the World Bank, James D. Wolfensohn, says that the struggle against terrorism "will not be won until we have come to grips with the problem of poverty and thus the sources of discontent."[10] Similarly, during a 2003 speech in Monterrey, Mexico, President George W. Bush said: "We fight against poverty because hope is an answer to terror. . . . We will challenge the poverty and hopelessness and lack of education and failed governments that too often allow conditions that terrorists can seize."[11] At the Council on Foreign Relations, Al Gore claimed that the anger that underlies terrorist states results from "the continued failure to thrive, as rates of economic growth stagnate, while the cohort of unemployed young men under 20 continues to increase." Public intellectuals such as Elie Wiesel concur, stating that, "[e]ducation is the way to eliminate terrorism."[12] And according to Nobel laureate Kim Dae Jung, "[a]t the bottom of terrorism is poverty."[13]

A consensus among this group is that poor conditions in impoverished nations engender feelings of alienation, resentment, and hopelessness. These feelings can lead to hostility, which puts wealthier nations at risk for terrorism. Thus, those who believe that poverty is the overriding cause of terrorism feel that there should be increased government spending on foreign aid, and that poorer countries should receive the bulk of available funds. Many are intensely interested in transforming major financial institutions into economic providers of efficiency, stability, and structure. These policy makers and observers view the financial sector, in particular international organizations, as the responsible parties capable of facilitating economic programs to foster social stability and peace.[14]

Amongst the group that believes poverty underlies violence and terrorism, many are proponents of globalization. A growing body of research suggests that globalization promotes free trade which, in turn, promotes peace. Recently, President George W. Bush has used the evidence to demonstrate why a liberal trade policy is a necessary part of a strong defense. According to the latest National Security Strategy of the United States of America, U.S. security depends on the economic success of other countries. On this view, free trade and open markets are equally as important for securing peace as robust military funding. In impoverished countries, a lack of economic stability undermines economic freedom, which produces the resentment discussed earlier. Terrorist organizations form and exploit impoverished and hostile environments to recruit more members. Thus, leaders of the poorer country continue to blame and resent a wealthier country, rather than accept responsibilities for the policies impoverishing their own people. As the Bush Administration states in its National Security Strategy platform, "[e]conomic growth supported by free trade and free markets creates new jobs and higher incomes. It allows people to lift their lives out of poverty, spurs economic and legal reform, and the fight against corruption, and it reinforces the habits of liberty."[15] The basic thesis underlying all of these pronouncements is that countries that trade with each other are far less likely to confront one another with violence.[16]

According to the International Institute for Sustainable Development, "[o]ver the last fifteen years Regional Trade Agreements (RTAs) have become defining features of the modern economy and a powerful force for globalization."[17] RTAs are treaties that promise cheaper imports and more valuable exports. In theory, they can also encourage foreign investment, enhance economic growth, improve a country's credit, and open roads to new skills and technology. By the beginning of 2005, more than 250 RTAs were integrated into the World Trade Organization.[18] The European Union is obviously an example of an economically successful trade agreement that has functioned under RTAs. However, not all RTAs follow the same trajectory as the EU. Poorly designed and implemented RTAs run the risk of increasing conflict. Failure is likely if there is a lack of transparency, consultation, and accountability in the negotiation of the agreement. Countries of largely different size, wealth, and influence run the risk of cementing inequalities between groups. Gains are rarely felt proportionally between the countries, and a shifted and unbalanced inter-state empowerment occurs. The political and economic adjustments that result from trade agreements can also undermine local economies and create a market of winners and losers. Competition between two groups leads to resentment and eventually to violence.[19]

An example of an unsuccessful negotiation occurred in the 1980s and 1990s in Francophone West Africa. During that time, the EU had encouraged rapid regional integration and structural policy changes in the area. Free transfer of goods was promoted, but no redistributive wealth mechanism was offered to balance the adjustment costs of trade liberalization and integration. This left people economically divided. Eventually, the process maximized unemployment and undermined government social programs as well, sparking regional conflict.[20]

Globalization itself is, at times, viewed as a catalyst for terrorism.[21] Many argue that governments of all political persuasions have been agreeing to agendas that essentially grant multinational corporations, banks, and speculative investors the right to move in and out of their countries freely. They have also agreed to agendas which force them to lower their standards in order to compete for the favors of the multinational corporations. The process results in millions of farmers and businesses going out of business. Hence, many businesses that have been functioning for years providing food, clothing, and shelter for the local communities, go bankrupt. Lawless shantytowns spring up around cities, collecting populations of unemployed and underemployed people. They sit in cafés and see the promise of globalized prosperity on television, but cannot enjoy it themselves. The opportunities that accompany globalization are just not available or accessible to some. The gulf between the rich and the poor widens, creating anger, violence, and instability.[22] In states like Pakistan, the government no longer offers basic services to the most impoverished people. Islamic parties, funded by Saudi Arabia, easily intervene, providing clinics, schools, and orphanages where the poor receive protection. The only product of raised but thwarted expectations is the harvesting of hatred.

Therefore, in the developing world there are several roads to terrorism. A major route connects with the frustrations arising out of poverty. It is not only the destitute who organize themselves and turn violent, nor solely the traditionally poor. It is those who have broken away from the cycle of poverty, yet have failed to find a role in the new scheme of things.[23] These are the people who have dreamt of success through symbols like Hollywood and Coca-Cola, but cannot find a place in that world. They are dislocated between an imaginary world created by symbols, and the reality of everyday life. Further, they end up living in shantytowns outside glittering cities, yet far from the misery of their origins. Thus they are stuck between home and dreams, yet disconnected from both. This is the point where envy and hatred stirs, and terrorism takes hold.

Many other politicians, analysts, and researchers, however, argue that poverty is not the sole generator of hate.[24] A study by Alberto Abadie found that much more than economic factors, a lack of political freedom can account for terrorism. According to Abadie, "[c]ountries with intermediate levels of political freedom are shown to be more prone to terrorism than countries with greater levels of political freedom, or countries with highly authoritarian regimes."[25] One reason for this may be that intermediate levels of political freedom are often the result of transitioning governments. Transitioning governments are often weak and unstable, which are conditions that tend to violence. Thus, a transition from an authoritarian regime to a democracy may be accompanied by a temporary increase in terrorism. On the other hand, oppressive and repressive autocratic regimes do not allow political dissent, and therefore are able to avert terrorist activity.[26]

Another view maintains that economic fluctuations may also lead to violence. Blomberg, Hess, and Weerapana, for example, argue that negative shocks that adversely affect an economy's resource base increase the incidence of conflict, leading to either rebellion or terrorist attack. In these circumstances, terrorist groups find fertile conditions to engender hatred in their effort to influence the course of political events. In distressed economic times, even solid governments with high defense capabilities may be subject to such terrorism.[27]

In light of this conflicting literature, one might argue that establishing post-modern institutions will not serve the strategic interests of the modern liberal democracies. First, there is very strong evidence that terroristic inclinations are immune to economic growth-based solutions. If terrorists are not bred by poverty, then there arguably is no point in further economic opportunity as a complement to the strategic struggle against terrorism. Second, the enablement of global economic opportunity is, by definition, an enterprise that does not guarantee minimum economic security to all. That entitlement was a hallmark of the modern nation-state and, as we have discussed, it will not work in the post-modern age. Terrorism is an activity conducted by the few. Even if there is a correlation between poverty and security, then, the enablement of global economic opportunity will always leave enough individuals outside of its reach to leave untouched a pool of recruits sufficient to fill the ranks of terrorist organizations. The same argument would apply to the claim that trade and enablement of global economic opportunity tend to stem religious fundamentalism.

However, our analysis bypasses the question whether economic security deters individuals from joining forces with terrorist organizations, and the conventional debate over the extent to which poor economic conditions breed crime, violent or other sociopath behavior. Instead, our analysis centers on Statecraft and the extent to which the international economic order of states supports the victors of World War II in establishing a system that accords with their legitimating drive. Just as Bretton Woods embedded modern liberal democratic welfare state Statecraft into a comparative advantage-driven international order, our proposals would, if adopted, embed modern liberal democratic post-modern Statecraft into the international system. As with Bretton Woods, the alternative to a system that works in harmony with the legitimating drive of the day is a fragmentizing, destructive, incoherent system that will inevitably lead to strategic catastrophes. To illustrate our point, consider the following alternative scenarios.

A Free Trade of the Americas Agreement (FTAA) has been contemplated for the past several years. The FTAA would extend the NAFTA all the way south to Tierra del Fuego, thereby encompassing the entire North and South American continent. The FTAA would be based on the NAFTA and GATT model. It would eliminate tariff barriers to trade among the participating states. It would allow for the free movement of goods and services unhindered by non-tariff barriers to trade. It would likely protect foreign investment in the less developed member states by adopting non-discriminatory rules of the type that we discussed in Chapter 7, and affording multinational corporations and other cross border investors a minimum level of economic security. In all likelihood, the FTAA would also include a side agreement on labor and the environment intended to require the participating states to maintain a minimum level of regulatory protection in these areas. For countries that already have "good laws" but do not enforce them, the FTAA would merely require enforcement. For countries that do not have laws that satisfy the modern sensibilities of its drafters, the FTAA might actually impose substantive standards that would require a regulatory overhaul.[28]

The establishment of the FTAA is sure to give foreign investors that currently do business in the maquiladoras the incentive to search for investment opportunities even more desirable than obtain in Mexico. Honeywell might establish plants in Guatemala, Nicaragua, and ship out of those countries to its ultimate points of sale. The plants established in those countries would be desirable from Honeywell's standpoint if the company could find labor of substantially comparable skills as in the maquiladoras, at a lower cost. Other factors might be taken into account including, for example, the company's ability to attract managers to the newly created industrial zones, transportation costs, the level of enforcement of regulation, the relative sophistication of banking systems, political stability, and generally the entire gamut of cost-benefit analysis considerations that are factored into the decision whether to move manufacturing operations to a new market.

The FTAA is the logical extension of the NAFTA. Politically and economically, it is viewed as a means of counter-balancing the increasing global market strength of the European Union. The world's centers of commercial power are shifting. American hegemony is waning, and we now have to share commercial strengths with the Europeans on the one side and, on the other, the emerging Asian powerhouses of China and India. In one or two generations, we might still be in the major league of economic players, but we may no longer hold the gold medal – or the silver or bronze, for that matter. In order to shore up and maintain American economic strength, Southward expansion is a logical project. If successful, the FTAA will expand the "American" market to include hundreds of millions of new consumers, start-up enterprises, skilled and unskilled workers, and generally create a powerhouse of the Western hemisphere capable of dealing with its European and Asian competitors for centuries to come.[29]

We submit that the success or failure of the FTAA (or, as we discuss below, economic enterprises in other parts of the world) depends on the extent to which it is grounded in the post-modern enablement of economic opportunity as an animating principle, as opposed to a modern (and obsolete) conception of welfare. To illustrate our point, let us assume that the American continents integrate into an FTAA using the GATT/NAFTA, modern view of welfare. If they do so, they would rely, as did the GATT and NAFTA, on participating states to redistribute the spoils of the increased economic pie and the proceeds of foreign investment. However, as we have demonstrated in earlier chapters, the governments of states like

Nicaragua or Guatemala would have as little ability as Mexico to accomplish the task. The FTAA would deprive them of the regulatory tools to apply performance requirements, which the post-modern diffuse market would avoid in all events when cross-border market players vote with their feet. The infrastructure of European style welfare is non-existent, because the states in question did not undergo a pre-modern stage of evolution of the type that Europe experienced. Instead of reaching its goal of creating an American market of consumers, producers, workers, and enterprises that counter-balance the European and Asian competition, the FTAA would essentially create a pan-American, diffuse and scattered aggregation of maquiladoras. At the end of the day, the system would continue to tell states that they should impose top-down regulation onto post-modern diffuse markets that do not respond to governance mechanisms from a bygone era. Where the King could decree, a Parliament must rule through democratic principles; no one would, barring some unique circumstances, expect the Parliament to follow the Kingly system of governance. Yet, today's policy planners continue to insist on modern principles that have lost their relevance in the new epoch.

The difference between an FTAA driven by modern concepts, and one governed by post-modern norms, boils down to a principle of governance. In the modern scenario, the vacuum created by the establishment of a post-modern market without post-modern institutions means that markets will operate and evolve based on the economic incentives of the post-modern enterprises: the benefits of the post-modern enterprise are unlikely to be used to build a cohesive, global post-modern market. Without the kind of incentives-based programs that we advocate, the post-modern markets of the FTAA will look like shifting sands of the maquiladoras. Post-modern, cross-border actors will identify the most efficient venues for manufacturing and other activities. They will leave behind a series of large geographical areas that tasted the benefits of post-modern economic opportunity but, as a result of the states' failure to shift to post-modern governance, were unable to build upon those benefits to erect solid post-modern zones of economic activities.

The Mexican maquiladoras, for instance, will in all likelihood be gradually abandoned in favor of new maquiladoras further south. The inability of the Mexican government to use the increased level of economic activities that came with the current maquiladora enterprise to create economic opportunity might leave behind economic zones that resemble the devastated post-industrial areas of, say, West Virginia. In both cases, the economic phenomenon is driven by the same cause: the end of an economic era associated with a specific age of Statecraft. A textiles factory or steel mill in West Virginia thrived in the modern era.[30] The economic undertaking was typical of the activities associated with the national industries of the modern age. When the GATT institutionalized comparative advantage, Asian (and other) competitors took over the markets of the firms engaged in those activities. The GATT solution, shifting the means of production to new areas of activity, did not work, in large part because such a solution would only make sense if (in the long run) the world remained modern. However, as we have shown, history has not ended and the post-modern era has arrived; and, with it, the shift away from welfare policies of the modern age.

The Mexican maquiladora problem would arise not because of the end of the post-modern era, but because without institutions for the post-modern age, the economic development phenomenon would shift across borders to the most efficient venue. The result and root cause, however, are the same as they were in West Virginia (except that the consequences of the abandonment of the maquiladoras will, as we discuss below, be more devastating in the case of the maquiladoras). Just like West Virginia's impoverished areas, these zones would be deprived of a core area of economic activity. The workforce that migrated north to the maquiladoras would find itself unemployed, without any substitute enterprises that could employ a meaningful part of the population. Unlike West Virginians, who at least have access to one of the most developed economies in the world, or the workers of Shenzhen, who would have access to one of the most rapidly growing markets, the Mexican maquiladora dwellers would be locked between a northern border that is legally closed to them, and a South that tends to shift opportunities to other states comprising the FTAA.

This state of affairs would defeat the core expectations of the NAFTA, result in a strategic nightmare and, if replicated throughout the FTAA, could result in a crisis of unprecedented scale in this hemisphere. As we explained, the NAFTA sought to raise standards of living in Mexico in order to, among other things, create economic opportunities at home that would make it less likely that illegal immigrants will cross the border to seek opportunity in the North. However, the NAFTA's modern regulatory framework has resulted in the establishment of a post-modern market, which itself necessitates that we revisit the institutions of trade. Unless regulated in accordance with the enablement of economic opportunity norm, the post-modern market would result in the mid to long run in the establishment of a large class of unemployed, disaffected classes. The emerging yet vulnerable classes of today would become the excluded classes of tomorrow. They would put pressure on the southern border of the United States of even greater magnitude than we have seen thus far.

Conceptually speaking, this state of affairs would be the functional equivalent of the collapse of worldwide markets exacerbated by the modern liberal democracies' insistence on pre-modern mercantilist policies. In both cases, Statecraft evolved to a new epoch. In both cases, the international society of states had to follow suit, and its failure to do so resulted in a fundamental disconnect between Statecraft and the international order of states. In the modern era, the choice was between a fractured concrete of states, battling one another into economic disjunction and chaos, and a cohesive compact able to maximize the production of resources for redistribution by the modern welfare State. In today's post-modern era, the choice is between a post-modern diffuse market with shifting pockets of temporary economic activity that create vulnerable trading classes that fall into economic despair as cross-border forces move without creating lasting economic opportunity, and the type of solidified global market that we further describe below.

From the strategic point of view, making the wrong choice will also have as dramatic an impact as it did in the modern era. Then, the modern liberal democratic world found itself fractured at the time when it needed cohesion most. Today, the failure to institutionalize the enablement of global economic opportunity could create no less of a strategic nightmare. The post-modern forces, fueled by the GATT, create trading classes that have raised expectations of entering the global market. They participate in the ultimate post-modern economic enterprise – the spread of economic activity with a connection to the nation bound up with cross-border economic actors. Yet, their vulnerability threatens to send them back two epochs, to the pre-modern world. If the Mexican maquiladoras are not shored up through a post-modern process of enablement of economic opportunity, they will revert back to pre-modernism, not modernism. The reason, as we have repeatedly explained, is that the Mexican state did not pass through a modern era akin to that which Europe experienced. Lacking an infrastructure capable of supporting a population like that of the maquiladoras, the fall to a pre-modern economic condition is assured.

While the plight of the vulnerable classes of Europe and North America also creates strategic problems (in particular in the Muslim immigrant suburbs of European capitals) the principal strategic danger associated with the failure to institutionalize post-modern enablement of comparative advantage arises from the regions that catapulted directly from pre-modern to post-modern status. The maquiladoras, for example, could become a breeding ground for terrorism-related smuggling at the very gates of America. If economic opportunity is not cultivated there, the maquiladoras could well experience classic spiraling down into violence and strategically dangerous activities. As we explain above, the raising of economic expectations is, somewhat ironically, one of the potential causes of violence and strategic activities that run counter to the interests of modern liberal democracies. The combination of raised expectations, vulnerability, and disappearance of economic opportunity without adequate substitute (and without a modern welfare net) is highly likely to generate a strategic threat.

Instead of being shored up by the NAFTA-generating of post-modern activities, the Mexican border could well become a zone akin to the infamous "Tri-Border Area" of Paraguay, Argentina, and Brazil.[31] That zone has become a breeding ground for underground or criminal activities of all sorts. Money launderers, drug smugglers, terrorists, and other post-modern threats operate in a border area that gives them a gateway to a large chunk of South America. The situation is so dangerous there that the U.S. government has entered into a collaboration agreement with the governments of Paraguay, Argentina, and Brazil to send federal agents charged with stemming the tide of potentially threatening activities at the source. The lack of economic opportunity in the maquiladoras could transplant the problem to our borders. Worse still, the continuous shifting of maquiladora-like zones of economic activities, and the failure to shore them up, would compound and multiply the problem throughout Central and South America. Instead of a growing, increasingly cohesive and fortifying cross border trading class, the post-modern FTAA would be a fractured aggregation of a large pre-modern class, lying alongside a dwindling post-modern set of economic classes.

BEYOND ECONOMIC CAUSALITY

Our argument does not depend on a correlation between economic opportunity and terrorism. The situation the world faces today is akin to that which prevailed before World War II. Then, there was no guarantee that the liberalization of trade through a system grounded in comparative advantage would increase the modern democracies' chance of defeating fascism and communism. Would Hitler have risen to power if Germany's economy had flourished instead of falling into the throes of inflation, depression, and pervasive gloom? Would France and Britain have stood up to Hitler earlier, instead of engaging in a failed policy of appeasement, had their economic strength and collaboration with each other and other democracies such as the United States been fostered by the abandonment of mercantilist policies? Would the United States have entered the war sooner had it started to recover from the Great Depression through internal policies that focused on welfare through reconstruction and an external trade policy based on free trade?

We submit that there was no need to answer these questions before World War II, because Statecraft dictated that in all events the GATT and Bretton Woods should come into effect. The inner face of Statecraft should have become embedded in the international economic order of states, regardless of whether Bretton Woods and comparative advantage would have prevented states from falling into the fascist camp. Comparative advantage worked in harmony with the modern welfare constitution to solidify a society of modern states, rather than a fractured alliance. The victors of World War II had the opportunity, before the war, to install a system of trade that would embed not just welfare and inner regulation, but democracy itself. Britain, France, the United States, and their allies had no meaningful choice but to establish a trade system that would accord with their modern liberal democratic form of Statecraft and, in the process, establish a structure that states such as pre-fascist Germany or Italy could join as they entered the alliance that would wrestle Statecraft away from communism. Their failure to do so did not necessarily change the course of history, but it failed to ensure that a system of trade that accords with inner Statecraft (and designed to work in harmony with the strategic needs of the State) would be effected.

The epochal nature of Statecraft drives not only the link between the inner and outer faces of the State, but also the relationship between strategy and trade. In the modern era, the United States, Britain, France, and other democracies should have put a comparative advantage-based system in place that would have consolidated their Statecraft and, additionally, might have brought within its fold pre-fascist Germany, Italy, and Spain. Today, the enablement of global economic opportunity will work to anchor the economic opportunities that the GATT has yielded throughout parts of the trading world. Using the regulatory tools that we have described, it will work to build and solidify a global post-modern market that, in turn, will ensure the survival of the modern liberal democracies and other states that comprise it.

In the FTAA example, instead of a fractured U.S. market, our program would contribute to the shoring up of economic development in the maquiladoras and other zones that will continue to be engendered through the development of post-modern enterprises. In the absence of a modern welfare system, post-modern enablement of economic opportunity will contribute to the continued entanglement, across national borders and above states, of the economic markets that are being integrated. Importantly, it will ensure the coordination of regulatory programs along the lines that we have described. Whereas comparative advantage helped the State unleash its powers to provide for the welfare of the nation, enablement of global economic opportunity will unleash the collective power of states, international organizations, and private actors, based on a system of incentives – not entitlements – to create a solidified pan-American market. Like the GATT, the post-modern institutionalization of the enablement of economic opportunity will embed the inner face of the State into the international economic order and contribute to the creation of a coherent whole, rather than its disintegration.

The enablement of economic opportunity on the globalized institutional level will deepen the relationship of inter-dependence and inter-connectedness among the victors of World War II and other states that are emerging as powerful economic and strategic actors. China, India, Indonesia, Brazil, Argentina, South Africa, and many other emerging economies, are the twenty-first century interlocutors of the modern liberal democracies. These states are bound to develop strong internal markets that may compensate for the failure of comparative advantage, working alone, to shore up the benefits of trade within their borders. China, for example, is in the process of building a massive internal market that will continue to supply demand for Chinese goods, no matter where comparative advantage leads foreign producers.[32] A system based on the enablement of global economic opportunity would ensure that China remains bound up and embedded in the global economy rather than retreat into itself.

For the United States and other World War II victors, it is vital to bring states like China into the fold of the modern liberal democratic alliance, as it has evolved in the post-modern era. The solidification of the post-modern global markets, and the relationships of inter-connectedness and inter-dependence that such solidification brings about, would serve the strategic interests of the modern liberal democracies in creating a post-modern bloc that includes a wide array of states, on every continent. The markets of all of these states, while faced with disparate economic conditions, would coalesce into a single whole that, as this epoch progresses, is more likely to coalesce into an association of like-minded market states that share strategic interests in market stability, combating terrorism, and containing religious fundamentalist Statecraft.

Conclusion

We live in an era of transition and transformation. The collapse of the Berlin Wall and the end of the Long War did not end history. Rather, the lull in foundational changes that followed the resolution of the great ideological battle of the twentieth century proved to be no more than a pause in the historical narrative. The victors of the war now face new, globalized, and diffuse chronic problems that threaten their continued ability to function as prosperous, liberal democratic states. Terrorist networks dedicated to suicide operations, the conflicts between the West and radical Islamic forces, and the volatile state of key geopolitical allies such as Pakistan, generate risks of protracted and diffuse military conflicts. Environmental and health threats are of a magnitude that make it impossible for any single state, however powerful, to control the outcome of threats that affect the collectivity. Global warming, viruses that can spread on the same schedule as a major airline's daily routes, staggering rates of infectious diseases in many poor countries, and myriad other health or environmental concerns, endanger virtually every inhabitant of the planet.

Markets, enterprises, and economic activities are also intertwined, spanning a mass that is best understood as a global market, where premodern, modern, and post-modern population segments live side-by-side. Private economic interests, networks of government officials, associations of professionals, coalitions of consumers, and other interests have enormous influence over issues that, in the modern era, would have fallen squarely within the competence of the State. Altogether, what has been called "globalization," the "flat world" or the post-modern world, is a phenomenon that has contributed to the gradual erosion of modern Statecraft and its reliance of sovereignty, welfare, the nation, and balance of power.

We have argued that each era of Statecraft implicates certain structural hallmarks that define the manner in which the State will operate, both internally as a matter of law and in its international strategic and trade orders. Rather than ending, the history of states and of Statecraft operates in a constant cycle that ushers in successive epochs containing the seeds of their own transformation. The pre-modern State drew on the power of its subjects to strengthen itself, thereby sowing the seeds of the nation and of the modern era in the process. The modern State valued open trade because it enlarged the global pie and fostered its national welfare architecture. By opening borders to trade, it flattened the world as the post-modern era dawned. This nascent post-modern era, we have argued, requires a new norm and institutional setting that will eliminate horizontal and vertical impediments to growth that are remnants of the twentieth century.

The modern world divided itself along horizontal and vertical lines. Horizontally, the nation-states constituted the basic ontological unit of analysis, relying on modern sovereignty to exclude other states from intruding in their territorial realm, and balancing each other's power to achieve a collective equilibrium. Vertically, nation-states sheltered themselves from intrusion by international or supra-national norms and institutions, and ensured that those would be confined to the extra-national realm. This basic framework manifested itself throughout the treaties that regulated the life of states in the twentieth century, including the GATT and its successor WTO, and the fundamental principles of modern international law enshrined in the United Nations charter provisions upholding each state's obligation to refrain from interfering in fellow states' internal affairs unless acting in self-defense or in the defense of its allies. "Embedded liberalism" – the poetry of Bretton Woods – expressed this foundational notion. Bretton Woods, however, transformed the world from a set of discrete economic units (states) trading with one another, speaking vertically to an international system aimed at liberalizing trade while respecting sovereignty and balance of power, to what may be termed a "horizontalizing system" where trading actors cut across borders to form international industries having more in common with each other than with the other players in the states in which they operate. Liberalism can no longer be embedded in such an international landscape. This is the essence of the post-modern trading world and, as we have explained, a constitutional moment is needed to create institutions and norms that will regulate this transformed global economy, and embed the new animating norm of the system.

The time has come for this constitutional moment to take place, in a public and highly visible conference that will install the Trade Council and the enablement of global economic opportunity as the pillars of the new global trading order. The ethos of the trade system has gradually shifted from a relatively pure focus on the elimination of protectionism and barriers to trade among the World War II victors to encompass the global lifting of standards of living. The Doha Declaration stated that "[i]nternational trade can play a major role in the promotion of economic development and the alleviation of poverty."[1] Following in the footsteps of the European commitment to a social and not merely economic union, Doha recognized the need for all people "to benefit from the increased opportunities and welfare gains that the multilateral trading system generates."[2]

We have argued that, regardless of whether greater economic opportunity and security further the security and strategic interests of the democratic world, the configuration of Statecraft in the post-modern world requires that the victors of World War II adopt the global enablement of economic opportunity as the animating principle of their trade system. Terrorists, militarily-inclined religious ideologues, and opportunistic leaders allying themselves with these forces, may prevail in post-modern battles regardless of the extent to which the populations they control or on whom they rely climb up the ladder of material progress. Structurally, however, if we do not construct a global trading order consistent with the architectural blueprint of the twenty-first century interloped markets, our expanding economic edifice will crumble and the enemies of democracy will be free to pick up the pieces and spread their totalitarian ideology of hate in the broken field that we will have made possible. At the beginning of this new era, we find ourselves at a crossroads and in a race against time, and we must write history rather than catch up to it. We have little choice: we can either spread economic opportunity, shore up as much of the global markets as possible, and bring as many stratas of the global collectivity into the fold, or wake up after the next global conflict to make these choices not a matter of foresight but the result of forced historical choice – much in the manner of Bretton Woods.

Yet, those at the helm of global trade and commercial policy, while acknowledging the goal, fail to avail themselves of the instruments of success. All the while recognizing that "the majority of WTO members are developing countries" and that "trade should equate with greater global economic opportunity," the WTO stubbornly holds fast to quintessentially modern tools. The Doha Round, even if it produces a wholesale adoption of its program, offers little more than the homily that modern "enhanced market access, balanced rules, and well targeted, sustainably financed technical assistance and capacity-building programmes have important roles to play." As we have demonstrated, this agenda is bound to fail in that it forces on a new international economic landscape policies of the past.

The WTO's lofty program of inclusion, as well as the continued use of trade to shore up the economic health of the Western victors of World

War II and their essential interest in fostering a globally integrated economy where emerging powers like China and India operate in harmony
with established economies, all depend on the ability of the global trading
partners to move beyond the hallmarks of the modern age. The failure of
the international trading system is directly linked to its continued adherence to modern welfare and comparative advantage in order to achieve
post-modern goals, and its imposition of a constitutional structure that
fertilized on Western soil in a world that never traversed the pre-modern
and modern European and American stages of development. Doha is correct that Benin's cotton or Morocco's tomatoes should compete in the
global markets free of the excessive subsidies granted to American or
European farmers. Doha, however, completely misses the point that the
economic interests that will benefit from the commercial exploitation of
Benin's cotton are the post-modern forces crisscrossing the evaporating
borders of the world, not the vulnerable classes of Benin and Morocco.
Welfare, as we know it, will not accomplish the redistribution of these benefits because there is no infrastructure in Benin and Morocco to accomplish the welfare enterprise, and because the resources to be derived from
freer and fairer trade are simply insufficient to realize a welfare state of the
type that France or other Western nations established after the Industrial
Revolution.

We have argued that the victors of war should establish a system of
trade that fits their needs in that it accords with their inner Statecraft, and
that they must account for changes in their inner constitutional structure and revise the global order in each epochal incarnation of the State.
While China, India, Brazil, and other emerging economies are rushing
with strength into the globalized markets of the post-modern world, the
international economic structure provides no regulatory framework for
prodding their development to encompass masses of people that, in the
twentieth century, looked as outsiders as the modern liberal democracies
traded toward advancement, wealth, and social stability. Further, the system of trade that the West adopted for itself has now run a course that
makes it necessary, as much for the West as for the rest of the world,
to adopt economic opportunity as the animating norm of the system
and push toward the future using this tool of trade policy as the main
driver.

In many respects, we find ourselves in the same position as the modern
liberal democracies in the 1930s. Strategic threats pose existential dangers to the democratic bloc. Then, fascism and communism knocked at
the door with takeover ambitions. Today, religiously grounded fundamentalism and global networked terrorism openly vow to destroy our markets
and more. Then, protectionism and the pre-modern states were difficult

policies to shed because of domestic pressures to shelter industrial sectors from competition. Today, a pure comparative advantage system insists on remaining the animating factor of international trade because of our attachment to welfare as the means to achieve prosperity for all. Then, protectionism was bound to cause the breakdown of the international trade system because protectionist policies were bound to yield trade regulatory wars that ultimately would cause the system to collapse. Today, the failure to recognize that the enablement of global economic opportunity is needed to unleash the forces of growth that will achieve development is bound to result in a system where crucial economic issues will be dealt with unilaterally in a way that, in the long run, will prove detrimental to the collective interests of the global markets.

The United States has been accused, in part legitimately, of failing as a global leader by imposing a power-based approach to international relations instead of seeking a more European, Kantian law-based approach. Like Kagan, we have vigorously protested that if the United States does not patrol the worst neighborhoods of the world, its thugs will soon threaten the gates of Europe, and that the European rules-based paradigm could not survive without an enforcer.[3] To a large extent, we subscribe to this view. However, even Kagan would concede that everywhere possible we should seek to impose order through law rather than power, and that putting aside morals we may not have the capacity to act as hegemon. Trade is an area where rules, collaboration and alliance building may achieve our core strategic goals in the age of the market state. Our proposals would create a structure that would unleash the forces of democracy to engage in a community- and incentives-based policing. Without such a foundational change, the road to hell will indeed be paved with the good intentions of welfare.

When we presented the ideas in this book on the academic road, we were constantly told both that welfare is a good thing and accused of subscribing to an unbridled theory of free market and unregulated trade. Underlying these accusations was the unspoken assumption that we believe, and that our arguments and proposals are premised on, the end of the State and the abdication of governmental authority over the well-being of its subjects. We believe that this criticism stems from more left-leaning attachment to welfare as a system, and that we are merely claiming that welfare no longer equates to well-being. Thus, the governments' new collective responsibility is to foster the global enablement of economic opportunity. We are as committed to the survival of liberal democracy as our critics. We recognize, though, that modern Statecraft has to give way to post-modern, and in the twenty-first century world well-being will not be achieved through obsolete and Euro-centric programs.

That is not to say that the institutions and foundational principles of modern liberal democracy have no place in the post-modern world and must all be discarded. Indeed, we have faced criticism from right-leaning colleagues for our insistence on institutional governance of the global market. That criticism, too, is unwarranted. What we are dealing with is the failure of the international community to establish cross-border leadership in a world where borders matter less and less. In this globalized world, there must be global leadership. We are not utopian: we simply do not see a global government as capable of functioning without bringing global tyranny along with worldwide legislation. Our analysis cuts through this Gordian knot with a proposal for an incentives-based, *ad hoc* system that will begin to solve the problems of the post-modern world. The world needs to be shifted toward a course that has the potential to succeed: top-down regulation will not do the job.

All life, we believe, is possibility. Unlike the welfare world, we do not purport to provide guarantees, but only the possibility that a peaceful, democratic, and prosperous world can be realized. It is in this spirit and with this hope that we have written this book.

Notes

Preface

1. The Atlantic Council (2007).

1. Introduction

1. The Atlantic Council's (2007) recent analysis continues to approach global trade in a "top-down" fashion, recommending solutions such as an expansion of G8 governance and merger of the World Bank and the IMF. The group maintains that the needs of developing countries are best addressed by global institutions such as the World Bank and the IMF:

> While the first step is a clearer delineation of roles, the real ambition must be to work together to provide a comprehensive set of strategies and resources that will move countries away from poverty and economic instability. A well-constructed merger will allow the institutions to reduce duplication in administration and elsewhere, while encouraging a coordinated approach to the micro- and macroeconomic needs of developing countries.

Ibid. at 12. We advocate a different approach to the challenges posed by developing nations. We agree with Paul Collier that, at least in the poorest countries, "failure of the growth process is the overwhelming problem we have to crack." Collier (2007a) at 190. In Chapter 6, we introduce our preferred institution, the Trade Council. For an attack on and rethinking of the very idea of "free trade," see Unger (2007).

2. One very recent debate in the news is over so-called "PTA" agreements. These regional agreements lead to increased trade within the trading bloc but less trade to those outside the bloc. Critics argue that this is "protectionism by another name" and condemn these agreements as undermining multilateralism. See Bhagwati (2007).

3. As we explain in more detail in Chapter 2, the "State" is an enduring entity that has gone through a series of metamorphoses we identify as "constitutional" in nature. Simply stated, while there are certainly different types of states in the world at any given time, the principal states of the trading regime all exemplify the same structure. The nation-state is a prime example of an important but by no means timeless form of the State.

4. We make no claim for the "necessity" of the story we tell. That is, we take no position on the question whether the history of global trade could have been different. We prescind from this discussion for two reasons. First, matters of explanatory historiography are very controversial. In itself, this is not a reason to refrain from taking a position. But the second reason leads us to believe that ours is the wiser course. The reason is quite simple: we do not need to take a position. Whether or not past events are in any sense "determined," we believe that we can see how the new global trading order requires

the sort of analysis we offer in this book. We can make our argument without taking a position on the question of historical necessity. Thus, we tell our story without reference to a controversial historiography.

5. Fukuyama has continued to massage his initial claim. Recently he had this to say:

> The End of History was never linked to a specifically American model of social or political organization. Following Alexandre Kojève, the Russian-French philosopher who inspired my original argument, I believe that the European Union more accurately reflects what the world will look like at the end of history than the contemporary United States. The EU's attempt to transcend sovereignty and traditional power politics by establishing a transnational rule of law is much more in line with a "post-historical" world than the Americans' continuing belief in God, national sovereignty, and their military.

> Francis Fukuyama, "The History at the End of History," http://www.project-syndicate .org/commentary/fukuyama3/English.

6. We use the term "post-modern" throughout this book in describing the form of the State that succeeds the nation-state. In choosing to use the term, we are mindful of the debates in architecture, literature and social theory over the continuing efficacy of claims for "postmodernism." We take no position on the question whether "postmodernism" or "postmodernity" are efficacious characterizations of any aspect of intellectual or artistic thought. Rather, we use the term "post-modern" because it enables us to contrast both forms of the State as well as different social formations that figure in our argument.

7. We are not alone in our opinion that the State continues to evolve. For our purposes, the most important focus is *how* the State is changing with respect to political economy and trade. See Levy (2006a) at 2:

> The state also rises. Rather than an eroding historical legacy, state intervention should be seen as a new response to some very contemporary economic, technological, social, and ideological developments. Whether state intervention is "increasing" or "decreasing," on balance, is ultimately unknowable – or, at least, unmeasurable. But it is clear that here is much more to the story than state decline, on the one hand, or path-dependent inertia, on the other hand. The essays in this book focus on the undertold story, on the transformation, adaptation, and transformation of state activities in the contemporary period.

> Ibid.

8. See Bobbitt (2002) at 178 ("The state-nation mobilized and exploited whatever national resources it happened to find itself in charge of . . . It was not responsible *to* the nation; rather it was responsible *for* the nation."). We discuss the state-nation in detail in Chapter 2. We believe that the state-nation is a distinct form of the State, one that immediately precedes the nation-state. Briefly, a central difference between the state-nation and the nation-state is the presence of a system of welfare (capaciously understood) in the nation-state.

9. The classic citation remains Weber's essay "Politics as a Vocation," in Gerth and Mills (1958).

10. This story is told in detail in Cooper (2003).

11. On the origin of the phrase "welfare state," see Johnson (2005):

> The phrase "welfare state" is one that emerged after the Second World War, and was first used to describe the complex of social policies enacted under the Labour government in Britain after 1945. From Britain, "the phrase made its way around the world." The welfare state possesses a unique institutional structure for the administration of social policy. In Weberian terms, the development of the welfare state may be linked to the process of rationalization, and the development of bureaucratic authority and the emergence of social clients. The expansion of the services provided by the welfare state in the twentieth century to cover a widening range of risks has also been described as a "general phenomenon of modernization". The growth of the number and kinds of social services provided by the state was a function of its ability to create procedures defining social policy, raise the funds (through taxation and contributions) to pay for these policies, identify recipients and distribute benefits and services. The welfare state may thus be conceived as a very advanced and developed state apparatus, functioning in

a political space that recognized its legitimacy, and in an economic space provided the means of paying for its output.

Ibid at 5.

12. Cooper writes: "The kind of world we have depends on the kind of states that compose it: for the pre-modern world, success is empire and failure is chaos. For the modern, success entails managing the balance of power and failure means falling back into war or empire. For the postmodern state, success means openness and transnational co-operation." Cooper (2003) at 76.

13. Martin Van Creveld has recently remarked that "[t]he principal function of the state, like that of all previous forms of government, has always been to fight other states, whether defensively, in an attempt to protect its interests, or offensively, in order to expand them." Van Creveld (2006) at 330.

14. See Barton et al. (2006) at 12: "The main purpose of the GATT was to lower trade barriers at the border: tariffs, quotas, countervailing duties, antidumping duties, safeguards measures, together with their administration."

15. This is what John Ruggie calls the bargain of "embedded liberalism." See Ruggie (1983).

16. The changing nature of welfare from a regime of entitlements to one of economic opportunity is discussed in Chapter 3.

17. As we explain, protection of minority rights is also a fundamental feature of "welfare."

18. Kent Jones describes these institutions in their historical context in Jones (2004):

Near the end of World War II, in 1944, representatives of the Allied powers met in Bretton Woods, New Hampshire, to discuss the future of world economic relations. The hope was to develop international economic institutions that would promote prosperity and peace in alignment with the foreign policy goals of the victorious Allies. As part of that plan, the Bretton Woods meeting led eventually to the establishment of the International Bank for Reconstruction and Development (World Bank), the International Monetary Fund (IMF) and the General Agreement on Tariffs and Trade (GATT).

Ibid at 68.

19. In its Policy Paper, the Atlantic Council also recommends convening a conference "aimed at restructuring the existing institutional architecture" of global trade. Atlantic Council (2007) at 3.

20. The Atlantic Council (2007) report confirms this.

2. The Evolving State

1. We use the word "state" in two different senses. When we write "State," we are referring to the conceptual political entity that has evolved in the Western world over roughly the last five hundred years. See McClelland (1996) at 280 (dating the birth of the modern state at 1500). The State is manifested in many territorially and politically distinct "states," like Italy or the Republic of Latvia. When we refer to these individual states, we refer to them as a "state." For discussion of the various phases of the State's development, and their relation to a variety of constitutional orders, see Bobbitt (2002) at 69–347.

2. Fukuyama (Summer 1989) at 3. As he had for so many intellectuals of his generation, Fukuyama's Hegel came by way of Alexandre Kojeve. See Kojeve (1969). For a general discussion, see Drury (1994) at 179–98.

3. See Fukuyama (Summer 1989) at 5–6.

4. The state-nation is the constitutional manifestation of a state characterized by a mobilization of a nation (a national, ethnocultural group) to benefit the State. ("State" as used herein is defined in note 1 above.) This form of the State, exemplified by Napoleonic France, dominated Europe and America in the nineteenth century and ultimately gave rise to the modern nation-state with the advent of World War I. For a general description, see Bobbitt (2002) 144–204. The classic definition of the nation-state, on the other hand, refers to "a relatively homogenous group of people with a feeling of common

nationality living within the defined boundaries of an independent and sovereign state: a state containing one as opposed to several nationalities." *Webster's Third New International Dictionary* 1505 (1986). As explained throughout, we use the term "nation-state," at times interchangeably with "modern state," to denote an era where the fundamental elements of Statecraft involved a State that harnessed itself to the nation, legitimized itself through the guarantee of the nation's welfare, adhered to relatively strong hallmarks of sovereignty and operated in an international system that valued balance of power. It is, of course, common for modern nation-states to include discrete minorities who are an integral part of the collectivity-state but do not necessarily belong to the dominant ethnicity. For our purposes, however, this nuance is irrelevant in that our use of the term nation-state is a shorthand for the hallmarks of Statecraft that are associated with a particular period and is not intended to address in any way the issues related to the rights of minorities in nation-states or like questions.

5. According to Fukuyama, the liberal democratic model soundly beat fascism and communism because, simply put, it was a better idea. The liberal democratic model had no problem besting the fascist ideology of expansionism and racial superiority. In time, it defeated the marxist ideology – in part because the growth of a strong and expansive middle class, resulting from (among other factors) the welfare policies of the nation-state – as it had radically changed the social reality in which Marx wrote. In the end, Fukuyama argued, all good government would be organized along the lines of the liberal democratic model, which would be applied to govern an ethnic or otherwise discrete nation and would protect the rights of minorities. See Fukuyama (1989) at 3–18.

6. The literature on the question of the State is vast. Not surprisingly, there exists a wide range of opinion on the question whether the State is dying, in a process of change, or neither. For discussion of the literature and the full range of opinions, see Levy (2006a).

7. See Slaughter (2004).

8. Some see the "end" of the State marked by a transition to other, more complicated organizing forms. See Van Creveld (1999) at vii ("Globally speaking, the international system is moving away from an assembly of distinct, territorial, sovereign, legally equal states toward different, more hierarchical, and in many ways more complicated structures."). See also Slaughter (2004) at 32 ("The conception of the unitary state is a fiction.").

9. For discussion of Kingly states, see Bobbitt (2002) *passim*.

10. We will shortly describe the state-nation in detail.

11. See Bobbitt (2002) at 178 ("The state-nation mobilized and exploited whatever national resources it happened to find itself in charge of . . . It was not responsible *to* the nation; rather it was responsible *for* the nation.").

12. Van Creveld (1999): "The first state to deliberately mobilize the masses for its own purposes was Revolutionary France; the magnitude of the task can be judged from the fact that, in 1789, the country was still divided into eighty provinces, each of which had it separate laws, customs, and political traditions." For an interesting (and amusing) discussion of the case of eighteenth century France (as well as other countries) and prevalence of tolls and customs throughout the provinces, see Blanning (2007) at 30–34.

13. See Bobbitt (2002) at 152.

14. We are both commercial lawyers and, so, are willing to entertain the proposition that Karl Llewellyn's Uniform Commercial Code might rival the Napoleonic Code in its achievements.

15. Van Creveld (1999) at 199.

16. The classic study is Breuilly (1982, 1994). He characterizes nationalist arguments for the State this way:

A nationalist argument is a political doctrine built upon three basis [sic] assertions:

a. There exists a nation with an explicit and peculiar character.
b. The interests and values of this nation take priority over all other interests and values.

c. The nation must be as independent as possible. This usually requires at least the attainment of political sovereignty.

Ibid at 2.

17. Deane (1978) at 2.

18. Preston (1967) at 22. For an accessible discussion of the origins of banking and the role of the Medici, see Parks (2005).

19. For discussion, see Vick (2003).

20. Cooper (2003) at 20 remarks: "National identities are usually created by states out of the raw material of history, culture and language."

21. Hegel (1975) at 331 ("[E]very state is sovereign and autonomous against its neighbours.").

22. When he wedded balance of power to the idea of "containment," George Kennan authored the US approach to the cold War. See Kennan (X) (July 1947) at 566–82.

23. For ease of reference, we will refer to these as "modern states."

24. Consider Bobbitt (2002) at xxv–xxvii.

25. Ibid.

26. Even marxists affirm the evolution of the State over claims for its demise. See Negri and Hardt (2004) and Negri and Hardt (2001).

27. For historical details, see Furet (1999).

28. See Cooper (2003) at 26 (attributing the beginning of "postmodern Europe" to The Treaty of Rome (1957) and the Treaty on Conventional Forces in Europe).

29. See Bobbitt, (2002) at 691, n39.

30. Cooper (2003) at 3.

31. Ibid at 27.

32. Bobbitt (2002) at 811.

33. As Machiavelli noted in 1519, "[n]o wall exists, however thick, that artillery cannot destroy in a few days."

34. For discussion of the idea of a "constitutional order" in the context of American constitutional law, see Tushnet (2003) at 1–7.

35. Even German fascists had a conception of the welfare state. See Aly (2006): ("The Nazi leadership made automobiles affordable to everyday Germans. It introduced the previously unknown idea of vacations. It doubled the number of days off for workers and began to develop large-scale tourism in Germany.")

36. For discussion and possible explanation, see Micklethwait and Woolridge (2004).

37. Ibid. See also Trebilcock and Howse (1999) at Chapter 1; Irwin (1996); Ruggie (1993a).

38. See Bobbitt (2002) 240–42.

39. Until recently, the situation was particularly acute in Germany. See Landler Feb. 3, (2005). The complexities of the German context are discussed in Bleses and Seeleib-Kaier (2004). See also Steingart (2004) (the story of Germany's rise and decline since 1945). Despite the pain of reform, or perhaps as a result of it, the German economy is now rebounding strongly. See Benoit (2007) (noting that Germany reported its first surplus since 1989). But, in the view of some, "the boom is over." See Rubisch, https://www.commerzbank.com/research/economic_research/pool/d_eur/d_konjunkturaktuell/d_eur_konjak_en_0607.pdf. See also Sinn (2007) for further doubts about Germany's future as a European welfare state.

40. 2004 HM Spending Review, PN A2 (July 12, 2004), available online at <http://www.hm-treasury.gov.uk/spending_review/spend_sr04/press/spend_sr04_press13.cfm> (visited Sept 19, 2005). See also Rachel Smithies, *Public and Private Welfare Activity in the United Kingdom, 1979 to 1999*, available online at <http://sticerd.lse.ac.uk/dps/case/cp/CASEpaper93.pdf> (visited Sept. 19, 2005).

41. See Levy, Miura, and Park (2006) at 94; OECD 2004a.

42. For data on European population issues, see United Nations Economic Commission for Europe Population Activities Unit, available online at <http://www.unece.org/ead/pau/pau/pau_h.htm> (visited Nov 1, 2005). Pension reform has been a topic of ongoing

discussion. In the case of France, for example, in 2006 the Bank of France reached agreement with trade unions to restructure a pension scheme that had been untouched since Napoleon created the central bank in 1800. See *Financial Times*, 11.27.06 at 4.

43. Razin and Sadka (2005).

44. Ibid at 1.

45. For a contrary view, see Wolf (2004) at 256 ("There is no sign of an inability to sustain tax revenue among the high-income countries."). The issue remains quite controversial. See Houlder (2007) at 11.

46. Quoted in Razin and Sadka (2005) at 4.

47. The importance of competitive tax rates has not gone unnoticed. Germany has recently moved to cut its corporate-tax rate to below 30 percent, undercutting the United States, France, Spain, Italy, Denmark, Netherlands, and the United Kingdom. See Walker (2006) at A6.

48. Razin and Sadka (2005) at 4.

49. Bobbitt (2002) at 284

50. Ibid at 670–71.

51. Ibid at 673.

52. Ibid at 672–76.

53. For excellent discussion of private law and the State's loss of control, see Caruso (2006).

54. Some even referred to international finance as a "dictatorship." See Evans (1997) at 62–87. Evans writes:

> The "dictatorship of international finance" is really closer to a mutual hostage situation. The operation of the international financial system would descend quickly into chaos without responsible fiscal and monetary policies on the part of international actors. Financial markets can easily punish deviant states, but in the long run their returns depend on the existence of an interstate system in which the principal national economies are under the control of competent and "responsible" state actors. Those who sit astride the international financial system need capable regulators. The lightning speed at which transactions of great magnitude can be completed makes for great allocational efficiency in theory, but it also makes for great volatility in practice.

> Ibid at 72.

55. Control was lost to the financial markets which, for example, imposed interest rate premiums on the currencies of governments pursuing policies deemed friendly to social democratic policies. See Garrett (1995) at 49.

56. See Frieden (2006) 392–412 for discussion of currency crises and their precipitation by growth in global computing and communications.

57. As Richard O'Brien explains (O'Brien (1992)), money is an "information product."

> Money is an 'information product.' The very essence of money is not so much in its physical appearance as in the information it conveys, whether as a debt, a store of value, or a medium of exchange. Its universality depends on the fact that everyone knows what money means, or can mean, even if it takes skills to manage it, to manipulate it, to use it. Money can exists in a physical state, or it can exist as an item of information, a record in a ledger, or even in an unwritten understanding between people and organizations. As soon as money goes beyond its physical state, its information characteristics come into play. Access to money depends on access to that information. Its existence as an information item also gives money its flexibility and its 'fungibility', the ability to be transferred from place to place, to move from purpose to purpose.

> Ibid at 7.

58. For an account of the role of European policymakers in the development of global capital, see Abdelal (2007).

59. The classic argument for this is made by Sassen. See Sassen (2006) and (1996).

60. See Goldsmith and Wu (2006).

61. The principal organizations for arbitration include: the International Chamber of Commerce in Paris (ICC); the American Arbitration Association (AAB); the London Court of

International Arbitration (LCIA); and the World Bank's International Center for Settlement of Investment Disputes (ICSID).

62. Sassen (2006) at 244, citing Smit and Pechota (2004); Dezalayn and Garth (1995); Aksen (1990).

63. Sassen (1996).

64. Ruggie (1993b) at 139–174.

65. See Sassen (1996) at 26.

66. Ibid at 29. Sassen writes:

> Sovereignty remains a feature of the system. But it is now located in a multiplicity of institutional arenas: the new emergent transnational private legal regimes, new supranational organizations (such as the WTO and the institutions of the European Union, and the various international human rights codes. All of these institutions constrain the autonomy of national states; states operating under the rule of law are caught in a web of obligations they cannot disregard easily (though they can to some extent, as illustrated by the United States' unpaid duties to the United Nations: if this were a personal credit card debt you or I would be in jail).

Ibid. at 30–31.

67. See Cooper (2003) at 65–69 (explaining that chaos and crime in the modern world are increasingly less localized and cannot be controlled through actions of individual states). Our argument on the changing nature of the relationship between states and welfare is in no way intended to imply that states are abandoning (or ought to abandon) policies intended to achieve the well-being of their people. Rather, we endorse the nuanced view that Statecraft, and the basis for legitimacy of the State in the post-modern era, are shifting and that, with that shift, comes a transformation of the fundamental goals and methods of the State in relation to its subjects' well-being. As Philip Bobbitt stated:

> [the] nation-state undertook to be responsible for economic planning for the society, income redistribution, and democratic accountability, and it promised to underwrite (in varying degrees) employment, heath care, education and old age security. The nation-state is rightly thought of as a new constitutional order, for not only are these responsibilities a significant departure from those of the state-nation, they also reflect the unique source of the nation-state's legitimacy, its promise to provide for the material well-being of the nation.

Bobbitt (2002) at 240. The shift in Statecraft that Bobbitt identifies challenges these fundamentals of the nation-state and leads the State towards its next incarnation, where the enablement of economic opportunity (itself intended in a broad sense to further the people's welfare) will be substituted for guarantees of a safety net with respect to the traditional components of the welfare package in the modern world that Bobbitt describes. As we observed earlier, even popular journalists such as Thomas Friedman have noted this shift in the social contract among the governed and the State. In a passage quoted earlier, Friedman writes: "The social contract that progressives should try to enforce between government and workers, and companies and workers, is one in which government and companies say, 'We cannot guarantee you any lifetime employment. But we can guarantee you that government and companies will focus on giving you the tools to make you more lifetime employable.'" In a flat world, "the individual worker is going to become more and more responsible for managing his or her own career, risks, and economic security, and the job of government and business is to help workers build the necessary muscles to do that." Friedman (2005) at 284. In our view, Friedman makes both a normative argument as to what government *should* do and a descriptive argument as to what the government *can or cannot* do. These ideas are neither the exclusive province of a deregulating Right nor a populist Left. Rather, they provide an insight into the transformative movements that have affected modern states, and the adjustment to the fundamentals of Statecraft that should obtain as a result of this metamorphosis.

68. Cooper (2003) at 27 ("The legitimate monopoly on force that is the essence of statehood is thus subject to international – but self-imposed – constraints").

69. Ibid at 102–13. "The essence of globalization is that it erodes the distinction between domestic and foreign events." Ibid at 110–11.
70. Ibid at 16–26.
71. Certain important players in the international scene, such as Indonesia and India, may still qualify as modern states. While operating in an increasingly post-modern world, these states continue to adhere to notions of sovereignty and nation, and they are not characterized by the same degree of diffuseness that is increasingly apparent in post-modern states. But see, for example, Gurcharan Das, *Is India Shining?* Wall St J A20 (May 3, 2004) (discussing India's drive to achieve "nation building" through economic success). For a more in-depth discussion, see Luce (2007).

3. The Changing Nature of Welfare

1. As mentioned in Chapter 2, financing of the modern welfare state is tied to demography and globalization. According to Razin et al. (2005), "[t]he combined forces of aging, low-skill migration and globalization seem to be too strong for the welfare state to survive in its present size." Ibid at 4.
2. In Chapter 4, we detail how these states developed their internal orders in the context of the institutions of Bretton Woods.
3. Levy, Miura, and Park (2006) at 98.
4. For a brief but incisive review of some of the structural problems with the French economy, see "The Art of the Impossible," *The Economist*, October 28, 2006, pp. 3–16 (Special Report on France).
5. Levy, Miura, and Park (2006) at 93–136.
6. The numbers are staggering: between 1974 and 1980, the number of early retirees more than tripled from 59,000 to 190,400 (DARES 1996: 100). The figure grew to over 700,000 workers in 1984. Ibid.
7. Ibid.
8. OECD (2004b).
9. Levy, Miura, and Park (2006) at 117.
10. For discussion of details and specific illustrations, see Levy, Miura, and Park (2006) at 117–123.
11. Abboud (2006) at A1.
12. Ibid.
13. The scheme described is also employed at other French companies like Total, the drug company Sanofi-Aventis, and Electricité de France.
14. As we have said often in this book, the logic of the GATT/WTO order is that welfare and distributional policies were left to individual nation-states as a matter of politi-cal ideology (embedded liberalism). The differences between European-style welfare and the Japanese approach are discussed, *inter alia*, in Estévez-Abe (2002) at 158. She writes:

> The Japanese case also shows how different institutional designs of welfare states produce different problems. Continental European countries use welfare programs to reduce labor supply. Germany, for example, uses old age pensions to encourage older workers to leave the labor force. Likewise, the Netherlands – at least until the recent reforms – used disability ben-efits for the same purpose. Japan did not use pensions, unemployment, or disability benefits as means to control labor supply, and thus what prompted welfare reforms in Japan was not the problem of *Welfare without Work*.
>
> Instead, by the end of the 1980s, Japanese policymakers were aware of three major problems: (1) the growing cost of benefits/services for the elderly; (2) rising inequity in cost allocation; and (3) skewed access to social services. In all cases, the problems resulted from a gap between those *paying* for welfare services/benefits and those *receiving* them, a gap embed-ded in the institutional structure of the welfare state.

Ibid.

15. Uzuhashi (2003) describes the Japanese approach as "an employment-centered welfare state." Ibid at 1. For a short and insightful summary of important, recent changes in the employment realm in Japan, see "Sayonara, Saiaryman," *The Economist* (2008).

16. We note that the outstanding performance of the Nikkei 225 since 2003 signals a turnaround in the Japanese economy. At least that is the judgment of global capital that is responsible for the rise in share prices. Of late, the market is faltering.

17. Levy, Miura and Park (2006) at 97.

18. Asia-Pacific Update (2002), Chapter 4 at 37.

19. Ibid.

20. Ibid.

21. Hane (2001) at 379. Also see generally Gordon (2003).

22. For a complete analysis, see Wood (1992).

23. *See* www.ecn.wfu.edu/~cottrell/OPE/itoh/itoh.pdf.

24. *See* http://www.imf.org/external/pubs/nft/2000/bubble/index.htm#over.

25. *See* www.ecn.wfu.edu/~cottrell/OPE/itoh/itoh.pdf.

26. *See* http://ideas.repec.org/a/fip/feddel/y2006ijannv.1no.1.html.

27. Cox and Koo (2006). As Amyx (2004) at 150 notes, "[t]he bursting of the bubble translated into the collective loss of $90 billion in latent stock values by Japan's top eleven city banks and thus heightened the chance of bank insolvency or collapse."

28. Cox and Koo (2006).

29. Ibid.

30. Ibid.

31. Levy, Miura and Park (2006) at 132.

32. In 2004, for women it was 85 and 78 years for men. See the OECD Country Statistical Profiles 2007, found at http://stats.oecd.org/wbos/viewhtml.aspx?queryname=314&querytype=view&lang=en.

33. For the statistics, see OECD Factbook (2007), Economic, Environmental and Social Statistics. For discussion of the European context, see Rosenthal (2006).

34. For discussion, see Papademetriou (2000).

35. Amyx (2004); Katz (1998).

36. Amyx (2004).

37. Tiberghien (2005) at 241–242 (citing Kanaya and Woo (2000)).

38. Ibid.

39. Tiberghien (2005) at 232 maintains that "foreign equity inflows provide the impetus for structural reforms."

40. Levy/Miura, and Park (2006) at 122.

41. Ibid at 125.

42. Statistics Bureau (1998, 2003).

43. One commentator writes:

> Some of the greatest costs of Japan's mediocre economic performance over the past fifteen years have been inflicted on young Japanese. They have disproportionately been unemployed or underemployed in part-time work. They are not receiving adequate on-the-job training. Many have stopped actively seeking work, or have dropped out of the labor market. Although some have deliberately chosen alternative life styles, most seek full-time work in a suitable occupation. New terms have entered the language: freeters (part-time and temporary workers), NEETs (those not in education, employment, or training). As of 2005, of those aged 15 to 34, 2,132,000 were unemployed (including about 640,000 NEETs), and another 2,010,000 were freeters, including many high school dropouts. Most NEETs come from poor families and have low educational attainment.

> Patrick (2006) at 7.

44. Vogel (2006). Vogel summarizes the results of reform efforts produced through the joint efforts of government and industry:

> In sum, the remodeled Japan differs from the earlier version in at least three important ways. It is more *selective*: in the face of hard times, companies have become more discriminating in

their partnerships. They have reevaluated their long-term relationships with workers, banks, and other firms, and they have loosened some and tightened others. They have shifted from a more reflexive acceptance of these long-term partnerships to a more rational assessment of their costs and benefits. It is more *differentiated*: companies have become more variable in their practices. There never was a uniform Japanese model that applied equally to all sectors and all companies, but the model has fragmented further. And it is more *open*: Japanese corporations have more foreign owners, managers, and business partners than ever before, and these foreign actors bring with them different practices and norms. Each of these trends has been driven not simply by companies freely choosing from a blank slate but through the interactive process of government reform and corporate adjustment described in detail in this book.

Ibid at 220.
45. Levy, Miura, and Park (2006) at 135.
46. Amyx (2004) at 253.
47. Known as "Japan Post," the postal savings system employs more than one-third of Japan's government workers and has savings deposits in excess of ¥225 trillion (more than $2 trillion).
48. OECD, Economic Survey of Japan (2005).
49. In the American system, many of the traditional welfare functions are tasked to individual state governments.
50. For an astute analysis of the present and future of the social security program in the United States, see Lowenstein (2005).
51. Bill Clinton, "Remarks on the Reinventing Government Initiative, Weekly Compilation of Presidential Documents," vol. 30, 1994, at 1763.
52. Bill Clinton, "Remarks to the Joint Session of the Louisiana State Legislature in Baton Rouge, Louisiana," Weekly Compilation of Presidential Documents, vol. 32, 1996, at 969.
53. Bill Clinton, "Inaugural Address," Weekly Compilation of Presidential Documents, vol. 33, 1997, at 60.
54. George W. Bush, State of the Union Address, January, 29, 2002.
55. President's Remarks at swearing in ceremony of Council of Economic Advisers Chairman Edward Lazear. http://www.whitehouse.gov/news/releases/2006/03/20060306.html (visited 2 May 2006).
56. Friedman (2005) at 84.
57. For a capacious view of the meaning of "work," with specific reference to the Clinton welfare-to-work program, see Zatz (2006).
58. Hacker (2006).
59. Ibid at 38.
60. Detail in diagram form in Hacker (2006) at 19 from proprietary data of ISR at www.isrinsight.com.
61. Lindsey is the author of *Against the Dead Hand: The Uncertain Struggle for Global Capitalism* (2002). His review appeared in the Wall Street Journal under the title "Poor Mouthing Prosperity," September 21, 2006, at p. D6.
62. See Brown, Haltiwanger and Lane (2006). They write:

The analysis of literally millions of worker histories and hundreds of career paths for workers and job ladders for firms leads to the reassuring finding that although turbulence imposes short-run costs, in the long-run job change leads to improved jobs for most workers. The evidence does not support the popular notion that *"low-wage workers churn from bad job to bad job "*-not even in retail food, where many workers leave the industry for better jobs, or in trucking, where a worker's alternative job is usually worse.

Ibid at 122.
63. Hacker (2006) at 125.
64. Hacker undercuts the credibility of his claims about the shortcomings of 401(k) plans with an anecdotal illustration of risk in stocks. He tells the story of "Jim Horner," an employee at MCI who put his entire 401(k) into company stock and lost it all. This story, Hacker claims, shows that while "the investment gurus" are right that stocks

deliver a better overall return than other asset classes, "[t]he problem is that this return comes with higher risk, and 401(k)s place all of this higher risk on workers. . . ." Ibid. at 126. The story of Jim Horner doesn't illustrate the risk inherent in stocks. What it shows is the foolishness of concentrating one's equity investments in a single firm (stock). The lesson is not that stocks are risky; rather, the lesson is the need for diversification.

65. See Weir, Orloff, and Skocpol (2007) at 37–80 and 137–198.

66. The situation of the excluded in France is dire. One astute commentator describes it this way:

> Millions of young people remain trapped in the unemployment and underemployment ghetto. Hundreds of thousands of youth of North African descent, especially young women, have never had the chance to work. The victims of the expensive system of "solidarity" which protects older, "Frencher" workers, these abandoned youth are also the scapegoat of the far Right, which portrays them as leeches on the public purse. The reality is that immigrants receive very little social spending – with two clear exceptions, derelict public housing which can hardly be considered a great social gain, and the RMI ("welfare") payment. The lion's share of social spending, however, goes to pensions and health care, not to the "welfare" or housing costs associated with the immigrant unemployed. Still, the majority of public housing units are indeed occupied by non-French-born citizens and non-citizens, and this is a powerful image in the minds of Le Pen supporters.

> Smith (2004) at 176–177.

4. Disaster and Redemption: 1930s and Bretton Woods

1. In fact, planning for the postwar economic order began soon after war broke out. See Frieden (2006) at 253 ("The Western Allies began to plan the peacetime economic order as soon as war broke out.").

2. For a brief history and chronology, see http://www.ll.georgetown.edu/intl/guides/gattwto/.

3. For a brief summary against the background of postwar European history, see Judt (2005) at 107–108.

4. Frieden (2006) at 261.

5. GDP grew from $101.4 billion in 1940 to $223.1 billion in 1945 and $293.8 billion in 1950 and continued to grow strongly thereafter. See http://eh.net/hmit/gdp/gdp_answer.php? CHKnominalGDP=on&CHKrealGDP=on&CHKGDPdeflator–on&CHKpopulation= on&CHKnominalGDP_percap=on&CHKrealGDP_percap=on&year1=1938&year2= 1960 and http://www.bea.gov/national/xls/gdplev.xls, last accessed August 17, 2007.

6. The Marshall Plan was embraced only after the initial plan for Germany – the Morgenthau Plan – had been abandoned. Designed by then American Secretary of the Treasury, Henry Morgenthau, Jr., Germany was to be partitioned and reduced to an agrarian society, all in an effort to prevent it from ever again posing a military threat. Among other things, the plan called for removal or destruction of industrial equipment and the flooding of mines. But the plan was abandoned when it became clear that the plan was wreaking havoc on the German economy, specifically wiping out agricultural productivity. Sent in 1947 to investigate the situation, former President Hoover concluded that the only way to make the plan work would be to move or exterminate 25,000,000 people in Germany. The Morgenthau Plan was abandoned and the Marshall Plan – a pro-growth plan – put in its place. See Balabkins (1964). A recent and fuller history of the Marshall Plan is found in Behrman (2007). For a contemporary German assessment of the Marshall Plan, see Stern, http://www.germany.info/relaunch/culture/history/marshall.html.

7. See, e.g., http://www.imf.org/external/np/exr/center/mm/eng/mm_dr_05.htm;. "The System of Bretton Woods" at 12, available at http://www.ww.uni-magdeburg.de/fwwdeka/student/arbeiten/006.pdf.

8. As the twentieth century progressed, the association between the ethos of the nation-state and welfare policies deepened. See Hart (1994).

9. For an example of how deregulating the currency market in Sweden (among other factors) changed the nature of the traditional Swedish welfare state, see http://zena .secureforum.com/znet/zmag/articles/june95wennerberg.htm. See also http://www.rsa .org.uk/acrobat/panic_100506.pdf, especially p. 5 *et seq* for a discussion of how the formation of the European Monetary Union changed the nature of states in Europe, last accessed August 20, 2007.

10. Jacob's ladder refers to a Biblical passage in Genesis where Jacob had a vision wherein he saw a ladder stretching from Earth to heaven with angels ascending and descending. Genesis 28:12.

11. We argue in Chapters 4 through 6 that such a constitutional moment has become necessary in the early part of the twenty-first century. As illustrated in various contexts below, we use the notion of constitutional moment as a conscious choice based on the interaction of Statecraft as inner law. It relates less to a change in the ordering of society that legitimizes the adoption of certain constitutional norms than it does to the infusion of new norms (recognizing the interaction between inner state order and the international order of states). But see Ackerman (1997) (defining a constitutional moment as a moment that "occurs when a rising political movement succeeds in placing a new problematic at the center of American political life.").

12. See Kemp (1982).

13. See Bagwell and Staiger (2000). It was Smith who, in *The Wealth of Nations*, married the private interests of individual agents to a theory of political economy. Smith's insight, of course, was that the pursuit of individual interest would collectively result in a stronger State because market efficiency would engender greater economic activity which devolved to the benefit of the State through taxation. Ricardo, in 1817, took Smith's insight and expanded the idea to foreign trade. Free trade, grounded in the theory of comparative advantage, would result in greater wealth for all nations. See Ricardo (1817).

14. Molle (2001) at Chapters 7 and 8, provides a thorough and accessible account of the economic theory underlying the formation of common markets, including free trade areas, customs unions and more integrated constitutional forms of union.

15. Alvarez and Howse (2002):

   A paramount goal is the avoidance of a protectionist summum malum – the situation where domestic social or economic pressures lead some states to increase or reinstate barriers to trade, thus triggering a competitive reaction in kind by other states, and eventually a "race to the bottom" that is disastrous for the global economy. This sort of behavior was widely perceived by the founders of the Bretton Woods system to have led eventually to perilous instability in the interstate system and economic catastrophe in the interwar years – which phenomena were seen as having contributed to the climate that made fascism, and the Second World War itself, possible.

   Ibid at 94–95.

16. For discussion, see Cho (2005).

17. This removal of barriers to trade spurred a sharp increase in cross-border economic activities among nation-states over the second half of the twentieth century. The GATT took off with 23 Contracting Parties, and gradually took hold in over 150 nations. It progressively expanded to new subject matter areas, such as intellectual property and trade in services. These developments are, in retrospect what grant Bretton Woods its status as a constitutional moment.

18. GATT, Article XXVIII.

19. The GATT sought to "tariffy" barriers to trade so as to establish a transparent framework for tariff reduction negotiations in successive "rounds." Over the course of the eight rounds that were completed since the GATT came into effect among its original twenty-three signatories, the average tariff among Contracting Parties has gone down from above 40 percent to less than 4 percent. See http://www.wto.org.

20. GATT, Article III.

21. See, for example, *Japan-Customs Duties, Taxes and Labeling Practices on Imported Wines and Alcoholic Beverages*, Nov 10, 1987, GATT BISD (34th Supp) 83, available online at <http://www.wto.org/ english/tratop_e/dispu_e/gt47ds_e.htm>.

22. See, for example, World Trade Organization, Report of the Panel, *Japan-Taxes on Alcoholic Beverages*, WTO Doc No WT DS-8-R (July 11, 1996). In this case, the WTO rejected the US argument to the effect that an aim and effect test should be applied to root out protectionism when determining whether the national treatment provisions of the GATT were violated. The literature and commentary on national treatment is voluminous and further comment lies beyond the scope of this discussion. Even with an explicit mandate to root out protectionism and to shelter national laws that furthers legitimate government purposes, national laws that involve both protectionist and legitimate purposes might be challenged. In *Reformulated Gasoline*, for example, the WTO was asked to evaluate the legality of a US regulation, promulgated pursuant to the Clean Air Act, which imposed more onerous requirements on foreign companies, ostensibly on the grounds that compliance with the substantive norm of the statute was difficult. While a protectionist purpose might be inferred from the record, it is also evident that the United States' interest in protecting its environment was at stake. See World Trade Organization, Report of the Appellate Body, *United States-Standards for Reformulated and Conventional Gasoline*, WTO Doc No WT/DS2/AB/R (Apr 29, 1996).

23. To illustrate this point, imagine that State A agrees not to impose a tariff on State B's cars in excess of 5 percent. If State A enacted a discriminatory sales tax, which burdens State B's cars by, say, 10 percent, it would have achieved a functionally equivalent economic result as a 10 percent tariff would accomplish. The difficult questions of interpretation arise when, for example, the internal sales tax applies to cars that consume more than a specified level of gasoline per mile, and State A's sales tax disproportionately burden State B's cars because they tend to belong the category of products that is affected by the (ostensibly neutral) definition.

24. GATT, Article XI.

25. See, for example, *Japanese Measures on Imports of Leather*, May 15, 1984 GATT BISD (31st Supp) 94, available online at http://www.wto.org/english/tratop_e/dispu_e/gt47ds_e.htm last accessed August 20, 2007.

26. For discussion, see Krugman (May Pt 2 362 1993). See also, Molle (2001) at 51; Bhagwati, (1971); Bhagwati and Ramaswami, (1963); Johnson (1965).

27. See Bretton Woods Project, *Background to the Issues*, available online at <http.//www.brettonwoodsproject.org/background/index.shtml> (stating that the forty three countries that met at Bretton Woods created the World Bank and IMF in order to help rebuild Europe after World War II), last accessed August 20, 2007.

28. See Alvarez and Howse (2002).

> The postwar trade and financial order was therefore mainly designed to enable states to manage their domestic economies, in a manner consistent with political and social stability and justice, without the risk of setting off a protectionist race to the bottom. States obligated themselves not to impose quotas or related import restrictions, of the sort strongly associated with the race to the bottom of the interwar years. On the other hand, they were not required to eliminate or reduce their import tariffs. The legal structure of the General Agreement on Tariffs and Trade (GATT) was designed to facilitate such concessions and make them binding, but it did not require them.

Ibid at 95.

29. But see Sassen (2006): "[T]he early Bretton Woods system aimed at protecting national economies from external forces, not at opening them up."

30. Alvarez and Howse (2002) at 97 (describing the move towards Ruggie's "embedded liberalism").

31. See Walling (2003/2004). Walling compares communist, socialist, and capitalist countries and briefly points out the differences between them that led to communism's downfall.

32. See Trebilcock and Howse (2001) at 7; Irwin (1996) at 5 (explaining that a free trade policy does not necessarily conform to free trade doctrine); and Ruggie (1993a).

33. This list illustrates the broad category of "welfare" which we discussed in previous chapters. Of course, a key feature of the society of nation-states is the fact that development of particular welfare schemes was left to individual states, thereby respecting the sovereignty of nations. In the post-modern era, this emphasis will change as the conception of sovereignty evolves (see Cooper (2003) on this) and the society of states comes to realize the trans-national nature of certain problems such as SARS, AIDS, and global warming.

34. See Alvarez and Howse (2002) at 95; Ruggie (1998) at 72, n 73.

35. See Ruggie (1993a) at 72–73.

36. See *The Columbia Encyclopedia, Hawley-Smoot Tarif Act* (Bartleby.com 6th ed 2005), available online at <http://www.bartleby.com/65/ha/HawleySm.html> ("The act brought *retaliatory* tariff acts from foreign countries, US foreign trade suffered a sharp decline, and the depression intensified."). See generally Irwin (1996) at 26–44, 193–99.

37. See Alvarez and Howse (2002).

38. As Professor Weiler has pointed out, the GATT's economic ethos largely resulted from the creation of a professional trade elite. This elite created a set of norms intended to project the impression that the GATT was grounded in "economic science" and insulated from crass politics:

   A dominant feature of GATT was its self-referential and even communitarian ethos explicable in constructivist terms. GATT successfully managed relative insulation from the "outside" world of international relations, and it established among its practitioners a closely knit environment revolving around shared normative values (of free trade) and shared institutional ambitions. GATT operatives became a classical "network" of first-name contacts and friendly relationships.

   Weiler (2002) at 336–337.

39. Alvarez and Howse (2002) at 96.

40. Consider GATT, Article VI (generally allowing anti-dumping practices even though they tend to be harmful to free trade); World Trade Organization, Agreement on Safeguards, WTO Doc No LT/UR/A-1A/8 (April 15, 1994).

41. Kant (1948). See also Kagan (2003). Consider Claude (1961).

42. Bobbitt (2002) at 144–45.

43. See generally Gordon and Sylvester (2004) at 11.

44. See generally Anderson (1991). This book is perhaps the most widely read book on nationalism, featuring Anderson's insightful argument to the effect that nations were born as indispensable components of societies that traversed industrialization and experienced print capitalism.

45. See generally Connor (1994) at 89, 97–100 (on the meaning of "nation" and related terms as "Terminological Chaos"); Tamir (1993) at 58, n69; Hobsbawm (1990) at 1, n 13; Seton-Watson (1977) at 3; Stalin (1934) at 8. This is true even though, under marxist theory, the nation-state would ultimately wither away in favor of rule by international workers.

46. See Ruggie (1998) at 76.

47. See Alvarez and Howse (2002) at 116.

48. See, for example, Krugman (1993) at 362. See also Molle (2001) at 47.

49. Hart details this well:

   Today we face a new reality. Advances in transportation and communications technology have made it possible to breach the territorial, social, and cultural integrity of the nation-state on a daily basis. The convergence of popular cultures and the crisis of the welfare state all point to the need to develop a new definition of sovereignty as well as a new set of norms and rules for inter-state relations. In short, we need a new set of rules that recognizes that the realm of goods, services, capital and technology has largely escaped from the effective regulation of the territorial nation-state, while its people remain largely attached to it.

Hart (1994) at 377.

50. Cooper (2003) at 23–26.
51. See Hall (1983) at 13.

5. The Transformation of the Bretton Woods World and the Rise of a New Economic Order

1. See Smith (2005) at 57; Moon (2000) at 33.
2. See Bayoumi (1995) at 5 ("The economic achievements of the postwar period were built year upon year, with the benefits accumulating steadily. Looking back on the past 50 years, it is clear that steady gains have added up to a period of extraordinary progress, unsurpassed in history. Other moves in this direction should generate high, sustained levels of economic growth worldwide. . . ."); Van Dormael (1978) (this book provides a detailed account of the negotiations that led to the establishment of the International Monetary Fund, making the point that the institution did not include the comprehensive regulatory body that Keynes desired).
3. See Curtin (1993) (in this famous and insightful article, Curtin criticizes the assault on the European Court of Justice and European constitutionalization process that characterized some of the debates over the Treaty of Maastricht).
4. See Curtin (1993) at 17.
5. See Mandelson (2003) (speech before the European Parliament Trade Committee arguing that at the credibility of the WTO as a multilateral organization is at stake in the Doha round, that Doha's success depends in large part on integrating developing countries in world markets and emphasizing the need to solve some of their pressing problems, such as access to affordable drugs). See also Cendrowicz (2005).
6. See Handelman (2001)(reporting on the Summit of the Americas).
7. See Rehn (2006) (address by former member of the European Commission emphasizing that the future of Europe lies in its enlargement to, among other territories, Southeastern Europe, and Turkey).
8. As explained in Chapter 2, we use the term "welfare" to refer broadly to a web of regulation intended to control the social and economic domestic realm in a wide array of subject matter areas, including health, labor, environmental protection, resource conservation, economic security, and morals.
9. See Cho (1998) at 311; Okediji (2003) at 819; Cho (2005) at 625.
10. As discussed later, this unsettled the balance of power of the twentieth century.
11. Barry and Reddy (2006) at 545; WTO, World Trade Report 2004: Exploring the Linkage Between Domestic Policy, Environment and International Trade. Available at http://www.wto.org/english/res_ e/booksp_e/anrep_e/world_trade_report04_e.pdf.
12. In the United States, for example, the *Lochner* era involved a clash between states' efforts to regulate the economy and freedom of contract. Starting with the Warren Court, defining the boundaries of personal autonomy became a central task of American constitutional law.
13. Driesen (2001) at 279.
14. Cho (2004) at 483.
15. The notion of importing regulation along with products, as well as the concept of regulatory comparative advantage, were gleaned from Professor Weiler's masterful lectures on trade by one of the co-authors, in his days as a Weiler student.
16. See Christensen (1990) (criticizing free movement of goods as undermining domestic regulation of food safety).
17. See Shaffer (2000) at 608.
18. See Yeh (2006) at 465; Knox (2004) at 1; Vautier (2003) at 218.

19. See Ortino (2004). This thoughtful Jean Monnet Working Paper explores the various standards of review that that have been applied by trade tribunals reviewing national measures that affect the free movement of goods.

20. See Afilalo (2005) at 279; Afilalo (2003) at 51.

21. See Wells (2006) at 357; Minton-Beddoes (2000) (discussing role that labor and environmental standards should play in trade negotiations); Clatanoff (2005) at 109.

22. For a general explanation of the issue and decision, see Kaczka (1998) at 308; Kaczka (1997) at 177; Bello (1997) (analyzing the Shrimp-Turtle dispute, which at the time had not been decided, and arguing that the challenged measures reflect increased unilateralism cloaked in the pretext of environmental and resource conservation).

23. For a critical review of the decision, see Stillwell and Arden-Clarke (1998) at 2.

24. See Munari (2001) at 157; Hudnall (1996) at 175.

25. For more on how this decision affects free trade, see Kelly (2005) at 496.

26. See Afilalo and Foster (2003) at 633.

27. For an extensive outline of the changes international trade has brought to the apparel industry, see Gereffi (2005).

28. See Quong (2004) (noting the shift away from the concentration of producers in one neighborhood toward outsourcing of both raw materials and finished products to China and other low-cost jurisdictions).

29. See Economy and Segal (2003); Rollo et al. (1993) at 139.

30. See Bradsher (2005) (detailing Chinese efforts to take over creation and design of branded products in addition to their manufacture).

31. Supplychainer (2007)(reporting on strategic choices made by Walmart and its French competitor Carrefour, whereby Walmart undertook to build its trademark retail outlets in China while Carrefour chose to sell its goods to local distributors and retailers and build a network using existing Chinese stores).

32. See Jeong-ju (2006).

33. In July of 2007, for example, Carrefour opened its 100th hypermarket in China and announced that it would open 23 outlets for 2007, as against the 15 stores planned by Walmart.

34. See, for example, Economical Services http://www.economicalservices.com (last visited August 12, 2007) (describing a New Delhi-based company that offers legal research services throughout the world).

35. See Ihde (2004) at 13; Bobbitt (2002) at 700; Burawoy (1999).

36. See Burawoy at 25, available online at http://sociology.berkeley.edu/faculty/burawoy/burawoy_pdf/transition.pdf.

37. Just one example is an op-ed by a senior adviser at the Federal Reserve Bank of Minnesota. See Edward C. Prescott, "Competitive Cooperation," Wall Street Journal, A19, February 15, 2007 ("Competitive openness is the key to bringing developing nations up to the standard of living enjoyed by citizens of wealthier countries.").

38. The crisis that surrounded the proposed European Constitution involved in part the power that Poland would wield as a Member State. In addition to voting rights and policy influence, some existing Member States feared that the Eastern European markets would successfully and aggressively compete with domestic industries, using cheaper and more abundant labor.

39. For perceptive analysis of the problems facing Africa, especially with respect to natural resources and governance, see Collier (2007a).

40. World Trade Organization, WTO Doha Ministerial declaration, adopted November 14, 2001. Available online http://www.wto.org/english/thewto_e/minist_e/min01_e/mindecl_e.htm#interaction (last visited August 12, 2007).

41. See Nardi (2005) (opening with the dramatic observation that Zambian cotton farmers must walk around in rags because they cannot buy the very clothes they are contributing to make, this essay highlights some of the gross inequities of the global trading system,

such as the payment of $12 billion in subsidies to 25,000 US farmers in 2003 and 2004, while millions of farmers in developing countries faced startling income reductions as global prices collapsed).

42. The Atlantic Council's (2007) recent Policy Paper confirms the widespread recognition of this fact.

43. See Reinert (2007) at 252 ("[T]he timing of the opening up of an economy is crucial.").

44. This is evidenced by the recent protests in France over the reform of employment laws.

6. The End of Bretton Woods and the Beginning of a New Global Trading Order

1. See Heckscher (1955) at 164 and 246. Heckscher uses the example of guilds in France and justices of the peace in England to demonstrate how this cohesive state economy coalesced out of numerous local governments. In France, guild officials were partly responsible for enforcing the standards created by the king that finished products must meet. In England, justices of the peace enforced industrial statutes that originated with the king. The justices of the peace were also appointed by the monarch and were loyal to the central government instead of the local government. These local officials helped create central ties, ultimately leading to the cohesive state economy.

2. See Van Creveld (2006) at 330.

3. See, e.g., France, 2007. In *Encyclopedia Britannica*, from Encyclopedia Britannica Online, available online at http://www.britannica.com/eb/article-40428 (last accessed August 13, 2007).

4. In international investment, for example, states used principally "gunboat diplomacy" to resolve conflicts during the mercantilist era. This resulted in a Darwinian playing field where imperial and other strong states would impose their will on weaker states. In that world, as La Fontaine would say, *"la raison du plus fort est toujours la meilleure."* (the reason of the strongest is always the better). The "Calvo Doctrine" (named after the Argentinian jurist Carlos Calvo, the idea is that the location of an investment decides the jurisdictional question for dispute resolution) was, in part, a reaction to the power-driven structure of the global trading order. That school of thought provided that each state (in particular a developing country) was free to impose its own rules, implemented through its own institutions, free of interference from foreign states. While the Calvo Doctrine rejected international institutions as legitimate law-makers and dispute resolution fora, it departed from the model of dispute resolution through force. See Cook (2007) at 1087–1089. See also Lekachman (1959) at 43 for discussion of the mercantilists' zero-sum view of the world.

5. See Angresano (1996) at 89.

6. The constitutional drive of colonizing states prompted them to view the establishment of colonies as the natural outlet for their commercial aspirations. The natural resources of colonies, be it sugar in Barbados or cotton in Benin, were regarded by the mother country as assets to draw upon and add to their balance sheet. The hemisphere thus viewed the periphery as an integral part of its panoply of resources, to be defended against other, competing states. See O'Melinn (1995) at 136–137. See also Barber (1967) at 18; Deane (1978) at 2.

7. See Low (1993) at 146.

8. See Roberts (2003) at 516.

> Throughout the 1960s and 1970s . . . dispute resolution mechanisms were increasingly perceived as being ineffective. The concerns were manifold. Delays were endemic at all stages of the process. The panel procedure, in particular, suffered from delays in the appointment of panel members, in setting the terms of reference relating to the adjudication . . . and in issuing and adopting the reports of the panels. In addition, objections were raised with regard to potential bias of panel members. Perhaps most importantly, because the GATT system relied heavily on consensus in rendering decisions, those nations against whom complaints were

filed could readily obstruct the process and make enforcement of any panel recommendations virtually non-existent.

Ibid. Compare the present day European Union where, among other decisions reaching deep into the national sovereign fabric, the European Court permitted Irish citizens to travel abroad to obtain abortions despite the Government of Ireland's prohibiting this. See also Van Creveld (2006) at 341.

9. See Vietor (2007) at 8–9.
10. Any tariff reduction below the binding that a Contracting State might elect to extend to another Contracting State would, under the Most Favored Nation Clause, be deemed automatically extended to all other GATT signatories. The GATT, however, authorized approved regional treaties to provide for the reduction or elimination of tariffs only among participating states.
11. See Barton et al. (2006) at 29–38 for a general discussion of the negotiations and the impetus leading to them.
12. Ibid at 61–62.
13. But see Ibid at 62. The authors discuss methods other than formal voting, that the GATT uses to achieve consensus by its parties.
14. WTO Members and Observers, website http://www.wto.org/english/thewto_e/whatis_e/tif_e/org6_e.htm.
15. Ibid. See Hudec (1987) at 4.
16. For discussion of the GATT's dispute settlement procedures, see Barton et al. (2006) at 68–69.
17. The GATT Uruguay Round Agreements: Report on Environmental Issues August 1994, 1994 WL 761804 (G.A.T.T.). Report of the Panel (DS21/R – 39S/155). Available online at http://www.worldtradelaw.net/reports/gattpanels/tunadolphinI.pdf.
18. Report of the Panel adopted on 6 November 1979 (L/4789 – 26S/320) available at http://www.worldtradelaw.net/reports/gattpanels/japanleather.pdf and Report of the Panel adopted on 10 November 1980 (L/5042 – 27S/118) available online at http://www.worldtradelaw.net/reports/gattpanels/japanleatherII.pdf.
19. In a classic article, Professor Weiler characterizes the establishment of the new GATT dispute resolution system, including compulsory adjudication, as a paradigm shift from diplomacy to law. Of course, as he insightfully observes, the system still retains hallmarks of diplomacy, thereby leaving lingering dissonance, and the system still faces foundational questions such as whether the "rule of lawyers" will overcome the rule of law. Weiler (2002) at 185–196. See generally Wald (2006).
20. Data on tariff concession since GATT's inception can be found at the WTO website: The GATT years: from Havana to Marrakesh, Available online at http://www.wto.org/English/thewto_e/whatis_e/tif_e/fact4_e.htm (last visited August 13, 2007); World Trade Organization Toolkit, Presented by Asian Development Bank, available online at http://www.adb.org/Documents/Others/OGC-Toolkits/WTO/wto0200.asp (last visited August 13, 2007).
21. See Agnew and Entrikin (2004) at 2 (the joint effect of the massive infusion of US aid to Europe and the implicit acceptance of open trade and investment were essential factors contributing to the Western European choice of a modern liberal democratic alliance with the United States).
22. See Wan (2001) at 22–70 and 186–204 (Wan argues that Japan competed with the United States on the economic level, at the same as it provided essential political collaboration and shored up the modern liberal democratic alliance on both the political and the economic level); See Horsley and Buckley (1990) for a general narrative of Japan's economic achievements since World War II.
23. See Ronen (1979); Thomson and Ronen (1986). Professor Ronen developed a theory that national identity is driven by external events rather than an inherent sense of belonging to the groupings that came to be associated with nation-states. In the West

African colonization context, the "activation of identity" of nation-states such as Nigeria, Ghana or Benin, resulted from the carving out of Africa by colonizing powers. The drawing of artificial boundaries cut through traditional ethnic and tribal lines, and resulted in a wide array of ethnic groups being lumped into a single state. A classic fault line separates Southern regions of African states, influenced by animist or Christian religions, from the Northern groups more associated with Islam and Arab influence from North Africa. These groups activated a joint identity to throw off the yoke of colonial oppression, often led by a strong political figure who dangled the branch of freedom and the good life if only the Nigeria or Benin that was created and ruled by foreigners would return to native hands. Once colonization ended, however, the newly independent states lost their activator of identity and had to deal with the widely disparate interests and ethnic affiliations vying for control of what in Ronen's words became a "prison-state" rather than a nation-state. Without the habit of peaceful democratic transition and sharing assets with successor parties, and in light of the dismal conditions that followed decolonization, loss of elections or other losses of power had such dire consequences for individual groupings that civil war at times was a better alternative than sitting out of the halls of government. This, in Ronen's view, is the best explanation of conflicts such as the Biafra war. Ronen's prescription for resolving this problem involves a combination of (i) political decentralization, with power devolving to regional and ethnic entities, and (ii) market integration through elimination of the artificial economic borders drawn during the colonization era.

24. See Ronen (1984); Ronen (1975). Ronen's case study of Benin illustrates the theoretical construct regarding self-determination and national identity described in note 22

25. See The World Bank, Data & Statistics – Country Groups, available online at http://web .worldbank.org/WBSITE/EXTERNAL/DATASTATISTICS/0,,contentMDK:20421402~ pagePK:64133150~piPK:64133175~theSitePK:239419,00.html#OECD_members

26. See Vietor (2007) at 127–46 for a discussion of how South Africa emerged to compete on the global scale.

27. See Ibid at 57–80.

28. See Ibid at 81–100.

29. See Mishra (2006). Articles such as this one reporting on India's economic boom have become commonplace. The prevailing theme, expressed through our Statecraft lens, is that India is achieving a remarkably post-modern economic status all the while continuing to be mired in pre-modern conditions in many sectors.

30. See Jellinck (2001)(addressing pre-modern conditions in Indonesia); Biasoto Jr. and Nishijima, Income Distribution of Brazil, available online at http://www.mre.gov.br/ CDBRASIL/ITAMARATY/WEB/INGLES/economia/merctrab/drenda/index.htm.

31. But see Bacoccina (2003) discussing Brazilian corporate and governmental initiatives aimed at providing youth in San Paolo with computer access and skills.

32. See United Nations Human Settlements Programme (2003); Kaplan (2002); Demery et al. (2002).

33. See Kochhar (2006). This study finds that India has followed an idiosyncratic pattern of economic development, emphasizing services over manufacturing, and within the manufacturing fields concentrating on labor intensive industries. The pattern of specialization leaves the Indian economy in need of foreign imports, at the same time as it contributes to the establishment of a trading class that generates increased demand for such goods.

34. See WTO website, World trade and output, Selected indicators 1948–98. Available online at http://www.wto.org/english/thewto_e/minist_e/min99_e/english/about_e/22fact_ e.htm#tariffcuts

35. See Marchak (1991). In this book, Marchak makes a now familiar argument that unrestrained global capitalism, which she associates with the "New Right," has created an unregulated mix of new markets, labor supplies and resources, which has benefited corporate interests and left masses in dire conditions. The catchy phrase that Marchak

coined – "Integrated Circus" – is intended to capture the unbridled aspect of the jungle capitalism that the author argues has come to dominate the global market. Marchak takes on various institutions, including the IMF and the GATT, to argue that globalized trade and conservative policies have resulted in an unmanageable global commons. We disagree with the over-used political polemic and the rather dogmatic assault on policies traditionally associated with the right wing of the political spectrum, but we agree with Marchak's view of the global marketplace as having transformed itself without overhauling its normative or institutional setting.

36. See Ronen (1986) for an explanation of how the colonization process of the pre-modern era has resulted in a chronic ability of the independent states to develop meaningfully.

37. Reinert (2007) observes that mere "openness" of an economy (i.e., unbridled comparative advantage) is positively dangerous. He writes:

> From the unification of Italy in the nineteenth century to the integration of Mongolia and Peru in the 1990s, historical experience has shown that free trade between nations at very different levels of development tends to destroy the most efficient industries in the least efficient countries. I have referred to this common phenomenon as the Vanik-Reinert effect. It was seen in France after the Napoleonic War, during the unification of Italy and – during the end of history – both in the Second and Third World. The first thing to die is advanced manufacturing, the last thing to die out is subsistence agriculture, the least advanced. The sequence is 1) deindustrialization, 2) deagriculturalization, 3) depopulation. This phenomenon can be observed in many countries, for example in the south of Mexico and in Moldova in the European periphery, where only the population over sixty and under fourteen stay behind while those in the working age bracket are working abroad.

> Ibid at 251. In a critical review of Reinert's book, Paul Collier praises what he describes as Reinert's "core idea," that "manufacturing industry offers much better long-term prospects of development than either agriculture or natural resource extraction." Collier (2007b) at 44. Collier chides Reinert for the latter's failure to analyze "the recent manufacturing successes of developing countries in global markets." Ibid. at 45. Although he does not make this point, it is fair to say that in his critique, Collier demonstrates that the issue in trade theory is not comparative advantage versus protectionism. Rather, it is engendering growth in underdeveloped countries in ways that enable those countries to enjoy the benefits of global trade. We read Collier as an advocate of what might be called "Enlightened Comparative Advantage" or "Comparative Advantage for the 21st Century." To the same effect is Ha-Joon Chang's recent book on the problems facing developing nations. Like Collier, Chang is critical of developing nations' overreliance on natural resources as a source of wealth. With respect to manufacturing, Chang writes: "History has repeatedly shown that the single most important thing that distinguishes rich countries from poor ones is basically their higher capabilities in manufacturing, where productivity is generally higher, and, more importantly, where productivity tends to (although does not always) grow faster than in agriculture or services." Chang (2007) at 213.

38. French Foreign Minister Robert Schuman, who is widely regarded as the Founding Father of Europe, announced his plan of preventing war by pooling the industrial resources of the original six member states of the European Economic Community: Italy, France, Germany, Belgium, the Netherlands, and Luxembourg. This statement was made on May 9, 1950 and is now referred to as Schuman's Declaration and is considered the beginning of the current European Union.

39. See generally Gomaa (1977) and MacDonald (1965) for narratives of the historical evolution of the Arab League. This regional organization arose in the days of the pan-Arab ideological attempts to unify the Arab nation. The divisions and ideological fractures among Arab states, however, have lingered. Today, among other profound divisions, Sunni states have grown suspicious of Shiite groups, Arab states like Syria, and even possibly Iraq, are cozying up to the Persian enemy of Saudi Arabia, and the secular/Islamic divide is causing increasing worries for regimes such as Egypt or Jordan. Depending on

the strategic direction of the Arab states, the League may or may not be an appropriate candidate for a seat on the Council.

40. The BBC reported that Chinese reserves reached $1 trillion in November 2006. See http://news.bbc.co.uk/2/hi/business/6120906.stm. The IMF gives the official reserve assets of many different countries and how these assets change monthly from March 2006 to February 2007. See http://www.imf.org/external/np/sta/ir/8802.pdf.

41. Sources state Chinese reserves are growing at rates of up to $20 billion per month: http://www.fxstreet.com/news/forex-news/article.aspx?StoryId=a928dc60-7128-4151-b9e6-9f9f0aa4b006; http://customwire.ap.org/dynamic/stories/C/CHINA_FOREIGN_RESERVES?SITE=FLROC&SECTION=BUSINESS&TEMPLATE=DEFAULT&CTIME=2007-03-10-18-08-42.

42. China's trade surplus passed $100 billion in 2005. See http://news.bbc.co.uk/2/hi/business/4602126.stm; The US-China Business Council reports a trade surplus of $178 billion in 2006. See http://www.uschina.org/info/forecast/2007/trade-performance.html.

43. The IMF has convened a forum for a select group of countries to promote dialogue on and, eventually, a common solution to deal with deficits in budgets and their impact on global financial stability. Delegates include the United States, China, the Euro Area, Japan, and Saudi Arabia all of whom were selected because of their likely ability to reduce the imbalance while sustaining increased world economic growth. While the parties invited to participate are eager to effect change, the IMF is having trouble incentivizing countries to cut deficits through trade measures. For more on the development of this body, see Robinson (2007).

44. See Corsi (2006) (reporting these numbers and noting that "[p]rior to Thanksgiving 2006, China's central banks suggested a possible move to diversify foreign exchange holdings away from the dollar. As a consequence, the dollar sold off on world currency markets, hitting a new 20-month low against the Euro, a currency which is beginning to compete with the dollar as an international foreign reserve currency"); D'Amato, Hon. C. Richard (2005), testimony available online at http://www.uscc.gov/testimonies_speeches/testimonies/2005/05_07_13_testi_damato.php; Capital Markets Transparency and Security: The Nexus Between U.S.-China Security Relations and America's Capital Markets, *U.S. – China Economic and Security Review Commission*, available online at http://www.uscc.gov/researchpapers/2000_2003/reports/cpmkex.php.

45. See Chen (2001) at 193–253 (detailing the growing domestic demand by Chinese actors, China's rise to prominence on the global markets, and the United States interests in a strong Chinese economy). See also Teunissen and Akkerman (2006) at 87–105 (discussing China's currency reserve buildup, currency asymmetry, and global imbalances).

46. The OECD and Fiscal Policy: Words of Warning. *The Economist* (2007).

47. See Hallwood and MacDonald (2000) at Parts VI and XXI (outlining international policy cooperation issues, including developing world issues). The incentives-based system that we are advocating would extend to manifold areas of international financial and economic coordination.

48. In addition, the success of industries such as textiles in China can lead to a backlash from competitors in Western states. The U.S. textiles industry, for example, has often lobbied for measures limiting access by Chinese-made garment to American markets. See, e.g., Becker (2004).

49. We have drawn the concept of "excluded" or *exclus* from the French context, where it has come to symbolize a socio-economic group that does not integrate into the economic and social framework where most subjects of the State find themselves. The question is intricately linked to the question of ethnicity and the lack of integration of North and sub-Saharan African immigrant communities in France. In Jennings (2000) at 575–585, the author explores whether traditional republican principles might be reconciled with a recognition of ethnic and cultural diversity. There are several schools of thought in France, which distinguish themselves from one another by the extent to which France

should accept multicultural diversity or insist on conformity. Regardless of the extent to which prejudice and lack of successful policies of integration contribute to the calcification of the excluded classes, the traditional French resistance to reforming modern welfare policies that have run their course and result in a rigid job market and relative lack of economic opportunity is a primary cause of the phenomenon. See Bolkestein and Rocard (2006) at 575.

50. North American Free Trade Agreement, Dec. 8–17, 1992, U.S.-Can.-Mex., ch. 11, 32 I.L.M. 605, 639 (1992) at article 1102 and 1105 (mandating national treatment of foreign investors and minimal levels of protection, including protection against arbitrary action).

51. See also www.kiva.org, an organization that facilitates loans between private citizens and small businesses in the developing world. Private lending to the third world is also described in Williamson (2007).

52. See, generally Grameen Bank, website http://www.grameen-info.org/index.html; Muhammad Yunus, website http://www.muhammadyunus.org/.

53. From a telephone interview with Adam Smith, Editor-in-Chief of nobelprize.org, on October 13, 2006, immediately following the announcement that Professor Yunus was to receive the 2006 Nobel Peace Price. This interview can be accessed at http://nobelprize.org/nobel_prizes/peace/laureates/2006/yunus-interview.html. Microcredit is so popular that even Hollywood and royalty are taking part. See Wighton (2007).

54. Professor Yunus made this statement and it is now quoted on Grameen Bank's website, http://www.grameen-info.org/bank/.

55. See the Grameen Bank's description of its "credit delivery system" on its website, http://www.grameen-info.org/bank/cds.html.

56. See Breaking the Vicious Cycle of Poverty, Grameen Bank website, http://www.grameen-info.org/bank/bcycle.html.

57. See Struggling Members Programme, Grameen Bank website, http://www.grameen-info.org/bank/BeggerProgram.html.

58. See Pitt and Khandker (1996) (documenting the impact of micro-credit on such household behaviors).

59. The ease of starting and running a business in Tunisia, relative to the region, is remarkable and makes the country an attractive place for European business. For more statistics, see Doing Business, Exploring Economies: Tunisia, Presented by The World Bank. Available online at http://rru.worldbank.org/DoingBusiness/ExploreEconomies/BusinessClimateSnapshot.aspx?economyid=190.

60. For a guide to proposed legislation in the 110th Congress of the United States, see Solving Global Warming: Your Guide to Legislation, *Natural Resource Defense Council*, available online at http://www.nrdc.org/legislation/factsheets/leg_07032601A.pdf (last visited August 13, 2007); Paulus-Jagrič (2007).

61. As Elkington and Lee (2005) point out, the United States and other Western powers have advocated free trade and open markets at the same time as they have increasingly complained about the emerging powers' access to their own economy. We would characterize this approach as reflective of the post-modern reluctance of Western powers to extend a modern framework of free trade, but in any events, as we point out, it is difficult for the West to sell such concepts as "sustainable developments" to emerging economies like China.

62. See Akcay (2006) at 29 (arguing that corruption reduces economic growth, hampers foreign investment, enhances inflation, depreciates currency, reduces health and other desirable expenditures, distorts job markets, and otherwise results in substantial political, social and economic inefficiencies).

63. The examples adduced by Rodgers (2006) illustrated the basic claim that corruption is one of the greatest obstacles to economic and social development because it undermines the rule of law and the institutions fostering growth.

64. See Hors (2001). This essay surveys corruption in customs services, and its effect on, among other things, trade expansion.
65. See also Buscaglia (2007), which explores corruption within the judicial branch of government in developing countries, finding that one of the predictors of corruption is also a dominant position of discretionary power.
66. See Hors (2000).
67. See Wei (1999).

7. The Enablement of Global Economic Opportunity

1. By "constitutional principle" we mean the emerging norm that will ground the global trading order. That principle – the global enablement of economic opportunity – is nascent, and its adoption on a global scale is in no way guaranteed. The arguments in this chapter serve to explain why we think this emerging norm should be nurtured and how the new institution of global trade will engender the growth and development of this norm.
2. Professor Cho has surveyed the principal academic views of the question of social legitimacy. See Cho (2005) at 625. Alvarez (2002) at 77 also discusses and categorizes the various "linkage" scenarios of conflict between free trade principles and domestic regulation of labor, environmental, health and other matters. The legitimacy of international law is intricately linked to its displacement of conflicting national norms, and the legitimacy question is often framed as whether and in what circumstances international legal norms trump countervailing national measures. Throughout this book, we have set forth our theory that the "linkage" issue is a GATT problem because the modern era featured sovereignty, the nation and welfare as foundational, animating norms, which provided the organic Statecraft reference for evaluating trade measures and their impact on national welfare.
3. Professor Weiler explored the evolution and formation of the European Union, and the relationship of the greater whole to the individual states. Weiler developed a powerful theory and axiom of international law holding that the less "Exit" states have the more "Voice" they will require in the formation of international law. Weiler illustrates this theory in the context of the European Union, showing how the Luxembourg Crisis of the mid-1960s was linked to Member State (France in particular) surprise at the extent to which the European Court of Justice "constitutionalized" European law, giving it direct effect and supremacy. Together with the Treaty framework giving individuals access to national courts for cases arising under European law, the European Court jurisprudence gave European law a presence within the European legal fabric akin to national law in a federated state, and, to a substantial extent, deprived the Member States of the ability to exit the European system. See Weiler (2005) at 2403. See also Cass (2005) (critiquing main conceptual paradigms for understanding the WTO: institutional managerialism (represented by J. H. H. Jackson), rights-based constitutionalization (represented by E.-U. Petersmann) and judicial norm-generation (represented by Weiler); and arguing that the WTO system is not constitutional in nature and should take into account to a greater extent the uneven playing field and the economic development needs of states in order to achieve democratic legitimacy). See Petersmann, 2000 (arguing that WTO should adopt human and civil rights as core constitutional values, in additional to economic rights).
4. See McGinnis (2004) at 353–365 (arguing that proposals for transfer of additional power to WTO to regulate substantively in areas such as labor or the environmental standards would create an unworkable "global government" and that the WTO should confine itself to its central task of reducing barriers to trade). Mc Ginnis and Movsesian, 2000, at 522–530 (one purpose of WTO is to remove national authorities' ability to adopt protectionist measures by transferring power of relevant subject-matter areas to international authority).

5. See Weiler (2005) at 2403.
6. Ibid.
7. Ibid.
8. Further, for example, United Nations Convention Against Torture, International Convention on Environment and Development, International Convention Against the Taking of Hostages.
9. See Buchanan (2004) at 1–13, 106–117 (presenting a moral critique of states' selective dismissal of their international obligations based on national perception of state interests and ability to further such interests through power in the international arena).
10. See Weiler (2005) at 2403.
11. In turn, the tariffs would be subject to gradual reduction based on consensual, successive agreements on lower tariff barriers for blocs of goods.
12. See Weiler (2005) at 2403.
13. See Shaw (2000) at 40–68.
14. See Weiler (2005) at 2403.
15. The concept of subsidiarity has, of course, been the subject of countless studies and analyses. For a good survey of the content of subsidiarity in both law and economics, see Pelkmans (2005) (also developing a multi-prong test blending law and economics and applying it to various subsidiarity cases). See also Begg (1993) at 35 (analyzing the strengths and weaknesses of centralized and decentralized forms of government).
16. MacShane's article highlights the increasing wealth and success of the European states, and attributes much success to cross-immigration between the countries. See MacShane (2007).
17. See WTO, website http://www.wto.org.
18. See Kocjan and Weiler (2004/5a) at 5–54 (excerpting rulings of the European Court of Justice that adopted a broad interpretation of the European Treaty provisions defining what constitutes a measure having an effect equivalent to a quantitative restriction, and of the case that, following a backlash and attacks on the perceived judicial activism of the Court, retreated from such interpretive stance).
19. Ibid. at 51–54.
20. See Strauss (2006) at 645.
21. See Govaere (1996) (in this thorough review of European competition and trade law affecting intellectual property rights, the author analyzes the regulatory and judicial norms that limit the application by national authorities of trademark, patent, copyright, and other intellectual property laws that hinder the free movement of goods across borders).
22. See National Euro Website – Glossary, website http://www.euro.cy/euro/euro.nsf/dmlglossary_en/dmlglossary_en?OpenDocument (providing a history of European monetary union).
23. See Farm Subsidy.org, website http://www.farmsubsidy.org/ (last accessed August 14, 2007); Gardner (1996) at 15. For a detailed description of the Common Agricultural Policy of the European Union, see Blumann (1996).
24. See Kocjan and Weiler (2004/5a) at 31-82 (excerpting rulings from the European Court of Justice applying the Treaty ban on discriminatory taxation).
25. See Kagan (2003) (Kagan further argues that the European ability to achieve some form of Kantian peace through integration may not have been possible without the United States' willingness to use power to achieve order in a Hobbesian universe).
26. See Afilalo (2005) at 279.
27. See Bilefsky (2007) (reporting that the election of Nicolas Sarkozy in France lessens Turkey's chances of accession); Wilson (2006)(thoughtful analysis of the debate between pro-admission politicians such as Tony Blair of England and opponents of Turkey's accession like mainstream French and German politicians who believe that bringing

Turkey within the fold of Europe would undermine the core cultural values of the continent and spell the beginning of its demise); Sciolino (2004).

28. The limitations on European integration found their latest expression in the rejection of the European constitutional draft by French and Dutch voters. It is posited that the Dutch rejected the 2005 referendum because of fears that the Netherlands, with its small population of 16.4 million people, would be engulfed by a superstate headquartered in Brussels and dominated by Germany, France, and Britain. Another suggestion was that some Dutch were harboring resentment over the adoption of the Euro as Europe's currency, even though they had voted against it. See Dutch reject EU constitution, CNN World Online, June 1, 2005. Available online at http://www.cnn.com/2005/WORLD/europe/06/01/dutch.poll/index.html. More reasons cited voters feeling that Brussels has too much power and that their national politicians were ceding control to a higher power. "No" supporters were also afraid of Brussels interfering in their liberal policies on soft drugs and gay marriage. Disillusionment with rapid EU expansion was also cited among the "No" supporters. See Dutch say 'No' to EU constitution, BBC News Europe, June 2, 2005. Available online at http://news.bbc.co.uk/2/hi/europe/4601439.stm. French rejection may have been caused by widespread disenchantment over a variety of issues, including the unpopularity of then President Jacques Chirac, the weakness of the French economy and fears that the country would lose its clout to a strengthened European central government. [See Whitlock, Craig, 2005. France Rejects European Constitution, *The Washington Post*, May 30, Page A01.] Opponents also worried about losing their national identity and sovereignty, and the influx of cheap labor during a time of high unemployment in France. See also Chirac accepts defeat on EU vote, CNN World, May 30, 2005. Available online at http://www.cnn.com/2005/WORLD/europe/05/29/france.eu/.

29. "The Convention establishes three main goals: the conservation of biological diversity, the sustainable use of its components, and the fair and equitable sharing of the benefits." Thus, in addition to ecological commitments, an aim of the Convention is economic and social growth in developing countries. See Convention on Biological Diversity, website http://www.cbd.int.

30. While this contract was signed shortly before the adoption of the treaty, it is often cited as a paradigmatic example of the type of incentives-driven framework the treaty is intended to foster.

31. For an outline of the agreement between Merck and INBio, and an exploration of the question of resource and biodiversity ownership, see http://www.american.edu/TED/lifepat.htm, (last accessed August 25, 2007).

32. Resor articulates the purpose and basis of debt-for-nature swapping, as well as its successes and limitations. See Resor (1997).

33. Thapa discusses the historical background of debt-for-nature swaps and their impact on economic stabilization in developing countries. See Thapa (2000).

34. See also Bequette (1992) (examining who ultimately benefits from debt-for-nature swaps and outlining the terms and conditions of the agreement entered into by Bolivia and Conservation International). See Bequette (1992).

35. Joseph argues that the Clinton administration aimed at "ensuring the potentially lucrative oil reserves in Azerbaijan and adjoining energy fields in the Caspian Sea flow through pipelines in a westward direction to the friendly markets of Turkey and Western Europe." See Joseph (2001) at 2.

36. Turkey's need for energy is increasing as a function of its growth rate. With 65 million people to service, a pipeline carrying a portion of the 100–200 billion barrels of Caspian crude oil through Turkey helps Turkey meet its energy needs. See Sasley (1998).

37. While billions of barrels of crude oil have been discovered in the Caspian Sea, the world's economic superpowers retain economic and strategic interest in the region. However,

Turkey's proximity to the area ensures that Turkey will own a large portion of the energy, Opposing Russian and Iranian plans, the United States pushed for a pipeline to be built through Turkey, which is sure to secure Turkish-American relations. See Kinzer (1998) at 11.

38. See Aftalion (1990) at 31–47 and 102–191 (describing economic conditions at the end of *Ancien Regime* and the economic consequences of the French Revolution).

39. See Ewald (1986); Culpepper et al. (2006).

40. See Araki (2006) at 251.

41. For a brief introduction, see Corporate Watch, Maquiladoras at a Glance (1999). Available online at http://www.corpwatch.org/article.php?id=1528; Baz, Aureliano Gonzalez Manufacturing In Mexico: The Mexican In-Bond (Maquila) Program.

42. About.com, 2007, Maquiladors in Mexico, http://geography.about.com/od/urbaneconomicgeography/a/maquiladoras.htm (reporting that the number of maquiladora workers has doubled since the 1990s and continues to grow and while foreign companies thrive and continue to raise more sweatshops along border towns, poor conditions inside many of the maquiladoras remain stagnant and without meaningful improvement).

43. Soriano describes the desperate conditions inside the maquiladoras, which are matched with wages ranging from $3.50–$5 a day. Workers are placed in dangerous conditions, experience sexual harassment, and are often exposed to toxic chemicals. Still, the workers hope for increased and fair wages that can ensure them more than minimal survival. See Soriano (1999); Although maquiladora workers along border towns collect higher wages than people working south of the cities, it is still not enough to cover the higher cost of living at the border. Bacon interviews a maquiladora worker who attests that his wages are not enough to sustain his family, and barely enough to put food on the table. Further, Bacon reveals the dirty sweatshops to be sites of toxic exposure. See Bacon (1997).

44. Table reproduced from Vogel, Richard D., 2006. Lessons from South of the Border, *Monthly Review Magazine*. Available online at www.monthlyreview.org/mrzine/vogel 121106.html (last accessed August 14, 2007).

45. See Honeywell, website, http://www.honeywell.com

46. In fact, the relocation for American managers and employees living in maquiladora towns has given rise to entire new industries. Consulting firms have tailored programs for making smooth cultural transitions. TraTec, Inc. is one such 'shelter company' – that is an American company with Maquila permits who can go into Mexico on behalf of an American company and get all transition matters in order for employees. *NAFTA Monitor*, 1994. Market Sector Develops Around NAFTA Business Expansion, February 15, vol. 1, no. 8.

47. See Friedman (2004) at 23.

48. See Robinson (1995) at 484 n. 31 (defining social dumping as a state of affairs "where the labour costs of production are held below the levels that they would attain in a regime of free and democratic unions and basic worker rights, owing to acts of corporate and/or government commission (e.g., repression of labour unions or worker rights) or government omission (e.g., failure to pass or enforce basic worker rights and labour standards"). Adams and Singh (1997), however, review the arguments advanced against the NAFTA and, in light of its early experience, argue that the treaty performed better than expected.

49. See Simon (2007) at 22 (while Mexico has protective labor laws, its institutions are often described as dictatorial and unfriendly to private party access).

50. Critics of the NAFTA argue that the treaty has done little to change this state of affairs. Proponents of the treaty, they claim, argued that labor rights, safety standards, and environmental laws would all be protected but the lack of access to effective dispute resolution meant that aggrieved workers did not gain the promised access to justice. See Bacon (2004).

51. See Lopez (1997) at 193–195.

52. See Englehart (1997) at 321–358.
53. See Ibid. at 358–373.
54. Ibid.
55. See Perez-Lopez (1995b) at 461–474 (examining how regional economic integration, including the NAFTA, can promote the adoption of international labor standards).
56. The following comment is an accurate, albeit provocative, statement of some of the challenges of the NAFTA's future:

   [G]overning class intellectuals in all three countries [the United States, Canada and Mexico] are thinking about NAFTA's next stage. It will require a much more intense level of integration among the three nations than even the people at the Independent Task Force on the Future of North America will publicly admit. Thus, in order to make a customs union effective, a whole host of economic policies have to be in some way harmonized – taxes, products, standards, and eventually currency. To say the least, this will raise a huge number of complicated and contentious issues, including those of sovereignty and the fate of what is left of each nation's social contract that cannot be avoided by repeating the mantra of "free trade," and for which the electorates of the countries – particularly the United States – are not prepared.

   Faux (2006) at 220.

57. "A Survey of Outsourcing: Men and Machines," *The Economist* (2004).
58. See Landes and Posner (1989) at 325.
59. Of course, we believe that the enablement of global economic opportunity will continue to develop into the gravamen of "welfare" for the State.
60. See WTO Doha Development Agenda, website http://www.wto.org/english/tratop_e/dda_e/dohasubjects_e.htm; Hilary (2006); Bello (2001).
61. See, generally, World Intellectual Property Organization (WIPO), website http://www.wipo.int. For member states, see Member States WIPO website, http://www.wipo.int/members/en/.
62. Hufbauer and Schott (2005) have argued that an overhaul of the immigration laws, in conjunction with the adoption of stronger core labor standards, is necessary to improve the effectiveness of the NAFTA and meaningfully increase the welfare of its intended beneficiaries. These measures would be candidates for the type of action by the Trade Council that we advocate below.
63. See Passel (2004).
64. See Bartlett and Steele (2006).
65. For example, in Arizona, 10 percent of the workforce is comprised of illegal workers. If a law were enforced that would alter this percentage, it logically follows that the state's economy would suffer as a result of the disruption. And with or without implementation of any immigration rules, life is difficult and uncomfortable for an illegal worker constantly dodging authorities and violating laws. See *The Economist* (2007), Illegal Immigration: Nowhere to Hide.
66. Griswold (2002) at 3 elaborates on the negative effects of the illegal labor market in the U.S. See Griswold (2002) at 3, for citation go to http://209.85.165.104/search?q=cache:R2w-Bd4wdREJ:www.freetrade.org/pubs/pas/tpa-019.pdf+what+do+illegal+mexicans+want+in+the+u.s.&hl=en&gl=us&ct=clnk&cd=17
67. For legislation in full, see Immigration Reform & Control Act of 1986, Office of Inspector General, website http://www.oig.lsc.gov/legis/irca86.htm.
68. Griswold (2002) at 2 details the background for these discussions. He argues that, despite increasingly close Mexican-American ties, the United States has persisted in discouraging labor migration, thereby creating a massive class of illegal immigrants. In turn, the illegal immigrant problem has caused grievous consequences on both sides of the border and has made it necessary for the leaders of the two countries to attempt to coordinate their policies.
69. From Presidents Vincente Fox and George W. Bush, Joint News Conference on the White House Lawn, September 6, 2001.
70. Ibid.

8. Trade and Security

1. See Shaw (2000) at Part I (outlining the roots of European integration, including among other things, the political climate change that followed the end of World War II and the Western realization that bringing Germany within the fold of Europe rather than punishing it would foster security, and providing an historical account of the continued legal, economic and political integration of Europe throughout the twentieth century, emphasizing the non-linear features of the integration process and the various crises (such as the Luxembourg crisis) that Europe faced).
2. Johnston, Taylor, and Watts (2002) at 144–148.
3. Kuhnle (2000) at 128–45.
4. For an insightful review of the history of the Communist Party in France, see Adereth (1985).
5. Gordon and Sylvester (2004) at 1–86 make a powerful case against the use of Western concepts, including the very notion of progress and development, to tackle the needs of countries that have traditionally been labeled as "developing," "Southern," "less developed," or "emerging." While we disagree with their assertion that economic growth will not shrink the gap between poor and rich countries, we endorse the claim that the Western policies towards states that did not experience a pre-modern and modern era have failed and that Western concepts cannot be forced upon cultures and polities that have not gone through the same transformative processes. Our own account of the issues at hand focuses on a critique of the Western states' insistence on imposing a road map that mirrors their own passage through pre-modern and modern epochs, and of the end of history narrative that it presumes. For a thorough account of the salient issues related to economic development, see Cypher and Dietz (2002).
6. We are of course approaching this question from the standpoint of the values that still characterize the Western liberal democratic victors of World War II, values we believe should be protected against the existential threats of the twenty-first century. We have essentially argued throughout this book that the international institutions and norms of trade may be structured by the victors of war to accord with their inner Statecraft. We also argue that the trade order should be harmonized with Statecraft before war makes such a move an inevitable historical choice. Like observers such as Mandelbaum (2002), our frame of reference is unapologetically Western in that we believe that democracies and democratic ideals like freedom of the press, religion or speech, and free markets, should be protected against the ideological threats of the day. However, our construct does not rely at all on clichés such as "exporting democracy" or imposing Western values on other cultures. Neither do we endorse the notion that any such values are superior to or should exclude others. We believe that post-modern Statecraft should be embedded in a new global trading order. The poets of Bretton Woods embedded liberalism in a modern comparative advantage system. Today's poetry should embed enduring democratic ideals into a post-modern order of economic opportunity.
7. Serafino discusses past experiences of global networked terrorism and how they influenced U.S. policy. See Serafino (2002) at 1.
8. Lawrence (2006) citing Remarks at the United Nations Financing for Development Conference in Monterrey, March 22, 2002, White House press release, www.whitehouse.gov (accessed September 15, 2006).
9. One of the most salient examples of terrorist intervention in the democratic process is the 2004 Madrid terrorist bombing. The terrorists' goal was widely perceived to entail the punishment of the government then in power for its support of the American invasion of Iraq and its aggressive investigations of Islamic groups. The indictment of 29 persons in connection with the bombing, which was part of a 1,500-page report on the attack, strongly suggested that the terrorists' motive was to influence the outcome of Spain's general elections, scheduled just three days after the bombing, Indeed, the ruling

conservative party of Jose Maria Aznar was defeated, despite a good showing in polls before the election. McLean (2006) at 13.

10. Wolfensohn (2002).

11. See Krueger and Maleckova (2003) (collecting statements of leaders in support of the claim that poverty is at the root of terrorism). See Lawrence (2006) citing Remarks at the United Nations Financing for Development Conference in Monterrey, March 22, 2002, White House press release, www.whitehouse.gov (last accessed September 15, 2006).

12. Quoted in Krueger and Maleckova (2003). See Atran (2003) citing Wiesel and Dalai Lama.

13. Quoted in Krueger and Maleckova (2003).

14. International Institute for Sustainable Development (2003), http://www.iisd.org/pdf/2003/natres_investing_stability.pdf, last accessed August 30, 2007(linking economic instability to world conflict, and proposing that financial institutions be utilized to strengthen and uphold areas struggling with poverty and violence).

15. White House Documents, National Strategy Council, http://www.whitehouse.gov/nsc/nss6.html (last accessed August 30, 2007).

16. O'Driscoll and Fitzgerald (2003) (arguing that international trade promotes prosperity and fosters a "habit of liberty" among disadvantaged segments of world population and that free trade should be a core foreign policy principle for economic as well as strategic reasons).

17. As quoted in Brown et al.(2005).

18. For discussion of RTAs, see Duina (2006).

19. Brown et al. (2005) at 4–15, outline the growth and history of regional trade agreements, citing instances where they have contributed to economic prosperity and stability as well as scenarios where individual member states have been adversely affected by the entry into force of an RTA.

20. Ibid.

21. Lizardo (2006) at 9–12 (outlining the "destructive globalization" thesis, which views terrorism as a reaction of the disaffected masses of the periphery to the globalization phenomenon).

22. Rodrik (2002)(arguing that globalization is ineffective in bringing true economic prosperity to countries suffering from financial crises and operating under the yoke of unfriendly monetary and financial burdens imposed by international financial institutions, and that Western governments often impose policies intended to benefit their economic interests under the pretext of globalization). See Rohter (2006).

23. Bartlett (2001) takes issue with what he claims to be the liberal claim that if poverty were eradicated, crime and terrorism would disappear. He uses the example of the wealthy Saudi hijackers involved in 9/11, whom he argues are representative of a class of well-off terrorists who cannot be said to act out of economic despair or lack of opportunity. See Becker and Posner (2005) (surveying studies showing that terrorists are oftentimes well educated and more advantaged economically than the classes of people whose interests they seek to further).

24. See Krueger (2003) (arguing that poverty and lack of education are not correlated with terrorism). Krueger's view is more fully developed in Krueger (2007).

25. Abadie (2004) at 3, http://ksghome.harvard.edu/~aabadie/povterr.pdf, (last accessed September 2, 2007). Abadie uses risk ratings to assess the "total amount of terrorist risk for every country in the world." The results of this analysis connect terrorism to political freedom and transitioning governments, as opposed to economic variables. Ibid. at 4. See Wessel (2007) (arguing that civil liberties reduce the incidence of terrorism).

26. Abadie (2004) at 4–9, http://ksghome.harvard.edu/~aabadie/povterr.pdf, (last accessed September 2, 2007).

27. Blomberg, Hess, and Weerapana (2003). The authors of this study find a positive correlation between economy and terrorism. Using GDP growth per capita and investment

variables, they find that dissident groups tend to proliferate in difficult economic times, although different types of economies are likely to see different forms of conflict.

28. Free Trade Area of the Americas, Third Draft Agreement, November 21, 2003. Available online at http://www.ftaa-alca.org/FTAADraft03/Index_e.asp.

29. See *The Economist* (2001). Breaking Barriers in the Americas.

30. See Fonda (2002).

31. See Waller (2001); Murphy (2005) at 375. Both articles report on the confluence of drug and terrorist related activities that are focused in this region, and the unusual concentration of law enforcement and security agencies gathered at the border area in an effort to combat crime and terrorism.

32. Nelson (2007) describes analysts' predictions that a Chinese middle class hungry for consumer products will arise and create an untapped, enormous market for producers of those goods.

Conclusion

1. Doha WTO Ministerial 2001: Ministerial Declaration of November 14, 2001, http://www.wto.org/English/thewto_e/minist_e/min01_e/mindecl_e.htm, last accessed August 28, 2007.

2. Ibid.

3. See Kagan (2003).

Bibliography

Abadie, Alberto, 2004. *Poverty, Political Freedom and the Roots of Terrorism*, Harvard University, Harvard University and NBER, available online at http://ksghome.harvard.edu/~aabadie/povterr.pdf.

Abboud, Leila, 2006. Exit Strategy. *Wall Street Journal*, August 14, p. A-1.

Abdelal, Rawi, 2007. *Capital Rules: The Construction of Global Finance* (Cambridge, Mass: Harvard University Press).

About.com, 2007. *Maquiladoras in Mexico*, Available online at: http://geography.about.com/od/urbaneconomicgeography/a/maquiladoras.htm (last viewed on August 30, 2007).

Ackerman, Bruce, 1997. A Generation of Betrayal? *Fordham Law Review*, Vol. 65, p. 1519.

Adereth, M., 1985. The French Communist Party: A Critical History (1920–84), *International Affairs (Royal Institute of International Affairs 1944-)*, Vol. 61, No. 4 (Autumn).

Afilalo, Ari and Sheila Foster, 2003. The World Trade Organization's Anti-Discrimination Jurisprudence: Free Trade, National Sovereignty, and Environmental Health in the Balance, *Georgetown International Environmental Law Review*, Vol. 15, p. 633.

Afilalo, Ari, 2004. Towards a Common Law of International Investment: How NAFTA Chapter 11 Panels Should Solve Their Legitimacy Crisis, *Georgetown International Environmental Law Review*, Vol. 17, p. 51.

Afilalo, Ari, 2005. Meaning, Ambiguity and Legitimacy: Judicial (Re-)Construction of NAFTA Chapter 11, *Northwestern Journal of International Law and Business*, Vol. 25, p. 279.

Afilalo, Ari and Dennis Patterson, 2006. Statecraft, Trade and the Order of States, *Chicago Journal of International Law*, Vol. 725, p. 6.

Aftalion, Florin, 1990. *The French Revolution: An Economic Interpretation* (Cambridge [England]; New York: Cambridge University Press; Paris: Editions de la Maison des sciences de l'homme).

Agnew, John and J. Nicholas Entrikin, 2004. *The Marshall Plan Today: Model and Metaphor* (London; New York: Routledge).

Akcay, Selcuk, 2006. Corruption and Human Development, *Cato Journal*, Vol. 26, No. 1, available online at http://www.cato.org/pubs/journal/cj26n1/cj26n1-2.pdf.

Aksen, Gerald, 1990. Arbitration and Other Means of Dispute Settlement in D. Goldsweig and R. Cummings (eds.), *International Joint Ventures: A Practical App.roach to Working With Foreign Investors in the U.S. and Abroad*, pp. 287–94 (Chicago: American Bar Association).

Allen, David, 1992. The Single European Market and Beyond: A Study of the Wider Implications of the Single European ACT 26, ed. Dennis Swan (New York: Routledge).

Alternate Trajectories: Options for Competitive Sourcing for the Space Shuttle, 2003 Final Report posted online at: http://www.rand.org/scitech/stpi/NASA/nasaFinalRpt.html (last viewed August 28, 2007).

Alvarez, José E., 2005. International Organizations as Law-Makers (Oxford; New York: Oxford University Press).

Alvarez, José E. and Joel Trachtman, 2002. International Linkage: Transcending "Trade and . . .", *American Journal of Int'l Law*, Vol. 96, p. 77.

Aly, Götz, 2006. *Hitler's Beneficiaries: Plunder, Racial War and the Nazi Welfare State* (New York: Metropolitan Books).

American University, The Mandala Projects, Life Patents and Trade, available online at: www.american.edu/TED/lifepat.htm (last viewed August 27, 2007).

Amyx, Jennifer, 2004. *Japan's Financial Crisis: Institutional Rigidity and Reluctant Change* (Princeton, NJ: Princeton University Press).

Anderson, Benedict R. O'G., 1991. Rev and extended ed., *Imagined Communities: Reflections on the Origin and Spread of Nationalism* (London, New York: Verso).

Anderson, Chris, 2006. *The Long Tail: Why the Future of Business is Selling Less of More* (New York: Hyperion).

Angresano, James, 1996. *Comparative Economics* (Upp.er Saddle River, NJ: Prentice Hall).

Antola, Esko and Allan Rosas, eds., 1995. *A Citizens' Europe: In Search of a New Order* (London; Thousand Oaks, CA: SAGE Publications).

Araki, Takashi, 2006. Changing Employment Practices, Corporate Governance, and the Role of Labor Law in Japan, *Comparative Labor Law and Policy Journal*, Vol. 28, p. 251.

Asia-Pacific Economic Update, 2002. Prepared by the U.S. Pacific Command's Strategic Planning and Policy Directorate and available online at: http://www.pacom.mil/publications/apeu02/apeu2002.htm.

Atlantic Council of the United States, April 2007 Policy Paper, *Transatlantic Leadership for a New Global Economy*, Co-chairs Stuart E. Eizenstat and Grant D. Aldonas.

Atran, Scott, 2003. Genesis of Suicide Terrorism in *Science* Magazine, Vol. 299, No. 5612, pp. 1534–1539. Available online at http://www.sciencemag.org/cgi/content/full/299/5612/1534 (last viewed August 22, 2007).

Bacevich, A. J., 2002. *American Empire: The Realities and Consequences of U.S. Diplomacy* (Cambridge, MA; London: Harvard University Press).

Bacoccina, Denize, 2003. Brazil Bets on Linux Cybercafes, *BBC News*, December 2, available online at http://news.bbc.co.uk/2/hi/technology/3250876.stm.

Bacon, David, 1997. Workers in maquiladoras from Tijuana to Juarez are fighting back against NAFTA-driven exploitation, *San Francisco Bay Guardian*, March 5, available online at http://www.hartford-hwp.com/archives/46/003.html.

Bacon, David, 2004. The Toxic Border: Environmental Injustice, *Foreign Policy in Focus Policy Report*, December 2004. Available online at http://www.fpif.org/papers/0412toxic_body.html (last visited August 18, 2007).

Bagwell, Kyle and Robert W. Staiger, 2000. *GATT-think, Natl.* Bureau of Economic Research, Discussion Paper 8005, Nov. Available online at http://www.nber.org/papers/w8005 (visited August 17, 2007).

Baker, Raymond W., 2005, *Capitalism's Achilles Heel: Dirty Money and How to Renew the Free-market System* (Hoboken, NJ: Wiley).

Balabkins, Nicholas, 1964. *Germany Under Direct Controls. Economic Aspects of Industrial Development 1945–1948* (New Brunswick: NJ: Rutgers University Press).

Barber, William, J., 1967. *A History of Economic Thought* (New York: Praeger Publishers).

Bard, Alexander and Jan Söderqvist, 2002. *Netocracy: The new power elite and life after capitalism* (London; New York: Pearson Education).

Bardhan, Pranab, and Samuel Bowles & Michael Wallerstein, editors. 2006. *Globalization and egalitarian redistribution* (Princeton, NJ: Princeton University Press).

Barrett, Kate, 2006. Philippines Boosts Marine Conservation, *Conservation International Online Journal*, November 8, available online at http://web.conservation.org/xp/frontlines/2006/11080603.xml (visited July 12, 2007).

Barry, Christian and Sanjay G. Reddy, 2006. International Trade and Labor Standards: A proposal for Linkage, *Cornell International Law Journal*, Vol. 39, p. 545.

Bartlett, Donald L. and James B. Steele, 2006. Who Left the Door Open?, *Time* Magazine, available online at http://www.time.com/time/magazine/article/0,9171,995145-18,00.html.

Barton, John H., Judith L. Goldstein, Timothy E. Josling, and Richard H. Steinberg, eds., 2006. *The Evolution of the Trade Regime: Politics, Law, and Economics of the GATT and the WTO* (Princeton, NJ: Princeton University Press).

Bauman, Zygmunt, 1998. *Globalization: The Human Consequences* (New York: Columbia University Press.

Bayoumi, Tamim, 1995. The postwar economic achievement. *International Monetary Fund Finance & Development*, June 1995, Vol. 32, No. 2, p. 48.

Baz, Aureliano Gonzalez Manufacturing In Mexico: The Mexican In-Bond (Maquila) Program. Available online at http://www.udel.edu/leipzig/texts2/vox128.htm (last visited July 12, 2007).

BBC News Europe, 2005. *Dutch Say No to EU Constitution*, June 2, 2005, Available online at http://news.bbc.co.uk/2/hi/europe/4601439.stm.

BBC, website http://news.bbc.co.uk/2/hi/business/6120906.stm (last visited March 26, 2007).

BBC, website http://news.bbc.co.uk/2/hi/business/4602126.stm (last visited March 27, 2007).

Beal, Dave, 1992. Honeywell: Leaner, Less Tied to Minnesota, *St. Paul Pioneer Press*, April 19, Business.

Becker, Elizabeth, 2004. Textile Industry To Request Limits On Chinese Goods, *The New York Times*, September 2, Section C.

Becker, Gary and Richard Posner, 2005. Poverty and Terrorism: Any Connection (Becker). *The Becker-Posner Blog*. May 29. Available online at http://www.becker-posner-blog.com/archives/2005/05/terrorism_and_p_1.html.

Begg, David et al., 1993. *Making Sense of Subsidiary: How Much Centralization for Europe?* (Centre for Economic Policy Research).

Behrman, Greg, 2007. *The Most Noble Adventure: The Marshall Plan and the Time When America Helped Save Europe* (New York: Free Press).

Bell, John Fred, 1967. *A History of Economic Thought* (New York: Ronald Press).

Bello, Walden, 1997. The "Shrimp-Turtle Controversy" and the Rise of Green Unilateralism. Available online at http://www.focusweb.org/publications/1997/The%20Shrimp-Turtle%20Controversy%20and%20the%20Rise%20of%20Green%20Unilateralism.htm.

Bello, Walton, 2001. WTO Talks Collapse: Good News for the Developing World, available online at http://www.focusweb.org/content/view/964/36/ (last visited July 15, 2007).

Benhabib, Seyla, 2002. *The Claims of Culture: Equality and Diversity in the Global Era* (Princeton, NJ: Princeton University Press).

Benoit, Bertrand, 2007. Germany Records Surplus for First Time since 1989, *Financial Times*, U.S. Edition, p. 4, August 25 2007.

Bequette, France, 1992. *Who Benefits from Debt-for-Nature Exchanges*, UNESCO Courier, September. Available online at: http://unesdoc.unesco.org/ulis/cgi-bin/ulis.pl?database=ged&lin=1&gp=0&look=new&sc1=1&sc2=1&nl=1&req=4&au=Bequette,%20France (last viewed August 30, 2007).

Beresford-Smith, Timothy, 2004. *France in Crisis: Welfare, Inequality, and Globalization Since 1980* (Cambridge; New York: Cambridge University Press).

Berman, Morris, 2000. *The Twilight of American Culture* (New York: London: Norton).

Bernstein, Edward M. and Orin Kirshner, 1996. *The Bretton Woods-GATT System: Retrospect and Prospect After Fifty Years* (Armonk, NY: M. E. Sharpe).

Bhagwati, Jagdish, N., 2007. America's Bipartisian Battle Against Free Trade, *Financial Times*, U.S. edition, April 8, 2007, p. 11.

Bhagwati, Jagdish N., 2005. A New Vocabulary for Trade, *Wall Street Journal*, A12, August 4.

Bhagwati, Jagdish N., 2004. *In Defense of Globalization* (New York: Oxford University Press).

Bhagwati, Jagdish N., 1971. The Generalized Theory of Distortions and Welfare, in Jagdish N. Ghagwati, et al., eds. *Trade, Balance of Payments and Growth: Papers in International Economics in Honor of Charles P. Kindleberger 69* (North-Holland).

Bhagwati, Jagdish N. and V. K. Ramaswami, 1963. Domestic Distortions, Tariffs and the Theory of Optimum Subsidy. *J Pol Econ*, Vol. 71, p. 44.

Bhala, Raj and David A. Gantz, 2005. WTO Case Review 2004, *Arizona Journal of International and Comparative Law*, Vol. 22, p. 99.

Biasoto Jr., Geraldo & Marisley Nishijima, Income Distribution, available online at http://www.mre.gov.br/CDBRASIL/ITAMARATY/WEB/INGLES/economia/merctrab/drenda/index.htm.

Biddle, Jo, 2005. Europeans seek to sew up luxury textile market before Chinese invasion, *Agence France Presse*, March 10, 2005.

Bilefsky, Dan, 2007. EU talks on Turkey blocked by Sarkozy French move lessens chances of accession, *International Herald Tribune*, June 27, News.

Bjorgo, Tore, 2005. *Root Causes of Terrorism: Myths, Reality and Ways Forward* (New York: Routledge).

Black, Cyril Edwin, 2000. *Rebirth: History of Europe Since World War II*, 2nd edition (Boulder, Colorado: Westview Press, Inc.).

Blanning, Tim, 2007. *The Pursuit of Glory: Europe 1648–1815.* (New York: Viking Press, Penguin Group).

Bleses, Peter and Martin Seeleib-Kaiser, 2004. *The Dual Transformation of the German Welfare State* (Basingstoke, Hampshire; New York: Palgrave Macmillan).

Blomberg, S. Brock, Hess, Gregory D., and Weerapana, Akila, 2003, *Economic Conditions and Terrorism*, Wellesley University, available online at http://209.85.165.104/search?q=cache:JyNSJI9TYSsJ:www.wellesley.edu/Economics/postscript/ejpeterr2.pdf+economic+conditions+affect+terrorism&hl=en&ct=clnk&cd=1&gl=us.

Blumann, Claude, 1996. *Politique Agricole Commune: Droit Communautaire Agricole et Agro-alimentaire* (France: Litec).

Bobbitt, Philip, 2002. *The Shield of Achilles* (New York: Knopf).

Bolkestein, Frits and Michel Rocard, 2006. *Peut-on Reformer la France* (Paris, France: Éditions Autrement, collection Frontières).

Bradsher, Keith, 2005. Chinese Apparel Makers Increasingly Seek the Creative Work, *New York Times*, C1, August 31.

Bradsher, Keith, 2006. Thanks to Detroit, China Is Poised to Lead, *The New York Times*, March 12, Section 3.

Brady, David, Jason Beckfield and Martin Seeleib-Kaiser, 2004. Economic Globalization and the Welfare State in Affluent Democracies, 1975–1998. Available online at http://www.apsoc.ox.ac.uk/Docs/ZesAP.pdf, last visited August 8, 2007.

Braithwaite, Rodric, 2002. *Moscow 1941: A City and its People at War* (New York: Knopf).

Brands, H. W., 2002. Ideas and Foreign Affairs, in Robert Schulzinger, ed., *A Companion to American Foreign Relations*, Vol. 1, p. 9 (Malden, MA: Blackwell Pub).

Brandt, Ron, 2003. Maquilas Throughout the Americas: Economic Development or Human Rights Nightmares?, available online at http://www.justice-and-peace.org/PolicyAdvocacy/pahome2.5.nsf/gereports/A4FC678BA27E35BB88256E46008361F4/$file/Maquilas4.pdf.

Brenner, Robert, 2002. *The Boom and the Bubble: The U.S. in the World Economy* (London; New York: Verso).

Bretton Woods, see http://www.ll.georgetown.edu/intl/guides/gattwto/.

Bretton Woods Project, *Background to the Issues*, available online at http://www.brettonwoodsproject.org/background/index.shtml (visited Nov 2005).

Breuilly, John, 1982. *Nationalism and the State* (London: Manchester University Press).

Breuilly, John, 1994. *Nationalism and the State*, 2nd edition, (c. 1982, 1985, 1993) (Chicago: University of Chicago Press).

Brenner, Robert, 2006. *The Economics of Global Turbulence* (London: New York: Verso Books).

Bretton Woods Project, *Background to the Issues*, available online at http://www.brettonwoodsproject.org/background/index.shtml (visited Nov. 8, 2005).

Bronckers, Marco C. E. J., 2001. More Power to the WTO?, *J Intl Econ L*, p. 41, 44.

Brooks, Stephen G., 2005. *Producing Security: Multinational Corporations, Globalization, and the Changing Calculus of Conflict* (Princeton, NJ: Princeton University Press).

Brown, Clair, John Haltiwanger, and Julia Lane, 2006. *Economic Turbulence: Is a Volatile Economy Good For America?* (Chicago: University of Chicago Press).

Brown, Oli, et. al., 2005. Regional Trade Agreements: Promoting Conflict or Building Peace?, *International Institution for Sustainable Development*, October 2005. Available online at http://www.iisd.org/pdf/2005/security_rta_conflict.pdf.

Brown, Oli, 2006. Continental Drift: Fractured Multilateralism, Regional, Trade Agreements, and the Prospects for Peace, *IISD Commentary: Opinions and Insights from the IISD*, June. Available online at http://www.iisd.org/pdf/2006/commentary_tas_4.pdf (last accessed July 23, 2007).

Brudny, Yitzhak M., Jonathan Frankel, and Stefani Hoffman, 2004. *Restructing Post-Communism Russia* (New York: Cambridge University Press).

Buchanan, Allan, 2004. *Justice, Legitimacy, and Self-Determination: Moral Foundations for International Law* (Oxford; New York: Oxford University Press).

Bunker, Robert J., editor. 2005. *Networks, Terrorism and Global Insurgency* (New York: Routledge).

Burawoy, Michael, 1999. *The Great Involution: Russia's Response to the Market* (Mar 28, 1999), available online at http://sociology.berkeley.edu/faculty/burawoy/burawoy_pdf/involution.pdf (last visited August 12, 2007).

Burawoy, Michael. *Transition Without Transformation: Russia's Involutionary Road to Capitalism*. Available online at http://sociology.berkeley.edu/faculty/burawoy/burawoy_pdf/transition.pdf (last visited August 12, 2007).

Buscaglia, Edgardo, 2007. Judicial Corruption in Developing Countries: Its Causes and Economic Consequences, *Hoover Institution Publications*. Available online at http://www.hoover.org/publications/epp/2846061.html?show=essay.

Bush, George W., 2002. State of the Union Address, January 29, 2002.

Bush, George W., 2006. Remarks at swearing in ceremony of Council of Economic Advisers Chairman, Edward Lazear. Available online at: http://www.whitehouse.gov/news/releases/2006/03/20060306.html (visited 2 May 2006).

Butler, Elisabeth, 2004. Tattered Apparel Industry Faces More Wear, Tear: Firms Brace for End of Trade Quotas, *Crain's NY Bus*, 4 (December 13).

Cable, Vincent, 1995. The Diminished Nation-State: A Study in the Loss of Economic Power, *Daedalus*, Vol. 124(2), pp. 23–53.

Capital Markets Transparency and Security: The Nexus Between U.S.-China Security Relations and America's Capital Markets, *U.S. – China Economic and Security Review Commission*, available online at http://www.uscc.gov/researchpapers/2000_2003/reports/cpmkex.php.

Caruso, Daniela, 2006. Private Law and State-making in the Age of Globalization, in *New York University Journal of International Law and Politics*, Vol 39, Fall, p. 1.

Cass, Deborah Z., 2005. *The Constitutionalization of the World Trade Organization: Legitimacy, Democracy, and Community in the International Trading System* (Oxford; New York: Oxford University Press).

Cendrowicz, Leo, 2005. Why Small Nations Hold Big Sway At Trade Talks, *Time Magazine*, December 14, 2005.

Cesarano, Filippo, 2006. *Monetary Theory and Bretton Woods: The Construction of an International Monetary Order* (New York: Cambridge University Press).

Chang, Ha-Joon, 2007. *Bad Samaritans: Rich Nations, Poor Policies and the Threat to the Developing World* (London: Random House Business Books).

Chen, Shuxun and Charles Wolf, 2001. *China, the United States and the Global Economy* (Santa Monica, CA: Rand).

Cho, Sung-Joon, 1998. GATT Non-Violation Issues In the WTO Framework: Are They the Achilles' Heel of the Dispute Settlement Process?, *Harvard International Law Journal*, Vol. 39, p. 311.

Cho, Sung-Joon, 2004. The WTO'S Gemeinschaft, *Alabama Law Review*, Vol. 56, p. 483.

Cho, Sung-Joon, 2005. Linkage of Free Trade and Social Regulation: Moving Beyond the Entropic Dilemma, *Chicago Journal of International Law*, Vol. 5, p. 625.

Christensen, Eric, 1990. Food Fight: How GATT Undermines Food Safety Regulations, *The Multinational Monitor*, Vol. 11, No. 11, November 1990.

Clatanoff, William (Bud), 2005. Labor Standards in Recent U.S. Trade Agreements, *Richmond Journal of Global Law and Business*, Vol. 5, p. 109.

Claude, Inis L., Jr., 1961. *Swords into Plowshares: The Problems and Progress of International Organization* (New York: Random House).

Clifford, Harlan C., 1994. Medicine Men Tropical Cures, *San Francisco Chronicle*, May 22, Section 2.

Clinton, Bill, 1994. Remarks on the Reinventing of Government Initiative, in Weekly Compilation of Presidential Documents, Vol. 30, 1994, p. 1763.

Clinton, Bill, 1996. Remarks to the Joint Session of the Louisiana State Legislature in Baton Rouge, Louisiana, in Weekly Compilation of Presidential Documents, Vol. 32, 1996, p. 969.

Clinton, Bill, 1997. Inaugural Address, in Weekly Compilation of Presidential Documents, Vol. 33, 1997, p. 60.

CNN World Online, 2005. *Dutch Reject EU Constitution*. Available online at http://www.cnn.com/2005/WORLD/europe/06/01/dutch.poll/index.html.

CNN World Online, 2005. *Chirac Accepts Defeat on EU Vote*, May 30, 2005. Available online at http://www.cnn.com/2005/WORLD/europe/05/29/france.eu/.

Cohen, Benjamin, J., 2004. *The Future of Money* (Princeton, NJ: Princeton University Press).

Cohen, Daniel, 2006. *Globalization and Its Enemies*, translated by Jessica B. Baker (Cambridge, MA: MIT Press).

Collier, Paul, 2007a. *The Bottom Billion: Why the Poorest Countries Are Failing And What Can Be Done About It* (New York; Oxford: Oxford University Press).

Collier, Paul, 2007b. For Richer and for Poorer, *Prospect*, June 2007, pp. 42–47.

Collier, Paul and Anthony Venables, 2007. *Trade Preferences and Manufacturing Export Response; Lessons from Theory and Policy*, January 30. Available at: http://users.ox.ac.uk/~econpco/research/pdfs/TradePrefs-Manufacturing.pdf.

Collins, Kimberly, 2003. Growth of the Maquiladora Industry in Baja California, *California Center for Border and Regional Economic Studies Bulletin*, November, Vol. 4, No. 11.

Columbia Encyclopedia, Hawley-Smoot Tariff Act (Bartleby.com 6th ed 2005), available online at http://www.bartleby.com/65/ha/HawleySm.html (visited April 5, 2005).

Commerzbank Economic Research at Commerzbank.com. https://www.commerzbank.com/research/economic_research/pool/d_eur/d_konjunkturaktuell/d_eur_konjak_en_0607.pdf.

Connor, Walker, 1994. *Ethnonationalism: The Quest for Understanding* (Princeton, NJ: Princeton University Press).

Conservation International, *CI mobilizes communities and presidents to preserve Andes treasure*, available online at http://web.conservation.org/xp/frontlines/partners/focus22-1.xml (visited July 12, 2007).

Conservation International, website http://www.conservation.org (last visited July 12, 2007).

Convention on Biological Diversity, website http://www.cbd.int (last visited July 12, 2007).

Cook, Jeffrey, T., 2007. Comment: The Evolution of Investment-State Dispute Resolution in NAFTA and CAFTA: Wild West to World Order, *Pepperdine Law Review*, Vol. 34, pp. 1087–89.

Cooper, Robert, 2003. *The Breaking of Nations: Order and Chaos in the Twenty-First Century* (London; New York: Atlantic Books).

Corporate Watch.org, 1999. *Maquiladoras at a Glance*, June 30, 1999. Available online at: http://www.corpwatch.org/article.php?id=1528 (last viewed August 30, 2007).

Corsi, Jermone, 2006. Could the Dollar's Collapse Prompt a New Currency? *Human Events.com*, December 20. Available online at http://www.humanevents.com/article.php?id=18564 (last visited August 13, 2007).

Cox, W. Michael and Jahyeong Koo, 2006. *Miracle to Malaise: What's Next for Japan?* In the Economic Letter – Insights from the Federal Reserve Bank of Dallas. Available from the Federal Reserve Bank of Dallas website at: http://www.dallasfed.org/research/eclett/2006/e10601.html.

Coyle, Diane, 2001. *Paradoxes of Prosperity: Why the New Capitalism Benefits All* (New York: Texere).

Craig, Paul and Grainne de Burca, 2002. *EU Law: Text, Cases and Materials* (Oxford; New York: Oxford University Press).

Craig, Tim, 2005a. Wal-Mart Closer to Entering India, *UPI*, June 6.

Craig, Tim, 2005b. Most Growth Potential Beyond U.S. Borders, *DSN Retailing Today*, June 13, Vol. 44, p. 48.

Crook, Clive, 2007. Unfounded New Fears on Free Trade. *Financial Times*, U.S. edition, May 10, p.11.

Culpepper, Pepper D., Hall, Peter A., and Bruno Palier, 2006. *La France en mutation, 1980–2005* (Paris: Presses de la fondation nationale des sciences politiques).

Curtin, Deirdre, 1993. The Constitutional Structure of the Union: A Europe of Bits and Pieces, *Common Market Law Review*, Vol. 30, No. 1, p. 17.

Cypher, James M. and James L. Dietz, 2002. *The Process of Economic Development* (London; New York: Routledge).

Daimler-Chrysler, 2002. *DaimlerChrysler, Hyundai, and Mitsubishi Motors to Form Global Engine Alliance* (May 5). Available online at http://www.daimlerchrysler.com/decom/o,,0-5-7153-1-9426-1-0-0-0-0-0-8-7145-0-0-0-0-0-0-1,00.html (visited September 13, 2005).

Daimer-Chryster, 1990. Courtship of Giants, *Time* Magazine available online at http://www.time.com/time/magazine/article/0,9171,969608,00.html.

D'Amato, Hon. C. Richard (2005). National Security Dimensions of the Possible Acquisition of UNOCAL by CNOOC and the Role of CFIUS, Testimony given July 13, 2005. Available online at http://www.uscc.gov/testimonies_speeches/testimonies/2005/05_07_13_testi_damato.php (last visited July 23, 2007).

Dammasch, Sabine, *The System of Bretton Woods: A lesson from history*. Available online at: http://www.ww.uni-magdeburg.de/fwwdeka/student/arbeiten/006.pdf (last viewed August 30, 2007).

DARES, 1996. Quarante ans de politique de l'emploi, Paris: l'Animation de la Recherche, des Etudes et des Statistiques.

DARES, 2000. La politique de l'emploi en 1999. Paris: Direction de l'Animation de la Recherche, des Etudes et des Statistiques. 52.2. December.

Das, Gurcharan, 2004. Is India Shining? *Wall Street Journal*, May 3, A-20.

Davis, Christina L., 2003. *Food Fights Over Free Trade: How International Institutions Promote Agricultural Trade Liberalization* (Princeton, NJ: Oxford: Princeton University Press).

Deane, Phyllis, 1978. *The Evolution of Economic Ideas* (Cambridge; New York: Cambridge University Press).

De Grazia, Victoria, 2005. *Irresistible Empire: America's Advance Through Twentieth-Century Europe* (Cambridge, MA: Belknap Press of Harvard University Press).

Demery, Lionel, Stefano Paternostro and Luc J. Christiaensen, 2002. *Growth Distribution and Poverty in Africa* (Washington, DC: World Bank).

Denes, Ivan Zoltan, 2006. *Liberty and the Search for Identity: Liberal Nationalisms and the Legacy of Empires* (New York: Central European Univ. Press).

Dezalay, Yves and Bryant Garth, 1995. Also Aksen, Gerald, 1990. Arbitration and Other Means of Dispute Settlement in D. Goldsweig and R. Cummings, eds., *International Joint Ventures: A Practical Approach to Working With Foreign Investors in the U.S. and Abroad*, pp. 287–94 (Chicago: American Bar Association).

Dezalay Yves and Bryant Garth, 1996. *Dealing in Virtue: International Commercial Arbitration and the Construction of a Transnational Legal Order* (CSLS) Chicago Series in Law and Society) (Chicago: Chicago University Press).

Dinnage, James D. and John F. Murphy, 1996. *Constitutional Law of the European Union* (Cincinnati: Anderson Publishing).

Doha Declaration, 2001. Doha WTO Ministerial Declaration, 14 2001 November Available online at http://www.wto.org/English/thewto_e/minist_e/min01_e/mindecl_e.htm (viewed August 20, 2007).

Doig, Alan and Stephen Riley, 1998. 'Corruption and Anti-Corruption Strategies: Issues and Case Studies from Developing Countries', in *Corruption and Integrity Improvement Initiatives in Developing Countries* (New York: UNDP).

Doing Business, Exploring Economies: Tunisia, Presented by The World Bank. Available online at http://rru.worldbank.org/DoingBusiness/ExploreEconomies/BusinessClimateSnapshot.aspx?economyid=190 (last visited August 13, 2007).

Dormois, Jean-Pierre, 2004. *The French Economy in the Twentieth Century*, prepared for the Economic History Society (Cambridge, UK; New York: Cambridge University Press).

Driesen, David M., 2001. What is Free Trade?: The Real Issue Lurking Behind the Trade and Environment Debate, *Virginia Journal of International Law*, Vol. 41, p. 279.

Drucker, Peter F., 1994. The Age of Social Transformation, *Atlantic Monthly*, November, pp. 72–73.

Drury, Shadia B., 1994. *Alexandre Kojeve: The Roots of Postmodern Politics* (New York: St. Martin's Press).

Duina, Francesco G., 2006. *The Social Construction of Free Trade: The European Union, NAFTA, and MERCOSUR* (Princeton, NJ: Princeton University Press).

Dunoff, Jeffrey L., 1999. The Death of the Trade Regime, *European Journal of International Law*, Vol. 10, p. 733.

Dunhoff, Jeffrey, 2006. Constitutional Conceits: The WTO's "Constitution" and the Discipline of International Law. *European Journal of International Law*, Vol. 17 No. 3, p. 675.

Easterly, William R., 2006. *The White Man's Burden: Why the West's Efforts to Aid the Rest Have Done So Much Ill and So Little Good* (New York: Penguin Press).

E. B. Williams Library Research Guides, *From GATT to the WTO*, John Wolff International and Comparative Law Library at the Georgetown University Law Center. Viewed at http://www.ll.georgetown.edu/intl/guides/gattwto/.

Economical Services, website http://www.economicalservices.com (last visited August 12, 2007).

The Economist, 2001. Breaking Barriers in the Americas, April 21, 2001 (London: The Economist Newspaper Limited).

The Economist, 2004. A Survey of Outsourcing: Men and Machines, November 13, 2004 (London: The Economist Newspaper Limited).

The Economist, 2006. The Art of the Impossible, Special Report on France, October 28, 2006 (London: The Economist Newspaper Limited).

The Economist, 2007. Illegal Immigration: Nowhere to Hide, Issue 950, July 7, 2007.

The Economist, 2007. The OECD and Fiscal Policy: Words of Warning, May 26 2007 (London: The Economist Newspaper Limited).

The Economist, 2008. Sayonara, Salaryman, January 5, 2008, pp. 68–70.

Economy, Elizabeth and Adam Segal, 2003. Trade tensions, *The Baltimore Sun*, December 11, 2003.

Eichengreen, Barry J., 1998. *Globalizing Capital: A History of the International Monetary System* (Princeton, NJ: Princeton University Press).

Eichengreen, Barry J., 2007a. *Global Imbalances and the Lessons of Bretton Woods* (Cambridge, MA: MIT Press).

Eichengreen, Barry J., 2007b. *The European Economy Since 1945* (Princeton, NJ: Princeton University Press).

Elazar, Daniel Judah, 1998. *Covenant and Civil Society: The Constitutional Matrix of Modern Democracy* (New Brunswick, NJ: Transaction).

Elkington, John and Mark Lee, 2005. China Syndromes: Will hard-won environmental and social gains survive China's economic rise?, *Grist Environmental News and Commentary*, August 23. Available online at http://www.grist.org/biz/fd/2005/08/23/china/index.html (last visited August 13, 2007).

Englehart, Fredrick, 1997, Withered Giants: Mexican and U.S. Organized Labor and the North American Agreement on Labor Cooperation, *Case Western Reserve Journal of International Law*, Vol. 20, p. 321.

Ernsberger Jr., Richard and Scott Johnson, 2003. Latin America: Darkest Before the Dawn, *Newsweek*, November 10. available online at http://www.msnbc.msn.com/id/3339617/site/newsweek/ (last visited July 15, 2007).

E-services Philippines, *Philippines to Showcase IT Services Edge in Outsourcing Expo*, available online at http://www.e-servicesphils.com/mediaroom/php?mrid=16 (Visited Oct 6, 2005).

Estevez-Abe, Margarita, 2002. Negotiating Welfare Reforms: Actors and Institutions in Japan, in Sven Steinmo and Bo Rothstein eds. *Institutionalism and Welfare Reforms*, pp. 157–183 (Palgrave 2002).

Evans, Peter, 1997. The Eclipse of the State. *World Politics*, Vol. 50, pp. 62–87.

Ewald, François, 1986. *L'Etat Providence* (Paris: B. Grasset).

Farm Subsidy.org, website http://www.farmsubsidy.org/ (last visited August 14, 2007).

Faux, Geoffrey P., 2006. *The Global Class War: How America's Bipartisan Elite Lost Our Future – And What It Will Take To Win It Back* (Hoboken, NJ: Wiley).

Feinstein, Lee and Anne-Marie Slaughter, 2004. A Duty to Prevent, *Foreign Affairs*, Vol. 83, (Jan.–Feb.) pp. 136–50.

Ferguson, Niall, 2001, *The Cash Nexus: Money and Power in the Modern World* (New York: Basic Books).

Financial Times, 2006. November 27, 2006, p. 4.

Fisher, William W., 2001. Theories of Intellectual Property, in Stephen Munzer ed. *New Essays in the Legal and Political Theory of Property* (New York: Cambridge University Press).

Fisk, Robert, 2005. *The Great War for Civilisation: The Conquest of the Middle East*, 1st American ed. (New York: Alfred A. Knopf).

Fitzgerald, Sara J., and Gerald P. O'Driscoll Jr., 2003. "Trade Brings Security," CATO Institute, February 11. Available online at http://www.cato.org/research/articles/fitzgerald-030211.html. (last accessed July 23, 2007).

Fonda, Daren, 2002. Steeling Jobs, *Time Magazine*, Vol. 159, No. 8, February 25.

Fontaine, Pascal, 2000. *A New Idea for Europe: The Schuman Declaration 1950–2000* (Luxembourg: Office for Official Publications of the European Communities).

For European Recovery: The Fiftieth Anniversary of the Marshall Plan, 1999 (Washington, DC: Library of Congress).

Fox, Vincente and George W. Bush, Presidents, Joint News Conference on White House Lawn, September 6, 2001. Transcript available online at http://transcripts.cnn.com/TRANSCRIPTS/0109/06/se.03.html.

France, 2007. In *Encyclopedia Britannica*, from Encyclopedia Britannica Online, available online at http://www.britannica.com/eb/article-40428 (last visited August 13, 2007).

Free Trade Area of the Americas, third draft agreement. Available online at http://www.ftaa-alca.org/FTAADraft03/Index_e.asp.

Frey, Bruno S., 2004. *Dealing with Terrorism: Stick or Carrot?* (Northhampton, MA: Edward Elgar Publishing).

Frieden, Jeffrey A., 2006. *Global Capitalism: Its Fall and Rise in the Twentieth Century* (New York: W. W. Norton).

Friedman, Thomas, J., 1999. *The Lexus and the Olive Tree* (New York: Farrar, Straus, Giroux).

Friedman, Thomas L., 2004. What's That Sound?, *The New York Times*, April 1, 2004, editorial section, p. 23.

Friedman, Thomas J., 2005. *The World is Flat: A Brief History of the Twenty-First Century* (New York: Farrar, Straus, Giroux).

Fukuyama, Francis, 1989. The End of History? *National Interest*, Issue 16 (Summer) pp. 3–18.

Fukuyama, Francis, 1992. *The End of History and the Last Man* (New York: Free Press)

Fukuyama, Francis, 2004. *State-Building: Governance and World Order in the 21st Century* (Ithaca, NY: Cornell University Press).

Fukuyama, Francis, 2007. The History at the End of History. Project Syndicate. Available at http://www.project-syndicate.org/commentary/fukuyama3/English. Viewed May 10, 2007.

Fung, Daniel R., 2004. Constitutional Reform in China: The Case of Hong Kong, *Texas International L J*, pp. 467, 468.

Furet, François, 1999. *The Passing of an Illusion: The Idea of Communism in the Twentieth Century* (translated by Deborah Furet) (Chicago: University of Chicago Press).

FXstreet.com, The Forex Market, 2007. Available online at: http://www.fxstreet.com/news/forex-news/article.aspx?StoryId=a928dc60-7128-4151-b9e6-9f9f0aa4b006; http://customwire.ap.org/dynamic/stories/C/CHINA_FOREIGN_RESERVES?SITE=FLROC&SECTION=BUSINESS&TEMPLATE=DEFAULT&CTIME=2007-03-10-18-08-42.

Gaddis, John Lewis, 2005. *The Cold War: A New History* (New York: Penguin Press).

Gallagher, Peter, 2005. *The First Ten Years of the WTO: 1995–2005* (Cambridge; New York: Cambridge University Press).

Gardner, Brian, 1996. *European Agriculture: Policies, Production and Trade* (London; New York: Routledge).

Garrett, Geoffrey, 1995. Capital Mobility, Trade, and Domestic Politics of Economic Policy in *International Organization*, Vol. 49.

Garrett, Geoffery and Deborah Mitchell, 1999. Globalization and the Welfare State, Available online at http://www.yale.edu/leitner/pdf/1999-04.pdf, last visited August 8, 2007.

GATT, http://www.wto.org.

GATT, General Agreement on Tariffs and Trade, 61 Stat A-11, TIAS 1700, 55 UN Treaty Ser 194 (1947).

GATT BISD, *Japan-Customs Duties, Taxes and Labeling Practices on Imported Wines and Alcoholic Beverages*, Nov 10, 1987 (34th Supp.) 83, available online at http://www.wto.org/english/tratop_e/dispu_e/gt47ds_e.htm.

GATT, *Japanese Measures on Imports of Leather*, May 15, 1984 GATT BISD (31st Supp.) 94, available online at http://www.wto.org/english/tratop_e/dispu_e/gt47ds_e.htm (visited Sept. 19, 2005).

GATT, Article VI, WTO, Agreement on Safeguards, WTO Doc No LT/UR/A-1A/8 (April 15, 1994.

GATT, Uruguay Round Agreements: Report on Environmental Issues, Aug 1994, available at 1994 WL 761804. Report of the Panel (DS21/R – 39S/155) available at http://www.worldtradelaw.net/reports/gattpanels/tunadolphinI.pdf.

GATT years: from Havana to Marrakesh. On WTO website. Available online at http://www.wto.org/English/thewto_e/whatis_e/tif_e/fact4_e.htm (last visited August 13, 2007);

Gellner, Ernest, 1983. *Nations and Nationalism* (Ithaca, NY: Cornell University Press).

Georgetown University Law Library, 2003. E. B. Williams Library Research Guides, *From the GATT to the WTO*. Available online at: http://www.ll.georgetown.edu/intl/guides/gattwto/ (last viewed August 28, 2007).

Gereffi, Gary, 2001. Outsourcing and Changing Patterns of International Competition in the Apparel Commodity Chain. Available online at http://www.colorado.edu/ibs/pec/gadconf/papers/gereffi.html (last visited August 13, 2007).

Gerth, H. H. and C. Wright Mills, 1958. *From Max Weber: Essays in Sociology* (New York: Oxford University Press, USA).

Globe and Mail, 2006. China ready to put brakes on runaway economy, July 25, 2006. http://www.imf.org/external/pubs/ft/survey/so/2007/SurveyartA.htm (last visited August 13, 2007).

Gildea, Robert, 2003. *Barricades and Borders: Europe 1800–1914*, 3d ed., c.1987, 1996 (Oxford [Oxfordshire]; New York: Oxford University Press).

Gilpin, Robert, 2001. *Global Political Economy: Understanding the International Economic Order* (Princeton, NJ: Princeton University Press).

Goldsmith, Jack L. and Eric A. Posner, 2005. *The Limits of International Law* (Oxford; New York: Oxford University Press).

Goldsmith, Jack and Tim Wu, 2006. *Who Controls the Internet? Illusions of a Borderless World* (New York: Oxford University Press).

Gomaa, Ahmed Mahmoud H., 1977. *The Foundation of the League of Arab States: Wartime Diplomacy and Inter-Arab Politics* (London; New York: Longman).

Gordon, Andrew, 2003. *A Modern History of Japan: From Tokugawa Times to the Present* (New York; Oxford: Oxford University Press).

Gordon, Ruth E. and Jon H. Sylvester, 2004. Deconstructing Development, *Wisconsin Intl L J*, Vol. 1, p. 11.

Govaere, Inge, 1996. The Use and Abuse of Intellectual Property Rights in EC Law (London: Sweet & Maxwell, Ltd.)

Grameen Bank, website http://www.grameen-info.org/index.html (last visited July 20, 2007).

Greider, William, 1997. *One World, Ready or No: The Manic Logic of Global Capitalism* (New York: Simon & Schuster).

Griswold, Daniel T., 2002. Willing Workers: Fixing the Problem of Illegal Mexican Migration, *CATO Institute: Trade Policy Analysis*, Available online at http://www.freetrade.org/pubs/pas/tpa-019.pdf.

Growth of the Maquiladora Industry in Baja California, 2003. *California Center for Border and Regional Economic Studies Bulletin*, November, Vol. 4, No. 11.

Guéhenno, Jean-Marie, 1995. *The End of the Nation-State*, translated by Victoria Elliott (Minneapolis: University of Minnesota Press).

Guzman, Andrew T., 2004. Global Governance and the WTO, *Harvard Intl L J*, Vol 45, pp. 303, 307.

Hacker, Jacob S., 2006. *The Great Risk Shift: The Assault on American Jobs, Families, Health Care, and Retirement – and How You Can Fight Back* (Oxford; New York: Oxford University Press).

Ha-Joon, Chang, 2007. *Bad Samaritans: Rich Nations, Poor Policies and the Threat to the Developing World* (New York: Random House Business Books).

Hall, Peter A. and David Soskice, eds. 2001. *Varieties of Capitalism: The Institutional Foundations of Comparative Advantage* (New York: Oxford University Press).

Hall, Robert Lowe, 1983. International Economic Co-operation after 1945. *History Today*, Vol. 33 (December), p. 13.

Hallwood, Paul and Ronald MacDonald, 2000. 3rd ed, *International Money and Finance* (Oxford, UK; Cambridge, MA: B. Blackwell).

Halofsky, Ada Lee, 2004. As even Pompoms Are Outsourced, A Fixture in the Field Bears Up. *New York Times*, 14.10 (December 5).

Handelman, Stephen, 2001. Special Report: Summit of the Americas, *Time Magazine*, April 19, 2001.

Hane, Mikiso, 2001. *Modern Japan: A Historical Survey*, 3d Ed., (Boulder: Westview Press).

Harrison, Lawrence E., 2006. *The Central Liberal Truth: How Politics Can Change a Culture and Save It from Itself* (New York, London: Oxford University Press).

Hart, Michael, 1994. Coercion or Cooperation: Social Policy and Future Trade Negotiations. *Can-US Law Journal*, Vol. 20, pp. 351–377.

Harvey, David, 1982. *The Limits to Capital* (Chicago: University of Chicago Press; Oxford [Oxfordshire]: B. Blackwell).

Haus, Leah, A., 1992. *Globalizing the GATT: The Soviet Union's Successor States, Eastern Europe, and the International Trading System* (Washington, DC: The Brookings Institution).

Heckscher, Eli, F., 1955. *Mercantilism* (New York: The Macmillan Company).

Hegel, G. W. F., 1975. *The Philosophy of Right*, §331 (T. M. Knox, trans) (Oxford).

Helleiner, Eric, 1994. *States and the Reemergence of Global Finance: From Bretton Woods to the 1990s* (Ithaca, NY: Cornell University Press).

Hempfling, Lee Kent, 2005. The Root of Terrorism, *The National Ledger*, Aug 21. Available online at http://www.nationalledger.com/cgi-bin/artman/exec/view.cgi?archive=1&num=346 (last visited August 14, 2007).

Heymann, Philip, 2003. *Terrorism, Freedom and Security: Winning Without War* (Cambridge, MA; London: MIT Press).

Hilary, John, 2006. No tears for Doha, *The Guardian*, July 25. Available online at http://commentisfree.guardian.co.uk/john_hilary/2006/07/no_tears_for_doha.html.

Hill, Charles W. L., 2003. *International Business: Competing in the Global Marketplace*, 4th ed (Boston: McGraw-Hill/Irwin).

Hirst, Paul Q., and Grahame Thompson, 1996. *Globalization in Question: The International Economy and the Possibilities of Governance* (Cambridge, UK: Polity Press; Oxford, UK; Cambridge, MA: Blackwell Publishers).

Hitchcock, William I., 2003. *The Struggle for Europe: The Turbulent History of a Divided Continent* (New York: Doubleday).

HM Spending Review, 2004. PN A2 (July 12, 2004), available online at http://www.hm-treasury.gov.uk/spending_review/spend_sr04/press/spend_sr04_press13.cfm.

Hobsbawm, E. J., 1990. *Nations and Nationalism Since 1780: Programme, Myth, Reality* (Cambridge [England]; New York: Cambridge University Press).

Hollis, Martin and Steve Smith, 1990. *Explaining and Understanding International Relations* (Oxford, England: Clarendon Press; New York: Oxford University Press).

Honeywell, website http://www.honeywell.com (last visited July 12, 2007).

Hors, Irene, 2000. Fighting corruption in the developing countries, *OECD Observer*, July 2000. Available online at http://www.oecdobserver.org/news/fullstory.php/aid/291/Fighting_corruption_in_the_developing_countries.html.

Hors, Irene, 2001. Fighting Corruption in Customs Administration: What Can We Learn From Recent Experiences? Available online at http://ideas.repec.org/p/oec/devaaa/175-en.html.

Horsley, William and Roger Buckley, 1990. *Nippon, New Superpower: Japan since 1945* (London: BBC Books).

Houlder, Vanessa, 2007. Europe's Tax Rivalry Keeps Multinationals on the Move. *Financial Times*, U.S. edition, January 19, p. 11.

Howard, Michael Eliot, 2002. *The First World War* (Oxford; New York: Oxford University Press).

Howard, Michael Eliot, 2002. *The Invention of Peace: Reflections on War and International Order* (New Haven, CT; London: Yale University Press).

Howard, Michael Eliot, 1983. *The Causes of War and Other Essays*, 2nd edition corr. with 2 additional ch. (London: Temple Smith).

Howse, Robert, and Jose E. Alvarez, 2002. From Politics to Technology – and Back Again: The Fate of the Multilateral Trading Regime. *American Journal of International Law*, Vol. 96, p. 94.

Hudec, Robert E., 1987. *Developing Countries in the GATT Legal System*. Published for the Trade Policy Research Centre (London: Gower).

Hudnall, Shannon, 1996. Towards a Greener International Trade System: Multilateral Environmental Agreements and The World Trade Organization, *Columbia Journal of Law and Social Problems*, Vol. 29, p. 175.

Hufbauer, Gary Clyde and Jeffrey J. Schott, 2005. *NAFTA Revisited: Achievements and Challenges* (Washington, DC: Institute for International Economics).

Hunt, Lynn A., 2007. *Inventing Human Rights: A History* (New York: W. W. Norton & Co.).

Huntington, Samuel P., 1996. *The Clash of Civilizations and the Remaking of World Order* (New York: Simon & Schuster).

Ihde, Erin, 2004. To Bank or Not to Bank: Edward Smith Hall on Free Trade and the Commodification of Money in Early New South Wales. The *Journal of Australian Studies*, Vol. 83, p. 13.

Immigration Reform & Control Act of 1986, Office of Inspector General, website http://www.oig.lsc.gov/legis/irca86.htm.

International Court of Justice, website http://www.icj-cij.org/jurisdiction/index.php?p1=5&p2=1&p3=2 (last visited July 11, 2007).

International Monetary Fund Survey, 2006, July 24. Vol. 35, No. 14.

International Monetary Fund, IMF website, *Money Matters: An IMF Exhibit – The Importance of Global Cooperation. Deconstruction and Reconstruction 1945–1958*. Available online at: http://www.imf.org/external/np/exr/center/mm/eng/mm_dr_05.htm (last viewed August 30, 2007).

International Monetary Fund, IMF, website http://www.imf.org/external/np/sta/ir/8802.pdf (last visited March 26, 2007).

International Monetary Fund, IMF, website. IMF-Backed Plan to Cut Global Imbalances, available online http://www.imf.org/external/pubs/ft/survey/so/2007/SurveyartA.htm (last visited August 13, 2007).

Iritani, Evelyn, 1998. Special Report: Europe's New Currency U.S. Firms Must Also Be Ready for the Change, *Los Angeles Times*, May 3, Business.

Irwin, Douglas A., 1996. *Against the Tide: An Intellectual History of Free Trade* (Princeton, NJ: Princeton University Press).

Irwin, Douglas A., 2002; 2005 2d ed. *Free Trade Under Fire* (Princeton, NJ: Princeton University Press).

Itoh, Makotoh, 1999. *The Burst of Bubble and Political Economy of the 1990's Depression*. Available online at: http://www.ecn.wfu.edu/~cottrell/OPE/itoh/itoh.pdf (last viewed August 28, 2007.

Jackson, John, 1998. *The World Trade Organization: Constitution and Jurisprudence* (London: Royal Institute of International Affairs).

Jackson, John H., 2000. *The Jurisprudence of GATT and The WTO Insights on Treaty Law and Economic Relations* (Cambridge: Cambridge University Press).

Jackson, John H., 2006. *Sovereignty, The WTO and Changing Fundamentals of International Law*, (Cambridge: Cambridge University Press).

Jai, Janet J., 2001. Getting at the Roots of Terrorism, *The Christian Science Monitor*, December 10, 2001 edition. Available online at http://www.csmonitor.com/2001/1210/p7s1-wogi.html (viewed August 20, 2007).

Jellinek, Lea, 2001. The New Poor, *Inside Indonesia*, No. 57 Jan.–March 1999, available online at http://www.insideindonesia.org/edit50/price.htm.

Jennings, Jeremy, 2000. Citizenship, Republicanism and Multiculturalism in Contemporary France, *British Journal of Political Science*, Vol. 30, No. 4, p. 575.

Jeong-ju, Na, 2006. Overseas Card Use Hits Record High, *Korean Times*, August 25, 2006.

Johnson, Ailish, 2005. *European Welfare States and Supranational Governance of Social policy* (Houndmills [England]; New York: Palgrave Macmillan in association with St. Antony's College Oxford).

Johnson, Harry G., 1965. Optimal Trade Intervention in the Presence of Domestic Distortions 9, in Robert E. Baldwin, et al, *Trade Growth and the Balance of Payments: Essays in Honor of Gottfried Haberler 3*(Chicago: Rand McNally).

Johnston, R. J., Peter James Taylor, and Michael J. Watts, 2002. *Geographies of Global Change: Remapping the World*. In 2d Edition, Global Regulation and Trans-State Organization, Susan M. Roberts ed., pp. 144–48 (Malden, MA: Blackwell Publishing).

Jones, Kent, 2004. *Who's Afraid of the WTO?* (Oxford; New York: Oxford University Press).

Joseph, Jofi, 2001. Pipeline Diplomacy: The Clinton Administration's Fight for Baku-Ceyhan, available online at http://www.wws.princeton.edu/cases/papers/pipeline.pdf.

Judt, Tony, 2005. Post War: A History of Europe Since 1945 (New York: Penguin Press).

Kaczka, David E., 1997. A Primer on the Shrimp-Sea Turtle Controversy, *Review of European Community & International Environmental Law*, Vol. 6, p. 171.

Kaczka, David E., 1998. WTO's Shrimp-Sea Turtle Decision, *Review of European Community & International Environmental Law* Vol. 7, p. 308.

Kagan, Frederick W., 2006. *The End of the Old Order: Napoleon and Europe, 1801–1805* (Cambridge, MA: Da Capo Press).

Kagan, Robert, 2003. *Of Paradise and Power: America vs. Europe in the New World Order* (New York: Knopf).

Kahler, Miles and David A. Lake, eds., 2003. *Governance in a Global Economy: Political Authority in Transition* (Princeton, NJ: Princeton University Press).

Kaldor, Mary, 1999. *New and Old Wars: Organized Violence in a Global Era* (Stanford, CA: Stanford University Press).

Kanaya, Akahiro and David Woo, 2000. *The Japanese Banking Crisis of the 1990s: Sources and Lessons* (Princeton, NJ: International Economics Section, Dept. of Economics, Princeton University).

Kant, Immanuel, 1948. *Perpetual Peace* (Liberal Arts).

Kaplan, David E., 2002. The Law of the Jungle, *U.S. News & World Report*, October 14.

Kapstein, Ethan B., 1999. *Sharing the Wealth: Workers and the World Economy* (New York; London: W. W. Norton).

Kapstein, Ethan, B., 2006. *Economic Justice in an Unfair World: Toward a Level Playing Field* (Princeton, NJ: Princeton University Press).

Katz, Richard, 1998. *Japan, The System That Soured: The Rise and Fall of the Japanese Economic Miracle* (Armonk, NY: M. E. Sharpe).

Keane, John, 2003. *Global Civil Society?* (Cambridge: Cambridge University Press).

Keith, K. J., 2004, Sovereignty at the Beginning of the 21st Century: Fundamental or Outmoded? *Cambridge Law Journal*, Vol. 63, p. 581.

Kell, George, Sandrine Tesner, 2000. *The United Nations and Business: A Partnership Recovered* (New York: St. Martin's Press).

Kelly, J. Patrick, 2005. The Seduction of the Appellate Body: Shrimp/Sea Turtle I and II and the Proper Role of States in WTO Governance, *Cornell International Law Journal*, Vol. 38, p. 459.

Kemp, Anthony, 1982. *The Maginot Line: Myth and Reality* (New York: Stein and Day).

Kenen, Peter B., 1995. *Economic and Monetary Union in Europe: Moving beyond Maastricht*, (Cambridge; New York: Cambridge University Press).

Kennan, George, 1947. X, The Sources of Soviet Conduct. *Foreign Affairs*, Vol. 25 (July), pp. 566–72.

Kennedy, Daniel L. M. and James D. Southwick, eds., 2002. *The Political Economy of International Trade Law: Essays in Honor of Robert E. Hudec* (Cambridge: Cambridge University Press).

Kennedy, Paul M., 1987. *The Rise and Fall of the Great Powers: Economic Change and Military Conflict From 1500 to 2000* (1989 1st Vintage ed.; New York: Vintage Books).

Keohane, Robert O. and Helen V. Milner, eds., 1996. *Internationalization and Domestic Politics* (Cambridge [England]; New York: Cambridge University Press).

Key, Sydney J., 1999. Trade Liberalization and Prudential Regulations: The International Framework for Financial Services, *Intl Affairs*, Vol. 75, p. 61.

Kindleberger, Charles, P., 1969. *American Business Abroad: Six Lectures on Direct Investment* (New Haven, CT: Yale University Pres).

Kinzer, Stephen, 1998. US, Pushing Its Route for Pipeline, Aides Turkey, *The New York Times*, October 22, Section A, p. 11.

Kinzer, Stephen, 1999. Summit in Turkey: The Caspian Accord, *New York Times*, November 19, Section A.

Kiva, www.kiva.org.

Knox, John H., 2004. The Judicial Resolution of Conflicts Between Trade and The Environment, *Harvard Environmental Law Review*, Vol. 28, p. 1.

Kochhar, Kalpana, 2006. *India's Pattern of Development: What Happened, What Follows* (Cambridge, MA: National Bureau of Economic Research).

Kocjan, Martina and J. H. H. Weiler, 2004/5a. *The Law of the European Union: Discriminatory Taxation and Measures Having an Effect Equivalent to Customs Duties*, available online at http://www.jeanmonnetprogram.org/eu/Units/documents/UNIT11-EU-2004-05.pdf.

Kocjan, Martina and J. H. H. Weiler, 2004/5b. The Law of the European Union: The Internal Market: Non-Tariff Barriers, available online at http://www.jeanmonnetprogram.org/eu/Units/documents/UNIT9-EU-2004-05.pdf.

Kojève, Alexandre, 1969, *Introduction to the Reading of Hegel: Lectures on the Phenomenology of Spirit* (Basic).

Kopstein, Jeffery, 2004. Let's Follow in the EU's footsteps, *Globe and Mail*, April 29, Commentary.

Koskenniemi, Martti, 2005 Reissue ed. *From Apology to Utopia: The Structure of International Legal Argument* (Cambridge: Cambridge University Press).

Krueger, Alan, 2003. To avoid terrorism, end poverty and ignorance. Right? Guess again. Debunking conventional wisdom about the roots of hate crime, *New York Times Economic Scene Columns*, December 13, 2003.

Krueger, Alan B. and Jitka Maleckova, 2003. Seeking the Roots of Terrorism, *The Chronicle Reviewer*, June 6, 2003. Available online at http://chronicle.com/free/v49/i39/39b01001.htm.

Krugman, Paul R., 1993. A Loss of (Theoretical) Nerve: The Narrow and Broad Arguments for Free Trade. *Am Econ Review*, Vol. 83 (May, Pt 2), p. 362.

Kuhnle, Stein, 2000. *Survival of the European Welfare State* (London; New York: Routledge).

Kupchan, Charles A., 2002. *The End of the American Era: U.S. Foreign Policy and the Geopolitics of the Twenty-First Century* (New York: Knopf: Distributed by Random House, Inc.).

Lafitee, H. I., 2003. Micro-Credit and Poverty Reduction, available online at http://www.grameen-info.org/grameen/gtrust/Microcredit%20and%20Poverty%20Reduction%20June%202003%20in%20TurkeyF.pdf.

Landes, William and Richard Posner, 1989. An Economic Analysis of Copyright Law, *Journal of Legal Studies*, Vol. 18, p. 325.

Landler, Mark, 2005. German Joblessness Rises As Benefits Are Reduced, *The New York Times*, February 3, C5.

Laqueur, Walter 2004. *No End to War: Terrorism in the Twenty-First Century* (New York: Continuum).

Larimer, Tim, 1995 A New Bourgeoisie Develops a Proletarian Taste. *New York Times*, November 16, A4.

Lawrence, Robert Z., 2006. *A US-Middle East Trade Agreement: A Circle of Opportunity?* (Washington, DC: Peterson Institute for International Economics).

Legrain, Phillippe, 2002. *Open World: The Truth about Globalization* (London: Abacus).

Lekachman, Robert, 1976, c1959. *A History of Economic Ideas* (New York: McGraw Hill).

Leonard, Mark, 2005. *Why Europe Will Run the 21st Century* (New York: Public Affairs, Fourth Estate, a division of Harper Collins).

Levy, Jonah D. ed., 2006. *The State After Statism: New State Activities in the Age of Liberalization* (London; Cambridge, MA: Harvard University Press).

Levy, Jonah D., 2006a. The State Also Rises: The Roots of Contemporary State Activism in *The State After Statism: New State Activities in the Age of Liberalization*, Jonah D. Levy ed. (London; Cambridge, MA: Harvard University Press).

Levy, Jonah D. and Mari Miura, and Gene Park, 2006. Exiting Etatisme?: New Directions in State Policy in France and Japan in *The State After Statism: New State Activities in the Age of Liberalization*, Jonah D. Levy ed. (London; Cambridge, MA: Harvard University Press).

Lewis, Bernard, *What Went Wrong: Western Impact and Middle Eastern Response* (Oxford; New York: Oxford University Press).

Lindsey, Brink, 2002. *Against the Dead Hand: The Uncertain Struggle for Global Capitalism* (New York: Wiley).

Lindsey, Brink, 2006. Poor Mouthing Prosperity, Review of *The Great Risk Shift* by Jacob S. Hacker, *The Wall Street Journal*, 21 September 2006, D6.

Lizardo, Omar, 2006. Effect of Economic and Cultural Globalization on Anti-US Transnational Terrorism 1971–2000. available online at http://www.nd.edu/~olizardo/papers/v12n1-lizardo-PRF2.pdf.

Lopez, David, 1997a, Dispute Resolution Under NAFTA: Lessons from the Early Experience, *Texas Journal of International Law*, Vol. 32.

Lopez, David, Thomas George Weiss, et. al., 1997b. *Political Gain and Citizen Pain* (Lanham: Rowman & Littlefield).

Low, Patrick, 1993. *Trading Free: The GATT and U.S. Trade Policy* (New York: Twentieth Century Fund Press).

Lowenstein, Roger, 2005. A Number of Questions: The Conservative New Deal, in *The New York Times Magazine*, January 16, 2005. Available online at: http://www.nytimes.com/2005/01/16/magazine/16SOCIAL.html?ex=1263704400&en=476a2ffc8bccd712&ei=5088&partner=rssnyt (last viewed August 17, 2007.

Luce, Edward, 2007. *In Spite of the Gods: The Strange Rise of Modern India* (New York: Doubleday).

Lynn, Barry C., 2005. *The End of the Line: The Rise and Coming Fall of the Global Corporation* (New York: Doubleday).

MacDonald, Robert W., 1965. *The League of Arab States; A Study in the Dynamics of Regional Organization* (Princeton, NJ: Princeton University Press).

MacMillan, Margaret Olwen, 2002. *Paris 1919: Six Months That Changed The World* (New York: Random House).

MacShane, Daniel, 2007. The Dynamic Duo. *Newsweek International*, available online at http://www.msnbc.msn.com/id/19388716/site/newsweek/.

Magnusson, Lars, 1994. *Mercantilism: The Shaping of an Economic Language* (London; New York: Routledge).

Mandelbaum, Michael, 2002. *The Ideas That Conquered The World: Peace, Democracy, and Free Markets in the Twenty-First Century* (New York: Public Affairs).

Mandelson, Peter, 2003. Doha: Goals for Hong Kong. Available online at http://trade.ec.europa.eu/doclib/docs/2005/november/tradoc_126121.pdf.

Mansfield, Edward D., and Jack L. Snyder, 2005. *Electing to Fight: Why Emerging Democracies Go To War* (Cambridge, MA: MIT Press).

Maquiladoras at a Glance, 1999. Corporate Watch, website. Available online at http://www.corpwatch.org/article.php?id=1528 (last visited July 24, 2007).

Marchak, M. Patricia, 1991. *The Integrated Circus: The New Right and the Restructuring of Global Markets* (Montreal; Buffalo: McGill-Queen's University).

Mattes, Robert, 1999. Do Diverse Social Identities Inhibit Nationhood and Democracy? Initial Considerations from South Africa, in Mai Palmberg ed., *National Identity and Democracy in Africa*, (Pretoria, S. A.: Human Sciences Research Council of South Africa; Bellville, S. A.: Mayibuye Centre at the University of the Western Cape; Uppsala: Nordic Africa Institute).

McClelland, J. S., 1996, *A History of Western Political Thought* (London; New York: Routledge).

McCrudden, Christopher and Stuart G. Gross, 2006. WTO Government Procurement Rules and the Local Dynamics of Procurement Policies: A Malaysian Case Study, *European Journal of International Law*, Vol. 17, p. 151.

McGinnis, John, and Mark Movsesian, 2000. The World Trade Constitution, *Harvard Law Review*, Vol. 114, p. 511.

McGinnis, John O. and Mark L. Movsesian, 2004. Response Against Global Governance in the WTO, *Harvard Intl L J*, Vol. 45, p. 353.

McManis, Charles R., 1996. Taking Trips on the Information Super Highway: International Intellectual Property Protection and Emerging Computer Technology, *Villanova Law Review*, Vol. 41, p. 207.

Mearsheimer, John J., 2001. *The Tragedy of Great Power Politics* (New York; London: Norton).

Melvin, Michael, 2004. *International Money and Finance* (Boston, MA: Pearson Addison-Wesley).

Meunier, Sophie, 2005. *Trading Voices: The European Union in International Commercial Negotiation* (Princeton, NJ: Princeton University Press).

Micklethwait, John and Adrian Woodridge, 2004. *The Right Nation: Conservative Power in America* (New York: Penguin).

Milanovic, Branko, 2005. *Worlds Apart: Measuring International and Global Inequality* (Princeton, NJ: Princeton University Press).

Minton-Beddoes, Zanny (moderator), 2000. Trade, Labor & the Environment, *Brookings/Resources for the Future Press Briefing*, April 11, 2000. Debate transcript available online at http://www.brook.edu/comm/transcripts/20000411.htm.

Mishkin, Frederic S, 2006. *The Next Great Globalization: How Disadvantaged Nations Can Harness Their Financial Systems To Get Rich* (Princeton, NJ: Princeton University Press).

Mishra, Pankaj, 2006. The Myth of The New India, *New York Times*, July 6, Section A.

Mizan, Ainon Nahar, 1996. *In Quest of Empowerment: The Grameen Bank Impact on Women's Power & Status* (Dhaka: University Press).

Molle, Willem, 2001. *The Economics of European Integration: Theory, Practice, Policy*, 4th ed (Aldershot, England; Vermont: Ashgate).

Moody, Kim, 1997. *Workers in a Lean World: Unions in the International Economy* (New York: Verso).

Moon, Bruce E., 2000. *Dilemmas of International Trade*, 2nd ed. (Boulder, CO: Westview Press).

Moore, Stephen and Julian Simon, 2006. *It's Getting Better All The Time: 100 Greatest Trends of the Last 100 Years* (Washington, DC: Cato Institute).

Morgan, Glyn, 2005. *The Idea of a European Superstate: Public Justification and European Integration* (Princeton, NJ: Princeton University Press).

Munari, Francesco, 2001. Technology Transfer and the Protection of the Environment, in Francesco Francioni, ed., *Environment, Human Rights and International Trade* (Oxford; Portland, OR: Hart Pub.).

Murphy, John F., 2005. Brave New World: U.S. Responses to the Rise in International Crime, *Villanova Law Review*, Vol. 50, p. 375.

Myles, John and Jill Quadagno, 2001. Political Theories of the Welfare State, *Social Service Review*, Vol. 76, p. 34.

NAFTA, 1992. North American Free Trade Agreement, Dec. 8–17, 1992, U.S.-Canada-Mexico, ch. 11, 32 I.L.M. 605, 639 (1992) at article 1102 and 1105.

NAFTA Monitor, 1993. Mexican Labor Unions Too Weak, December 20, Vol. 1, No. 1.

NAFTA Monitor, 1994. Market Sector Develops Around NAFTA Business Expansion, February 15, Vol. 1, No. 8.

Nardi, Jason, 2005. WTO-SPECIAL: Cotton, Acid Test for Doha Round, *IPS News Network*, December 15, 2005. Available online at http://ipsnews.net/news.asp?idnews=31430 (last visited August 12, 2007).

National Euro Website – Glossary, website http://www.euro.cy/euro/euro nsf/dmlglossary_en/dmlglossary_en?OpenDocument (last visited July 11, 2007).

Nichols, Philip M., 1996. Corruption in the World Trade Organization: Discerning the Limits of the World Trade Organization's Authority, *NYU Journal of International Law & Politics*, Vol. 28, pp. 711–14.

Negri, Antonio and Michael Hardt, 2001. *Empire* (Cambridge, MA; London: Harvard University Press).

Negri, Antonio and Michael Hardt, 2004. *Multitude: War and Democracy in the Age of Empire* (New York: Penguin Press).

Nelson, Andy, 2007. Consumer tidal wave on the way: China's middle class, *Christian Science Monitor*, January 2. Available online at http://www.csmonitor.com/2007/0102/p01s02-woap.html.

Nobel Foundation, 2006, Interview with 2006 Nobel Peace Prize Laureate Muhammad Yunus. Available at http://nobelprize.org/nobel_prizes/peace/laureates/2006/yunus-interview .html.

Noble, Charles, 1997. *Welfare As We Knew It: A Political History of the American Welfare State* (New York: Oxford University Press).

North American Free Trade Agreement, Dec. 8–17, 1992, U.S.-Can.-Mex., ch. 11, 32 I.L.M. 605, 639 (1992) at article 1110.

Nye, John V. C., 1998. European Economic Union in Historical Perspective: The View From The Nineteenth Century, *Columbia Journal of European Law*, Vol. 4, p. 479.

O'Brien, Richard, 1992. *Global Financial Integration: The End of Geography* (The Royal Institute of International Affairs Council on Foreign Relations Press).

O'Driscoll Jr., Gerald and Sara J. Fitzgerald, 2003. Trade Brings Security, *CATO Institute*, February 11, 2003. Available online at http://www.cato.org/research/articles/fitzgerald-030211.html.

OECD, 2002. OECD Statistics Database: Total Social Expenditures 2002. Available at http://www.oecd.org/document/2/0,2340,en_2825_497118_31612994_1_1_1_1,00.html.

OECD, 2004a. Economic Outlook #75: Annual and Quarterly Data. Paris: OECD.

OECD, 2004b. Social Expenditure Database. Paris: OECD.

OECD, 2005. Economic Survey of Japan 2005: Removing the Obstacles to Faster Growth at http://www.OECD.org/document/15/0,2340,EN_33873108_33873539_34287887_1_1_1_1,00.html.

OECD, 2007. Factbook, Economic, Environmental and Social Statistics, available at http://www.lysander.sourceoecd.org/vl=7994578/cl=22/nw=1/rpsv/factbook/01-01-01-g02.htm.

OECD Country Statistical Profiles 2007, found at http://stats.oecd.org/wbos/viewhtml.aspx?queryname=314&querytype=view&lang=en.

Ohmae, Kenichi, 1991. *The Borderless World: Power and Strategy in the Internet Economy* (New York: Harper and Row).

Ohmae, Kenichi, 1995. *The End of the Nation State: The Rise of Regional Economies* (New York: Simon and Schuster, Inc.).

Ohmae, Kenichi, 2005. *The Next Global Stage: Challenges and Opportunities in our Borderless World* (Upper Saddle River, NJ: Wharton School Pub.)

Okediji, Ruth L., 2003. Public Welfare and the Role of the WTO: Reconsidering the TRIPS Agreement, *Emory Law Review*, Vol. 17, p. 819.

O'Melinn, Liam Seamus, 1995. The American Revolution and Constitutionalism in the Seventeenth-Century West Indies, *Columbia Law Review*, Vol. 95, pp. 136–37.

Ortino, Federico, 2004. From 'non-discrimination' to 'reasonableness': a paradigm shift in international economic law? Available online at http://www.jeanmonnetprogram.org/ as part of the Jean Monnet Working Papers program.

Owabukeruyele, Worgu Stanley, 2000. Hydrocarbon Exploitation, Environmental Degradation and Poverty in the Niger Delta Region of Nigeria, *Lund University, Sweden*. Available online at http://www.waado.org/Environment/PetrolPolution/EnvEconomics.htm.

Palmer, Glenn and T. Clifton Morgan, 2006. *A Theory of Foreign Policy* (Princeton, NJ: Princeton University Press).

Papademetriou, Demetrios and Kimberly Hamilton, 2000. *Reinventing Japan: Immigration's Role in Shaping Japan's Future* (Washington, DC: Carnegie Endowment for International Peace).

Parks, Tim, 2005. *Medici Money: Banking, Metaphysics, and Art in Fifteenth-Century Florence* (New York: W. W. Norton & Co.).

Passel, Jeffrey, March 2004. Mexican Immigration to the US: The Latest Estimates, *Migration Information Source*, website, available online at http://www.migrationinformation.org/usfocus/display.cfm?ID=208.

Patrick, Hugh, 2006. Working Paper #249, "Japan's Economy: Finally Finding It's Way to Full Employment and Sustained Growth," Working Paper Series, Center on Japanese Economy and Business, Columbia University Business School. Site: http://digitalcommons/libraries.columbia.edu/japan_wps/241.

Paulus-Jagrič, Deborah, 2007. Global Warming: A Comparative Guide to the E.U. and the U.S. and Their Approaches to the U.N. Framework Convention on Climate Change and the Kyoto Protocol. Available online at http://www.nyulawglobal.org/globalex/Climate_Change_Kyoto_Protocol.htm (last visited August 13, 2007).

Pauwelyn, J., 2005. The Transformation of World Trade. *Michigan Law Review*, Vol. 104, p. 1.

Pear, Robert and Jim Rutenberg, 2007. Senators in Bipartisan Deal On Broad Immigration Bill, *New York Times*, May 18, Section A.

Pelkmans, Jacques, 2005. Subsidiarity between Law and Economics, *European Legal Studies of College of Europe*, Paper No. 1/2005.

Perez-Lopez, Jorge F., 1995a. Implementation of the North American Agreement on Labor Cooperation: A Perspective from the Signatory Countries, *NAFTA: Law and Business Review of the Americas*, Autumn ed., p. 3.

Perez-Lopez, Jorge F., 1995b. The Promotion of International Labor Standards and NAFTA: Retrospect and Prospects, *Connecticut Journal of International Law*, Vol. 10, p. 427.

Perez-Lopez, Jorge F. and Eric Griego, 1995. The Labor Dimension of the NAFTA: Reflections on the First Year, *Arizona Journal of International and Comparative Law*, Vol. 12, p. 473.

Petersmann, Ernst-Ulrich, 2000. The WTO Constitution and Human Rights, *Journal of International Economic Law*, Vol. 3(1), p. 19.

Pierson, Paul, 1994. *Dismantling the Welfare State?: Reagan, Thatcher, and the Politics of Retrenchment* (Cambridge, England; New York: Cambridge University Press).

Piana, Pilar, 2004. Maquiladoras in Mexico: Cheap Labor, Worker Abuse and Environmental Degradation, *Concrete Magazine* available online at http://www.hartford-hwp.com/archives/46/003.html.

Pitt, M. M. and S. R. Khandker, 1996. Household and Intrahousehold Impact of the Grameen Bank and Similar Targeted Credit Programs in Bangladesh, *World Bank Discussion Papers*, available online at http://ideas.repec.org/p/fth/wobadi/320.html.

Portes, Alejandro, and Jose Itzigsohn and Carlos Dore-Cabral, 1994. Urbanization in the Caribbean Basin: Social Change During the Years of the Crisis. *Lat Am Res R*, Vol 3, p. 21.

Posner, Eric, 2007. What the Cold War Taught Us, *Wall Street Journal*, April 22, Op-Ed.

Posner, Eric A. and Adrian Vermeule. 2007. *Terror in the Balance: Security, Liberty, and the Courts* (Oxford; New York: Oxford University Press).

Prescott, Edward C., 2007. Competitive Cooperation. *The Wall Street Journal*, February 15, A-19.

Preston, Nathaniel Stone, 1967. *Politics, Economics, and Power; Ideology and Practice under Capitalism, Socialism, Communism, and Fascism* (New York: The Macmillan Company).

Prins, Gwyn, 2002. *The Heart of War: On Power, Conflict and Obligation in the Twenty-First Century* (London: Routledge).

Quong, Andrea A., 2004. Brushing off Paris clothiers, *International Herald Tribune*, March 5.

Rabkin, Jeremy A., 2005, *Law Without Nations? Why Constitutional Government Requires Sovereign States* (Princeton, NJ: Princeton University Press).

Rand Corporation, 2002. *Alternate Trajectories: Options for Competitive Sourcing for the Space Shuttle Program*, Final Report. Available at http://www.rand.org/scitech/stpi/nasa/.

Razin, Assaf and Efraim Sadka, 2005, in cooperation with Chang Woon Nam. *The Decline of the Welfare State: Demography and Globalization* (Cambridge, MA: MIT Press).

Rehn, Olli, 2006. 'Europe's Next Frontiers,' Lecture at the Finnish Institute of International Affairs Helsinki, 27 October 2006. Available online at http://europa.eu/rapid/pressReleasesAction.do?reference=SPEECH/06/654&format=HTML&aged=1&language=EN&guiLanguage=en.

Reinert, Erik S., 2007. *How Rich Countries Got Rich and Why Poor Countries Stay Poor* (London: Constable & Robinson).

Resor, James P., 1997. Debt-for-nature swaps: a decade of experience and new directions for the future, *Unasylva*, No. 188.

Ricardo, David, 1817. *The Principles of Political Economy and Taxation* (London: J. M. Dent & Son, Ltd, 1911).

Richburg, Keith B., 2004. Madrid Attacks May Have Targeted Election, *The Washington Post*, October 17, Page A16.

Risse, Mathias, 2005. How Does the Global Order Harm the Poor? *Philosophy and Public Affairs*, Vol. 33 Issue 4, pp. 349–76.

Robb, John, 2007. *Brave New War: The Next Stage of Terrorism and the End of Globalization* (New York: Wiley).

Roberts, Lawrence D., 2003. Beyond Notions of Diplomacy and Legalism: Building a Just Mechanism for WTO Dispute Resolution, *American Business Law Journal*, p. 516.

Robertson, Jamie, 2006. Acquisitions drive markets talk, *BBC News*, April 3, 2006. available online at http://news.bbc.co.uk/2/hi/business/4871526.stm.

Robinson, David, 2007. IMF-Backed Plan to Cut Global Imbalances, available online at http://www.imf.org/external/pubs/ft/survey/so/2007/SurveyartA.htm (last visited August 13, 2007).

Robinson, Ian, 1995, The NAFTA Labour Accord in Canada: Experience, Prospects, and Alternatives, *Connecticut Journal of International Law*, Vol. 10, p. 474.

Robinson, Nick, 2005. Is a Madrid-style atrocity going to happen here? Or is it overheated talk? *The Times (UK)*, February 26.

Robinson, William I., 2003. *Transnational Conflicts: Central America, Social Change, and Globalization* (London; New York: Verso).

Roger, John J., 2000. *From A Welfare State To A Welfare Society: The Changing Context of Social Policy in a Postmodern Era* (New York: St. Martin's Press).

Rodgers, Bill, 2006. Worldwide Corruption Continues to Block Development, July 24. Available online at http://www.voanews.com/english/archive/2006-07/2006-07-24-voa25.cfm?CFID=102413079&CFTOKEN=89286557.

Rohter, Larry, 2006. A Widening Gap Erodes Argentina's Egalitarian Image, *The New York Times*, December 26.

Rollo, Jim, Alasdair Smith, John S. Flemming, and Hans-Werner Sinn, 1993. The Political Economy of Eastern European Trade with the European Community: Why so Sensitive?, *Economic Policy*, Vol. 8, No. 16, p. 139.

Ronen, Dov, 1975. *Dahomey: Between Tradition and Modernity* (Ithaca: Cornell University Press).

Ronen, Dov, 1979. *The Quest For Self-Determination* (New Haven, CT: Yale University Press).

Ronen, Dov, 1984. *Ethnicity, ideology and the military in the People's Republic of Benin* (Boston, MA: African-American Issues Center).

Ronen, Dov, 1986. *Democracy and Pluralism in Africa* (Boulder, CO: L. Rienner; Sevenoaks, KY: Hodder and Stoughton).

Rosecrance, Richard N., 1999. *The Rise of the Virtual State: Wealth and Power in the Coming Century* (New York: Basic Books).

Rosenberg, Justin, 2000. *The Follies of Globalization Theory: Polemical Essays* (London; New York: Verso).

Rosenthal, Elisabeth, Europe, East and West, wrestles with falling birthrates, *International Herald Tribune*, September 3, 2006, available at:http://www.iht.com/articles/2006/09/03/news/birth.php.

Rotberg, Robert I., editor. 2004. *When States Fail: Causes and Consequences* (Princeton, NJ; Oxford: Princeton University Press).

Rothermund, Diet, 1996. *The Global Impact of the Great Depression, 1929–1939* (New York: Routlege).

RSA.org, 2006, *The Euro, the Welfare State and the EU. Manifesto Challenge: Advancing Global Citizenship*, May 10, 2006. Available online at: http://www.rsa.org.uk/acrobat/panic_100506.pdf (last viewed August 30, 2007).

Rubisch, Matthias, 2007. *Germany: The Boom is Over*. Commerzbank Economic Research, April 2. Available at: https://www.commerzbank.com/research/economic_research/pool/d_eur/d_konjunkturaktuell/d_eur_konjak_en_0607.pdf.

Rudra, Nita, 2002. Globalization and the Decline of the Welfare State in Less-Developed Countries, *International Organization*, Vol. 56, n. 2, p. 411. Available online at http://cps.sagepub.com/cgi/content/abstract/38/9/1015.

Ruggie, John, 1983. International Regimes, Transactions, and Change: Embedded liberalism in the Postwar Economic Order, in *International Regimes*, ed. Stephen Krasner (Ithaca, NY: Cornell University Press).

Ruggie, John Gerard, 1993a. *Multilateralism Matters: The Theory and Praxis of an Institutional Form* (New York: Columbia University Press).

Ruggie, John Gerard, 1993b. Territoriality and beyond: problematizing modernity in International Relations. *International Organization*, Vol. 47 (No. 1, Winter) pp. 139–74.

Ruggie, John Gerard, 1996. *Winning the Peace: America and World Order in the New Era* (New York: Columbia University Press).

Ruggie, John Gerard, 1998. *Constructing the World Polity: Essays on International Institutionalization* (London, New York: Routledge).

Sachs, Jeffrey D., 2005. *The End of Poverty: Economic Possibilities for Our Time* (New York: Penguin Press).

Sasley, Brent, 1998. Turkey's Energy Politics in the Post-Cold War Era, *Middle East Review of International Affairs (MERIA)*,Vol. 2, No. 4, November. Available online at http://meria.idc .ac.il/journal/1998/issue4/jv2n4a4.html.

Sassen, Saskia, 1991. *The Global City: New York, London, Tokyo* (Princeton, NJ: Princeton University Press).

Sassen, Saskia, 2001. *The Global City: New York, London, Tokyo*, 2nd edition (Princeton, NJ; Oxford: Princeton University Press).

Sassen, Saskia, 1996. *Losing Control?: Sovereignty in an Age of Globalization* (New York: Columbia University Press).

Sassen, Saskia, 1998. *Globalization and its Discontents; Essays on the New Mobility of People and Money* (New York: New Press).

Sassen, Saskia (ed.), 2002a. *Global Networks, Linked Cities* (New York: Routledge).

Sassen, Saskia, 2002b. The State and Globalization. In Rodney B. Hall and Thomas J. Biersteker, eds, *The Emergence of Private Authority in Global Governance*, pp. 91–110 (Cambridge, UK; New York: Cambridge University Press).

Sassen, Saskia, 2006, *Territory, Authority, Rights: From Medieval to Global Assemblages* (Princeton, NJ: Princeton University Press).

Saul, John Ralston, 2005. *The Collapse of Globalism: and the Reinvention of the World* (Woodstock: Overlook Press).

Schmoller, Gustav von, 1967. *The Mercantile System and its Historical Significance*. 1884. (New York: A. M. Kelley Publishers).

Sciolino, Elaine, 2004. European Public Uneasy Over Turkey's Bid to Join Union. *New York Times*, October 2, Section 1.

Sciolino, Elaine, 2006a. French Youth at Barricades, but It's No Revolution, *The New York Times*, March 28, Section A.

Sciolino, Elaine, 2006b. Chirac Will Rescind Labor Law That Caused Wide French Riots, *The New York Times*, April 11, Section A.

Seeleib-Kaiser, Martin, 2002. Globalization, Political Discourse, and Welfare Systems in a Comparative Perspective: Germany, Japan and the USA, *Centre for Social Policy Research, Bremen University Germany*. Available online at http://sreview.soc.cas.cz/upl/archiv/files/ 106_64seel41.pdf, last visited August 9, 2007.

Sen, Raj Kumar, 2006. *Indian Economic Development: Globalization, Transformation, Equity, Crime and Economic Thinking* (New Delhi: Deep & Deep Publications).

Seton-Watson, Hugh, 1977. *Nations and States: An Enquiry into the Origins of Nations and the Politics of Nationalism* (Boulder, Colorado: Westview Press).

Settimi, Stella Maris, Patricia Audino and Fernando Tohme, 2004. The Road from Orthodoxy towards Structuralism: The Influence of John Maynard Keynes on the Economics of Raul Prebisch, *Departemento de Economia Universidad Nacional del Sur*.

Shaffer, Gregory, 2000. WTO Blue-Green Blues: The Impact of US Domestic Policies on Trade-Labor, Trade-Environment Linkages for the WTO's Future, *Fordham International Law Journal*, Vol. 24, p. 608.

Shaw, Josephine, 2000. *Law of the European Union*, (Houndmills, Basingstoke; New York: Palgrave).

Shonfield, Andrew, 1965. *Modern Capitalism: The Changing Balance of Public and Private Power* (London: Oxford University Press).

Siebert, Horst, 2003. Germany's Social Market Economy: How Sustainable is the Welfare State? Available online at http://www.uni-kiel.de/IfW/pub/siebert/pdf/Washington2003.pdf, last visited August 8, 2007.

Simon, Suzanne, 2007. Framing the Nation: Law and the Cultivation of National Character Stereotypes in the NAFTA Debate and Beyond, *PoLAR: Political and Legal Anthropology Review*, Vol. 30, p. 22.

Singer, Peter, 2002. *One World: The Ethics of Globalization* (New Haven, CT: Yale University Press).

Sinn, Hans-Werner, 2007. *Can Germany Be Saved?: The Malaise of the World's First Welfare State* (Cambridge, MA: MIT Press).

Slaughter, Anne-Marie, 2004. *A New World Order* (Princeton, NJ; Oxford: Princeton University Press).

Smit, Hans and Vratislav Pechota, eds. 2004. *Smit's Guides to International Arbitration: The Roster of International Arbitrators* (Huntington, NY: Juris Publishing).

Smith, Adam, *The Wealth of Nations*, (Author). 2000 new edition. Robert B. Reich (Introduction), Robert Reich (Author) (Modern Library).

Smith, Anthony D., 1971. *Theories of Nationalism* (London: Duckworth).

Smith, Clint E., 2000. *Inevitable Partnership: Understanding Mexico-US Relations* (Boulder, CO: Lynne Rienner Publishers).

Smith, J. W., 2005. *Economic Democracy: The Political Struggle for the 21st Century*, 4th ed. (New York: M. E. Sharpe).

Smith, Timothy B., 2004, *France in Crisis: Welfare, Inequality, and Globalitzation since 1980* (Cambridge, UK; New York: Cambridge University Press).

Smithies, Rachel, 2005. *Public and Private Welfare Activity in the United Kingdom, 1979 to 1999*. Available online at http://sticerd.lse.ac.uk/dps/case/cp/CASEpaper93.pdf.

Solving Global Warming: Your Guide to Legislation, *Natural Resource Defense Council*, available online at http://www.nrdc.org/legislation/factsheets/leg_07032601A.pdf (last visited August 13, 2007).

Soriano, Jen, 1999. Globalization and the Maquiladoras, *Mother Jones*, Nov. 24, Available online at http://www.motherjones.com/news/special_reports/wto/soriano1.html.

Stalin, Joseph, 1934. *Marxism and the National and Colonial Question* (New York: International Publishers).

Steinmo, Sven. Globalization and Taxation: Challenges to the Swedish Welfare State. Available online at http://stripe.colorado.edu/~steinmo/cpsfinal.pdf, last visited August 8, 2007.

Statistics Bureau, 1998–2003. *Employment Status Basic Survey*, Ministry of Public Management, Home Affairs, Posts and Telecommunications. http://www.stat.go.jp/data/shugyou/index.htm.

Stein, Eric, 2001. International Integration and Democracy: No Love at First Sight, *American Journal of International Law*, Vol. 95, p. 489.

Stein, Mark A., 2005. Export Opportunities Aren't Just for the Big Guys, *New York Times*, March 24, C8.

Steingart, Gabor, 2004. *Deutschland: Der Abstieg eines Superstars* (Munich: Piper Verlag).

Stern, Susan, *Marshall Plan 1947–1997: A German View*. Available at: http://www.germany.info/relaunch/culture/history/marshall.html.

Stiglitz, Joseph, 2006. Economic Crisis or Global Malaise in 2006? *The Economists' Voice*, 3.2. Available at: http://works.bepress.com/joseph_stiglitz/2.

Stillwell, Matthew and Charles Arden-Clarke, 1998. Dispute Settlement in the WTO: A Crisis for Sustainable Development. *Center for International Environmental Law* (CIEL), p. 2

Stoffaës, Christian and William James Adams eds., 1986 *Politique Industrielle, Paris, Les Cours de Droit* (French Industrial Policy) (Washington, DC: Brookings Institution).

Strange, Susan, 1995. The Defective "State", *Daedalus*, Vol. 124(2), pp. 55–74.

Strange, Susan, 1996. *The Retreat of the "State": The Diffusion of Power in the Economy* (Cambridge: Cambridge University Press).

Strauss, Peter L., 2006. Rulemaking in the Ages of Globalization and Information: What America Can Learn from Europe, and Vice Versa, *Columbia Journal of European Law*, Vol. 12, p. 645.

Struggling Members Programme, Grameen Bank website http://www.grameen-info.org/bank/BeggerProgram.html (last visited July 20, 2007).

Supplychainer.com, 2007. *Walmart and Carrefour in China: Whose Strategy is Better?* February 23, 2007. Available online at: www.supplychainer.com/50226711/walmart_and_carrefour_in_china_whose_strategy_is_better.php (last viewed August 29, 2007).

Swann, Dennis, 1992. *The Single European Market and Beyond: A Study of the Wider Implications of the Single European Act* (London; New York: Routledge).

Swarns, Rachel L., 2006. Bipartisan Effort to Draft Immigration Bill, *The New York Times*, December 26, Section A.

Tamanaha, Brian Z., 2004. *On The Rule of Law: History, Politics, Theory* (Cambridge, UK; New York: Cambridge University Press).

Tamir, Yael, 1993. *Liberal Nationalism* (Princeton, NJ: Princeton University Press).

Teò, Mario, 1995. Démocratie Internationale et Démocratie Supranationale en Europe, in Mario Teò, ed., *Démocratie et Construction Européenne* (Editions de l'Université de Bruxelles).

Teunissen, Jan Joost and Age Akkerman, 2006. *Global Imbalances and the US Debt Problem: Should Developing Countries Support the US Dollar?* (The Hague: FONDAD).

Thapa, Brijesh, 2000. *The Relationship Between Debt-For-Nature Swaps and Protected Area Tourism: A Plausible Strategy for Developing Countries.* Available online at: http://64.233.169.104/search?q=cache:RIy8_6E5U6QJ:www.fs.fed.us/rm/pubs/rmrs_p015_2/rmrs_p015_2_268_272.pdf+debt-for-nature+swaps+-+Boliva&hl=en&ct=clnk&cd=6&gl=us) (last viewed August 30, 2007).

The GATT Years: from Havana to Marrakesh, WTO website. Available online at http://www.wto.org/English/thewto_e/whatis_e/tif_e/fact4_e.htm (last visited August 13, 2007).

The Marshall Plan and The Future of U.S. European Relations, 1973 (New York: German Information Center).

The World Bank, Data & Statistics – Country Groups, available online at http://web.worldbank.org/WBSITE/EXTERNAL/DATASTATISTICS/0,,contentMDK:20421402~pagePK:64133150~piPK:64133175~theSitePK:239419,00.html#OECD_members.

The World Bank. *Doing Business, Exploring Economics: Tunisia, Presented by The World Bank* Available online at http://rru.worldbank.org/DoingBusiness/ExploreEconomies/BusinessClimateSnapshot.aspx?economyid=190

Thomson, Dennis L. and Dov Ronen, 1986. *Ethnicity, politics, and development* (Boulder, CO: L. Rienner, 1986).

Tiberghien, Yves, 2005. *Invisible Reforms: Globalization, State Mediation and Corporate Restructuring*, PhD Dissertation, Harvard Academy, April 2005.

Tooze, Adam, 2006. *The Wages of Destruction: The Making and Breaking of the Nazi Economy* (London: Allen Lane; Viking).

Trebilcock, Michael J. and Robert Howse, 1999. *The Regulation of International Trade*, (New York: Routledge).

Trebilcock, Michael J. and Robert Howse, 2005. *The Regulation of International Trade*, 3rd ed. (New York: Routledge).

Tsuzuki, Chåushichi, 2000. *The Pursuit of Power in Modern Japan: 1825–1995* (New York: Oxford University Press).

Tully, L. Danielle, 2003. Prospects for Progress: The TRIPS Agreement and Developing Countries After the DOHA Conference, *Boston College International and Comparative Law Review*, Vol. 26, p. 129.

Tushnet, Mark, 2003. *The New Constitutional Order* (Princeton, NJ; Oxford: Princeton University Press).

Unger, Roberto Mangabeira, 2007. *Free Trade Reimagined* (Princeton, NJ; Oxford: Princeton University Press).

United Nations Economic Commission for Europe Population Activities Unit, available online at http://www.unece.org/ead/pau/pau/pau_h.htm (visited Nov 1, 2005).

United Nations Human Settlements Programme, 2003. *The Challenge of Slums: Global Report on Human Settlements* (London; Sterling, VA: Earthscan Publications).

United Nations, *Trade and Development Report 2005*, ch IV, available online at http://www
.unctad.org/Templates/webflyer.asp?docid=6086&intItemID=345& lang=1&mode=toc
(visited Nov 17, 2005).

USCC.gov, 2007, US-China Economic and Security Review Commission. Available
at http://www.uscc.gov/testimonies_speeches/testimonies/2005/05_07_13_testi_damato.php
(last visited April 11, 2007).

U.S.-China Business Council, website http://www.uschina.org/info/forecast/2007/trade-
performance.html (last visited March 27, 2007).

Uzuhashi, Takafumi, 2003. Japanese Model of Welfare State: How it was changed throughout
"The lost decade" of the 1990's? in *Japanese Journal of Social Security Policy*, Vol. 2, No. 2,
December 2003.

Van Creveld, Martin L., 1999, *The Rise and Decline of the State* (Cambridge, U.K.; New York:
Cambridge University Press).

Van Creveld, Martin, 2006. The Fate of the State Revisited, *Global Crime*, Vol. 7, #3–4, Aug–
Nov, pp. 329–50.

Van Dormael, Armand, 1978. *Bretton Woods: Birth of a Monetary System* (New York: Holmes
& Meier).

Vautier, Kerrin M., Peter Lloyd, and Ing-Wen Tsai, 2003. Competition Policies, Developing
Countries and the WTO, in Will Martin, et. al., eds. *Options for Global Trade Reform: A View
from the Asia-Pacific* (Cambridge, UK; New York: Cambridge University Press).

Venter, Al J., 2007. *Allah's Bomb: The Islamic Question of Nuclear Weapons* (Guilford, CT:
Lyons Press).

Vick, Brian, 2003. The Origins of the German Volk: Cultural Purity and National Identity in
Nineteenth-Century Germany, *German Studies Review*, Vol. 26 No 2, pp. 241–56.

Vietor, Richard, H. K., 2007. *How Countries Compete: Strategy, Structure, and Government in
the Global Economy* (Cambridge, MA: Harvard Business School Press).

Villarreal, M. Angeles, 2005. U.S.-Mexico Economic Relations: Trends, Issues and Implications. CRS Report for Congress, available online at http://www.fas.org/sgp/crs/row/
RL32934.pdf.

Vogel, Richard D., 2006. Lessons From South of the Boarder, *Monthly Review Magazine*. Available online at www.monthlyreview.org/mrzine/vogel121106.html (last visited August 14,
2007).

Vogel, Steven, 2006. *Japan Remodeled: How Government and Industry are Reforming Japanese
Capitalism* (Ithaca, NY: Cornell University Press).

Von Hagen, Jürgen and Christopher J. Waller, eds., 1999. *Regional Aspects of Monetary Policy
in Europe*, (Boston: Kluwer Academic).

Wald, Patricia M., 2006. The Judicial Evolution of the WTO App.ellate Body, presented to
"WTO at 10 Conference," April 2006. Available online at www.sipa.columbia.edu/wto/pdf/
PatriciaWaldWTORemarks.pdf (last visited August 13, 2007).

Walker, Marcus, 2006. Politics & Economics: Germany Plans Corporate Tax Cut. In *Wall
Street Journal*, June 22, A6.

Waller, Douglas, 2001. A Terror Threat From The South, *Time Magazine*, Vol. 158, No. 25,
December 10.

Walling, Alastar, J., 2003. Early to Bed, Early to Rise, Work Like Hell and Globalize, *Kansas
Journal of Law and Public Policy*, vol 13 (Winter 2003/2004).

Wan, Ming, 2001. *Japan Between Asia and the West: Economic Power and Strategic Balance*
(Armonk, NY: M. E. Sharpe).

Warsh, David, 2006. *Knowledge and the Wealth of Nations: A Story of Economic Discovery*
(New York: W. W. Norton).

Weber, Lauren, 2005. Our Global Closet: End of Trade Pact Likely Means More Americans
Will be 'Dressed' by Chinese, Other Exporters – Pay Less. *Newsday*, January 30, A50.

Webster's, 1986. *Webster's Third New International Dictionary*.

Wei, Shang-Jin, 1999. Corruption and Economic Development: Beneficial Grease, Minor
Annoyance, or Major Obstacle? *World Bank Publications*. Available online at http://www
.worldbank.org/wbi/governance/pdf/wei.pdf.

Weiler, J. H. H., 2002. The Rule of Lawyers and the Ethos of Diplomats: Reflections on WTO Dispute Settlement, *American Review of International Arbitration*, vol 13, p. 177.

Weiler, J. H. H. and Martina Kocjan, 2004. *European Community System: The Historical Perspective and the Basics of Economic Integration*, available online at http://www.jeanmonnetprogram.org/eu/Units/documents/UNIT1-1-EU-2004-05.pdf.

Weiler, J. H. H., 2005. The Transformation of Europe, *Yale Law Journal*, Vol. 100, p. 2403.

Weir, M., Orloff, A., and Skocpol, T., (2007). *The Politics of Social Policy in the United States* (Princeton: Princeton University Press).

Wennerberg, Tor, 1995. Undermining the Welfare State in Sweden, in *Z Magazine*, June 1995. Available online at: http://zena.secureforum.com/Znet/zmag/articles/june95wennerberg.htm (last viewed August 30, 2007).

Wells, Don, 2006. "Best Practice" in the Regulation of International Labor Standards: Lessons of the U.S. – Cambodia Textile Agreement, *Comparative Labor Law and Policy Journal*, Vol. 27, p. 357.

Wessel, David, 2007. Princeton Economist Says Lack of Civil Liberties, Not Poverty, Breeds Terrorism. *Wall Street Journal*, July 5, p. A-2.

Whitlock, Craig, 2005. France Rejects European Constitution, *The Washington Post*, May 30, 2005, p. A-01.

Wighton, David, 2007. Hollywood joins royalty to seek $200m for microfinance, *The Financial Times Limited*, May 7.

Williamson, Hugh, 2007. Germany proposes micro-credit fund for Africa, *The Financial Times Limited*, February 14.

Wilson, Scott, 2006. Can Turkey come on side? *Northern Echo (UK)*, October 20.

Wolf, Martin, 2004. *Why Globalization Works* (New Haven, CT; London: Yale University Press).

Wolfensohn, James D., 2002. America's Might: What To Do With It?: Fight Terrorism by Ending Poverty, *New Perspectives Quarterly*, Vol. 19, n. 2 (Abingdon, UK: Blackwell Publishing).

Wood, Christopher, 1989. *Boom and Bust: The Rise and Fall of the World's Financial Markets* (New York: Atheneum).

Wood, Christopher, 1992. *The Bubble Economy: Japan's Extraordinary Speculative Boom of the '80s and the Dramatic Bust of the '90s* (New York: Atlantic Monthly Press).

Wood, Christopher, 1994. *The End of Japan, Inc.: And How the New Japan Will Look* (New York: Simon & Shuster).

World Intellectual Property Organization (WIPO), website http://www.wipo.int (last visited July 15, 2007).

WTO, website http://www.wto.org/english/thewto_e/minist_e/min99_e/english/about_e/22fact_e.htm#tariffcuts (last visited July 10, 2007).

World Trade Organization, WTO Doha Development Agenda, website http://www.wto.org/english/tratop_e/dda_e/dohasubjects_e.htm. (last visited July 15, 2007).

World Trade Organization, WTO Doha Ministerial declaration, adopted November 14, 2001. Available online http://www.wto.org/english/thewto_e/minist_e/min01_e/mindecl_e.htm#interaction (last visited August 12, 2007).

World Trade Organization, WTO, http://www.econ.iastate.edu/classes/econ355/choi/wtoroots.htm.

World Trade Organization, WTO, http://www.wto.org/english/thewto_e/thewto_e.htm.

World Trade Organization, July 11, 1996. Report of the Panel, *Japan – Taxes on Alcoholic Beverages*, WTO Doc No WT DS-8-R.

World Trade Organization, April 29, 1996. Report of the Appellate Body, *United States – Standards for Reformulated and Conventional Gasoline*, WTO Doc No WT/DS2/AB/R.

WTO Members and Observers, website http://www.wto.org/english/thewto_e/whatis_e/tif_e/org6_e.htm. Updated July 27, 2007, (last visited August 13, 2007).

WTO, World trade and output, Selected indicators 1948–98. Available online at http://www.wto.org/english/thewto_e/minist_e/min99_e/english/about_e/22fact_e.htm#tariffcuts.

WTO, World Trade Report 2004: Exploring the Linkage Between Domestic Policy, Environment and International Trade. Available at http://www.wto.org/english/res_e/booksp_e/anrep_e/world_trade_report04_e.pdf.

WTO, World Trade Organization Toolkit, Presented by Asian Development Bank, available online at http://www.adb.org/Documents/Others/OGC-Toolkits/WTO/wto0200.asp (last visited August 13, 2007).

Yeh, Shun-yong, 2006. Dragging out of or Deeper into Another Impasse of the Political Economy of the World Trade Organization? A Critic of the Findings of the Dispute Settlement Body in European Communities-Conditions for the Granting of Tariff Preferences to Developing Countries, *Asian Journal of WTO & International Health Law and Policy*, Vol. 1, p. 465.

Yunus, Muhammad.Website http://www.muhammadyunus.org/ (last visited July 20, 2007).

Zakaria, Fareed, 2003. *The Future of Freedom: Illiberal Democracy At Home and Abroad* (New York; London: W. W. Norton & Co.).

Zatz, Noah D. 2006. What Welfare Requires From Work, *UCLA Law Review*, Vol. 54, Issue 2, p. 373. Available at: http://www.law.ucla.edu/docs/zatz-what_welfare_requires.pdf or http://www.uclalawreview.org/articles/?view=54/2/1-3

Zeiler, Thomas W., 1999. *Free Trade Free World: The Advent of the GATT* (Chapel Hill, NC and London: University of North Carolina Press).

Ziblatt, Daniel, 2006. *Structuring the State: The Formation of Italy and Germany and the Puzzle of Federalism* (Princeton, NJ: Princeton University Press).

Index

Abadie, Alberto, 194, 237, 239
acid rain, 142
acquis social, 32, 82
Africa, 17, 83, 105, 118, 119, 121, 123, 129, 130, 190, 193, 202, 224, 227, 245, 254, 258, 263
aid to families with dependent children, 26, 65
American Revolution, 17, 256
Anglo-American common law, 38
Annan, Kofi, 192
Argentina, 104, 119, 123, 200, 202, 258
Asia, 17, 42, 67, 69, 83, 91, 104, 118, 123, 217, 240, 262
Austria, 33, 68, 112
Axis Powers, 12, 67

Baku-Tbilisi-Ceyhan pipeline, 163
balance of power, 3, 4, 16, 26, 28, 30, 74, 79, 211, 223
ballistic missile, 31
Bangladesh, 133, 135, 145, 257
Bank of Japan, 53
beggar thy neighbor, 22
Belgium, 33, 112, 228
Benin, 104, 106, 144, 206, 225, 227, 258
Berlin, 3, 4, 29, 31, 68, 131, 156, 203
Berlin Wall, 3, 4, 29, 68, 203
Biafran massacres, 130
Blomberg, Brock, Gregory Hess, and Akila Weerapana, 194
Bobbitt, Philip, x, 3, 5, 16, 29, 30, 31, 60, 74, 210, 211, 212, 213, 214, 215, 222, 224, 242
Bolivia, 144, 161, 233
BP (British Petroleum), 163

Brazil, 5, 102, 104, 106, 107, 119, 121, 123, 128, 130, 142, 143, 170, 175, 190, 200, 202, 206, 227, 240
Bretton Woods, i, ix, 2, 7, 8, 9, 10, 66, 67, 68, 69, 70, 72, 73, 75, 76, 77, 78, 79, 80, 81, 84, 85, 86, 87, 93, 94, 98, 99, 100, 101, 102, 103, 110, 114, 115, 117, 124, 158, 188, 189, 190, 195, 201, 204, 205, 211, 216, 219, 220, 221, 223, 236, 241, 242, 243, 245, 246, 249, 262
Britain, 12, 32, 68, 112, 169, 200, 201, 210, 233
Bulgaria, 83
Bush, George W., 61, 184, 191, 192, 218, 235, 243, 247

Cameroon, 169
Canada, 33, 166, 170, 173, 176, 179, 181, 235, 255, 258
capital, 26, 35, 36, 38, 46, 48, 55, 57, 79, 97, 126, 130, 131, 132, 144, 154, 156, 214, 217, 223
Carrefour, 96, 97, 141, 224, 261
Caspian Sea, 162, 233
Central America, 123
centralized planning, 75
CFE Treaty, 30
China, 5, 7, 80, 96, 97, 99, 101, 102, 104, 106, 107, 118, 121, 123, 125, 126, 128, 130, 131, 136, 137, 139, 140, 141, 145, 165, 170, 175, 196, 202, 206, 224, 229, 230, 242, 243, 246, 248, 255, 261, 262
Yuan, 126, 127
Clean Air Act, 142, 221
Clinton, William Jefferson, 60, 61, 62, 171, 172, 173, 174, 193, 218, 233, 244, 251

colonization, 17, 81, 100, 112, 118, 129, 227, 228

communism, 3, 4, 12, 13, 24, 28, 29, 31, 69, 74, 79, 108, 165, 188, 200, 206, 212, 221

comparative advantage, 2, 3, 7, 8, 9, 12, 13, 16, 19, 21, 22, 27, 36, 40, 42, 48, 67, 69, 71, 72, 73, 74, 75, 76, 78, 79, 80, 81, 82, 85, 88, 89, 90, 91, 92, 93, 94, 95, 96, 97, 98, 99, 103, 104, 106, 108, 113, 114, 115, 116, 117, 118, 119, 120, 121, 126, 128, 132, 137, 142, 150, 151, 152, 153, 158, 161, 169, 170, 171, 173, 176, 180, 182, 187, 189, 190, 195, 198, 199, 200, 201, 202, 206, 207, 220, 223, 228, 236

Conservation International, 161, 244

constitutional moment, 8, 9, 69, 71, 73, 76, 77, 78, 79, 84, 103, 109, 110, 121, 124, 204, 220

constitutional order of states, 2, 3, 11, 13, 14, 16, 17, 81, 82

constitutional principle, 147, 231

Cooper, Robert, 3, 5, 15, 29, 30, 31, 39, 60, 79, 210, 211, 213, 215, 216, 222, 223, 244

corporate governance, 49

corruption, 8, 123, 144, 145, 192, 230, 231, 239, 243, 246, 250, 255, 258, 262

Costa Rica
    Merck, 160, 161, 162, 233
    National Institute of Biodiversity of Costa Rica (INBio), 160, 161, 233

Council on Foreign Relations, 191, 256

Cunningham, Randy, 144

De Gaulle, Charles, 151, 154

decolonization, 87, 121, 169, 227

developing countries, 5, 7, 32, 35, 36, 92, 102, 106, 115, 124, 132, 172, 173, 205, 209, 223, 225, 228, 231, 233, 250

Dezalayn, Yves, 38

Dickens, Charles, 164

dirigisme, 45, 46

dirigiste, 45, 46, 47, 48

disability benefits, 26, 216

discrimination, 17, 72, 73, 89, 91, 92, 106, 132, 172, 173, 176

Doha, 83, 84, 102, 103, 104, 105, 106, 107, 108, 180, 205, 206, 223, 224, 235, 238, 246, 250, 254, 255, 263

Ecuador, 161

education, 5, 26, 34, 102, 120, 134, 145, 191, 215, 217, 237

Egypt, 105, 123, 135, 136, 139, 228

embedded liberalism, 40, 76, 84, 93, 188, 204, 211, 216, 221, 236, 258

enablement of economic opportunity, i, 6, 7, 8, 9, 40, 42, 43, 44, 58, 60, 64, 65, 66, 80, 81, 103, 107, 117, 121, 124, 137, 138, 141, 146, 147, 154, 155, 158, 159, 160, 162, 170, 171, 177, 178, 179, 180, 187, 191, 195, 196, 198, 199, 201, 202, 204, 205, 207, 231, 235

endangered species, 142

England, 12, 24, 38, 148, 169, 225, 232, 239, 250, 251, 252, 255, 257

Ethiopia, 123, 135

Europe, 7, 12, 15, 16, 17, 21, 26, 27, 30, 31, 32, 33, 34, 37, 42, 65, 67, 68, 69, 73, 75, 77, 79, 82, 83, 101, 105, 106, 117, 118, 119, 120, 121, 122, 127, 129, 130, 132, 136, 139, 140, 150, 151, 152, 153, 154, 155, 156, 157, 158, 159, 160, 162, 163, 178, 179, 186, 197, 199, 207, 211, 213, 220, 221, 223, 226, 228, 233, 236, 240, 241, 242, 245, 247, 248, 249, 250, 251, 252, 253, 256, 257, 258, 260, 261, 262, 263

European Court of Justice, 114, 150, 223, 231, 232

European Union, 5, 6, 13, 49, 54, 83, 89, 105, 122, 123, 125, 127, 148, 150, 152, 153, 155, 156, 157, 158, 193, 196, 210, 215, 226, 228, 231, 232, 245, 246, 252, 254, 259

Export Processing Zones, 13

Far East, 96, 139

Fascism, 3, 4, 12, 13, 24, 28, 29, 31, 69, 73, 74, 76, 78, 108, 188, 200, 206, 212, 220

Fichte, Johann Gottlieb, 25

flat world, 60, 61, 85, 100, 108, 203, 215

Ford, Gerald R., 105

Fortress Europe, 153

Fortress France, 21

Fox, Vincente, 184, 235, 247

France, 12, 20, 21, 24, 32, 33, 42, 44, 45, 46, 47, 48, 49, 50, 60, 66, 68, 82, 87, 88, 89, 92, 95, 99, 107, 108, 112, 118, 121, 131, 141, 148, 153, 163, 164, 169, 188, 200, 201, 206, 211, 212, 214, 216, 219, 225, 228, 229, 231, 232, 233, 236, 241, 242, 245, 246, 247, 251, 253, 260, 263
    Communist Party of, 188
    Etat Providence (welfare state), 188
    Lille, 165
    Marseillaise, 21
    Socialist Party, 12

France Télécom, 47, 48
free trade zones, 136, 137, 171
French garment industry, 95, 96, 140
French state, 20, 43, 44, 45, 46, 47, 48
Friedman, Thomas, 60, 61, 215, 218, 234, 247
FTAA (Free Trade of the Americas Act), 195, 196, 197, 198, 200, 201
Fujimori, Alberto, 144
Fukuyama, Francis, 3, 11, 12, 13, 25, 29, 71, 77, 78, 83, 129, 189, 210, 211, 212, 247, 248
    end of history, 3, 11, 12, 13, 25, 29, 31, 75, 77, 78, 80, 82, 83, 115, 129, 172, 173, 210, 228, 236

GATT, 5, 7, 9, 12, 28, 43, 67, 69, 72, 73, 74, 76, 78, 79, 81, 85, 86, 87, 88, 89, 90, 91, 92, 93, 94, 95, 98, 103, 104, 105, 106, 107, 108, 113, 114, 115, 116, 117, 118, 120, 121, 125, 128, 135, 140, 148, 150, 152, 153, 154, 157, 158, 168, 173, 181, 187, 195, 196, 198, 199, 201, 202, 204, 211, 216, 220, 221, 222, 225, 226, 228, 231, 240, 241, 243, 244, 246, 248, 249, 250, 251, 254, 261, 264
General Electric, 174
General Motors (GM), 140
Genoa, 86, 108
Germany, 12, 33, 61, 72, 73, 82, 112, 118, 121, 153, 188, 200, 201, 213, 214, 216, 219, 228, 233, 236, 240, 241, 258, 259, 260, 262, 263, 264
    Social-Democratic Party, 12
global warming, 142, 203
Gore, Albert A., Jr (Al), 191
Grameen Bank, 133, 134, 135, 230, 249, 255, 257, 260
Guatemala, 140, 175, 196, 197

Hacker, Jacob, 62, 63, 218, 249, 253
Hawley-Smoot Tariff Act, 76, 244
health and safety, 16, 27
Hegel, Georg Wilhelm Friedrich, 11, 13, 71, 77, 211, 213, 249, 253
Herder, Johann Gottfried von, 25
Hollywood, 194, 230, 263
Honeywell, 166, 167, 168, 173, 174, 175, 177, 178, 179, 180, 181, 182, 196, 234, 241, 250
Hong Kong, 119, 128, 248, 254
Horn of Africa, 135
Hors, Irene, 144, 145, 231, 250
Hungary, 33, 112

IMF, 36, 57, 127, 128, 209, 211, 221, 228, 229, 251, 258
Immigration Reform and Control Act, 184
incentives, 6, 41, 42, 45, 47, 49, 62, 64, 65, 80, 113, 123, 126, 128, 134, 136, 137, 138, 139, 140, 142, 143, 147, 160, 161, 162, 167, 176, 177, 178, 180, 181, 187, 197, 202, 207, 208, 229, 233
India, 5, 80, 99, 102, 104, 106, 107, 119, 120, 121, 123, 128, 130, 131, 137, 145, 165, 170, 175, 196, 202, 206, 216, 227, 245, 252, 254, 255
    Bombay, 165
Indonesia, 91, 93, 104, 106, 107, 108, 119, 123, 130, 142, 143, 175, 190, 202, 216, 227, 251
intellectual property rights, 155, 178, 181, 232
Internal Revenue Code, 63
International Court of Justice, 115, 250
International Criminal Court, 9, 146
International Institute for Sustainable Development (IISD), 192
international law, 38, 132, 148, 149, 150, 231
    Voice and Exit, 148
International Monetary Fund, 67, 126, 211, 220, 223, 241, 251
international private law, 38
Iran, 122, 135, 163, 191
Iron Curtain, 12, 31
Islam, 130, 136, 227
Italy
    Milan, 165

Jacob's Ladder, 71
Jakarta, 119
Japan, 6, 12, 33, 34, 42, 43, 49, 50, 51, 52, 53, 54, 55, 56, 57, 58, 60, 61, 67, 68, 69, 72, 75, 79, 97, 101, 106, 116, 118, 121, 123, 125, 127, 164, 216, 217, 218, 221, 224, 226, 229, 240, 244, 247, 248, 249, 250, 252, 253, 256, 259, 261, 262, 263
Japanese Basic Environmental Law, 225
Japanese indicative planning, 64
Johnson, Lyndon B., 59
Jordan, 105, 123, 135, 136, 228

Kant, Immanuel, 208, 222, 252
keiretsu, 49, 51, 52, 54, 56, 58
Kenya, 169
Keynes, 72, 76, 78, 98, 223, 259
Keynesian welfare state, 76
Kim Dae Jung, 192
Kingly states, 15, 19, 212
Korea, 33, 36, 50, 97, 104

Korean War, 51
Krueger, Alan, 194, 237, 253
Kurdistan, 122

labor regulation, 16, 26
Latin America, 123
legitimacy, 4, 5, 28, 30, 32, 41, 42, 57, 66, 89,
    102, 106, 108, 110, 111, 117, 141, 147,
    148, 151, 157, 158, 159, 160, 211, 215,
    231, 239, 243
less developed (Nations), 13, 107, 115, 119,
    195, 236
levée en masse, 20
Lindsey, Brink, 62, 218, 253
linkage, 8, 73, 84, 85, 86, 87, 88, 90, 93, 114,
    223, 231, 240, 244, 264
Long War, 16, 31, 79, 170, 188, 189, 203
loss of control,
Luxembourg Accords, 151, 154, 158
Luxembourg Crisis, 151, 154, 231

Maginot Line, 71, 252
Malaysia, 36, 90
Malaysian Prime Minister Mahathir, 36
Marrakesh, 116, 117, 226, 248, 261
    Marrakesh Agreement, 150
Marshall Plan, 68, 79, 118, 124, 188, 189,
    219, 239, 241, 247, 260, 261
Marx, Karl, 19, 164, 189, 212
Marxism, 15, 24, 25, 78, 260
May 1968, 55
Medicaid, 60
Medicare, 59, 63
Merari, Ariel
    Tel Aviv University Political Violence
    Research Center, 194
mercantilism, 2, 3, 16, 18, 22, 23, 65, 69, 76,
    78, 81, 82, 93, 104, 108, 111, 112, 169,
    175, 188, 189
Mexico, 33, 104, 116, 123, 128, 139, 140,
    165, 166, 168, 170, 171, 173, 175, 176,
    178, 179, 181, 182, 183, 191, 196, 197,
    198, 228, 234, 235, 239, 241, 255, 257,
    260, 262
    maquiladoras, 139, 140, 165, 166, 167,
    168, 169, 170, 171, 173, 175, 176, 177,
    178, 179, 180, 181, 182, 183, 185, 187,
    196, 197, 198, 199, 200, 201, 234, 239,
    240
    Peso, 182
middle classes, 139
minimum wage, 26, 165, 172
mining, 21, 23, 24, 36, 149
    sea bed, 149

MITI, Ministry of International Trade and
    Industry, 51, 52, 164
Mitterrand, François, 45
monetary policy, 6, 101
Montesinos, Vladimiro, 144
Morocco, 87, 88, 89, 144, 206
Most Favored Nation Clause, 72, 226

NAFTA, 89, 168, 170, 171, 172, 173, 174,
    176, 179, 182, 183, 195, 196, 198, 200,
    234, 235, 239, 240, 244, 246, 250, 253,
    255, 257, 258, 259
Napoleonic code, 20
Nationalism, 25, 240, 242, 248, 250, 259,
    260, 261
Nation-State, 2, 3, 5, 6, 7, 8, 9, 11, 13, 14,
    15, 16, 17, 18, 21, 22, 25, 26, 27, 29, 30,
    31, 34, 35, 37, 40, 41, 42, 43, 61, 64, 65,
    67, 74, 75, 78, 81, 83, 86, 94, 98, 103,
    105, 114, 115, 117, 119, 125, 127, 139,
    142, 153, 157, 158, 160, 165, 189, 195,
    209, 210, 211, 212, 215, 219, 222, 223,
    227
Nazi Germany, 72, 188, 213, 240, 261
negative integration, 88, 89
Netherlands, 33, 112, 155, 214, 216, 228,
    233
new constitutional order, 31, 150, 215
New Deal, 59, 254
New Marshall Plan, 132, 135, 136, 143
New York Garment District, 96, 106
Nicaragua, 175, 196, 197
Nigeria, 118, 119, 123, 130, 143, 144, 227,
    256
Nixon, Richard M., 68
Nobel Peace Prize, 133, 255

OECD, 5, 32, 33, 47, 58, 127, 144, 213, 216,
    217, 218, 227, 229, 246, 250, 256, 261
    Doig, Alan and Stephen Riley, 145
    Final Report of the Ad Hoc Working
    Group on Participatory Development
    and Good Governance of the
    Development Assistance Committee,
    145
Organization of African States, 143

Pakistan, 119, 123, 135, 140, 144, 193, 203
Palestine, 169
Paraguay, 200
Paris, 66, 95, 102, 106, 131, 156, 214, 239,
    242, 245, 247, 254, 256, 257, 260
    District 5, 131
    excluded suburbs, 66

patents, 181, 240
  U.S. and Canadian patent offices, 181
Peace of Westphalia, 25
Perot, Ross, 170, 171
perpetual peace, 25, 77
Personal Responsibility Crusade, 62
Peru, 144, 228
Philippines, 36, 99, 100, 144, 145, 161, 240,
  247
Poland, 33, 83, 105, 224
Portugal, 33, 96, 112, 148, 153
post-*dirigiste*, 46
post-modern diffuseness, 132
post-modern epoch, 42–44, 137, 154, 183
price controls, 54
proportionality, 88, 92
protectionism, 73, 87, 89, 91, 104, 106, 157,
  204, 206, 209, 221, 228
public debt, 6, 101

quotas, 22, 51, 72, 211, 221

railroad, 23, 24, 36
rain forests, 142
Razin, Assaf, 33
Realizability,
Regional Trade Agreements (RTAs), 192,
  193, 237
regulations, 6, 22, 41, 75, 87, 94, 142, 155,
  156, 172, 175
resource conservation, 28, 75, 86, 90, 92, 93,
  142, 171, 223, 224
retirement, 26, 32, 33, 42, 46, 48, 55, 59, 63,
  65, 83, 175
Ricardo, David, 72, 73, 98, 220, 257
Rio Convention on Biological Diversity,
  160
Rodgers, Bill, 144
Romania, 83, 100
Roosevelt, Franklin D., 59
Ruggie, John, 8, 38, 40, 76, 78, 211, 213,
  215, 221, 222, 258, 259
Russia, 112, 122, 163, 243

Sadka, Efraim, 33, 257
Sarkozy, Nicolas, 32, 232
Sassen, Saskia, 38, 39, 214, 215, 221,
  259
SCAP, Supreme Commander of the Allied
  Powers, 50
Schuman, Robert, 82, 121, 146, 186, 228,
  247
Seattle, 86, 108
Sentier, 95, 106

Shelley, Louise, 144
Shenzhen, 120, 125, 138, 139, 163, 165, 179,
  198
shipbuilding, 23, 24
Shrimp and Turtle, 90, 91
Side Agreements, 172, 173, 174, 176
  NAO (National Administrative Office),
  173, 174
Silicon Valley, 99
Sinclair, Upton, 164
Singapore, i, 145
Single European Act, 151, 157, 261
SME, 47
Smith, Adam, 72, 73
social contract, 61, 136, 138, 139, 140, 179,
  181, 215, 235
social entitlements, 31
Social Security Act of 1935, 59
society of states, 2, 6, 14, 39, 67, 71, 79, 113,
  169, 222
Somalia, 135, 138, 140
Sony, 57, 166, 173, 174, 182
Soros, George, 36
South, 5, 83, 102, 104, 106, 107, 108, 115,
  119, 121, 123, 130, 179, 180, 185, 187,
  195, 197, 198, 200, 202, 227, 235, 250,
  254, 262
South Africa, 119
South Korea, 5, 102
sovereignty, 3, 4, 5, 6, 13, 16, 23, 27, 28, 29,
  30, 37, 39, 68, 76, 79, 81, 84, 86, 88, 89,
  91, 92, 93, 101, 103, 107, 113, 114, 115,
  116, 117, 151, 152, 203, 204, 210, 212,
  213, 216, 222, 231, 233, 235
Soviet bloc, 12, 104, 188, 189
Soviet republics, 128
Spain, 33, 108, 112, 201, 214, 236
Sprint, 174
State
  inner face, 3
  outer face, 3
Statecraft, i, ix, x, 2, 3, 4, 7, 8, 9, 13, 14, 15,
  16, 17, 18, 19, 21, 23, 25, 26, 27, 28, 29,
  30, 31, 34, 35, 36, 37, 39, 40, 41, 42, 43,
  49, 60, 64, 65, 66, 68, 69, 71, 74, 75, 76,
  77, 78, 79, 81, 82, 84, 85, 86, 87, 88, 91,
  93, 100, 101, 104, 106, 107, 108, 110,
  111, 112, 113, 114, 117, 118, 119, 121,
  122, 128, 129, 130, 132, 138, 142, 146,
  148, 150, 151, 152, 153, 157, 158, 165,
  169, 170, 171, 175, 176, 179, 180, 186,
  188, 189, 190, 195, 197, 199, 201, 202,
  203, 205, 206, 212, 215, 220, 227, 231,
  236, 239

State-Nation, 3, 7, 11, 15, 16, 17, 18, 19, 20,
    21, 22, 23, 24, 25, 26, 27, 31, 78, 81, 94,
    103, 175, 210, 211, 212, 215
steel, 23, 24, 36, 51, 52, 85, 99, 104, 105,
    119, 156, 186, 197
Struggling Members Programme, 134
Sudan, 161
suitcase bomb, 31
Supreme Court, 64, 149
Sweden, 33, 47, 220, 256, 263

Taiwan, 36, 50, 119
Tanaka, Kakuei, 55
tariff bindings, 72
terrorism, 5, 9, 30, 103, 108, 136, 191, 192,
    193, 194, 195, 199, 200, 202, 206, 236,
    237, 238, 239, 240, 241, 242, 243, 247,
    249, 250, 251, 253, 257, 263
The Economist, 34, 216, 229, 246
The Free Trade of the Americas Agreement,
    83
Third World, 13, 115, 161, 228
third worldists, 108
tiers-mondistes, 108
Trade Council, i, ix, 8, 9, 121, 122, 123, 124,
    128, 131, 132, 133, 135, 136, 138, 140,
    141, 143, 145, 146, 160, 162, 163, 176,
    181, 182, 183, 184, 204, 209, 235
transportation, 23
Treaty of Maastricht, 158, 223
Treaty of Versailles, 73, 188, 190
Tri-Border Area, 200
Tunisia, 37, 96, 100, 123, 135, 136, 139, 230,
    246, 261
Turkey, 33, 83, 122, 159, 162, 223, 232, 233,
    234, 242, 252, 259, 263
turtle excluder devices, TEDs, 90

U.S. long-term bonds, 126
unemployment benefits, 26
United Nations, 13, 92, 102, 192, 194, 204,
    213, 215, 227, 232, 236, 237, 252, 261,
    262
United Nations Environment Programme
    Finance Initiative (UNEP FI), 192
universal health care, 26

Venezuela, 144

Wal-Mart, 96, 97, 98, 245
weapons of mass destruction, 5, 30, 31, 103

Wei, Shang-Jin, 145, 231, 262
Weil Law, 83
Weiler, Joseph, 148, 149, 150, 151, 152, 154,
    222, 223, 226, 231, 232, 252, 263
welfare, 3, 4, 5, 6, 7, 8, 12, 15, 16, 17, 18, 19,
    20, 21, 24, 25, 26, 27, 28, 29, 30, 31, 32,
    33, 34, 36, 37, 39, 40, 41, 42, 43, 44, 45,
    47, 48, 49, 55, 57, 58, 59, 60, 61, 62, 63,
    64, 65, 66, 68, 70, 71, 74, 76, 78, 79, 82,
    83, 84, 85, 86, 87, 88, 92, 94, 100, 101,
    102, 103, 104, 106, 107, 108, 110, 111,
    117, 121, 124, 129, 131, 132, 135, 139,
    141, 142, 151, 154, 155, 156, 157, 158,
    159, 160, 163, 164, 165, 167, 169, 170,
    171, 172, 173, 174, 175, 176, 178, 179,
    180, 183, 185, 187, 188, 189, 191, 195,
    196, 198, 199, 200, 201, 203, 204, 205,
    206, 207, 208, 210, 211, 212, 213, 215,
    216, 217, 218, 219, 220, 222, 223, 230,
    231, 235, 264
    decline of, 6, 13, 21, 32, 108, 117, 187
welfare state, 15, 26, 28, 32, 74
welfare-to-work, 62
West Virginia, 139, 197, 198
Wiesel, Elie, 192, 237
WMD, 30, 31
Wolfensohn, James D., 191, 237, 263
World Bank, 36, 135, 144, 191, 209, 211,
    215, 221, 227, 230, 245, 246, 257, 261,
    262
World War I, 28, 71, 211
World War II, i, 1, 2, 3, 5, 8, 12, 16, 29, 36,
    42, 49, 51, 64, 67, 68, 69, 70, 71, 72,
    73, 75, 76, 79, 80, 81, 82, 84, 93, 104,
    106, 107, 108, 118, 120, 122, 132, 135,
    147, 151, 158, 164, 170, 178, 180, 185,
    186, 187, 188, 189, 190, 195, 200, 201,
    202, 205, 206, 211, 220, 221, 226, 236,
    242
World Wildlife Fund (WWF), 161
WTO, ix, 5, 7, 8, 9, 13, 28, 72, 89, 90, 95,
    102, 105, 204, 205, 215, 216, 221, 222,
    223, 224, 226, 227, 231, 232, 235, 238,
    241, 242, 243, 244, 246, 248, 249, 251,
    252, 254, 255, 256, 257, 259, 260, 261,
    262, 263, 264
    Dispute Settlement Body, 105, 264

Yunus, Muhammad, 133, 230, 255, 264

Zola, Emile, 164